The Transmission of Culture
in Early Modern Europe

D0026531

Published under the auspices of the
Shelby Cullom Davis Center for Historical Studies
Princeton University

Gerald L. Geison, ed. *Professions and the French State, 1700–1900.* 1984
Sean Wilentz, ed. *Rites of Power: Symbolism, Ritual, and Politics Since the Middle
    Ages.* 1985
Peter J. Mandler, ed. *The Uses of Charity: The Poor on Relief in the Nineteenth-
    Century Metropolis.* 1990
Anthony Grafton and Ann Blair, eds. *The Transmission of Culture in Early Modern
    Europe.* 1990

The Transmission
of Culture in Early
Modern Europe

Anthony Grafton and
Ann Blair, editors

upp

University of Pennsylvania Press
Philadelphia

Copyright © 1990 by the University of Pennsylvania Press
All rights reserved
Printed in the United States of America

Library of Congress Cataloging-in-Publication Data

The Transmission of culture in early modern Europe / Anthony Grafton
and Ann Blair, editors.
    p. cm.
  "Published under the auspices of the Shelby Cullom Davis Center
for Historical Studies, Princeton University."
  Includes bibliographical references.
  ISBN 0-8122-8191-8
    1. Europe—Civilization. 2. Europe—Intellectual life.
3. Culture diffusion—Europe—History. 4. Grafton, Anthony.
5. Blair, Ann. 6. Shelby Cullom Davis Center for Historical Studies.
CB203.T3 1990
940.2—dc20   89-70750
                                                         CIP

CB
203
.T73
1990

Contents

JAN 1 9 1994

Acknowledgments

We would like to thank Lawrence Stone and Joan Daviduk for help of many kinds; also the Department of Rare Books and Manuscripts of Princeton University Library, whose staff provided most of the illustrations with miraculous speed and efficiency.

Anthony Grafton
Ann Blair

Princeton, New Jersey
11 September 1989

Anthony Grafton

Introduction: Notes from Underground on Cultural Transmission

I was in a Printing house in Hell, & saw the method in which knowledge is transmitted from generation to generation.

In the first chamber was a Dragon-Man, clearing away the rubbish from a cave's mouth; within, a number of Dragons were hollowing the cave.

In the second chamber was a Viper folding round the rock & the cave, and others adorning it with gold, silver and precious stones.

In the third chamber was an Eagle with wings and feathers of air: he caused the inside of the cave to be infinite; around were numbers of Eagle-like men who built palaces in the immense cliffs.

In the fourth chamber were Lions of flaming fire, raging around & melting the metals into living fluids.

In the fifth chamber were Unman'd forms, which cast the metals into the expanse.

There they were reciev'd by Men who occupied the sixth chamber, and took the forms of books & were arranged in libraries.[1]

William Blake, *The Marriage of Heaven and Hell*

Unlike Blake, most nineteenth-century scholars saw the creation of culture as distinct from and more interesting than its transmission.[2] Jacob Burckhardt, for example, treated the culture of the Renaissance as an essentially new creation rather than a mere revival of an ancient one, and deliberately relegated the study of the classics to a late and subordinate position in his work. "The essence of the phenomena," he remarked, "might have been the same without the classical revival."[3] This attitude, rooted in Romantic beliefs about originality and intensity, died hard; but between 1870 and 1914 it gave up the ghost. In its place arose a new scholarship centrally concerned with the transmission of texts, images, and ideas.

Aby Warburg and the scholars associated with the institute he founded traced with the zest and intuition of detectives the shifting paths taken by classical ideas and forms in the worlds of Islam and the Western Middle Ages. Literary scholars tracked classical topoi from text to text. Iconographers mapped the visual and literary deformation of myths and fables. And historians of the Renaissance and Reformation took the individuals they studied at their word and ceased to dismiss the central importance of the retrieval of texts and other ancient models to early modern culture. The medieval and early modern scholarship that resulted from this reorientation of interests and assumptions was both rich in specific results and prolific in further applications. It inspired many of the German humanists whose transplantation to England and North America in the 1930s transformed historical scholarship in the English-speaking world; its results have shaped undergraduate teaching on the history of Western culture from the 1930s to the present.

This new scholarship, however, accepted and transmitted its own problematic and largely unexamined assumptions. It treated transmission as a simple, one-directional process rather like high-fidelity broadcasting of classical music. The original message was assumed to be pure and perfect. The changes and revisions introduced into it in the course of time were defined as interference—something to be studied with meticulous care, but also to be treated with regret, as a corruption, not an enhancement, of the original. In general, only a limited set of adaptations of inherited forms and ideas seemed to be organic expressions of genuine thoughts and feelings; others were dismissed, for no evident reason, as banal and sterile. And the humanists of the Renaissance emerged as heroes not for the originality of mind and spirit that had attracted Burckhardt but for their painstaking efforts to restore the signal to its initial, correct form. The transmission of culture, in other words, turned out to be rather like the Decline and Fall of the Roman Empire: a protracted and fascinating process, but one only gloomily illuminated by the glow of decay. If transmission equaled corruption of a primal light, however, retrieval equaled restoration. The new historical insight of early modern intellectuals was assumed—rather than proved—to be a triumph of culture over barbarism and reason over superstition.[4]

The high-cultural scholarship which the Davis Center has sampled in 1986–88 still draws inspiration and information from the rich traditions of Burckhardt and Warburg, but it rests on its own new foundations. It assumes that changes in an original form, text, or idea were charged with meaning unless the contrary can be proved—that they normally represent conscious artistic and intellectual decisions rather than failures to reproduce a primal truth. More specifically, medieval and Renaissance changes in classical and biblical originals are themselves not simply innovations, but moves in a game some of whose rules were established in antiquity itself. All literary or artistic creations—classical as well as postclassical—result from choices among preexisting genres and elements and take effect only by the grace of scribes and printers and the conscious activity of readers. The history of cultural transmission has been extended backward into the ancient world itself; even Homer has come to seem an Alexandrian poet, playing nostalgically with tradition. And the assumption that any given stage in the history of culture deserves intellectual priority over others has largely been abandoned. Changed scripts, artistic forms, methods of commentary, and modes of appropriation are the outward and visible signs of life in a tradition that would have the marmoreal perfection of death if it froze in a stable form instead of continuing to undergo creative adaptation. Transmission thus becomes central to the story of high culture in the West; and several of the essays that follow take off from the assumption that alteration in a powerful message is just alteration, not degradation.

Burckhardt denigrated the study of transmission because he envisioned cultures as organically unified—as coherent beings that could be studied in any social or individual manifestation. And he found much grist for his analytical mill entirely outside the high world of literature and ideas. He scrutinized a vast range of social and cultural institutions and activities—from waging war to holding festivals, from raising taxes to making jokes—in his *Civilization of the Renaissance,* treating all of them as expressions of a common cultural spirit inhabiting an entire society. His catholic interests and generous learning still inspire us; but here, too, his assumptions and methods need scrutiny and revision. Burckhardt assumed that nonliterary forms within a culture—ways of eating or fighting or assembling in public—are simply shared, not elaborately learned. He was more interested in calling them back to life than in investigating whether they had been dominated or shaped by single powerful groups in a larger society—for example, by members of a profession or social order bent on making forms of behavior or public institutions serve their own interest. And he was not fully attentive to the fact—well known to the classicists of his time—that such forms of conduct have their own long-term history, which also involves creative adaptation from an existing repertoire and frequently allows the survival of ideas and attitudes that would otherwise seem obsolete or harmful.[5]

Many of the sociocultural essays presented to the Davis Center have implicitly or explicitly suggested analogies between the fates of rituals and practices and those of texts. Here, too, conscious, active choices are the dominant model for interpreting cultural developments—not unconscious obedience to the spirit of an age or passive acceptance of a hegemonic culture imposed from above. The diachronic story of transmission—its reasons, its modalities, its frequent paradoxes—proves as fascinating as the frozen tableaux offered by an earlier social history. The forms of transmission prove as many in number and as varied in form as the institutions of the complex societies we have studied. Warfare, like cricket, proves to have its own complex, formal rules which encode larger social values, and its conduct proves to be a complex system for passing on diverse messages about these values. As so often in recent historiography, legal sources have yielded particularly rich results. The courtroom and the lawyer's study have turned out to be historical alembics where the methods of social and intellectual historians can be mingled in new forms, producing results of unsuspected richness. And in all cases, transmission across the barriers of class and profession has proved as complex and absorbing as transmission from one period to the next. The passage of chivalric ideas from noble authors to upwardly mobile artisans, the passage of new ideas of honor and sensibility from writers and women of rank to lawyers—and from lawyers to writers and women of rank—offer a rich and rewarding vision of creative adaptation of a world of social practices and spoken and unspoken assumptions.

Transmission of culture, then, has proved a productive rubric for discussion—one that has enabled historians of the high and the low, the ritual and the textual, the legal and the scholarly to find common methodological ground and suggestively shared approaches. It has shown that many of the methodological polemics that take up so much space in journals and win so much attention from readers—new sociocultural history berating the old history of ideas for its sterility, old history of ideas berating the new cultural history for its superficiality—no longer reflect the practice of serious historians in any of the fields concerned with transmission. And it has stimulated historians of many different stripes to join in finding good historical reasons for the apparently unreasonable in past practices and arguments. Transmission will never replace creation in the historian's romantic heart. It will not produce new causal explanations for the great events in Western history or the seismic shifts in the landscape of Western thought, but it does provide us with a set of hard, unromantic and revealing questions to ask about many received truths and tenets.

In the realm of intellectual history, for example, the study of transmission has led us to see that the canon of texts now considered central to the intellectual history of the West does not include some of the most original and influential texts ever written. Works of fundamental originality and import have been defined as peripheral by critics and historians whose criteria of evaluation had more to do with the literary appeal of a work in their own time than with the extent or influence of its original readership. My study of the transmission of rules for judging historical sources shows that the forger Annius of Viterbo played a role comparable in size and impact to those of sober scholars like Valla and Bodin in the creation of modern historiography. Jardine's study of the massive advertising campaign waged on behalf of Rudolph Agricola's *De inventione dialectica* by intellectuals and printers shows that pedagogical and professional concerns of a very down-to-earth kind did more than innovations in dialectic to make that technical and rebarbative book a publishing success in the early sixteenth century. Valensi's study of Venetian reports on the Ottoman empire shows that their patrician authors came to see that organism as monstrous rather than healthy, as a classic case of "despotism"—a phenomenon they described exactly as Montesquieu would two centuries later—less because the empire itself had changed, though it had, than because they were incorporating different theoretical assumptions, drawn from Botero rather than Bodin, into their supposedly untheoretical and objective reports. And Kors's study of the printed and manuscript debates of French theologians, those driest and least appealing of writers, reveals them—rather than the philosophes who attacked them so wittily—as the creators of modern atheism. Valla remains central to the history of historiography, Agricola to the history of logic, Montesquieu to the history of political thought, and the philosophes to the history of religion; but in each case a concerted effort to find out who read, published, or advertised what, and when, and where enlarges the traditional context and qualifies the traditional certainties of the field.

In the wider realm of sociocultural history, concentrating on transmission can transform one's view of familiar problems and events—can reveal the vital importance of learned skills and artificial codes that traditional historiography has ignored. Clendinnen's vivid recreation of the battle for Tenochtitlan restores the logic to Spanish and Aztec attack and counterattack, discovering in their battle to the death the clash not only of men but of whole culturally distinct systems of fighting. It reveals the Aztecs, in particular, as far more determined and coherent individuals than they are portrayed in traditional historiography. Hunt's reading of preachers and playwrights, militia company rules and manuals for education, demonstrates the survival of a late form of the chivalric ideal among the urban youth of seventeenth-century England. More strikingly still, it reinterprets the outbreak of the English Revolution, once thought a triumph for the bourgeoisie, as the triumph of a set of feudal values and practices without which the New Model Army could never have been raised. Kelley's investigation of the legal idea of "custom" uses the afterlife of a single concept as a way into a history of genuinely *longue durée*—a history that follows the persistent ambiguity of one basic concept from its theoretical formulation by ancient jurists and philosophers, through its practical application by officers of the French crown, to its final assimilation into the modern social sciences. It thus sheds a new light on basic problems of Western social thought and organization. And Stone's study of the action for criminal conversation ("crim. con.") in eighteenth- and nineteenth-century England uses the growth and final abandonment of a single method for obtaining divorce as a key to the transformation of basic views about morality, honor, and religion and their relation to marriage.

These studies differ widely in substance, emphasis, and method. Some deal with transmission of ideas within, some with transmission across cultural and linguistic barriers. Kelley and I follow ideas over many centuries of deformation and revision, Stone and Valensi over shorter spans, Jardine, Hunt, Kors, and Clendinnen over still shorter ones. Some of these studies offer readings of texts, others readings of social actions as well. And two years of discussion in the Davis Center did little to establish the existence of a shared model of culture to which the authors of these and the other papers discussed there would subscribe. Still, all of them converge in their interest in identifying the barriers that impede and the pores that allow the passage of rituals and reasoning from group to group.

These new approaches hardly replace Burckhardt's effort to visualize a past culture as a whole. They force us to contemplate texts and artifacts less appealing than the canonical ones of the older cultural history. They divert our attention from familiar and evidently rewarding enterprises, like decoding for ourselves the message of *The Praise of Folly,* to less familiar and evidently difficult ones, like reconstructing the various ways in which sixteenth-century readers decoded the texts of the ancients or the mores of their Turkish contemporaries. By necessity, they concentrate more on the process of transmission than on the cultural products that are transmitted; they do not offer new definitions of culture and operate on the basis of highly diverse, implied definitions of it. And by their nature, they are less apt than more traditional approaches to produce satisfying generalizations. Yet they also give us a fresh look at texts and topics so worn by familiarity that they seem to offer few rewards to inquirers. They enable us to envision the transmission of skills and ideas as a human rather than a textual process. And they challenge and qualify the holistic visions, even if they cannot replace them. That would seem to be enough.

Notes

1. *The Portable Blake,* ed. A. Kazin (New York, 1946), 258 ("A Memorable Fancy").

2. Blake was in fact so concerned with the process of dissemination that he tried to control every aspect of the production and distribution of his work. See J. McGann, *A Critique of Modern Textual Criticism* (Chicago and London, 1983), 44–47.

3. Quoted by W. K. Ferguson, *The Renaissance in Historical Thought* (Boston, 1948), 191.

4. This account is necessarily very abbreviated and does not try to do justice to the work of individuals. For a much more nuanced approach and rich bibliography, see C. Ginzburg's discussion of the Warburg Institute in his *Miti emblemi spie* (Turin, 1986).

5. Cf. E. H. Gombrich, *In Search of Cultural History* (Oxford, 1969); F. Gilbert, "Jacob Burckhardt's Student Years: The Road to Cultural History," *Journal of the History of Ideas* 47 (1986), 249–74.

Anthony Grafton

1. Invention of Traditions and Traditions of Invention in Renaissance Europe: The Strange Case of Annius of Viterbo

A Scientific Prelude

Joseph Scaliger encountered two supernatural beings in the course of his long and well-spent life. He saw one of them, a black man on a horse, as he rode by a marsh with some friends. He only read about the other, a monster named Oannês with the body of a fish and the voice of a man. Yet as so often happened in the Renaissance, the encounter with Art had far more lasting consequences than that with Life. The black man tried to lure Scaliger into the marsh, failed, and disappeared, leaving him confirmed in his contempt for the devil and all his works: "My father didn't fear the Devil, neither do I. I'm worse than the devil."[1] Oannês, in the book that Scaliger read, climbed out of the ocean and taught humanity the arts and sciences. "Devil Tempts Man" was no headline to excite the Renaissance public; but "Amphibian Creates Culture" was something very far out of the ordinary.

The fish who gave us civilization appeared at the beginning of the account of Babylonian mythology and history written by Berosus, a priest of Bel, early in the third century BC. Berosus drew on genuine Babylonian records but wrote in Greek, for the benefit of the Seleucid king Antiochus I Soter. He and other Near Eastern writers, like the Egyptian Manetho and many Jews, tried to avenge in the realm of the archive their defeat on the battlefield, using documents and inscriptions to show that Babylon, Israel, and Egypt were older and wiser than Greece. Jewish and Christian writers preserved his Babyloniaca. It was in the unpublished world chronicle of one of them, George Syncellus (c. AD 800), that Scaliger met Berosus and his fishy pet, in 1602–1603.[2]

The most remarkable thing about the encounter was Scaliger's reaction to it. As a good Calvinist he considered Babylonian gods to be abhorrent and Babylonian boasts of the great antiquity of their state to be fanciful. As a good scholar he knew that Berosus was not a name to inspire trust. In fact, as his disciple John Selden pointed out, a century earlier than Scaliger "THERE came forth, and in Buskins too (I mean with Pomp and State) . . . an Author, called *Berosus* a *Chaldee* Priest"—a forged text that had become a sixteenth-century best-seller and perverted the early histories of every country in Europe.[3] Scaliger had been one of pseudo-Berosus's sharpest critics. Yet in this case he showed respectful interest in what he had every reason to dismiss as mad forgeries. Taking his first notes on the story of Oannês, he remarked only that in another account the same fish was called Oês and added a note on Berosus himself from the early Christian writer Tatian.[4] Compiling his last large work on world history, the *Thesaurus temporum* of 1606, he included all the Berosus he could find, dated the material as precisely as he could, and boasted of the service he had performed by collecting these previously unknown texts.[5] He did not even remark—as his close friend Isaac Casaubon mildly did, when taking his own notes on the same manuscript chronicle—that "the nature of a certain animal, *Oannês,* is particularly curious [*in primis mira*]."[6] Instead, he defended the work of Berosus—like that of Manetho, which he also recovered and published—as genuine Near Eastern historiography. True, the early sections of these texts seemed fabulous, but they still deserved the reverence that goes with genuine antiquity, and they also linked up neatly with the ancients' true accounts of later history. Challenged by the Heidelberg theologian David Pareus, Scaliger developed the latter argument into the more polemical thesis, hardly a new one in this context, that the apparently fabulous histories of the pagans clothed real events in mythical form.[7] He thus preserved and defended what we now know to have been the first genuine large-scale products of the ancient Near East to reach the modern West—works so alien to the Western tradition that they could hardly be interpreted at all until the discovery and decipherment of parallel records in cuneiform, more than two hundred years later.

How then do we account for Scaliger's divinatory prowess—his ability to shake off the prejudices normal to his period and place and see that his Near Eastern fragments, if unintelligible, were also unimpeachable? The rich historiographical scholarship of the 1960s and 1970s offers us an answer. The humanists of the early Renaissance—notably Petrarch and Valla—tested and rejected many medieval forgeries. They showed that texts like the charter of Julius Caesar that exempted Austria from imperial jurisdiction or the Donation of Constantine that gave the Pope control of the western empire used a language different from the attested language of their supposed authors, ignored facts recounted by reputable historians, and contradicted the beliefs and aims of well-known historical actors associated with them.[8]

The theologians and jurists of the mid-sixteenth century, men like Melchior Cano and Jean Bodin, were confronted by a much wider range of supposedly authoritative texts and an even more pressing set of religious and political problems. Accordingly, they went much further than their predecessors. They had not only to purify the canon of its fakes but to weigh the authority of its genuine components. Accepting the humanists' isolated but valid insights, Cano and Bodin tried to fuse them into a general art of choosing and reading authorities about the past. Rather than providing empirical case studies they formulated universally applicable rules for evaluating sources. And by applying these consistently to a wide range of texts, slightly later scholars like Henri Estienne, Joseph Scaliger, and Isaac Casaubon purged the classical corpus of its fakes and pseudepigrapha. They made clear the priority of Homer to his spurious Latin rivals, Dictys and Dares; the priority of Plato to his supposed Egyptian source, Hermes Trismegistus; the priority of Hesiod, who really composed for an audience of shepherds, to Musaeus, who wrote for an audience of Alexandrian grammarians. The image conjured up is of a train in which Greeks and Latins, spurious and genuine authorities, sit side by side until they reach a stop marked "Renaissance." Then grim-faced humanists climb aboard, check tickets, and expel fakes in hordes through doors and windows alike. Their destination, of course, is Oblivion, the wrecking yard to which History and Humanism conduct all canons—and certainly consign all fakes.[9]

This vision suggests that humanist critical method was both new and modern. Two centuries and more after the Renaissance, when Karl Otfried Müller confronted the Greek account of Phoenician antiquities forged by Wagenfeld, attributed to a mysterious disappearing manuscript from Portugal (and accepted by the epigrapher and orientalist Grotefend), he needed only to apply the humanists' touchstones to make the odor of authenticity vanish. Pseudo-Philo of Byblos, as presented by Wagenfeld, misunderstood and contradicted the fragments of his own work preserved by Eusebius (though he faithfully retained typographical errors from printed texts). He made many unlikely grammatical and syntactical errors, large and small ("Auch im Gebrauche der Partikeln ist manche Unrichtigkeit zu bemerken"). And he believed in the gods (though he had really been an atheist). Müller transcended the humanists only in his sympathy for forgery as a work of art. He praised Wagenfeld's *Geist* and *Phantasie*, the splendid aptness with which he had caught "the spirit of ancient, Greek-Oriental historiography." In other respects, however, he was merely doing what came humanistically.[10]

Happily, a still more recent generation of scholarship has introduced some attractive loops and swerves into this rectilinear and teleological account. Joseph Levine and others have shown that the simple accumulation of data, generation after generation, did more than method could to catalyze the fixing of a modern canon of classic texts and objects.[11] Others have emphasized the distance that lies between the humanists' exposures of fakes and those of the modern philologist. We now know, for example, that Isaac Casaubon obtained one of the great "modern" results of humanist philology—the inauthenticity of Hermes Trismegistus—precisely because he believed firmly in a traditional dogma, that no pagan could have written a book as pure, clear, and theologically correct as the *Hermetic Corpus* at the early date traditionally assigned to it.[12] History often offered not the subversion but the confirmation of dogma.

But by far the most fetching of these new directions of research is that opened up in two elegant articles by Werner Goez. Goez argues that previous historians have omitted not just an important way station, but the crucial one, from their account of the journey of the ancients. The Dominican Annius of Viterbo, who forged the fake Berosus at the end of the fifteenth century, created not only texts but general rules for the choice of texts as well. These rules in turn formed the basis of all later systematic reflection on the choice and evaluation of sources. Some of the mid-sixteenth-century theorists, like Melchior Cano, rejected Annius and all his works; others, like Jean Bodin, accepted them. But all of them developed their theories of reading in direct response to the challenge he presented. Thus, a forger emerges as the first really modern theorist of critical reading of historians—a paradox that only a heart of stone could reject.[13] If Scaliger could tell that his Berosus was real, he owed his perceptiveness in large part to the creator of the false Berosus he despised.

In this chapter I propose to examine Annius's role in the development of historical and philological method, both by analyzing his own work and by inspecting the mid-sixteenth-century reactions to it. I hope by doing so to reveal my own ignorance *de omni re scibili et quibusdam aliis*—and to suggest that the development of modern response to classical histories, real and fake, is even more crooked and complex than the tale told by Goez.

Mystery, Ancient and Modern, with Seaography

In 1498 Eucharius Silber published Annius's *Commentaries on Various Authors Discussing Antiquities*. This elegant volume contained original sources by real Greek authors like Archilochus, Berosus, and Manetho; by imaginary Greek authors like Metasthenes (a perversion of Megasthenes, the name of a Greek who wrote c. 300 BC about India); and by noble Romans like Cato, Fabius Pictor, and Propertius (exceptionally, this last text was genuine). These texts, cut up into neat gobbets set in a large and impressive Gothic type, swam on a rich foam of commentary by Annius himself, giving a nice impression of classical or biblical status.[14] They looked—and read—like a comprehensive and powerful history of the world. They wove biblical history, ancient myths, and medieval Trojan legends together into a single story. Noah—the only pious member of the race of giants that inhabited the prelapsarian world—became the father not just of Shem, Ham, and Japhet but of a pride of other giants. His sons in turn insinuated themselves into national mythologies of the most diverse kinds, which Berosus neatly laid out in genealogical diagrams ("the lawyers," Annius helpfully remarks, "imitated this example in their use of the form of trees to set out degrees of consanguinity").[15] The Tuyscon whom Tacitus made the ancestor of the Germans, the Hercules whom Spanish legend made the founder of Iberia, the Etruscans whom Tuscan scholars from Leonardo Bruni on had seen as the true, non-Roman progenitors of the modern Italian city-states, and the Dryius who founded the learned Anglo-Gallic order of Druids all found places in a rich if chaotic story. And spicy details—like the story, perhaps derived from the rabbinical tradition in which it also occurs, of how Ham touched Noah's genitals, murmured an incantation, and made him sterile—gave entertainment value to what might otherwise have seemed an austere and tedious narrative.[16]

Annius made his story vivid with devices too many to list. A neat illustration (Fig. 1.1) gave material form to pseudo-Fabius's account of early Rome. An introductory appeal to the Catholic kings of Spain—those possessors of the "bravery, victory, chastity, courtesy, prudence, modesty, piety, solicitude" of Moses and David—gave the works powerful patronage.[17] A reference to two Armenian friars as the source of Annius's new texts—and the Armenian oral tradition that Noah was there called Sale "Aramea lingua"—gave it an exotic flavor highly appropriate to that age of lovers of hieroglyphs and readers of the *Hypnerotomachia Poliphili*.[18]

Above all, the content of the work made a powerful appeal to at least

Figure 1.1. Annius's Vision of Ancient Rome. Source: Berosus, *Berosus Babilonicus* (Paris, 1510). Courtesy of Princeton University Library.

three period forms of historical imagination. Like one of his principal sources, Josephus, whose *Antiquitates* he plundered, Annius offered new details about Noah and the early kingdoms.[19] These provided precisely the rich context for the biblical history of man that the Bible itself lacks. Martin Luther, for example, urges readers of his *Supputatio annorum mundi* to realize that events now forgotten had filled the "vacua spatia" of his chronicle. Many kings and institutions had flourished in biblical times besides those mentioned in the Bible, and most of the patriarchs—as their long life spans showed—had lived simultaneously, not successively.[20] The Annian texts offered precisely the richly detailed backdrop in front of which Luther would have preferred to see the family dramas of ancient Israel performed. No wonder that he found Annius his richest nonbiblical source—despite his discovery of occasional errors and inconsistencies in the texts. No wonder either that the chronologist Ioannes Lucidus Samotheus explicitly defended Berosus's enlarged version of the Mosaic account of the origins of the nations: "Berosus described more [founders of nations than Moses did in Genesis X] because Berosus the Chaldean described as many rulers as there were founders of kingdoms and peoples; Moses, however, described those who had different languages." Differences in forms, he explained, stemmed from the two authors' use of different languages, Hebrew and Chaldean—the latter in any case changed by the Latin translator.[21] On the whole, after all, Berosus stood out among ancient historians for the large amount of material he had in common with Moses; Guillaume Postel insisted that Berosus had a bad reputation precisely because "he passed down to posterity an account similar to that in the sacred [books], and thus is despised and ridiculed by men poorly disposed towards divine things, because of the very quality for which he ought to be praised and preferred to all other authors."[22]

Annius's constant emphasis on Egypt as the source of civilization, on the great journeys and achievements of Osiris, appealed as strongly to that widespread Egyptomania that inspired collectors of hieroglyphs, composers of emblem books, and painters of historical scenes from the late fifteenth-century Vatican to the other extremes of Renaissance Europe, Jacobean London, and Rudolphine Prague.[23] Annius's heavy emphasis on the connections between the biblical Orient, Troy, and the states of fifteenth-century Europe opened up an even more fruitful field for wild speculations. Every nation and city from Novgorod to Naples felt the need for an early history that rivaled or surpassed the ancient histories of Greece and Rome, to which the humanists had given such prominence. No wonder that scholars from Toledo to Trier leaped with alacrity down the rabbit hole where Annius preceded them. True, he offered his richest rewards to his native Viterbo, that cradle of world civilization where Osiris had taught the arts and left inscriptions; to Spain, where his patrons the Borgia came from; and to the reputation of Egypt. But he also had much to offer the French, English, Germans, and other Italians. Hence, he became omnipresent in the historical fantasies and historical frescoes of the early sixteenth century—though, to be sure, the particular interests of those who vulgarized his work had the normal transformative effect.[24] Geoffroy Tory complained that greedy readers coerced him to print an edition of the Annian texts without commentary—already a notable change—for his Parisian public in 1510. Something of the nature of that demand can be glimpsed in the Princeton copy, bought hot from the press in 1510 by Robert Nicolson of London, who carefully underlined every passage dealing with the early history of the British (while either he or another reader also marked the sterilization of Noah with a lurid marginal sign).[25]

Until recently, serious scholars have occasionally tried to clear Annius of the charge of forgery—to make him a genuine transmitter of early texts preserved in Armenia or, more plausibly, the gullible victim of a forger. But in the last twenty years research on him has intensified. Italian scholars have dug out and published some of his *inedita*. And by doing so they have demonstrated that he not only commented on but wrote his *Antiquities*. Eduardo Fumagalli has exposed him citing in early letters a recognizable (but not finished) version of the pseudo-Cato that he printed.[26] A work of 1491–92, the *Epitome of Viterbese History,* shows him already at work on Fabius Pictor. Describing the rape of the Sabine women, he writes: "according to Fabius, an audacious crime in the form of a rape of women took place four months after the founding of the city, 11 days before the Kalends of September (22 August)."[27] Here Annius conflates two passages from one ancient source, Plutarch's life of Romulus, where he read both that the founding took place eleven days before the Kalends of May (21 April) (12.1) and that Fabius Pictor had dated the rape to the fourth month after the foundation (14.1). By combining these two bits of Plutarch, no connection between which is evident in context, he gave an event more lurid than the foundation a nice—if spurious—precision. Later, however, he thought better of this tactic, perhaps because he noticed that his Plutarchan source gave a precise date—quite possibly Fabius Pictor's own—of 18 August for the same event. Accordingly, he made his published Fabius Pictor say only that the rape fell in the fourth month after the foundation, and he transferred precise discussion of the founding date itself to another of his *auctores,* pseudo-Sempronius.[28] Tactics like these reveal a Chatterton, not a

Walpole, hard at work. Annius was no innocent agent or victim but a conscious artist creating a coherent piece of work.

Annius, of course, was no fly-by-night forger but a very serious man—the possessor, indeed, of two of the ultimate accolades for a Renaissance Dominican, a miraculous cure that won mention in the *Acta Sanctorum* and a death by poisoning at the hands of Cesare Borgia. His fakes apparently won him papal attention, Spanish financial and personal support, and even his high office as *magister sacri palatii*.[29] The question, then, is how to appreciate and assess a fine piece of high Renaissance scholarship and art.

Here, too, debate has recently flared up. Goez stressed the modernity of Annius's approach, the theoretical sophistication of the arguments by which he tried to validate his fakes. But Bernard Guenée has tried to find in Annius's critical technique not the triumph of modernity but the culmination of medieval historical method. Annius merely stated in a general form rules long applied in practice by medieval scholars—especially when they needed historical evidence to adjudicate the rival claims of quarreling religious institutions or orders to a privilege or a relic. Further evidence—like Beryl Smalley's discovery that a medieval forger had been inspired long before Annius to invent a pseudo-Berosus, who described the eclipse that accompanied the crucifixion—seems to confirm the traditional flavor of Annius's heady historical concoction.[30]

AMBITION

Ambition, more than any other term, conveys the basic flavor of Annius's stew. He set out, as he says, on a Herculean journey, to do the "duty of a theologian: to seek, discover, confirm, reveal, and so far as possible to explicate, teach and pass on the truth." He claims to offer *nuda veritas*, unadorned by rhetoric and uncontaminated by falsehood. And he claims that this truth embraces all events in human history, the creation of all significant arts and sciences, and the origins of all peoples. This effort to enfold in a single encyclopedic history the origins of society and culture harks back to the world of the Fathers of the Church, when Julius Africanus, Eusebius, and Isidore of Seville set out to provide similarly comprehensive records. Like them, Annius is a compiler with an ideology. He wishes to reveal the truth; but the truth he reveals is as polemical as it is comprehensive. It displaces Greek culture from its central place in human history and connects the modern West directly to the biblical Near East.[31]

Annius's ambition, moreover, makes itself felt in many details as well as in the larger framework of his enterprise: chiefly when he forges ancient precedent for practices and institutions of his own time. A theologian of distinction, he had opinions on many controverted problems of his day: the licitness of the *monte di pietà,* the freedom of the will, and the influence of the stars on history.[32] And in the last case at least, Annius built into his ancient texts support for a highly up-to-date practice. In 1480, as Cesare Vasoli has shown, Annius reacted to the Turkish landing at Otranto by issuing a back-dated prediction, based both on the *Revelation* of John and the revelations of the stars, that the time of Muslim dominance had reached its end and a Christian triumph was approaching. He supported this view with a general argument about the role of the stars as intermediaries between God and this world and a specific argument about the role of the zodiacal sign of Leo in the victories of the Turks. These prophecies—like the many others that circulated through Italy in the last two decades of the fifteenth century, heralded by the preaching of Savonarola and the strange street-corner agitation of men like Giovanni Mercurio—were entirely serious both in detail and in their underlying assumptions. In his *Antiquities,* almost twenty years later, Annius defended his early position retroactively. He made Berosus describe Noah as foreseeing the Flood *ex astris,* seventy-eight years in advance; his commentary made other giants predict the Flood from the stars; he even quoted the "more competent Talmudists'" opinion that Noah was an expert astronomer as well as a giant. He thus made the kind of astrology he practiced not merely old but antediluvian— an enviable disciplinary history, since it chartered astrological prediction as a part of the primeval knowledge of the patriarchs.[33]

DERISION

If Annius hoped to replace the texts of the ancients with his own new canon, he had to prove the fallibility of his opponents as well as the antiquity and purity of his own authors. That he did, ad nauseam, at every opportunity conceivable and some that were not. Sometimes he gives the Greeks the lie direct, as in this comment on his forged Xenophon *De equivocis:*

Berosus writes in Antiquities 5: "In the fourth year of Ninus (king of Babylon) Tuyscon the giant trained the Germans in letters and laws, Samotes trained the Celts, and Tubal trained the Celtiberians." . . . Therefore the Iberians, Samotheans and Tuyscons were clearly the fathers of letters and philosophy, more than a thousand years before the Greeks, as Aristotle attests rightly in his Magic, and Senon, and not the Greeks, as lying Ephorus and the dreamer Diogenes Laertius imagine but do not prove.[34]

Annius often gave free rein to his enviable talent as a composer of invective. Graecia for him was preeminently Graecia mendax; the Greeks stood guilty of inventing new doctrines instead of sticking to the old ones of the giants, and were accused of vanity, levity, and virtually every crime but mopery: "Greece and the Peloponnesus were called in antiquity Aegialea, that is, Goaty (*Hircina*), because they produce many goats and because the race of men there is dirty, fetid and goatish (*hircinum*)."[35] Elsewhere, though, he took a more measured tone, using the Greeks' inability to agree as the outward and visible sign of their interior corruption: "The Greeks fight and disagree with one another, as is not surprising, and they have entirely ruined history as well as philosophy with their civil war."[36] This combination of invective and argument gives texts and commentary alike a hectoring, even menacing tone, which helped to ensure Annius and his boys a friendly reception not only in the Catholic Italy he knew but also in the Protestant and puritanical north a few decades later. No wonder that Luther, who believed that all of Aristotle compared to the Bible as darkness compares to light, preferred Annius's Berosus to Herodotus and his ilk.

UGLIFICATION

For our purposes, however, Annius's methods matter more than his attitudes. Some of his tools were simple enough. Composing the history of "Myrsilus of Lesbos," he derived his matter from the extraordinarily rich first book of Dionysius of Halicarnassus's Roman history, recently translated into Latin. He then admitted the similarity of their accounts— "quamvis qui Dionisium in primo libro legit, etiam Myrsilum videatur legere"—and explained them handily: "Dionysius follows Myrsilus consistently in the first book, save in the time of Enotrius' arrival in Italy." "In any event," he wound up for the benefit of the unconvinced, "both of them will be clarified by my commentary."[37] Composing Berosus on Germany, he borrowed Tyscon from Tacitus and went on his way rejoicing.[38]

Elsewhere he transplanted what he read in one source to alien ground. If Diodorus Siculus described the pillar on which Osiris recorded his expeditions, Annius both forged an inscription left by Osiris in Viterbo and made his Xenophon—not the proper Xenophon, of course, but another writer of the same name—describe the similar inscription of Ninus of Babylon.[39] Much of the grist for his mill came from the great Jewish and Christian writers who had assembled evidence to prove the antiquity and priority of the Judeo-Christian tradition—above all Josephus and Eusebius, from whom he took the very names of Berosus and Manetho and much else. One of his handiest multi-application tools, the euhemerist interpretation of classical myths as reworkings of genuine events, had already proved an interpretative Swiss army knife to legions of interpreters pagan and Christian, from whom Annius could learn how great men did great things and then became gods.[40]

Sometimes Annius moved from the low plane of craft to the higher one of art. When it came to tying the early histories of modern nations to the Bible, the ancient sources left him cast up on a dry beach, clueless and uninformed. Accordingly, he invented, assuming that etymology provided the key that could decipher any tribe's or city's name, making it reveal the lost name of its founder. Text and commentator work together closely in these cases.

In the time of Mancaleus [says Berosus] . . . Lugdus ruled the Celts; province and people took their name from him.
Lugdus [says Annius] was the one who settled the province of Lugdunum, as his name proves.[41]

"He invents kings like this whenever he has to," so Annius's most brilliant critic in the next generation, Beatus Rhenanus, cried in disgust: "But Lugdunum isn't derived from Lugdus. Dunum is a suffix, like German *berg* or *burg*."[42] But such reservations were rare. On the whole, Annius's method—itself no doubt derived from a careful reading of another ancient source, the *Etymologies* of Isidore—carried conviction, even when he went to the imaginative extreme of deriving Hercules from Egyptian *Her*, "covered with skin," and Hebrew *Col*, "all," "since he used wild beasts' skins to cover his whole body in place of arms, since arms were not yet invented."[43] Etymology ensured authority.

It would be wrong to assume—as some interpreters have—that Annius's novel information all came from his mother wit. Sometimes he made creative use of others' mistakes. In book 5 of his histories, Diodorus Siculus mentions those wise men "whom the Gauls call Druids." Poggio Bracciolini rendered the clause in question as "quos vocant Saronidas"—

"whom they call Saronidae."[44] It was from this very up-to-date textual foundation, built of only the best sand, that Annius derived his wise King Sarron, who taught the barbarous Celts their letters.

Sometimes, too, his information comes straight from sources that were to him classic—but that we have ceased to read. One problem modern scholarship has not solved is this: why does Annius make Archilochus—a poet rather than a scholar, and one about whose character the most alarming information circulated—tell the story of the eight different Homers who inhabited the ancient world, the last of whom, Archilochus's contemporary, won at the Olympics and became the official reformer of the Greek alphabet? Who ever heard of a scholarly Archilochus? The answer here is simple. At some point in the Hellenistic age, a scholar compiled several divergent opinions about the date of Homer. He attributed these, using a normal late Greek phrase, to *hoi peri* Aristarchus, *hoi peri* Eratosthenes, and others. Literally, *hoi peri* means "those about" or "the school of," but in late Greek it is often merely an elegant periphrasis for the proper name that follows the pronoun *peri*. This is probably the sense required here. The anonymous scholar also noted that others date Homer to the time of Archilochus. His compilation, in turn, found a place in Tatian's *Oration Against the Greeks* (c. AD 150) and in Eusebius's *Chronicle* two centuries later, in condensed form: *heteroi kata Archilochon* ("others date him to the time of Archilochus").[45] The problem arose when St. Jerome translated Eusebius into Latin. Quite reasonably, he turned *hoi peri Aristarchon* into "Aristarchus," *hoi peri Eratosthenen* into "Eratosthenes"; but when he came to the end of the list, he misread *heteroi kata Archilochon* as an elegant variation on the earlier construction, and made Archilochus the author of the last opinion rather than its chronological benchmark.[46] In this case, Annius's mistake was by no means his own. It came from that dramatic era, the late fourth and fifth centuries AD, when Christian scholars like Jerome treated the classical heritage much as their unlearned followers were treating the pagan philosopher Hypatia.

In a larger sense, too, Annius's effort to fill in and add color to the biblical narrative has deep roots in scholarly tradition. Jewish scholars had spent centuries devising *aggadot*, supplementary tales about the characters in the Old Testament that rounded out their lives and clarified their motives—like the tale of Ham's enchantment of Noah. And late medieval Mendicants, of course, had done the same for the characters in the New Testament and their favorite saints. It was the late medieval Dominicans who enriched the biography of St. Jerome with the story that he had pushed an insufficiently respectful abbot to the edge of a cliff and allowed him to live only when he promised to dedicate a church to St. Jerome. Swiss Dominicans in Bern just after Annius's time adorned a statue of the Virgin Mary with drops of varnish, to show that it wept (and thus possessed holy powers); they even put a speaking tube between its lips and made it issue prophecies and commands.[47] The production of serious fiction designed to fill out the holiest of records was no novelty in 1498. Annius's methods of uglification, then, do not qualify him as either medieval or modern. Classical, patristic and medieval, popular and learned, Christian and non-Christian ingredients are blended here into a stew so rich and complex that the original ingredients and spices are often beyond retrieval.

DISTRACTION

Like any forger, Annius had to keep his readers' confidence—to distract them from the holes in his material, the contradictions in his texts, and the obvious anachronisms of his style ("Alexander," writes Metasthenes, ". . . transtulit imperium in Graecos"—a splendid piece of Greek historical writing).[48] He used a variety of means. Some were the normal resources of the ancient and medieval forger—like the claim to have derived his information from a source so distant as to discourage verification and so exotic as to compel belief. If Geoffrey of Monmouth could attribute his account of Brutus et al. to "a very ancient book in the British tongue" offered him by Walter, Archdeacon of Oxford, Annius could certainly borrow some texts from his Armenian confreres and ask advice on Hebrew and Aramaic from his Jewish friend, the still unidentified "Samuel the Talmudist" who told him that "Alemannus" comes from Scythian Ale (river) and the name Mannus.[49]

But Annius was both more polemical and more imperious than most medieval forgers. Like other defenders of oral tradition in a scholarly age, he had to provide his own textual warrants of authority. Moreover, he was a scholar in his own right, one who wanted not only to complement but to replace the Greek historians. To bring this about he insinuated, into both his forged texts and his commentaries, a set of rules for the choice of reliable sources. Metasthenes states these clearly:

Those who write on chronology must not do so on the basis of hearsay and opinion. For if they write by opinion, like the Greeks, they will deceive themselves and others and waste their lives in error. But error will be avoided if we follow only the annals of the two kingdoms and reject the rest as fabulous. For these contain the dates, kings, and names, set out as clearly and truly as their kings ruled splendidly. But we must not accept everyone who writes about these kings, but only the priests of the kingdom, whose annals have public and incontrovertible authority, like Berosus. For that Chaldean set out the entire Assyrian history on the basis of the ancients' annals, and we Persians now follow him alone, or above all.[50]

Annius's comment described the ancient priests as "publici notarii rerum gestarum et temporum," whose records deserved as ready belief as the notarial records in a modern archive. And his other authors referred to, repeated, and expanded on these injunctions, creating a sticky, cohesive web of mutually supportive fictions about authority. After working his way through Myrsilus, Berosus, and Philo, the reader knew that each of the Four Monarchies, Assyrian, Persian, Greek, and Roman, had had its own priestly caste and produced its own sacred annals. Only histories based on these deserved credit; and any given historian deserved credit only for those sections where he drew on an authoritative set of records.[51] For example, Ctesias the Greek "is accepted for Persian history and rejected from Assyrian history," since he drew his account of the former from the Persian archives (in fact, of course, he invented it) and made the latter up.[52] These principles have attracted more attention than any other segment of the corpus Annianum. Rightly, too; for they do seem a prescient effort to separate history, the record of events, *res gestae*, from history, the literary work of an individual, *historia*. Certainly they mark an effort to replace the empirical, case-by-case practices of the early humanists with a general theory. Yet at the same time they have an eerily traditional quality. Guenée points out that when the monks of Saint-Denis and the canons of Notre-Dame disputed around 1400 on the burning question of which of them had which bits of Saint Denis, both sides cited and assessed historical evidence. One of the advocates of Saint-Denis argued that the *Grandes Chroniques de France,* which supported his case, should prevail. After all, it was an "approved and authorized" history, preserved in a "public archive." Was new humanist old canonist rewritten in fetching macaronic Latin?[53]

In fact, here, too, Annius drew on a one-time classic now read only by specialists, as Stephens has now shown in detail.[54] In the last years of his life, the Jewish historian and honest traitor Josephus wrote a polemical work in two books against the grammarian Apion, who had defamed the Jews. In the course of this he repeatedly emphasized the novelty of Greek and the antiquity of Jewish civilization. And to nail this point home he emphasized that the Jewish and Near Eastern texts he quoted rested not on individual opinion but on archival documents recorded by a caste of priests:

> The Egyptians, the Chaldeans, and the Phoenicians (to say nothing for the moment of ourselves) have by their own account an historical record rooted in tradition of extreme antiquity and stability. For all these peoples live in places where the climate causes little decay, and they take care not to let any of their historical experiences pass out of their memory. On the contrary, they religiously preserve it in their public records, written by their most able scholars. In the Greek world, however, the memory of past events has been blotted out. (1.8–10)

Josephus elsewhere praises Berosus for "following the most ancient records" (1.130), the people of Tyre for keeping careful "public records" (1.107), and the Egyptians for entrusting the care of their records to their priests (1.28). If the *contra Apionem,* available in Latin since the time of Cassiodorus, was little read in the Middle Ages, Annius certainly used it heavily. In fact, in his comment on Metasthenes, Annius made clear—*more suo*—what his source was. He explains that "Josephus used Metasthenes' rules to make a most valid argument" against Greek views on the origin of the Greek alphabet.[55]

This reuse of ancient scholarship, though unusually extended, is far from unique in the corpus. In pseudo-Sempronius, Annius lists a series of opinions, including that of the astrologer L. Tarrutius Firmanus, about the year of Rome's foundation. He draws his datings, as O. A. Danielsson showed long ago in what remains a very useful article, from the Roman compiler Solinus (third century AD).[56] He then declares his—or Sempronius's—preference for *Eratosthenis invicta regula,* "the unvanquished rule of Eratosthenes." Danielsson read with amusement what he took to be this "echt annianische Phrase." In fact, Annius took it directly from L. Biragus's Latin translation of Dionysius of Halicarnassus's *Roman Antiquities.* At 1.63 Dionysius explains that he has elsewhere shown the *canones* (chronological canons or tables) of Eratosthenes to be sound; Biragus rendered Greek *canones* as Latin *regulae,* rather than *tabulae* or *laterculi,* and thus misled at least one reader. Annius's rules, then, were neither medieval nor modern. They were instead a classical revival, for the most part a restatement of that partly justified Near Eastern pride in great longevity and accurate records that animated so much of the resistance to Hellenization and to Rome—and gave rise in its own right to so many forgeries. We will not find in Annius the culmination of medieval historical scholarship or the origins of modern historical hermeneutics.

Nothing ages so quickly as one period's convincing version of a still earlier period. Annius's antiquity looks intensely quaint and entirely Renaissance now. Indeed, it looked quite modern to some of his early readers. Beatus Rhenanus, for example, had no trouble seeing the single authorship of texts and commentary. "While the one milks the he-goat," he dryly commented, "the other holds out the sieve." Pietro Crinito, who preferred to take his fragments of Cato from genuine Roman sources like Macrobius, had no trouble condemning Annius. Nor did Juan Luis Vives, who inserted a powerful attack into his commentary on Augustine's *City of God,* where it found a surprising number of readers. Nor did the anonymous skeptics of whom Postel bitterly complained.[57] But these exceptions do not disturb the general rule. For every Rhenanus there was at least one Trithemius, eager and willing to embroider on Annius in the most fanciful ways (Trithemius's version of *broderie allemande* took the form of his own invented text, that of the Scythian historian Hunibald, who recounted the deeds of the Germans from Marcomir on)—even if he did point out, in an uncharacteristically critical moment, that it was absurd for everyone in Europe to boast of Trojan ancestry, as if there weren't a good many older families in Europe and as if the Trojans hadn't included some rascals.[58] In history as in the economy, bad currency drives out the good.

Seven Types of Assiduity: Readers, Rules, and Annius in the Mid-Century

More than seventy years ago, Friedrich von Bezold called attention in a brilliant essay to the great vitality and interest of mid-sixteenth-century historical thought. As he saw, intellectuals of very different origins and types—from the Spanish Dominican Melchior Cano to the irenic Calvinist lawyer François Baudouin—all confronted the same set of theoretical and practical problems. All had to find guidance for churches split on points of dogma, kingdoms split along multiple social and religious fault lines, and families divided by both religious and political questions. All agreed that the authoritative canon of ancient texts, biblical and classical, should provide the remedies needed to heal the fissures in church and state and quell the European trend toward religious and civil war. Reading was urgent; but reading unguided by rules led only to chaos, as the Reformation clearly showed. Accordingly, the mid-century saw a massive effort to rethink and regulate the reading of the ancients—particularly the historians, those preeminent guides for practical action in the present. Which sources are which? This simple question burned and stimulated for two decades.[59]

Some modern scholars have made even larger claims. They have taken the mid-century theoretical writers, especially Cano, Baudouin, and Bodin, as doing more than raising questions—as formulating a modern set of rules for weighing sources.[60] But they have not in general examined these in detail in the light of the Annian rules that their authors knew, and they have abstracted the texts on historical method from the wider body of sixteenth-century scholarly literature on related points, as if visionaries like Guillaume Postel and chronologers like Johann Funck did not attack the same problems, respond to the same Annian stimuli, and profoundly influence the theorists. A broad look at mid-century scholars' use of Annius will enable us, I think, to refine and moderate some of the claims that have been made on behalf of individuals or about the modernity of the movement they supposedly made up.

We can begin with Postel, that strange man, half visionary and half philologist, who started out in religious life in the early Jesuit order and wound up honorably confined as a madman in a French convent. A real scholar, a man who knew Greek well enough to compile a pioneering study of Athenian institutions and knew Hebrew and other Eastern languages better than almost any other European of his time, Postel had prejudices even more overpowering than his erudition.[61] He saw classical Greek and Roman culture as a perversion of an earlier, Near Eastern revelation, best entrusted in his own day to the virtuous Gauls; he condemned Romulus as a descendant of Ham who had tried to extirpate the virtuous laws and customs established in Italy by Noah, also known as Janus. He knew that some doubted the authenticity of Berosus and the rest, but he maintained the positive stoutly, accepting the texts and Metasthenic rules as givens:

> Though Berosus the Chaldean is preserved in fragments, and is disliked by Atheists or enemies of Moses, he is approved of by innumerable men and authors expert in every language and field of learning. Hence I grant him the faith deserved by any accurate author.[62]

At the other end of the spectrum we find Baudouin, writing in 1560, expressing his surprise that so many of his contemporaries had accepted as genuine the "farrago" of Berosus, with its many obvious falsehoods.[63] On the one hand we have Postel's unquestioning faith and reverence, on the other Baudouin's disgust, like that of a gardener confronted by a poisonous spider; neither position, as one would expect, rests on elaborate argument. Neither, of course, can be simply taken as "modern." Postel, for all his literalist insistence that Berosus's closeness to Genesis was his great virtue, also made an elegant historiographical point: Berosus sometimes told stories that redounded to the discredit of the Chaldeans, and a witness testifying against his own interest deserves belief.[64] Baudouin, by contrast, enjoys great credit now as a theorist of source criticism. Yet his modern-sounding argument that while all historians tell lies and make mistakes, all histories are not therefore fabulous, was in fact a quotation from an ancient forgery—the *Scriptores historiae Augustae*.[65] Baudouin took it from the bravura dialogue at the beginning of "Flavius Vopiscus'" life of Aurelian (*Divus Aurelianus* ii)—one of the several reflections on *fides historica*, good sources and archival documents that adorn the *Scriptores*. In fact, the "rogue scholar" who forged these texts, with their alluring references to what could be found in "Bookcase 6 of the Ulpian Library," may well have taught Baudouin the principle that a good historian relies on original documents—something that "Vopicus" claimed that he had systematically done (Flavius Vopiscus, *Divus Aurelianus* i; *Tacitus* viii.1; *Probus* ii). Still, on Annius at least, Postel and Baudouin took uncompromisingly opposed positions.

Between the extremes positions grow even more complex, and the supporting arguments—or at least the supporting attitudes—became more subtle. On the side of credulity we find a writer like John Caius of Cambridge—a skilled Hellenist, like many sixteenth-century medical writers, and one with a sharp interest in questions about lost and inauthentic medical works from the ancient world. In the 1560s he became embroiled in a dispute with Thomas Caius of Oxford about the antiquity of the two universities.[66] Trying to prove the antiquity of learning in England, he cited Berosus copiously about the giants Sarron, Druys, et al., who founded public institutions of learning in England and Gaul around the year 1829 after the Creation, a bit more than 150 years after the Flood. Yet for all his apparent belief in the learned Sarronidae and Berosus "antiquae memoriae scriptor," he took care to indicate that the giants had not founded Cambridge—that came later—and, more important, that the giants had been so called not because they were huge but because they were aborigines, *gêgeneis*.[67] True, one or two of them, like Polyphemus and Gogmagog, had reached great heights, but on the whole "giants, like modern men, came in a variety of sizes," even if nature brought forth stronger and bigger offspring in those purer days. By confining his use of Berosus to this very early period, by rationalizing away some of his more bizarre ideas, and by faith, John Caius could avoid applying to the myths that supported his own position the cutting-edge philological *Kritik* he applied to Oxford myths about the academic beneficence of Good King Alfred. And a similar attitude—of distrust mingled with unwillingness to give up such rich material—can be found in others, like the historian Sleidanus, the historical theorist Chytraeus, and, perhaps, Caius's younger Oxford contemporary Henry Savile.[68]

On the side of criticism we find a number of writers—such as the theologian Cano, the Portuguese scholar Gasper Barreiros, and the Florentine antiquary Vincenzo Borghini—piling up evidence to prove the falsity of the Annian texts. They rapidly found in his richest ancient sources ample evidence of his mistakes. Berosus, in Josephus, explicitly denied the Greek story that Semiramis had converted Babylon from a small town to a great city; the Berosus in Annius affirmed it. Josephus's Berosus wrote three books, Annius's five.[69] And, in any event, Josephus's Berosus knew only about events before his own time, while Annius's Berosus mentioned the founding of Lugdunum which took place two hundred years after his death.[70] These critics, moreover, did not confine themselves to pointing out blunders of organization and detail. They also showed that Berosus wrote the wrong kind of history for his age and place. The Greeks of his time, after all, knew nothing about Western lands like Spain; how could Berosus, still farther east than they, know more?[71] As to the "annals" of the Greeks and Romans, Cano pointed out in a brilliant historiographical essay that none existed. Josephus, Annius's main source, denied that the Greeks had had designated public historians. Livy, the main source for early Roman history, showed by his infrequent citation of public records and his many errors and hesitations that "there were no public annals in the libraries and temples of the gods." Cano's conclusion was lapidary and remorseless:

They who say that the Greek and Roman monarchies had public annals against which other histories must be checked say nothing. . . . For it has been shown that no Greek or Roman public annals existed. Therefore there were no authors who described deeds or times in accordance with those Greek and Roman annals.[72]

Here the limits of Annius's own historical imagination told against him. A more modern notion of the practice of classical historians revealed that they were rarely if ever "public recorders of events."

Still more complex were the reactions of the Wittenberg chronologer Johann Funck. A student of Philipp Melanchthon and a friend of Andreas

Osiander, who wrote the celebrated and misleading preface to Copernicus's *De revolutionibus,* Funck attacked the records of the ancient world with both philological and scientific tools. These soon enabled him to chip away the authority of one of the deadliest Annian writers, Metasthenes, who covered the centuries after the Babylonian exile of the Jews for which neither the Bible nor any pagan author offered a full, coherent, and acceptable narrative. Like Copernicus—and some earlier Byzantine writers— Funck set out to use the data preserved by Ptolemy, the great ancient astronomer. Like them, he wrongly identified Salmanassar, a king of Assyria mentioned in the Bible, with Nabonassar, the king of Babylon from whose accession on 26 February 747 BC the Babylonian astronomical records used by Ptolemy began. Unlike them, he systematically teased out the implications of astronomy for history. He identified the biblical Nabuchodonosor (incorrectly by modern standards) with the king Nabopolassar mentioned by Ptolemy. He pointed out that Ptolemy fixed the beginning of Nabopolassar's reign absolutely, since he dated a lunar eclipse to "the fifth year of Nabopolassar, which is the 127th year from Nabonassar (= 21/2 April 621 BC)" (*Almagest* 5.14, tr. Toomer). He found a different epoch date for Nabuchodonosor in Metasthenes. And he concluded that Metasthenes—or the archives he had used—must be rejected:

Do not let his authority stand in your way. Rather examine how far he stands in agreement with Holy Scripture and Ptolemy's absolutely certain observations of times. That way, even if you do not manage to reach the absolute truth you may approach it as closely as is possible.[73]

Having examined a full range of texts, he also decided that ancient historians could lead where astronomical records gave out, so long as they were critically chosen: Herodotus and Eusebius, not Ctesias and Metasthenes, should be preferred.[74] Funck thus pioneered the way along what remains the only path to absolute dates in ancient history. Though he, like the reader he addresses, did not reach the absolute truth, his footing was remarkably sure. Yet Funck found no stimulus in his examination of Metasthenes to raise wider questions about Annius's writers or their archives. Where the early pages of Luther's *Supputatio* offered white spaces, Funck's swarm with the deeds of the giants and the first seven Homers, all derived from Annian sources. He considered Berosus "the most approved history of the Babylonians" and copied him out joyfully, invention by invention.[75] Thus technical methods of a strikingly modern kind could coexist with a credulity so complete as to be surprising.

Bodin, whose *Method for the Easy Comprehension of History* of 1566 has proved a textual Greenland that has killed off interpreters for centuries, struggled mightily with Annius's texts and Funck's ideas. He knew enough to add guarded references to the possible falsity of Berosus's and Manetho's fragments in his bibliography of historians—but not enough to do the same for Metasthenes or pseudo-Philo (or, indeed, for Dictys and Dares).[76] He quoted Metasthenes' advice about choosing historians without a word of caution, and praised Metasthenes as a historian who used archival sources and wrote about a people not his own (about which he could be objective).[77] When it came to the problems Funck raised, he showed a shattering lack of perceptiveness. Berosus and Metasthenes disagreed with "the rule of celestial motions" not because they made mistakes or used bad sources, he argued, but because they had not recorded the years and months of interregna. If only they had done so, like that "scriptor diligens" Ctesias, all discrepancies would drop away and all good sources hang together in one great Happy Historical Family.[78] If Bodin's willingness to accept pagan attacks on Christianity as the product of milieu and education rather than moral debility marks him out as an unusually perceptive reader, his use of Metasthenes sets narrow limits on his critical faculties and reveals that Annius helped to inspire—and even to shape—his notion of critical method. Even his insistence that the accuracy of historians be judged case by case, not assessed for all time by a single verdict cast in stone—his belief that Dionysius of Halicarnassus, for example, described Roman foreigners more objectively than his fellow Greeks and therefore should be read in different ways at different points—even this is no more than a development of Annius's argument that a single historian could be accepted for one kingdom and still rejected from the reliable sources for another. Bodin's rich tapestry of methodological admonitions reveals many gaudy Annian splotches when held up to the light. Despite his comprehensive curiosity and psychological insight, Bodin's limits are more striking than his strengths—especially when he is compared with the forgotten Johann Funck, whose work he knew so well.

The most complex—and one of the most influential—of all the mid-century readers was Joannes Goropius Becanus, the Flemish doctor whose *Origines Antwerpianae* of 1569 mounted the shrewdest attack of all on Annius, and in doing so drew on much of the literature we have surveyed. To refute the forgeries he collected, in Greek, as many as possible of the fragments of the real authors Annius had travestied and as many collateral testimonia as he could find. Some of his finds were conventional—and perhaps derivative—like his use of Josephus to show that the real Berosus did not think that Semiramis made Babylon great.[79] Others, however, showed far more penetration. Attacking Archilochus—from whom his predecessors had discreetly withheld their fire—he showed that no one ascribed a work on chronology to him. Finding in Tatian the original of the passage on the eight Homers that had inspired Annius to create pseudo-Archilochus, Goropius printed it, showed that Eusebius must have quoted it in the form that Tatian gave, and argued that the Latin text of Jerome's translation of Eusebius was corrupt and must be corrected or filled out "not as our antiquity-hawker wished, but by reference to what Tatian recounts."[80] The original reference had been not to Archilochus's theory that Homer lived in his own time but to someone else's theory that Homer and Archilochus were contemporaries. By diligent search in Clement of Alexandria, Goropius even managed to give that someone a name, Theopompus.[81] Goropius, in short, found inspiration in Annius not to advance theories but to collect fragments and elucidate them. The *Origines Antwerpianae* are the distant ancestor of *Die Fragmente der griechischen Historiker.*

Yet Goropius had more in mind than negative criticism and technical philology. He had his own new history of the ancient world to advance— one in which the Dutch were the remnant of the antediluvian peoples and their language, with its many monosyllables, was the primal speech of Adam. To prove this he offered evidence of many kinds—notably the famous experiment of king Psammetichus, who locked up two children, did not let them learn any words, and found that they spontaneously asked for "*Becos,*" the Phrygian word for bread—thereby identifying the Phrygians rather than the Egyptians as the primeval race (Hdt. 2.2). This showed, Goropius reasonably argued, that the Dutch were the oldest; after all, "they call the man who makes bread a *Becker.* That king's ancient experiment shows that the language of the inhabitants of Antwerp must be considered the oldest, and therefore the noblest."[82] This revision of world history—which, as even Goropius admitted, rested on novel readings of the sources—was closely related to Goropius's attack on Annius. An essential element of his history of the migrations lay in the denial that Noah and his fellows had been giants; and thus prejudice as well as precision inspired Goropius's sedulous work as collector and exegete.

Enough has been said to make several points clear. The mid-century certainly saw a concerted effort to reshape the history of the world and to rethink the sources it should be derived from. But this effort took place as much in the tedious and technical pages of chronologies—and the terrifying and bizarre ones of historical fantasies—as it did in those of writers on the uses of human historians. No single writer, no single genre, held a monopoly on the relevant forms of criticism; fantasts on some points were the grimmest and most exacting of realists on others. Twenty years of ardent speculation, most of it provoked by Annius, left his forged texts and his tarted-up ancient rules firmly in command of large parts of the historical field as most scholars viewed it. Even those who attacked him most ardently often did so in a partial and half-hearted way; even those who accepted some of his forgeries did splendidly at unmasking others.

Goez is triumphantly right to point to the pervasive stimulus Annius afforded, but wrong to overemphasize Annius's isolation and originality. And any effort to ground in the thought of the mid-sixteenth century the rise of a new and operational method of source criticism risks committing what has well been called a "hagiographical anachronism"—the fallacy of attributing to the original and learned of the past ideas and methods consistent with what we now believe in.[83] Baudouin and Bodin, Postel and Goropius are thinkers individual and original enough to need no ex post facto rescue operations designed to prove that they were modern as well.

An Unscientific Postscript

Meanwhile, back in Leiden, how did Joseph Scaliger manage not to reject the real Berosus as he had the false one? None of the writers we have examined could have taught him to accept as somehow generally reliable a text much of whose factual content was false. Whence came enlightenment?

The answer is clear and definite, though unexpected: it came from nearby Friesland. There earlier sixteenth-century intellectuals had developed a model *Urgeschichte* of the province. They argued that three Indian gentlemen, Friso, Saxo, and Bruno, had left their native country in the fourth century BC. They studied with Plato, fought for Philip and Alexander of Macedon, and then settled in Frisia, where they drove off the aboriginal giants and founded Groningen. The image is enchanting: three gentlemen in frock coats sitting around a peat fire, murmuring politely in Sanskrit.[84] But around 1600 it enflamed the temper of a critical humanist Scaliger esteemed, Ubbo Emmius. He denounced Friso and his friends as fables and the sources they came from as spurious.[85] And Suffridus Petri, who had given the Frisian tales currency in elegant Latin, mounted a brilliant defense. He claimed that ancient texts now lost and popular songs like the *Carmina* of the early Romans and Germans, long familiar from Livy and Tacitus, could have preserved the origins of Frisia even if formal historians did not. He insisted that even if such popular sources contained fables, they should be analyzed not scarified: "A good historian should not simply abandon the antiquities because of the fables, but should cleanse the fables for the sake of the antiquities."[86] Oral tradition, in short, needed critical reworking, not contempt.[87]

Scaliger knew these debates because Leiden friends of his like Janus Dousa plunged into them, trying to purify Holland of its origin myths as Scaliger tried to purify Egypt and Babylon. What is remarkable, again, is his reaction. He praised Emmius but imitated Petri. The tolerant and eclectic attitude Petri recommended for Friso informed Scaliger's approach to Berosus and Manetho. When Scaliger published the Babylonian *Urgeschichte* and defended it, urging that it deserved at least the *reverentia* that Livy had shown for ancient stories and arguing that it was a mythical transfiguration of real events, he used a forger's and a fantast's tools to integrate the real ancient Near East into the Western tradition. Even if the forger was Petri rather than Annius, he, too, was a forger who gave philology new intellectual worlds to conquer.

Forgery and philology fell and rose together, in the Renaissance as in Hellenistic Alexandria; sometimes the forgers were the first to create or restate elegant critical methods, sometimes the philologists beat them to it. But in either event one conclusion emerges. The rediscovery of the classical tradition in the Renaissance was as much an act of imagination as of criticism, as much an invention as a rediscovery; yet many of the instruments by which it was carried out were themselves classical products rediscovered by the humanists. Paradox, contradiction, and confusion hold illimitable dominion over all; we wanted the humanists to give us a ticket for Birmingham but they have sent us on to Crewe. The only consolation is to sit back, relax, and enjoy the leather upholstery and gaslights that made old-fashioned journeys so much more pleasant than modern ones.[88]

My thanks are owed to many friends who have commented on earlier drafts of this article—especially Susanna Barrows, Peter Brown, Jill Kraye, Glenn Most, and David Quint; Carlotta Dionisotti and James Hankins, neither of whom believes a word of it, offered especially searching criticisms, to many of which I can as yet provide no adequate reply.

Notes

1. *Scaligerana* (Cologne, 1695), 123.
2. For Berosus see *FrGrHist* 680 F 1; modern translation and commentary by

S. M. Burstein (1978). For the general context see S. K. Eddy, *The King Is Dead* (Lincoln, 1961).

3. J. Selden, *The Reverse . . . of the English Janus,* tr. R. Westcot, quoted by A. L. Owen, *The Famous Druids* (Oxford, 1962), 36.

4. Leiden University Library MS Scal. 10, fol. 2 recto, quoting Helladius from Photius, *Bibliotheca,* cod. 279 and Tatian *Ad Graecos* 36 (= Eus. *Praep. ev.* 10. 11. 8 = *FrGrHist* 680 T 2).

5. *Thesaurus temporum,* 2d ed. (Amsterdam, 1658), *Notae in Graeca Eusebii,* 407–8.

6. Bodleian Library MS Casaubon 32, fol. 52 verso: "Multa ex Beroso ipsis verbis recitantur, quae non memini reperire neque apud Eusebium, neque apud Iosephum. Eiusmodi est pericopa de Babylonia et eius mira ubertate. Sed in primis mira natura animalis cuiusdam *oanne,* ex multis composito monstro: cuius vox hominem sonat." For the date and significance of these notes—like those in Leiden MS Scal. 10, not discussed in the recent Teubner ed. of Syncellus (Leipzig, 1984) by A. A. Mosshammer—see A. Grafton, "Protestant versus Prophet: Isaac Casaubon on Hermes Trismegistus," *Journal of the Warburg and Courtauld Institutes* 46 (1983), 93.

7. Scaliger, *Notae in Graeca Eusebii* (n. 5 above), 408: "Haec quanquam in dubium merito revocari possunt, propter prodigiosa vetustatis et longissimi temporis curricula, tam Chaldaica Berosi, quam Aegyptiaca Manethonis, tamen non solum retinenda sunt, sed etiam in precio habenda propter reverentiam vetustatis, tum etiam, quia medii temporis vera cum illis fabulosis continuantur." For Scaliger's late, polemical euhemerism see A. Grafton, "Renaissance Readers and Ancient Texts: Comments on some Commentaries," *Renaissance Quarterly* 38 (1985), 636.

8. Petrarch, *Seniles* 15.5; *Opera* (Basel, 1554), II, 1055–58; tr. and discussed by P. Burke, *The Renaissance Sense of the Past* (New York, 1970), 50–54; for a text and discussion of Valla's work see W. Setz, *Lorenzo Vallas Schrift gegen die Konstantinische Schenkung* (Tübingen, 1975). See also the standard—and splendid—work of W. Speyer, *Die literarische Fälschung im heidnischen und christlichen Altertum* (Munich, 1971), 99–102.

9. See, e.g., Burke (n. 8 above); M. P. Gilmore, *Humanists and Jurists* (Cambridge, Mass., 1963); J. Franklin, *Jean Bodin and the Sixteenth-Century Revolution in the Methodology of Law and History* (New York and London, 1963); D. R. Kelley, *Foundations of Modern Historical Scholarship* (New York and London, 1970).

10. K. O. Müller, *Kleine deutsche Schriften,* I (Breslau, 1847), 445–52 (first published 1837).

11. J. Levine, *Doctor Woodward's Shield* (Berkeley, 1977).

12. Grafton (n. 6 above); G. Parry, "Puritanism, Science, and Capitalism: William Harrison and the Rejection of Hermes Trismegistus," *History of Science* 22 (1984), 245–70.

13. W. Goez, "Die Anfänge der historischen Methoden-Reflexion im italienischen Humanismus," *Geschichte in der Gegenwart: Festschrift für Kurt Kluxen,* ed. E. Heinen and H. J. Schoeps (Paderborn, 1972), 3–21; "Die Anfänge der historischen Methoden-Reflexion in der italienischen Renaissance und ihre Aufnahme in der Geschichtsschreibung des deutschen Humanismus," *Archiv für Kulturgeschichte* 56 (1974), 25–48. See also the more recent interpretation of W. Stephens,

Jr., "The Etruscans and the Ancient Theology in Annius of Viterbo," *Umanesimo a Roma nel Quattrocento,* ed. P. Brezzi et al. (New York and Rome, 1984), 309–22; Stephens, "*De historia gigantum:* Theological Anthropology before Rabelais," *Traditio* 40 (1984), esp. 70–89.

14. A good description of the Rome 1498 edition can be found in the British Museum catalog of incunabula, IV, 118–19; I use the texts in the first edition but identify them, for simplicity's sake, by the page numbers of the well-edited and -indexed edition of Antwerp 1552.

15. Annius, *Commentaria,* 59.

16. Ibid., 80 (the magic took the form of an illusion).

17. Ibid., ep. ded.

18. Ibid., 76–77.

19. For Josephus see F. Blatt, *The Latin Josephus,* I (Aarhus and Copenhagen, 1958), 13–15.

20. M. Luther, *Supputatio annorum mundi,* ed. J. Cohrs; *Werke* (WA), 53 (1920), 33–34, 36, 26–27.

21. Io. Lucidus Samotheus, *Opusculum de emendationibus temporum,* 2d ed. (Venice, 1546), II.3, 19 recto.

22. G. Postel, *De Etruriae regionis originibus, institutis, religione et moribus,* ed. G. Cipriani (Rome, 1986), ch. xliii, 173.

23. See in general E. Iversen, *The Myth of Egypt and Its Hieroglyphs in European Tradition* (Copenhagen, 1961); D. C. Allen, *Mysteriously Meant* (Baltimore, 1970), ch. v; R. Wittkower, "Hieroglyphics in the Early Renaissance," *Allegory and the Migration of Symbols* (London, 1977), 113–28.

24. For Viterbo see esp. R. Weiss, "An Unknown Epigraphic Tract by Annius of Viterbo," *Italian Studies Presented to E. R. Vincent* (Cambridge, 1962), 101–20; for Spain, R. B. Tate, "Mitología en la historiografía española de la edad media e del renacimento," *Ensayos sobre la historiografía peninsular del siglo xv,* tr. J. Diaz (Madrid, 1970), 13–32; for France, R. E. Asher, "Myth, Legend and History in Renaissance France," *Studi francesi* 39 (1969), 409–19; for England, Owen (n. 3 above) and T. D. Kendrick, *British Antiquity* (London, 1950); for Germany, F. Borchardt, *Germany Antiquity in Renaissance Myth* (Baltimore, 1970); for Italy, E. Cochrane, *Historians and Historiography in the Italian Renaissance* (Chicago and London, 1981), 432–35, and G. Cipriani, *Il mito etrusco nel rinascimento fiorentino* (Florence, 1980). Stephens's articles (n. 13 above) emphasize the transformation that Annius's ideas underwent in the course of being vulgarized and rewritten in the sixteenth century.

25. Princeton University Library Ex 2613.1510, with this note on the title page: "Roberti Nicolsoni Londinensis liber Parrhisiis: 1510."

26. See Fumagalli's fine case study, "Un falso tardo-quattrocentesco: Lo pseudo-Catone di Annio da Viterbo," *Vestigia. Studi in onore di Giuseppe Billanovich,* ed. R. Avesani et al. (Rome, 1984), I, 337–60.

27. Annius, *Viterbiae historiae epitoma,* ed. with useful commentary by G. Baffioni in *Annio da Viterbo. Documenti e ricerche,* I (Rome, 1981), 130–31. Baffioni indicates Annius's sources but does not exhaustively interpret his manipulation of them.

28. Annius, *Commentaria,* 432 (Fabius Pictor on the Sabines); 577 (Sempronius on the date and horoscope of the foundation of Rome).

29. The standard account of Annius's life remains R. Weiss, "Traccia per una biografia di Annio da Viterbo," *Italia Medioevale e Umanistica* 5 (1962), 425–41.

30. B. Guenée, *Histoire et culture historique dans l'Occident médiéval* (Paris, 1980), 133–40; B. Smalley, *English Friars and Antiquity in the Early Fourteenth Century* (Oxford, 1960), 233–35, 360–61 (Lathbury, quoting bk. III, ch. 1 of the Athenian historian "Verosus"; as Smalley points out, the forger took off from the elder Pliny's reference to the Athenians' respect for Berosus's skill in astronomy [*Natural History* 7.123]; chronology, like astronomy, was not this forger's long suit).

31. Annius, *Commentaria,* praef.

32. E. Fumagalli, "Aneddoti della vita di Annio da Viterbo O.P. . . . ," *Archivum Fratrum Praedicatorum* 50 (1980), 167–99, and 52 (1982), 197–218; V. Meneghin, *Bernardino da Feltre e i Monti di Pietà* (Vicenza, 1974), 545–50; *Giovanni Rucellai ed il suo Zibaldone,* I: "*Il Zibaldone Quaresimale,*" ed. A. Perosa (London, 1960), 164–70, 179–80.

33. C. Vasoli, *I miti e gli astri* (Naples, 1977), ch. i; Annius, *Commentaria,* 48–52, in and on Berosus.

34. Ibid., 16.

35. Ibid., 463, on Cato.

36. Ibid., 238, on Metasthenes. Cf. in general E. N. Tigerstedt, "Ioannes Annius and *Graecia Mendax,*" in *Classical, Mediaeval and Renaissance Studies in Honor of Berthold Louis Ullman,* ed. C. Henderson, Jr. (Rome, 1964), II, 293–310.

37. Annius, *Commentaria,* 453.

38. Borchardt (n. 24 above), 89–91.

39. Diodorus Siculus 1.20.1, 1.27.3–6; Annius, *Commentaria,* 12 (Xenophon on Ninus's monument).

40. See Allen (n. 23 above); O. Gruppe, *Geschichte der klassischen Mythologie und Religionsgeschichte* (Leipzig, 1921), 29–31; J. Seznec, *The Survival of the Pagan Gods,* tr. B. F. Sessions (New York, 1953), ch. i.

41. Annius, *Commentaria,* 188.

42. Beatus Rhenanus, *Rerum Germanicarum libri tres,* 2d ed. (Basel, 1551), 191.

43. Annius, *Commentaria,* 518–19, on Cato; amusingly pulverized by G. Barreiros, *Censura in quendam auctorem qui sub falsa inscriptione Berosi Chaldaei circunfertur* (Rome, 1565), 71.

44. Owen (n. 3 above), 37, using a printed text of the translation (at 5.31.2). The very early manuscript of Poggio's version in Princeton University Library, Garrett 105, already offers the text in the form that I cite (fol. 144 recto; according to A. C. de la Mare, whose opinion was kindly conveyed to me by J. Preston, the manuscript was prepared in the circle of Tortelli and contains indexing notes by Poggio himself).

45. Tatian, *Oratio ad Graecos* 31; Clement of Alexandria, *Stromateis* 1.117; Eusebius in Syncellus 211 M.

46. Jerome-Eusebius, *Chronicle* 108, Fotheringham: "licet Archilocus . . . supputet"; the same error is in the Armenian version. The origin of the eight Homers—though not their Olympic victories and achievements in magic and medicine, painting and sculpture—can easily be explained. Jerome gives seven possible dates for Homer; euhemerism turns these into eight Homers who lived at different times.

47. E. F. Rice, Jr., *St. Jerome in the Renaissance* (Baltimore and London, 1985); M. Baxandall, *The Limewood Sculptors of Renaissance Germany* (New Haven and London, 1980).

48. Annius, *Commentaria*, 246.

49. For Geoffrey, see G. Gordon, "The Trojans in Britain," *The Discipline of Letters* (Oxford, 1946), 35–58; for Alemannus see Annius, *Commentaria*, 125 on Berosus.

50. Ibid., 239.

51. Ibid., 460 (Myrsilus); 75–76 (Berosus); 281 (Philo).

52. Ibid., 244 (on Metasthenes).

53. Guenée (n. 30 above).

54. Stephens (n. 13 above). For Josephus, see J. R. Bartlett, *Jews in the Hellenistic World* (Cambridge, 1985), 86–89; the translation given below is to be found ibid., 171–76, with useful commentary. The importance of Josephus for Annius had previously received due attention from A. Biondi in the introduction to his translation of M. Cano, *L'autorità della storia profana* (Turin, 1973), xxxviii.

55. Annius, *Commentaria*, 240 (on Metasthenes).

56. O. A. Danielsson, "Annius von Viterbo über die Gründungsgeschichte Roms," *Corolla Archaeologica* (Lund, 1932), 1–16.

57. Beatus Rhenanus (n. 42 above), 39; P. Crinito, *De honesta disciplina*, ed. C. Angeleri (Rome, 1955), 460; for Vives's comment on Augustine, *City of God* 18, see the interesting transcript made by C. Peutinger in his copy of Annius, published by P. Joachimsen, *Geschichtsauffassung und Geschichtschreibung in Deutschland unter dem Einfluss des Humanismus*, I (Leipzig, 1910; repr. Aalen, 1968), 271 n. 24.

58. K. Arnold, *Johannes Trithemius (1462–1516)* (Würzburg, 1971), 167–79; J. Trithemius, "Chronologia Mystica," *Opera historica*, I (Frankfurt, 1601), unpaginated.

59. F. von Bezold, "Zur Entstehungsgeschichte der historischen Methodik [1914]," *Aus Mittelalter und Renaissance* (Munich and Berlin, 1918), 362–83.

60. See the literature cited in n. 9 above. Most previous critiques—e.g., the powerful one of E. Hassinger, *Empirisch-rationaler Historismus* (Bern, 1978)—have addressed issues different from those to be discussed below.

61. See, e.g., W. J. Bouwsma, *Concordia Mundi* (Cambridge, Mass., 1957); H. J. Erasmus, *The Origins of Rome in Historiography from Petrarch to Perizonius* (Assen, 1962).

62. G. Postel, *Le Thrésor des Prophéties de l'Univers*, ed. F. Secret (The Hague, 1969), 67. See also 76, where he describes the Annian Cato as drawing material "des monuments publikes," and Postel (n. 22 above).

63. F. Baudouin, *De institutione historiae universae et eius cum iurisprudentia coniunctione* prolegomenôn *libri duo* (Paris, 1561), 48–49.

64. Postel (n. 22 above), 195–99. Cipriani shows that Postel's beliefs were shared by many members of that intellectually advanced institution, the Florentine Academy; one of them, Pier Francesco Giambullari, found what seemed vital corroborative evidence in a then unpublished passage in Athenaeus, for which Postel thanked him fervently. It is a pity that Postel's own full-scale defense of the forgeries does not survive. See ibid., esp. 15–23.

65. Baudouin (n. 63 above), 44.

66. For Caius see V. Nutton, "John Caius and the Eton Galen: Medical Philology in the Renaissance," *Medizinhistorisches Journal* 20 (1985), 227–52; for the Oxford/Cambridge debate, a distant ancestor of the Boat Race, see Kendrick (n. 24 above).

67. J. Caius, *De antiquitate Cantabrigiensis Academiae libri duo* (London, 1568), 21–25; Caius's etymology of "giant" is an ancient one.

68. See, respectively, J. Sleidanus, *De quatuor monarchiis libri tres* (Leiden, 1669), 11; Franklin (n. 9 above), 124–25; Savile in Bodleian Library MS Savile 29 (his "Prooemium mathematicum" of 1570), fol. 32 recto, where a reference to Berosus's *defloratio* of Chaldean history is underlined and bracketed. An afterthought?

69. M. Cano, *Loci theologici* 11.6; *Opera* (Venice, 1776), 234; Barreiros, *Censura* (n. 43 above), 26–30.

70. Ibid., 35–37; V. Borghini, *Discorsi* (Florence, 1584–85), I, 229. Borghini had help from O. Panvinio (II, 305).

71. Barreiros (n. 43 above), 56–59, where Barreiros's own chronology seems a bit shaky. For an effort to reply see Postel (n. 22 above).

72. Cano (n. 69 above), 230–32.

73. J. Funck, *Commentariorum in praecedentem chronologiam libri decem* (Wittenberg, 1601), fol. B iiij recto.

74. Ibid., fol. [B v verso].

75. Ibid., fol. [A v verso]. Funck says that he has taken his matter "ad verbum fere" from Berosus and the Bible; his genealogy of the descendants of Noah (fols. A iiij verso–[A v recto]) confirms this.

76. J. Bodin, *Methodus,* ch. x; *Oeuvres philosophiques,* ed. P. Mesnard (Paris, 1951), 254–57.

77. Ibid., iv, 126, praising Metasthenes, Polybius, and Ammianus Marcellinus for their use of *acta publica* and their objectivity when discussing other nations.

78. Ibid., viii, 240. For a modern view of Ctesias, whose ancient critics Bodin knew, see R. Drews, *The Greek Accounts of Near Eastern History* (Cambridge, Mass., 1973), 103–16 (109: "all the details were invented").

79. J. Goropius Becanus, *Origines Antwerpianae* (Antwerp, 1569), 344–45.

80. Ibid., 357–62.

81. Ibid., 362; Goropius goes on to quote a fragment from bk. 43 of Theopompus's *Philippica,* in Latin; this dates Homer 500 years after the fall of Troy (Clement of Alexandria *Stromateis* 1.117.8 = *FrGrHist* 115 F 205)—that is, to the time of Archilochus.

82. Ibid., ep. ded. See in general A. Borst, *Der Turmbau von Babel* (Stuttgart, 1957–63), III.1, 1215–19.

83. N. Swerdlow, "Pseudodoxia Copernicana: or, Enquiries into very many received tenents and commonly presumed truths, mostly concerning spheres," *Archives internationales pour l'histoire des sciences* 26 (1976), 108–58.

84. S. Petri, *Apologia . . . pro antiquitate et origine Frisiorum* (Franeker, 1603), 15–17, summarizes the Frisian *Urgeschichte.*

85. U. Emmius, *De origine atque antiquitatibus Frisiorum,* in his *Rerum Frisicarum historia* (Leiden, 1616), 7ff.

86. Petri (n. 84 above), 40–41.

87. See further E. H. Waterbolk, "Zeventiende-eeuwers in de Republiek over de grondslagen van het geschiedverhaal. Mondelinge of schriftelijke overlevering," *Bijdragen voor de Geschiedenis der Nederlanden* 12 (1957), 26–44; "Reacties op het historisch pyrrhonisme," ibid., 15 (1960), 81–102; cf. in general S. Schama, *The Embarrassment of Riches* (New York, 1987), ch. ii.

88. See further the classical article by C. Mitchell, "Archaeology and Romance in Renaissance Italy," in *Italian Renaissance Studies,* ed. E. F. Jacob (London, 1960), 455–83.

Lisa Jardine

2. Inventing Rudolph Agricola: Cultural Transmission, Renaissance Dialectic, and the Emerging Humanities

Introduction

This piece of work attempts a study of the transmission of high culture which sets the traditional internal account of continuity and change amongst texts in a broader historical context.[1] My study singles out an individual—Erasmus of Rotterdam—in an unfamiliar way: not as a Renaissance "self" (however fashioned), but as the center to which a large, specific part of the print-related activities of a much less well-known group of authors, *commendatores, emendatores,* and *castigatores,* was directed.

It is into this textual, Erasmian context that I reinsert the published works of Rudolph Agricola. I argue that the external, shaping pressures on the production of Agricola's *De inventione dialectica* (a work whose influence on Renaissance developments in dialectic is generally agreed to have been considerable) have consequences for our understanding and analysis of the text as subsequently transmitted. We are looking at a particular, crucial moment in the northern Renaissance of learning, and the particular preoccupations of that moment, in the Netherlands, have a necessary part to play in our understanding of the texts it produced.

Underlying this study is my concern that we traditional intellectual historians should revise the history of the transmission of high culture so as to be able to integrate it with the powerful and vigorous recent work on cultural transmission as a whole, and to contribute to an account that registers "cultural currents" as continuously producing parallel and interactive transmission and impact.[2] The present study is something like my own first attempt to indicate what such a revised history of the transmission of high culture would be like.[3]

Rudolph Agricola's *De inventione dialectica* was the higher-education manual of *argumentatio* (argumentation) most widely specified, bought, and used in schools and universities throughout Protestant Europe, between the early decades of the sixteenth century and the mid-seventeenth century (when attitudes toward logic/dialectic in the curriculum altered so as to render it irrelevant).[4] The first printed edition appeared in 1515, published in Louvain and with the name of the distinguished theologian Martin Dorp on the title page. Between 1515 and 1600 it went through more than seventy (known) editions (including epitomes).[5] Not surprisingly, therefore, Agricola's *De inventione dialectica* has been the object of a considerable amount of attention from intellectual historians (particularly historians of logic) and from historians of education. One might cite three key works as initiating Agricola as a focus for interest: W. J. Ong's extremely readable and influential book, *Ramus, Method, and the Decay of Dialogue* (Cambridge, Mass., 1958); W. S. Howell's much-cited *Logic and Rhetoric in England 1500 –1700* (New York, 1961); and C. Vasoli's monumental and highly regarded *La dialettica e la retorica dell'umanesimo* (Milan, 1968).[6] I stress the readability and monumental nature of such work in order to indicate that although this was specialist work, it had a considerable impact beyond the histories of logic and "method," so that Agricola's name crops up (with these bibliographical items attached) quite widely in Renaissance intellectual history and in histories of humanism.

In the "hard" (i.e., difficult to penetrate) history of logic, Agricola's name, his textbook, and its influence were already firmly established by Prantl in the late nineteenth century, and the high assessment of his importance (though without a very consistent version of *how* he was important) has been sustained to the present in a whole sequence of "authoritative" publications, including work of my own.[7] These authorities have tended to divide into two camps: those who have regarded Agricola's *De inventione dialectica* as an integrated part of developing Renaissance logic and dialectic (a camp that includes Vasoli and myself), and those who have regarded it as an aberration or a distraction, diverting "Renaissance thought" from knotty technical problems of validity and inference (the camp led by the Kneales, who notoriously blame Agricola for "starting the corruption" in logic but cannot even get his name right).[8]

Who was Rudolph Agricola? He was a distinguished teacher, born in Bafflo, near Groningen in the Low Countries, in 1444. He trained with Battista Guarino, son of the great Guarino, in Ferrara. He taught Alexander Hegius Greek, who in turn taught Erasmus at Deventer. In addition to being a considerable scholar of Latin and Greek, he was a poet, musician, and painter of note. He died in Heidelberg, where he had gone to teach at the invitation of Johann von Dalberg, Bishop of Worms, in 1485.[9] All secondary sources are agreed that he was an extremely important influence on the development of northern European humanism.[10]

As early as 1971, however, in an important article Terrence Heath drew attention to the curious lag of nearly forty years between the completion of Agricola's best-known work, *De inventione dialectica* (around 1479), and its availability in printed form.[11] Furthermore, Heath suggested that in the first instance the influence of that text in the early decades of the sixteenth century (its prominence in northern European curricula and university statutes) had to do precisely with its availability. It went into print at the moment when more orthodox Aristotelian and scholastic texts were discarded both because of their explicitly Catholic scholia and because those commentaries assumed a student body destined for the study of philosophy and canon law, rather than one simply gaining an education in the liberal arts.[12]

So we have an author, an acknowledged influential humanist teacher of the late fifteenth century. We have a key text, judged to be a crucial connecting link in a chronological development (assumed linear and direct) of western European thought, at its logical core. And we have a gap, which is noticed by one such scholar, and judged to be significant—the gap between Agricola's writing the work and its appearance in print. That is where this study begins.

"What has a dog to do with a bath?"

In 1503 Jacobus Faber of Deventer published the *Carmina* and assorted minor works of his and Erasmus's old schoolmaster Alexander Hegius (who had died in 1498).[13] The prefatory letter to the *Carmina* was addressed to Erasmus and drew attention to the proverb "Canis in balneo" ("A dog in a bath") in the 1500 Paris edition of Erasmus's *Adages* (*Adagiorum collectanea*)[14] (Fig. 2.1). (The phrase indicates irrelevance or inappropriateness: "That is about as appropriate as a dog in a bath," i.e., it doesn't belong there at all.) Faber was anxious to draw the reader's attention to Erasmus's linking of the names of Hegius and Agricola in a digressionary note in the adage.[15]

On the face of it, it seems clear what Faber is doing. He wishes to enhance the reputation (and historical importance) of Alexander Hegius

Figure 2.1. Erasmus and his tools—detail of Albrecht Dürer's woodcut portrait of Erasmus. Source: *Engravings reproduced by the heliotype process chiefly from the Gray Collection, Harvard College* (Boston, n.d.). Courtesy of Princeton University Library.

by pointing out a connection between Hegius and the already well-known humanist Erasmus.[16] In the aside in the "canis in balneo" adage, Erasmus had indicated that Hegius had been part of his own intellectual heritage (though Faber wishes to stress that Hegius's importance is greater than that assigned him by Erasmus, thus rhetorically magnifying the eulogy by association).[17] But if Erasmus "validates" Hegius's reputation in this way, the prefatory letter serves *his* purposes as well. It closes with the following:

Enough on this subject. For the rest, dearest Erasmus, I fail to comprehend why you have not given me, as we agreed, the Greek oration of Libanius when you have done it into Latin; I am waiting for it. I can glimpse your intention; you have decided to add to my Libanius the books you are now engaged upon: on famous metaphors, on ecclesiastical allegories, on allusions in classical authors, and on witty sayings and replies. This is the one thought I console myself with that I may bear patiently the rather long delay. So now accept our teacher's most important poems, to which will also be added, when I see that it would please you and my other kindly readers, his enquiries into a variety of topics, composed in dialogue form; in this respect he follows the example of Plato, who was most intimately known to him. Finally I shall see to it that any of Rodolphus Agricola's works that come to hand here are sent to you, except those that have been published in previous years and are now in the booksellers' shops.[18]

So the letter provides a "puff" for Erasmus—in particular his forthcoming Libanius (but also promising a number of other, vaguely specified works, none of which in fact ever saw print under such titles). It also responds, apparently, to Erasmus's tribute to Agricola (in the "canis in balneo" adage), by indicating that some collection of unpublished Agricola works ("praeter ea que superioribus annis edita apud bibliopolas exponuntur") is also forthcoming.[19]

In fact, I think that Faber's prefatory letter to Hegius's *Carmina* is a more purposive document even than this, and that the final paragraph actually tells us that any "events" with which the letter deals have to do with books and in particular with constructing reputations out of genealogies of books.[20] The last paragraph of Faber's letter, I suggest, seeks to establish a coterie within a printing community. "I fail to comprehend why you have not given me, as we agreed, the Greek oration of Libanius when you have done it into Latin. . . . I shall see to it that any of Rodolphus Agricola's works that come to hand here are sent to you, except those that have been published in previous years and are now in the booksellers' shops." Faber is in Deventer, where the school, at which he teaches, is closely associated with the publishing houses of Paffraet and de Breda.[21] Erasmus is publishing his Libanius with Martens at Louvain. They have "agreed" to exchange "in press" volumes. And indeed, as we shall see, a volume of Agricola works largely identical with Faber's was published by Martens (with Erasmus's support) at Louvain in 1511.[22]

In the 1508 much expanded edition of the *Adages* (*Adagiorum chiliades tres* . . .), published by Aldus Manutius in Venice, "Quid cani et balneo" (as it now became) contains a much enlarged reminiscence on Erasmus's teachers and becomes, in effect, an extended conventional panegyric, addressed in the first place to Agricola and then to Hegius.[23] But in spite of its touchingly intimate tone (on which several Erasmus scholars remark), this long "digression," as Erasmus himself calls it, is actually a curiously precise account of the published remains of Agricola currently available, of which the following forms the core:

There are a few literary remains of his work, some letters, poems of various kinds; the *Axiochus* of Plato translated into Latin, and a version of Isocrates' *To Demonicus*. Then there are a couple of lectures given in public session in the University of Ferrara, for it was there he both learnt and gave open lectures. There are lying hidden in some people's possession his treatises on dialectic. He had also translated some of Lucian's dialogues.[24]

These are indeed precisely the works of Agricola which were available at that moment, more than twenty years after his death. The translation of pseudo-Plato's *Axiochus* was printed by Richard Paffraet around 1480. Hegius lived in Paffraet's house during his time as head teacher at the Deventer school, and Paffraet was the publisher of his *Farrago* (1480–85, 1490, 1495),[25] as well as of Jacobus Faber's posthumous edition of his *Carmina* and *Dialogi* which carried the prefatory letter to Erasmus discussed above.[26] The translation of Isocrates' *Praecepta ad Demonicum* appeared around 1480.[27] The "Anna mater" poem, and individual letters were in print, generally as additional items in other people's volumes.[28] The juxtaposition of the *De inventione dialectica* "lying hidden in some people's possession," and the Lucian translations ("He had also translated some of Lucian's dialogues") suggests Erasmus had not seen the latter, but inferred their existence from one of Agricola's (published) letters, in which he promises to send a Lucian translation to Hegius.[29] And, indeed, the information that "at the very end of his life [Agricola] had bent his whole mind on the study of Hebrew and the Holy Scripture" (one of the few "facts" the panegyric contains) is to be found in that same published letter.[30] The lectures (delivered at Pavia and Ferrara in 1473, 1474, and 1476) were widely spoken of and acclaimed.[31] In other words, the additional information about Agricola's life and works, with which Erasmus embellishes the expanded adage, is derived entirely from *printed* remains (rather than from personal reminiscences, though the tone certainly suggests the latter).

In 1508 Jacobus Faber brought out a small (and, contrary to his promise, almost entirely derivative) volume of Agricola's works.[32] Its title page manages to refer both to Alexander Hegius and to Ermolao Barbaro's epitaph for Agricola, which had figured prominently in Faber's earlier attempt to link his *Carmina* with Erasmus's *Adagia*. It runs as follows:

Rudolph Agricola's "Paraenesis," or advice on the method by which study should be pursued, and which authors ought to be followed; together with a letter from the same to Alexander Hegius, headmaster at Deventer school. And Isocrates's "Paraenesis ad Demonicum," translated from the Greek by Rudolph Agricola. The verses of Ermolao Barbaro on the tomb of Rudolph Agricola of Groningen run:

Under this stone, the jealous Fates decreed
  The Frisian hope, his country's light, should come,
Rudolph Agricola; in life, indeed,
  He brought such praise to Germany his home
  As ever Greece could have, or ever Rome.[33]

But the contents of the volume had largely been available in print before. So the volume makes a *gesture* toward fulfilling Faber's previous, rather grander commitment to Erasmus, that he will "see to it that any of Rodolphus Agricola's works that come to hand are sent to you, except those that have been published in previous years and are now in the booksellers' shops." I am arguing that such "gestures" are "purposive"—are part of a kind of publishing performance (which appears to fulfill a commitment to the public on behalf of Erasmus to make good the deficiency in the available works of the man supposed to be a major influence on northern European humanist pedagogy, but actually provides no new foundation to build on at all).

Erasmus's own next "press" pronouncement on the subject was more prominently placed. In the new prefatory letter to the 1514 edition of the popular *De copia* addressed to the printer Matthias Schürer, he wrote: "We are eagerly expecting at any moment the *Lucubrationes* of Rudolph Agricola (a truly inspired man). Whenever I read his writings, I venerate and give fervent praise to that sacred and heavenly spirit."[34] This is, in fact, a fragment of a more extended and rather curious exchange with the Schürer publishing house about an Agricola volume. In February 1514, in the preface to an edition of Pliny's *Letters,* which he had seen through the Schürer press, Beatus Rhenanus had referred to some unpublished "Lucubrationes" of Agricola as being in his possession.[35] Erasmus's *De copia* preface is in effect a response to that announcement (placed equivalently prominently).[36] A year later, however, Rhenanus had apparently made no progress, for we find another Schürer corrector, Nicholas Gerbell, telling Erasmus in a letter that Schürer is anxious for Rhenanus to send him the works, so they can be corrected and published without delay.[37] In July 1517 Erasmus was still asking the Schürer printing house "why the publication of Rodolphus Agricola's papers is so long postponed,"[38] and in August Erasmus himself is offering to "do his duty as a friend," and correct them himself, if Schürer will send them to him.[39] At this point Schürer himself informed Erasmus that he had mislaid a crucial item from the collection while moving house, but would send the whole thing the moment he could find it ("I have been through the whole house looking for it!")[40] Did Schürer ever have such a manuscript (no such collection ever appeared)? Or was he hoping to keep Erasmus interested enough in his publishing house to place some of his own works there (as indeed he subsequently did)?[41]

Two months before the publication of the new *De copia* preface, in August 1514, Erasmus had himself published a minor work by Agricola— his Latin translation of Isocrates' *Paraenesis ad demonicum*—in the edition of his own *Opuscula* published in Louvain by Thierry Martens, thus apparently making his own contribution to the retrieval of the "truly inspired man"'s works.[42]

However, in spite of the assurance of the title page of this work ("quibus primae aetati nihil prelegi potest neque utilius neque elegantius"), the Agricola translation from Isocrates did not in fact appear for the first time in this volume. It had been printed twice before since 1500 (and several times before 1500), in both cases with Erasmus's own explicit encouragement. In 1508 Jacobus Faber had included it in his Agricola volume.[43] In 1511 it also appeared in a volume of Agricola *opuscula* edited by Peter Gilles and published by Thierry Martens (the publisher of the Erasmus *Opuscula* volume, as of many other of his works) at Antwerp.[44]

There is further evidence that this annexing of an already available Agricola fragment was something of a token gesture, in the prefatory letter that accompanies it in editions from 1517 onward.[45] In it Erasmus tells the reader that he has "collated this treatise afresh with the Greek copies" and has "found one sentence missing, which in any case [he] suspected might be spurious." He continues: "It has, however, been inserted, with a note [or mark], for fear anyone might suppose it omitted by accident, since it appears in current texts. Further, in another passage Rodolphus seems to have read $\psi v \chi \hat{\eta} s$ where the printed Greek copies have $\tau \dot{v} \chi \eta s$."[46] In fact, neither the note nor the emendation is to be found in the printed text (presumably Erasmus did not have time, or did not care to bother himself with it).[47]

In 1505 or thereabouts Erasmus had written from Paris to Peter Gilles, urging him to collect together such of Agricola's works as he could for publication: "Vale et vndecunque potes collige Rodolphi Agricolae opuscula tecumque deporta."[48] In 1511 Gilles did indeed edit and see through the Martens press such a volume; once again the volume is apparently a compilation of scattered, already published works.[49] We should note that the prefatory letter to this volume is addressed by Peter Gilles to Martin Dorp, a printing-house colleague of his, and another friend of, and proof corrector for, Erasmus.[50]

It was not until 1528 that Erasmus was able himself to lay his hands on and publish a "first edition" of an Agricola *opusculum* in a volume of his own works.[51] This was the "Oratio in laudem Matthiae Richili," which appeared in a collection of popular Erasmus teaching works, published by Frobenius in Basel, and including the *De recta pronuntiatione* and the *Ciceronianus*.[52] In neither this nor any of the three subsequent editions of this volume does Agricola's name, or the title of his oration, figure on the title page. But Erasmus includes another textual note expressing his earnest desire that more of Agricola's works should be brought to light, and the *Ciceronianus* itself contains another fulsome tribute to Agricola's standing as a Ciceronian and a humanist in the roll call of great "modern" figures in humane learning.[53]

But by this time, as we shall see, Agricola publishing had opened up, largely owing to the efforts of Alardus of Amsterdam (Fig. 2.2), another proof corrector for the Thierry Martens publishing house, and another friend and protégé of Erasmus. Alardus, however, belongs in the section on the recovery of the *De inventione dialectica*. He is crucial to our story, and perhaps its picaresque hero.

I have labored this publishing history in order to insist that Erasmus's published references to Agricola, and his subsequent inclusion of minor works by Agricola alongside his own, constitute a narrative to which we need to give attention. As I have tried to develop this narrative, the tale which seems to be unfolding is one of a series of publishing gestures, simulating spontaneous tributes to one's (Erasmus's) intellectual antecedents, and matching textual "discoveries": printed pronouncements about the great heritage of Agricola/Hegius; calls for making accessible Agricola's works after the appearance of Hegius's; the appearance of collections apparently answering such calls, sponsored by individuals standing in a direct (printing) relationship to Erasmus, but which are actually collations of existing incunabula fragments.

This is not a linear narrative, however—at least, I have been unable to think of a way of telling it in linear fashion. So at this point we have to go back to 1503 and that letter from Faber to Erasmus concerning Hegius and what the dog has to do with the bath.

"I think immediately of Rodolphus Agricola, the former teacher of my own teacher Alexander"

In addition to the highly specific bibliographical printer's material, Erasmus's adage "What has a dog to do with a bath?" launches two important

ALARDVS AMSTELREDAMVS
Philosophus.

Si Logicâ laus est præcellere in arte, Rodolphum
Par laus Agricolam debita, meq̃ manet,

Figure 2.2. Alardus of Amsterdam (1491–1544). Source: Nicolaus Reusner, *Icones sive imagines virorum literis illustrium* (Strasbourg, 1587), f. G V verso. Courtesy of Princeton University Library.

general themes, championed by Europe's most popular and prolific educationalist. The first is the "genealogy of teachers" theme—a kind of humanist laying on of hands: Agricola taught Hegius taught Erasmus. The second is the "can anyone find me the great man's lost works?" theme. As twentieth-century readers, we might feel that buried in a digression in a compendious reference work, the latter could hardly be guaranteed the reader's attention. But as we have seen, this textual addition, orchestrated in collaboration with an editor friend from the same academic stable, is only one of a number of careful moves establishing an intellectual pedigree for Agricola (and thereby Erasmus), and advertising for those in possession of Agricola's unpublished works in manuscript to come forward.[54]

Jacobus Faber links Hegius to Agricola, around the tag from Erasmus's *Adages*. When Erasmus expands that reference in the revised edition of his work, he specifies that the link is a letter from Agricola via Hegius, read to Erasmus apparently while he was at the Deventer school:

I remember having learnt [this adage] from a certain very learned letter of my beloved Rodolphus, at a time when I was a mere child and as yet ignorant of Greek. In this letter he is trying to persuade the town council of Antwerp, with conviction and eloquence, that they should appoint as master of their school someone proficient in liberal studies, and not (as they usually do) entrust this office to an inarticulate theologian or naturalist, the sort of man who is sure he has something to say about everything but has no notion of what it is to speak. "What good would he be in a school? As much good, to use the Greek repartee, as a dog in a bath."

Transmission, in other words, is rigorously textual here—not the great man to his pupil, who in his turn passes it on to his pupil, but a letter from a remote great man, sent to his one-time pupil (not in fact a letter to Hegius, but to Barbarianus),[55] and then read to the young Erasmus. However, this is not at all the way Erasmus chooses to emphasize the story:

I quote this adage with all the more pleasure because it refreshes and renews my memory, and my affection, for Rodolphus Agricola of Friesland, whom I name as the man in all Germany and Italy most worthy of the highest public honour. . . . Such full and ungrudging praise of this man has, I confess, a singular charm for me, because I happened while yet a boy to have his disciple Alexander Hegius as my teacher. . . . Now to turn to the adage, which I remember having learnt from a certain very learned letter of my beloved Rodolphus, at a time when I was a mere child and as yet ignorant of Greek.

"A certain very learned letter of my beloved Rodolphus" gives no hint that the letter in question is addressed neither to Erasmus nor to Hegius, but transmitted by the latter to the former in class. What Erasmus emphasizes here is above all the bond of affection between master and pupil, a bond which certainly suggests personal contact. And, indeed, scholars have expended a good deal of ingenuity on specifying exactly when Erasmus had this personal contact with Agricola. What I shall argue in this section is that there was no personal contact—perhaps one brief meeting—but that the story of the affective bond is crucial for Erasmus's version of emerging humane studies.

It is interesting to compare the *Adages* digression with a much earlier letter to Cornelius Gerard, written around 1489–90, after Erasmus had entered the monastery at Steyn:[56]

I am most surprised that you describe [Girolamo Balbi] as the only writer who follows the tracks of antiquity; for, not to mention yourself, it seems to me that I see countless well-schooled writers of the present day who approach quite closely the ancient ideal of eloquence. I think immediately of Rodolphus Agricola, the former teacher of my own teacher Alexander. He was a man not only exceptionally highly educated in all the liberal arts, but extremely proficient in oratory and poetic theory, and moreover as well acquainted with Greek as with Latin. To him may be added Alexander himself, a worthy pupil of so great a master; so elegantly did he reproduce the style of the ancients that one might easily mistake the authorship of a poem by him if the book's title page were missing; and he, too, is not quite devoid of Greek.[57]

Here the intimacy of the *Adages* reminiscence is entirely absent, the link between Agricola and Hegius conventional and formal: "the former teacher of my own teacher"; "a worthy pupil of so great a master." And the link itself is naturally made by Erasmus around Hegius's ability as a poet, and a poet on the written page: "one might easily mistake the authorship of a poem by him if the book's title page were missing." At this stage in his life, I suggest, Erasmus's version of a humanistic chain of influence beginning with Agricola and passing via Hegius to himself is a limited one, centering on the imitative technique of neo-Latin poetry, which we know Agricola had published at this date, which Hegius fostered at Deventer school, and in which both the young Erasmus and Cornelius Gerard participated—a production that nevertheless depended on the circulation of written texts from Agricola to Hegius and his pupils, and possibly back again for comment.[58]

My crucial point here is one of absence. There are no biographical details to support those memories and the affection of Erasmus for his "beloved Agricola" that are not already firmly rooted in text. Nothing, in fact, shows this more clearly than that crucial adage: "Quid cani in balneo?" For the story about the Agricola letter containing the "what has a dog to do with a bath?" tag is disturbingly closely related to the printing history of Agricola's works (disturbingly, that is, if what one wants to claim is intimacy amongst these three landmark figures in humane learning). The letter from Agricola to Barbarianus about the school at Antwerp, which Hegius read out in assembly at Deventer, was already printed in 1483, in the incunabulum of pseudo-Plato's *Axiochus*.[59] So Erasmus is drawing the reader of the *Adages*'s attention to a letter that was read to him but addressed neither to him nor to the teacher who read it to him, which is available to the reader himself in the extremely limited printed works of Agricola, soon to be made conveniently available in Peter Gilles's edition of Agricola *opuscula*.[60]

That Erasmus succeeded in convincing successive generations of readers that he had genuinely had some inspirational contact with Agricola is beyond doubt. By 1539 (the year of publication of Alardus's definitive edition of Agricola's works), Melanchthon had taken up the "great heritage of Agricola" theme; and by 1557, in his "Oratio de Erasmo Roterodamo," he had embellished the reference by Erasmus to a brief encounter at Deventer school, so that Agricola singled out the young Erasmus as a boy with a glorious future.[61] Hyma, the author of the classic *The Youth of Erasmus*, provides a perfect example of the intellectual investment generations of scholars have given to this incident:

A halo of almost supernatural learning seemed to surround those favored beings [early humanists] who told with rapture how they had actually heard the voice of the great Ficino or of the famous Pico. When ambitious boys of twelve or thirteen saw such a scholar, freshly arrived from the land of intellectual giants, they were nearly struck dumb with awe. This happened one day to Erasmus when he beheld the beaming features of Rudolph Agricola, "who was one of the first to bring a breath of the new learning from Italy."[62]

As astute a reader as the great Erasmus scholar P. S. Allen, however, is more reticent, but equally revealing:

As to the meeting with Agricola certainty is not to be attained. Erasmus' estimate of his age quoted above cannot be correct, if 1466 is rightly taken for his birth-year; for Agricola did not return from Italy until 1479. But between 1480 and 1484 Agricola probably passed through Deventer many times on his way to and from Groningen. He mentions a visit in Oct. 1480; and in April 1484 he was staying there, perhaps with Hegius in the house of the printer, Richard Paffraet. From the close connexion which existed in Erasmus' mind between Hegius and Agricola, whom he frequently mentions together, there is some ground for supposing that it was on this occasion that he saw the great scholar, whom he afterwards regarded as the teacher of his own master.[63]

"From the close connexion which existed in Erasmus' mind between Hegius and Agricola" it appears that we can only infer that Erasmus *wished to establish* (canonically) that there had been some crucial meeting with "the great scholar, whom he afterwards regarded as the teacher of his own master"—some laying on of hands which made him the direct heir to the tradition of humane learning which Agricola had been the first (so the story went) to bring from Italy.[64]

"Unfortunately in the *De copia* we were unable to consult the *De inventione dialectica*"

I am arguing that the accumulating textual reference to Agricola as intellectual and spiritual ancestor to Erasmus of Rotterdam is part of a purposive narrative, emanating from Erasmus himself. In the story so far the so-called central Agricola text, the *De inventione dialectica,* has been noticeable by its absence (Fig. 2.3). In the systematic search for publishable material (essentially, as we have seen, a publishing search by printers and editors) it had disappeared entirely from sight.[65] But I think it will be clear by now that Erasmus and his "circle" of correctors and editors were not waiting for a particular Agricola work: they were anxious to publish *any* Agricola texts compatible with a version of him as the key intermediary in the transmission of Italian humanism to northern Europe—and of Erasmus as heir to that inheritance.

In fact, if we scrutinize the surviving traces of the *De inventione dialectica* in scholarly correspondence and in prefatory letters, it begins to look as if there was a problem associated with that text—a problem of corruption in the text, illegibility, or, at the least, serious difficulty for the "castigator."[66] This is where Alardus Amstelredamus comes into the story. Alardus was a scholar in the Erasmus "circle" who had taught at the school at Alkmaar, who later lived and worked in Louvain, and was, naturally, a corrector for the Martens printing house, and who became the individual most closely associated with the quest for Agricola's lost works.[67] He came

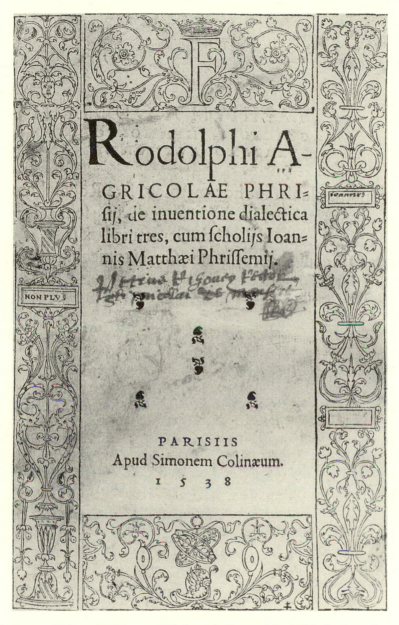

Figure 2.3. Title page of the 1538 "Phrissemius" text of Agricola's *De inventione dialectica*. Source: Rudolph Agricola, *De inventione dialectica* (Paris, 1538). Courtesy of Princeton University Library.

to Louvain from Alkmaar in the second half of 1514.[68] and immediately began to work as a corrector for Martens, which brought him to the attention of Erasmus, who renewed his involvement with Louvain (after an extended period in England) at the same moment.[69]

The publication of the *De inventione dialectica* evidently met with Erasmus's approval: that volume came out with Martens in January, and in June we find Alardus providing a prefatory letter to Erasmus's *Enchiridion militis christiani*.[70] So although the discovery of the lost manuscript of Agricola's treatise on dialectic supposedly antedates Alardus's connection with the Martens press and Erasmus, the editorial work is apparently exactly contemporary with it. This suggests that in our attempt to unravel the "transmission" of the cultural heritage of Agricola we should go back to that "discovery" and its consequences. All the detail concerning the pursuit of a manuscript of the *De inventione dialectica* suitable for printing comes from Alardus's dense commentary to his 1539 two-volume edition of Agricola's surviving *Opera*.[71]

Jacobus Faber's volume of Agricola *Opuscula,* published in 1508, had carried a prefatory letter to "Guillelmus medicus," in which Faber claimed to have in his possession a manuscript of the *De inventione dialectica* "in six books."[72] The important thing to notice is that there is a specific reason for Faber's preface including such a boast: the *Opuscula* printed the Agricola letter known as the "De formando studio," which is indeed an epistolary program for an education in humane letters. As the culmination of his graded program of study, Agricola briefly sketches two techniques for ensuring that the body of knowledge acquired is not sterile, but may be redeployed fruitfully and extended. Both techniques concern the classification of material for easy retrieval: storage under headings or common places to adduce illustratively, and storage under the "loci" of dialectic to facilitate argumentation. On the latter he concludes:

And if anyone wishes to pursue this more broadly, and through all the dialectical places, as far as the nature of the thing allows, he will certainly provide himself with a vast wealth of matter both for speaking and for inventing. How, and in what manner this ought to be done is more than can be arrived at in a letter, and I have discussed this matter at length in those three books which I wrote *De inventione dialectica*.[73]

It is because of this direct allusion by Agricola to one of his own (as yet unpublished) works that Faber feels it necessary to include the prefatory information that he has a copy in his possession.[74] The fact that he (a) does not include the text in the volume and (b) makes an entirely erroneous remark about the number of books in his copy, suggests that there were problems with his manuscript.[75]

Alardus, dedicatedly assembling Agricola's complete works for publication, went straight to Deventer in pursuit of Faber's copy of the *De inventione dialectica*. Although he found that the manuscript was (a) of three books, as all previous reports had suggested, and (b) a corrupt copy, he paid Faber twenty ducats for permission to publish the text with Martens in Louvain.[76] It was another seven years, however, before the edited text appeared, with Dorp's name (and not Alardus's) on the title page.[77]

The only satisfactory explanation for the story of a wild goose chase and a disappointment, followed by a delay in publication,[78] is that neither Faber, who had chosen not to include the text in his *Opuscula,* nor Alardus was equipped to put the manuscript they had into publishable form. The most likely reason for this is the state of the manuscript—it was a transcription by several hands and Agricola's own bad handwriting was notorious.[79] Another is that a good deal of the text was technical and conceptually innovative. Dorp, in contrast to Faber and Alardus, was both a professional corrector[80] and a professional theologian and logician by training.[81]

It was another thirteen years before a supposedly substantially revised text became available[82] and nearly twenty-five years before Alardus published his definitive commented edition.[83] There is, moreover, really no plausible explanation for the long delay. Alardus located Agricola's missing papers in 1516 in the possession of the prominent banker Pompeius Occo, nephew of the doctor and distinguished poet Adolphus Occo, the close friend to whom Agricola had bequeathed them at his death.[84] In the *Lucubrationes* Alardus claims that the manuscript of the *De inventione dialectica* had been lent by Occo to a passing dignitary and was not returned until 1528 (when Alardus publicly announced his intention to publish a commented edition). Like other colorful details concerning the retrieval of the text scattered through the commentary to his edition, this accounts for the dates without being terribly convincing.[85] In the meantime, Alardus took employment with Occo and saw several elaborately illustrated devotional volumes through the press on his behalf.[86]

One of Alardus's problems was, in the end, finding a publisher. It seems significant that after 1519 Erasmus was apparently on more distant terms with Alardus. When, sometime after 1529, Alardus had finally completed his two-volume *Opera,* he could not get Erasmus's support for its publication.[87]

All of this must surely give us pause for thought when we are considering the "diffusion" and "influence" of the *De inventione dialectica* as a key text in the development of humanist dialectic and humanist pedagogy. For, as far as I am aware, the secondary literature that focuses determinedly on Agricola's *De inventione dialectica* as the significant bridging work between the "old" dialectic and the "new" has no anxieties whatsoever about the integrity and authenticity of the text, never alludes to the commentaries or corrections of the "*castigatores,*" and barely even mentions the name of Desiderius Erasmus.[88]

Coda: Which "German" Sat at the Feet of Guarino? A Tale of Intellectual Legitimation

A good deal of this story has hinged on biography and autobiography and who constructs them. It has emerged that there is a "Life" of Erasmus, circulating in the history of the recovery and printing of Agricola's works, that is woven into the prefatory and other letters. I have argued that out of this "Life" a meaning is being constructed for Erasmus in the history of northern humanism. Since Agricola is a crucial component in this construction of meaning, it follows that intellectual historians who trace the emerging humanities and their distinctive discipline from Petrarch and Valla (say) to the schools and universities of Protestant Europe, via Agricola's *De inventione dialectica,* cannot afford to ignore the purposive "Vita Erasmi."

But the meticulousness with which this story must be told, if traditional intellectual history is to be convinced and is to be persuaded to take on board the story I have been telling, has, I am afraid, obscured one of its salient features. There is a real flair and virtuosity, a kind of exuberance about this "inventing" of an intellectual pedigree for northern humanism on the part of its authors—maybe a kind of nerve which makes the scholar gasp. I would like to close with a couple of examples.

Gerardus [Erasmus's father] took himself off to Rome. There he made his living by writing (for at that time there was not yet an art of printing): he had a most elegant hand. He lived in a youthful fashion. Soon he applied himself to worthy study. He was well-versed in fine Greek and Latin. Moreover in knowledge of law he made more than usual progress. For Rome at that time boasted an extraordinary number of learned men. He heard Guarino. He had transcribed all kinds of authors with his own hand. (Erasmus [1524])[89]

Alexander Hegius of Westphalia, presided over that school of humane learning, a man profoundly skilled in "bonae litterae," and somewhat skilled in Greek literature, thanks to the teaching of Rudolph Agricola, whose friend he became, shortly after Agricola's return from Italy, where he had heard Guarino Veronese lecture at Ferrara and several others distinguished for their erudition. Erasmus's talent soon made itself apparent, since he understood immediately whatever he was taught, and retained it perfectly, surpassing all his peers. (Beatus Rhenanus 1540)[90]

Sent next to Deventer, we heard Alexander Hegius, follower of Rudolph Agricola and of Guarino Veronese, a most pious man, both eloquent and learned, and a despiser of wordly glory. I was the equal of any of my contemporaries or colleagues in following and remembering lectures. . . . These were, inestimable men, the principles of instruction of our childhood, it was fashioned by these teachers, and in boyhood I was instructed by these sorts of methods. ("Erasmus," in Johann Herold, *Philopseudes, sive Prodes Erasmo Roterodamo v.c. contra Dialogum famosum Anonymi cuiusdam, Declamatio* [Basel, 1542])[91]

I begin by juxtaposing these three biographical fragments, one supposedly by Erasmus himself, at a time when his fame was established, the other two after his death, as his posthumous reputation was being consolidated in the authorized editions of his works. What interests me, of course, is the similarity in phrasing concerning the intellectual formation of Erasmus's two "fathers": his natural father, Gerardus, and his spiritual father, Agricola. (Remember how Erasmus characterized that spiritual relationship in the "Quid cani et balneo?" adage: "So it was not without thought that I plunged into this digression; not to boast of the glory of Germany, but to perform the duty of a grateful pupil, and acquit myself of the debt I owe to the memory of both these men, because I owe one the loving respect of a son, and to the other the affection of a grandson.")

Rudolph Agricola certainly (insofar as there is any certainty in this story) studied with Battista Guarino, son of Guarino Veronese, in Ferrara. There he abandoned legal studies, the original purpose of his educational journey to Pavia and Ferrara, and dedicated his life to the *bonae litterae,* becoming one of the first major intellectual links between Italy and northern Europe. That became Agricola's figurative position in northern humanistic hagiography:

Rudolph Agricola made this distinction in the first book of his *De inventione dialectica,* and Ramus follows him in this, to the extent that he came to rival Agricola's achievement in this art especially, whom Ramus himself was wont to rank in logical studies immediately after the ancient school of Socratic logic (in which the practical application of that art is handled, as much as the science), and ahead of all subsequent logicians. And he used to say publicly that thanks to Agricola the true study of genuine [*germana*] logic had first been established in Germany [*Germania*], and thence, by way of its disciples and emulators had spread throughout the whole world.[92]

The germaneness of being German is also crucial here (as Ramus, with his usual nose for the good publicity line, accurately reflects). In fact Agricola was Frisian, and proud of it. It was Erasmus who abandoned his Dutch origins and "became" a German.[93] In the Johann Herold version, it is Hegius who has become the disciple of Guarino. Clearly a Guarino of some sort or another is necessary to the story of trans-alpine transmission.[94]

The story of Erasmus's father, Gerardus, however, as told in the *Compendium vitae Erasmi,* is rather different. When Erasmus's mother was pregnant with him (so Erasmus tells us) his father (an ordained priest, or about to become an ordained priest—Erasmus is deliberately vague)[95] fled to Rome, returning only when her family wrote and informed him falsely that she had died in childbirth. It is during this ignominious flight that Erasmus represents his father as "listening to Guarino"—yet textually, I think, this Guarino reference also "figures" northward transmission from intellectual father to his heir.[96]

The second example relates to Agricola himself. In his *Life of Petrarch,* describing how Petrarch decided to abandon study of the law and devote himself to "bonae litterae," "Agricola expanded the account given by his source by adding: 'His mind was too noble to be wasted on things of slight and small importance like those of which the civil law consists for the most part, and he did not take lightly his being tied down to them.'"[97] The Stuttgart manuscript which contains the *Life of Petrarch* also contains a sketch for a biography of Agricola by Johann von Plenningen. In that biography, Agricola's decision to abandon the study of the law and devote himself to the *studia humanitatis* is described as follows:

In his early years he followed civil law, and did this more as one who was submitting to the wishes of others than because that subject pleased him. For "his mind was too noble to be wasted on things of slight and small importance like those of which the civil law consists for the most part" (if I may borrow his own words), "and he did not take lightly his being tied down to them," especially since he believed that it could scarcely be trusted by anyone. So abandoning the study of law, he applied his mind to polite letters and to those arts which are called humane.[98]

The mantle of Petrarch falls directly onto the shoulders of Agricola: the mantle of Italian humanism onto the shoulders of the "German."

Finally, in a prefatory letter to Peter Nannius (a former pupil of his at

Alkmaar and now the school's rector), in his collection of Agricola's works (the *Lucubrationes*), Alardus eulogizes the great rhetorician Aphthonius, whose *Progymnasmata* Agricola had translated into Latin. His praise of Aphthonius is extravagant:

One can hardly express how distinguished a practitioner of the liberal arts Aphthonius the Sophist is, who attracts and entices the reader with his fitting brevity, his clarity, his orderliness, and with other synoptic aids of this kind. Who acts in the interest of the student with no less diligence than conviction, not attempting immediately to appear learned himself, but to make the reader learned. In these *Progymnasmata,* with what brilliant conciseness, with how admirable a method [*ordo*], with what simplicity is the whole aim of rhetoric comprehended, as if some clear image were drawn out before us? [99]

In the prefatory letter to Goclenius, in the volume of Agricola's works containing the *De inventione dialectica,* we find Alardus inveighing against those who make Plato's teaching inaccessible and obscure to students,

who would more appropriately be attracted and enticed with fitting brevity, clarity, orderliness, and with other attractive features of this kind.[100] And Agricola is the one man above all who is everywhere consistent; on any topic whatsoever a distinguished practitioner of the liberal arts, who acts in the interest of the student with no less judgement than conviction, not attempting immediately to appear learned himself, but to make the reader learned.[101]

I do not think it would have bothered Alardus at all that we have found him out transposing compliments from one "distinguished practitioner of the liberal arts" to another—from the antique exemplar, Aphthonius, to the figurehead of northern humanism, Rudolph Agricola. If he had annotated his own prefatory letters as assiduously as he annotated Agricola's, he would probably have drawn attention to the "self-quotation" himself. Cumulatively, every such textual echo, every virtuoso print elision, contributes to the construction of the Erasmian cultural tradition, which we might now wish to call: *De inventione Agricolae.*[102]

The tale this virtuosity tells—this exuberant shuffling of the flash cards to provide self-confirming testimony for northern humanism—is in the end a tale of legitimation. Outside the universities (which cannot, or will not, provide a place for them), in print, Erasmus and his circle compose the history of their own intellectual movement: the intellectual pedigree; the testimonies of excellence; the corroborating evidence for and confirming allusions to the seminal influence and lasting impact of a small band of Dutch educators. Four centuries later, the scholarly community still takes them entirely at their word.

Endnote

In 1523, in the polemical *Spongia,* Erasmus once more referred to the "Quid cani et balneo?" adage and drew attention to his eulogy of Agricola and Hegius: "Did not I praise Rudolph Agricola and Alexander Hegius fulsomely, to whom I owed absolutely nothing?"[103] By then, of course, he himself no longer needed to stand on the shoulders of giants. By then the print story of the preeminence of Erasmus was in any case canonical.

Appendix 1

LETTER FROM JACOBUS FABER TO ERASMUS, 1503

IACOBVS ERASMO SVO VTRIUSQVE LINGVE PREDOCTO CANONICO
REGVLARI SALVTEM

⟨C⟩ommunis preceptoris viri doctissimi lucubratiunculas, Erasme suauissime, dignissimas quas edam tuo auspicio, politioribus characteribus exprimantur, quantum in me erit, curabo quam diligentissime. Impietatis non iniuria aget me quispiam, immo studiosis adolescentulis inuidere asseueret, quando hanc prouinciam subire suorum videam neminem subterfugientium laborem, si vigilias illas a blattis corrodentibus non vindicarem situ squalentes, tenebris abstrusas; opera certe cedro tingenda Pallados, penitiore ex adyto deprompta Alcide nostro. Non sum nescius quantum preceptori, sub quo meruimus non tempore vno eodemque, debeam; cuius beneficiis quis respondit aliquando? eo plura cui referam accepta, quo mihi deuinctus magis. In quem quam pium te prestiteris, Adagia Graeca a te iampridem traducta docent luculentissime. Non longe enim a principio, in adagio (vt mens fert) Quid canis in balneo, vt de eo memineris, haud tibi mente excidit: Rodolfus, inquam, Agricola, "quem ego virum totius Germaniae publico honore nomino: nominoque hoc libentius quod puellus huius discipulo sum vsus preceptore, Alexandro Westphalo, vt huic ⟨filii⟩ pietatem, illi tanquam nepoti⟨s⟩ debeam charitatem. Verum ne Rhodolfi nostri gloriam Germanus preco faciam inuidiosam, Hermolai Barbari, quem nemo (vt opinor) negat inter Italos preter summam morum innocentiam et eruditionis arcem tenuisse, epitaphium de eo subscribam:

Inuida clauserunt hoc marmore fata Rodolfum
  Agricola, Phrisii spemque decusque soli:
Scilicet hoc viuo meruit Germania laudis
  Quicquid habet Latium, Graecia quicquid habet."

Quanti autem is ipse nostrum fecerit, hinc profecto clarum; siquidem nostrum sibi persuasit pro eius summo studiorum amore proque eius candore animi (qualem sibi exoptabat) studiorum fuisse acerrimum et exactorem et stimulum et socium, quocum communicaret gratissimum fuit quicquid cogitando inuenerat, quicquid scribendo effecerat, quicquid legendo didicerat, quicquid vel laude vel acriori dignum iudicio annotauerat; que in eius aures ipse, vt itidem in suas ille, deposuit. Semper vel ingerebat aliquid vel contabatur vel dubitabat vel disceptabat, nunc negligentiam liberiori reprehensione castigabat, nunc conatum benigniori prouehebat laude, verum et dicere et audire qui et sciuit et voluit. Itaque quocum etatem vna degere hoc nostro maluerit habuit neminem; id quod per res vtriusque non licuisse tulit egerrime.

   Que nostrum commendant quis dixerit facile? qui et dignitate et auctoritate pre ceteris valens infimos quosque facilitate incredibili aequauit. Vigilantissimus negociosam vitam et quietae et tranquillae pretulit semper; mirum in modum sollicitus qua ratione iuuentuti studiosae consulendum optime; cui bene instituendae vt se natum duxerit vita acta docet. Solida queque summo sudore amplexus, quantopere luctandum non preuidit. De hac enim bene mereretur, hanc sibi conciliaret, laborem omnem duxit minimi. Hunc quesiuit prodesse desiderans, non caeco Midac stolidi captus auro. Quos pauperes esse perspicuum erat, haud ab aliis idipsum pretendentibus mercede defraudari eque passus, celum sibi proponens admisit facillime; quos bonis artibus, aeque atque diuites quosque, instituit diligentissime. Vnde ad vitam bene modesteque transigendam quid ei in viuis defuit? Deo incumbens non est spe frustratus, cui is ipse respondit abunde virtute consumatus. Cuius illam [Curam illius?] admouit accuratissime, ad quam colendam inuitauit maiorem in modum, hanc predicans, hanc extollens, a viciis dehortatus, vicia detestans. Quibus quam infestum se prestiterit, pleraque eius carmina grauissima, que quotannis vt moris est dedit, luce clarius ostendunt; que consilio aliis sudoribus eius longe et melioribus premittenda censui. Cognoscetur enim hinc quo vultu, quo animo suscipientur. Que vbi placuisse videro, que nulli non, et qui litteris affectus et qui doctus, ob tum singularem doctrinam tum admonitiones modestas futura sunt gratissima, facilius (non vt modo) calchographi importunitate improba victus librarie officine alia imprimenda dabo. Hec quidem:

De vera Paschae inueniendi ratione, que Bibliae innititur: quam ex Isaac Argyro Greco excepisse apparet, adiunctis plaerisque de incarnationis mysterio.

De scientia et eo quod scitur, contra Academicos.

De philosophia.

Erotemata interloquutoribus insertis de triplici anima, vegetabili, sensibili, rationali.

De arte et inertia.

De rhetorica.

De moribus.

De sensu et sensili.   Et alia non nulla.

Quocirca mentis bona rebus et fluxis et caducis quo prestantiora sunt, laus eius eo magis solidis ex bonis surgat semper; qui docendo de suis meritus est quam optime, quos non ambagibus, non inuolucris, non inanibus argutiunculis nihil ad rem facientibus suspendebat, qui lumen soli ingerere non didicit, qui luce clariora crassis velaminibus non obtexit, intellectum inutilibus adductis interimens. Sed contra in medium obscura queque misit clarissime; adeo vt nemo non, cui haud gelidus circum precordia sanguis, intelligat quam facillime. Dignus igitur cuius apud posteriores, que liquit monimenta extent semper.

Haec hactenus. Ceterum nescio quid sibi velit, Erasme dulcissime, quo minus Libanii orationem Graecam, vbi Latinam feceris, quam expecto, ad me (vt conuenimus) dederis. Preuideo consilium tuum; quos in manibus habes De illustribus metaphoris, De allegoriis ecclesiasticis, De auctorum allusionibus, De scite et dictis et responsis libros, Libanio meo addere instituisti. Quo vno me consolor, vt moram longiusculam haud feram animo iniquo. Accipe nunc preceptoris nostri carmina grauissima, ad que accedent, vbi et tibi et candidis lectoribus grata viderim, eius insuper de diuersis Erotemata colloquutoribus insertis, Platoni se in hoc accommodans, qui erat ei quam familiarissimus. Dabo tandem operam, quicquid de Rodolfi Agricolae operibus ad manus hic veniet, preter ea que superioribus annis edita apud bibliopolas exponuntur, te adeant. Non absurdum rursus putaui subiicere epicedion incultum, quod ei vita defuncto inueni, in quo prestinguntur quedam quibus ille noster miratur, qui tuis commendatus sit semper.[104]

[Jacob to his Friend Erasmus, an accomplished scholar in Latin and Greek and a Canon regular, Greetings

The writings of that excellent scholar, your teacher and mine, dearest Erasmus, are well worth my editing with your blessing; and I shall take every possible care to see that as far as in me lies they are reproduced in elegant characters. I could justifiably be held guilty of disloyalty, indeed of malice, towards studious youth, if, observing as I do that none of his close friends is undertaking this charge and that they shrink from the toil it involves, I were to fail to rescue those products of his pen, filthy with dust and buried in darkness, from the devouring worm; for they are works that deserve to be preserved by the cedar oil of Pallas Athene, drawn by our Hercules from an inner shrine. I recognize how much I am indebted to the teacher under whom you and I served, though at different times. Who has ever responded worthily to all he did for us? I have even more for which to be grateful, inasmuch as he was closer to me personally. How loyal you yourself have been to him the Greek adages which you translated some time ago show very clearly; for, near the beginning of that work, in the adage called, as I remember, "Quid canis in balneo," you did not forget to mention him in these terms: Rodolphus Agricola, "whom I name to the general honor of the entire German nation; and name all the more gladly because as a boy I had for my own teacher his pupil Alexander [Hegius] of Westphalia, so that I owe to the latter filial duty, to the former as it were a grandson's affection. But, in case I as a German should arouse resentment by singing the praises of my fellow-countryman Rodolphus, I shall add the epitaph composed by Ermolao Barbaro, whom everyone, I think, must agree to have occupied the preeminent place among Italians, both for personal honour and for scholarship:

In this cold tomb hath envious fate sealed up
  The hope and glory of the Frisian name;
Whate'er of praise to Rome or Greece belong,
  He, living, won for Germany that same."

How highly Agricola himself respected Hegius is made clear by the following: he was convinced that by virtue of his intense enthusiasm for study and his sincere goodwill, such as he himself longed to possess, our master was most effective in evoking, prompting, and assisting others' studies. With him he loved to share whatever he had discovered by reflection, or created in writing, or learned by reading, or marked as deserving either praise or censure. And these things he poured into our master's ears, just as Hegius did into his. He always made some relevant point, or expressed reluctance or hesitation, or debated the matter, sometimes chiding carelessness with an outspoken rebuke and sometimes encouraging an attempt with kindly words of praise, but always both able and willing to speak and to listen. And therefore there was nobody with whom he would have preferred to spend his life than with our master; and he was very sorry that their circumstances made it impossible.

Who could easily chronicle all our master's good qualities? Though he surpassed others in rank and authority, he showed exceptional affability in condescending to men of low estate. He was extremely energetic, and always preferred a busy life to a quiet and restful one; he was extraordinarily anxious to find the best way of serving the interests of studious youth, and his life-story shows that he regarded it as his destined task to educate youth well. He took infinite pains to achieve what would be most permanent without calculating what struggles it would cost him; for in order to deserve well of youth and win its affection, he thought no kind of fatigue was of any consequence, and when he sought hard work, he did so not under the spell of foolish Midas's hidden gold, but out of a longing to do good. In fairness he would not allow those who were obviously poor to be disappointed by others who claimed the same benefits in return for fees, and was very ready to admit them, regarding Heaven as his recompense; and he taught the liberal arts to them with the same careful attention as to the rich. Thus while he was alive he did all that one could do to live a virtuous and unselfish life; he relied on God, and did not hope in vain; indeed he lived up to his own hopes in generous measure, for he was filled with goodness and made perfect in goodness. He was most assiduous in encouraging the pursuit of virtue, to the exercise of which he earnestly called his pupils; he preached and praised virtue, exhorting them to abandon vice, which he hated. The extent of his hostility to it is shown with perfect clarity in the many deeply serious poems he published each year, as was his custom; these I have deliberately decided to issue in advance of his other productions, even though the latter are far more accomplished, for I shall thereby come to know what reception they can expect. When I perceive that they have won approval (and they are sure to receive a warm welcome from every educated person with any taste for literature, both for their profound learning and for their restrained moral exhortations), I shall then be more ready, without suffering the printer's importunate insistence as I do now, to send his other works to the press to be printed. They consist of the following:

An enquiry in the form of a dialogue on the true method of determining the date of Easter, which depends upon the Bible; this he evidently derived from the Greek, Isaac Argyros; together with a lengthy treatment of the mystery of the incarnation.

On knowledge and [that which can be] known; against the philosophers of the academic school

On philosophy

On the tripartite soul: vegetable, sensory, and rational

On ability and its absence

On rhetoric

On morals

On sensation and its object; also several other writings

And thus, as treasures of the mind are finer than transitory and ephemeral possessions, so may his glory ever grow greater from his enduring achievements; for by his teaching he deserved excellently well of his pupils, whom he never teased with circumlocutions, obscurities, or vain and petty cleverness of no relevance to the subject; who never learned the art of adding light to the sun; who did not wrap up in thick veils matters that were clearer than daylight, blunting the understanding with useless additions. On the contrary, he set whatever was obscure in the clearest possible light, in such a way that anyone save he whose "blood within his breast did coldly run" [*Georgics* 2.484] could understand it with the greatest ease. For this reason he deserves to enjoy eternal remembrance among posterity through the literary memorials he has left.

Enough on this subject. For the rest, dearest Erasmus, I fail to comprehend why you have not given me, as we agreed, the Greek oration of Libanius when you have done it into Latin; I am waiting for it. I can glimpse your intention; you have decided to add to my Libanius the books you are now engaged upon: on famous metaphors, on ecclesiastical allegories, on allusions in classical authors, and on witty sayings and replies. This is the one thought I console myself with that I may bear patiently the rather long delay. So now accept our teacher's most important poems, to which will also be added, when I see that it would please you and my other kindly readers, his enquiries into a variety of topics, composed in dialogue form; in this respect he follows the example of Plato, who was most intimately known to him. Finally I shall see to it that any of Rodolphus Agricola's works that come to hand here are sent to you, except those that have been published in previous years and are now in the booksellers' shops. Also I thought it not inappropriate to add a rough-and-ready dirge that I composed in honor of our departed friend, which touches on certain admirable qualities in him, which may ever serve to commend him to your friends.[105]]

ERASMUS, ADAGES (1508), "WHAT HAS A DOG TO DO WITH A BATH?"

What has a dog to do with a bath? I quote this adage with all the more pleasure because it refreshes and renews my memory, and my affection, for Rodolphus Agricola of Friesland, whom I name as the man in all Germany and Italy most worthy of the highest public honor: in Germany, because she gave him birth, in Italy, because she made him a great scholar. No one was ever born this side of the Alps more completely endowed with all literary gifts; let this be said without prejudice. There was no branch of fine learning in which that great man could not vie with the most eminent masters. Among the Greeks he was the best Greek of them all, among the Latins the best Latin. As a poet you would have said he was a second Virgil; as a writer of prose he had the charm of a Poliziano, but more dignity. His style, even extempore, had such purity, such naturalness, you would maintain that it was not a Frisian who spoke, but a native of ancient Rome herself. Such perfect eloquence was paired with the same degree of learning. He had delved into all the mysteries of philosophy. There was no part of music in which he was not accurately versed. At the very end of his life he had bent his whole mind on the study of Hebrew and the Holy Scripture. In the midst of these efforts he was snatched from this world by the envy of the Fates, not yet forty years old, as I am told. There are a few literary remains of his work, some letters, poems of various kinds; the *Axiochus* of Plato translated into Latin, and a version of Isocrates' *To Demonicus*. Then there are a couple of lectures given in public session in the University of Ferrara, for it was there he both learnt and gave open lectures. There are lying hidden in some people's possession his treatises on dialectic.[106] He had also translated some of Lucian's dialogues. But since he himself cared little for glory, and most mortals are, to say the least of it, careless in looking after the work of others, none of these have yet seen the light. But the works which are extant, even if not published by himself, give plain proof of something divine about the man.

Let it not be thought that I as a German am blinded by patriotic feeling; to avoid this I will transcribe the epitaph written for him by Ermolao Barbaro for Venice. It is superb, and one might find it difficult to decide whether it was more worthy of the man who wrote it or the man it was written about. Here it is:

Under this stone, the jealous Fates decreed
  The Frisian hope, his country's light, should come,
Rudolph Agricola; in life, indeed,
  He brought such praise to Germany his home
  As ever Greece could have, or ever Rome.

What ampler or more magnificent tribute could be paid to our dear Rodolphus than this splendid testimony, so complete, and offered not to a living man but to one already dead—so there is no question of its proceeding from affection rather than from judgment? and to a German, so there is no possibility that love for a country they both shared should diminish the weight of the testimony? And it came from that man who had brought glory not only to his native Italy, but to this whole age of ours; whose authority is such among all learned men that it would be most impertinent to disagree with him; whose work in restoring literature is so outstandingly valuable that anyone would have to be utterly impervious to culture, or at least utterly ungrateful, who did not hold the memory of Ermolao as sacrosanct.

Such full and ungrudging praise of this man has, I confess, a singular charm for me, because I happened while yet a boy to have his disciple Alexander Hegius as my teacher. He was headmaster of the once famous school of the town of Deventer, where I learned the rudiments of both languages when I was almost a child. To put it in a few words, he was a man just like his master: as upright in his life as he was serious in his teaching. Momus himself could have found no fault with him except one, that he cared less for fame than he need have done, and took no heed of posterity. If he wrote anything, he wrote as if he were playing a game rather than doing something serious. And yet these writings, so written, are of the sort which the learned world votes worthy of immortality.

So it was not without thought that I plunged into this digression; not to boast of the glory of Germany, but to perform the duty of a grateful pupil, and acquit myself of the debt I owe to the memory of both these men, because I owe one the loving respect of a son, and to the other the affection of a grandson.

Now to turn to the adage, which I remember having learnt from a certain very learned letter of my beloved Rodolphus, at a time when I was a mere child and as yet ignorant of Greek. In this letter he is trying to persuade the town council of Antwerp, with conviction and eloquence, that they should appoint as master of their school someone proficient in liberal studies, and not (as they usually do) entrust this office to an inarticulate theologian or naturalist, the sort of man who is sure he has something to say about everything but has no notion of what it is to speak. "What good would he be in a school? As much good, to use the Greek repartee, as a dog in a bath."

Lucian *Against an Ignoramus:* "And each one of the onlookers immediately voices that very handy proverb: what do a dog and a bath have in common?" Again in the *Parasite:* "But to my way of thinking, a philosopher at a drinking-party is just like a dog in a bath." So this is to be applied to those who are totally useless for certain purposes, just as there is no use for dogs in a bath.[107]

Appendix 2

EARLY PRINTING HISTORY OF AGRICOLA'S WORKS

The following account is based on a search of L. Hain, *Repertorium Bibliographicum, in quo libri omnes ab arte typographica inventa usque ad annum MD,* 2 vols. in 4 (Paris, 1826–38), and W. A. Copinger, *Supplement to Hain's Repertorium Bibliographicum. or corrections towards a new edition of that work,* 3 vols. (Milan, 1950). I have also made use of G. van Thienen, *Incunabula in Dutch Libraries: A Census of Fifteenth-Century Printed Books in Dutch Public Collections,* 2 vols. ('s-Gravenhage, 1983), with additional information from J. C. T. Oates, *A Catalogue of the Fifteenth-Century Printed Books in the University Library Cambridge* (Cambridge, 1954). Finally, as always, I have derived a good deal of guidance by careful reading of P. S. Allen's header notes and footnotes in his edition of Erasmus's letters, *Opus epistolarum Des. Erasmi Roterodami,* 12 vols. (Oxford, 1906–58), as well as from his "The Letters of Rudolph Agricola," *English Historical Review* 21 (1906), 302–17.

The only original work of Agricola's published in his lifetime seems to have been the long Latin poem, "Anna mater" (Alardus II, 297–309), and a small number of individual letters. The "Anna mater" was published by Richard Paffraet:

On 7 April 1484 Richard Paffraet and his wife Stine were honored by

a visit to their home by the great man Agricola. In his luggage the humanist had a panegyric to St. Anne, the mother of the Virgin Mary. Paffraet
hastened to his workshop and returned with Agricola's *Anna Mater* in ten
pages of print. Agricola, in a hurry to continue his journey, had to overlook the printing errors.[108]

This volume is recorded in Copinger as item 133, as follows:

Agricola (Rodolphus) Anna mater.—Epicedion, epitaphium et epigramma [Da-
ventriae, Rich. Paffroet, 1485.] 4°. Goth. . . . 10ff.

It corresponds to Huisman 141 (where it has strayed into a post–1500
bibliography): [109]

S.A. (Deventer. R. Paffraet.)
4°. a¹⁰.

a2	Rodolphi Agricolae / Anna mater incipit
a7	Rodolphi Agricolae / Mauricio comiti spegelbergi
	epicedion.
a10	Epitaphium. / Eiusdem epigram[m]a

The "Epicedion" is printed in Alardus II, 314–19; the epitaph to the same
is printed in Alardus II, 319. Copinger 134 is another edition of the "Anna
mater," "Carmina in divae Annae laudem" [Swollis, Petr. Os de Breda,
1500] (also 10ff.).

Hain 15923 gives the following:

Vegius (Maphaeus) Vita divi Antonii. F. Ia: Uita diui Antonii a Mapheo Vegio
Laudensi viro si quisq[ue] fuit etate nostra eruditissimo tam vere quam eleganter
conscripta unacum suauissimis quibusdam carminibus de Sancte Marie et beate
Anne laudibus pulcherrimis. . . . Impressum Liptzk per Gregorium Werman et per
magistrum Ioannem Cubitensem diligenter emendatum. 1492.

I take it this is Huisman 140 (also pre-1500):

1492. s.l. s.n.
In Annam matrem carmen.
1492.
in: Mapheus Vegius: Vita Divi Antonii.[110]

The "de Sancte Marie" poem here suggests a link with Copinger, item 5753,
Jodocus Beysselius, *Rosacea augustissimae christiferae Mariae corona* (Ant-

werp, Govaert Bac, [1493–   ]), which van Thienen lists as "with other tracts" (item 808), and which Oates indexes as containing "Anna mater" (Oates, item 3980 and page 702).

In addition to prefatory letters in his own volumes, two Agricola letters, to Rudolphus Langen and Antonius Liber (Vrye) were published around 1477 in a volume edited by Liber, *Familiarum epistolarum compendium* (Cologne, J. Koelhoff, c. 1477).[111]

Two of Agricola's translations from Greek (at least) were also published during his lifetime. His translation of Isocrates' *Praecepta ad demonicum* appears as item 3328 in Copinger as follows:

Isocrates. Praecepta ad Demonicum. *Sine notâ* [1480.] 4°. . . . 8ff. Praecepta Isocratis per eruditissimum virum Rudolphu[m] agricola[m] e graeco sermone in latinum traducta.

It was apparently reprinted in Heidelberg (Heinrich Knoblochtzer, about 1495) and Nuremberg (Friedrich Creussner, about 1497).[112] His translation of pseudo-Plato's *Axiochus de contemnenda morte* appears as item 4766 in Copinger as follows:

Plato Axiochus de contemnenda morte. Daventriae, In platea episcopi [Rich. Paffraet, c. 1480] 4°. Goth. . . . 6ff.

In a characteristic printer's move, Paffraet later used this six-folio work to fill out the end of another publication. Copinger 2953 gives the following:

Hieronymus s. Epistolae duae ad Athletam et Heliodorum etc. [Deventer, Rich. Pafraet, ca. 1500] 4°. Cont. Hieronymus s. Epistolae duae ad Athletam et Heliodorum—Marcus Tullius Cicero: Epistolarum ad familiares libri tres ultimi—Basilius Magnus s.: De legendis libris gentilium—pseudo-Plato: Axiochus, seu De contemnenda morte.—Quintus Flaccus Horatius: Satirae, seu sermonum liber primus.

Copinger item 4768 is a more interesting volume for my purposes, since it includes, in addition to the *Axiochus,* Agricola's translation from French of the letter "de congressu Imperatoris Friderici et Caroli Burgundiorum ducis" (Alardus, *Lucubrationes,* 221–27), and the letter to Barbarianus containing the "canis in balneo" tag, as well as some "carmina":

Plato. Dialogus de contemnenda morte qui Axiochus inscribitur, vertit Rodolphus Agricola.—Rod. Agricolae Traductio in epistolam de congressu Imperatoris Friderici et Karoli Burgundionum ducis etc. [Lovanii, Joh. de Westfalia, c. 1483.] 4°. Goth. . . . 28ff. including 1st and last blank.

Oates's version of the same volume runs: "Traductio in epistolam de congressu Friderici et Karoli. Epistola ad Barbirianum. Carmina. [Louvain, J. de Paderborn]" (Oates, item 3777 and page 702).

Copinger item 4767 is also an edition of the *Axiochus,* listed as follows:

Plato [Moguntiae, P. Friedberg, 149–.] 4°. Goth. . . . 8FF.
F.1ª: (Title) Axiochus Platonis de con \\ temnenda morte. \\ Infracto ut possis animo contemnere morte \\ ad nomen cuius vulgus mane tremuit: Divini Socratis verba haec lege quis moriente \\ Axiochum monuit: illico tutus eris \\
F.1ᵇ (Text) Jacobus Canter Phrysius artiu[m] ingeniaru[m] p[ro]fessor: \\ Poeta Laureatus . . . \\ End. Finit dialogus Platonis de contemnenda \\ morte qui Axiochus inscribitur Feliciter.\\

According to Allen (*Opus epistolarum* I, 126), Jacobus Canter's preface to this edition can be dated as after 26 March 1496 (death of Hermann Rinck), thus confirming a publishing date in the 1490s (after Agricola's death). Canter corresponded with Erasmus around 1489 (see my discussion of the neo-Latin poetry link between Erasmus as possibly the original stimulus for his interest, above).

Hain, item 6692, lists the following, undated and without place of provenance:

Eucherivs Episcop. Lugduneus. Epistola ad Valerianum de Philosophia Christiana.

Allen identifies this as the "Epistola Valerii episcopi ad propinquum suum ex Greco in Latinum sermonem per magistrum Rodolphum Agricolam traducta" (J. de Breda [Deventer c. 1485]) (Allen, *Opus epistolarum* III, [introduction to letter 676]). In 1517 Erasmus printed this work in an edition by Martens of his *Cato.* In his prefatory letter to Alardus he identifies the letter as being from Eucherius to Valerianus, rather than vice versa, and points out that it was a Latin original and not translated from the Greek, but he used Alardus's text (possibly the edition just described) to prepare his own edition.[113]

Finally, in pursuit of the elusive Lucian, Copinger, items 3655, 3656, 3657, gives Lucian editions by de Breda and Paffraet in Deventer, c. 1485 to c. 1497, which would be worth closer inspection. A. F. van Iseghem (*Biographie de Thierry Martens d'Alost, premier imprimeur de la Belgique* [Alost,

1852]) refers to a record of a volume *Rodolphi Agricolae varia*, Martens, 1511, which supposedly contains Agricola translations of two Lucian dialogues, but of which there appears to be no trace apart from this one citation.[114]

Notes

1. I would like to thank all those members of the Princeton History Department who contributed to my own understanding of "broader historical context," in vigorous and stimulating debate, during my tenure there of a Shelby Cullom Davis Center Fellowship.

2. See, e.g., Robert Darnton, *The Great Cat Massacre and Other Episodes in French Cultural History* (New York, 1984), 63: "Cultural currents intermingled, moving up as well as down, while passing through different media and connecting groups as far apart as peasants and salon sophisticates. These groups did not inhabit completely separate mental worlds."

3. For a preliminary skirmish with such problems on my part see L. Jardine, "Distinctive Discipline: Rudolph Agricola's Influence on Methodical Thinking in the Humanities," in F. Akkerman and A. J. Vanderjagt, eds., *Rodolphus Agricola Phrisius 1444–1485* (Proceedings of the International Conference at the University of Groningen, 28–30 October 1985) (Leiden, 1988).

4. For the case for the persistence of a more traditionally scholastic view of logic/dialectic, however, see J. M. Fletcher, "Change and Resistance to Change: A Consideration of the Development of English and German Universities During the Sixteenth Century," *History of Universities* I (1981), 1–36; J. K. McConica, "Humanism and Aristotle in Tudor Oxford," *English Historical Review* 94 (1979), 291–317.

5. G. C. Huisman, *Rudolph Agricola: A Bibliography of Printed Works and Translations* (Groningen, 1985). This work replaces W. J. Ong, *Ramus and Talon Inventory* (Cambridge, Mass., 1958), and W. Risse, *Bibliographia Logica. Verzeichnis der Druckschriften zur Logik mit Angabe ihrer Fundorte. Band I 1473–1800* (Hildesheim, 1965), for Agricola editions, since Huisman incorporates these authors' works.

6. Inevitably one's view of precisely who were the influential originators of the sustained study of Agricola will be subjective, and in my case probably related directly to my own initiation into the subject. One should probably add N. W. Gilbert, *Renaissance Concepts of Method* (New York, 1960), and W. Risse's *Die Logik der Neuzeit*, vol. I (Stuttgart, 1964).

7. C. Prantl, *Geschichte der Logik im Abendlande* (Leipzig, 1870), IV, ch. 21; W. and M. Kneale, *The Development of Logic* (Oxford, 1962) (though they cite him as "Agrippa"!); Risse, *Die Logik der Neuzeit;* Vasoli, *La dialettica;* Vasoli, "La retorica e la dialettica umanistiche e le origini delle concezioni moderne del 'metodo'," *Il Verri* 35/6 (1970), 250–306; L. Jardine, *Francis Bacon: Discovery and the Art of Discourse* (Cambridge, 1974), ch. 1; "The Place of Dialectic Teaching in Sixteenth-Century Cambridge," *Studies in the Renaissance* 21 (1974), 31–62; "Humanism and the Sixteenth-Century Cambridge Arts Course," *History of Education* 4 (1975),

16–31; "Lorenzo Valla and the Intellectual Origins of Humanist Dialectic," *Journal of the History of Philosophy* 15 (1977), 143–63; "Humanism and the Teaching of Logic," in N. Kretzmann, A. Kenny, and J. Pinborg, eds., *The Cambridge History of Later Medieval Philosophy* (Cambridge, 1982), section 43, 797–807; "Humanist Logic," in C. B. Schmitt, E. Kessler, and Q. R. D. Skinner, eds., *The Cambridge History of Renaissance Philosophy,* section II.2 (Cambridge, 1988).

8. Kneale, *Development,* 300.

9. Agricola biographies tend to be in Dutch. The standard such ones are: H. E. J. M. van der Velden, *Rodolphus Agricola (Roelof Huusman) een Nederlandsch Humanist der vijftiende Eeuw* (Leiden, 1911), and M. A. Nauwelaerts, *Rodolphus Agricola* (Kruseman den Haag, 1963). Such detail as there is concerning his life (and much of this paper will be concerned with the sources of such detail) is to be found in the following places: F. G. Adelmann, "Dr. Dietrich von Plieningen zu Schaubeck," *Ludwigsburger Geschichtsblätter* 28 (1976), 9–139; R. Pfeiffer, *History of Classical Scholarship 1300–1850* (Oxford, 1976); J. E. Sandys, *A History of Classical Scholarship,* 3 vols. (Cambridge, 1903–1908), II; R. Radouant, "L'union de l'éloquence et de la philosophie au temps de Ramus," *Revue d'Histoire littéraire de la France* 31 (1924), 161–92; P. S. Allen, "The Letters of Rudolph Agricola," *English Historical Review* 21 (1906), 302–17; K. Hartfelder, ed., *Unedierte Briefe von Rudolf Agricola: Ein Beitrag zur Geschichte des Humanismus, Festschrift der Badischen Gymnasien, gewidmet der Universität Heidelberg* (Karlsruhe, 1886); P. Pfeifer, ed., *Commentarii seu index vitae Rudolphi Agricolae Phrisii . . . , Serapeum* 10 (1849), 97–107. On Agricola as a painter see M. Baxandall, "Rudolph Agricola and the Visual Arts," Sonderdruck aus *Institution und Kunstwissenschaft: Festschrift für Hans Swarzenski,* 409–18. See also L. W. Spitz, *The Religious Renaissance of the German Humanists* (Cambridge, Mass., 1963), 20–40; H. de Vocht, *History of the Foundation and the Rise of the Collegium Trilingue Lovaniense 1517–1550,* 4 vols. (Louvain, 1951–55), especially vol. 1.

10. For a good example of this type of generalized argument for Agricola's importance, see Spitz, op. cit. The classic, influential account, of course, is W. H. Woodward, *Studies in Education During the Age of the Renaissance 1400–1600* (Cambridge, 1924), where twenty-odd pages on Agricola (79–103) are dovetailed neatly in between Guarino Veronese, Leon Battista Alberti, and Matteo Palmieri on the one hand, and Erasmus, Budé, Vives, and Melanchthon on the other. Woodward also has a helpful chronological table which confirms this seamless development from Italy to northern Europe via Agricola.

11. There is another candidate for "best-known work": a letter which became known as the *De formando studio,* first published by Jacobus Faber (Deventer, 1508), and frequently reprinted with corresponding works by Erasmus and Melanchthon.

12. T. Heath, "Logical Grammar, Grammatical Logic, and Humanism in Three German Universities," *Studies in the Renaissance* 18 (1971), 9–64.

13. Faber brought Hegius's works out in two volumes. The first, containing Hegius's poems, is somewhat confusingly entitled: *Alexandri Hegii Gymnasi / archae iampridem Daventriensis diligentissimi ar / tium professoris clarissimi philosophi presbyteri / poetae utriusque linguae docti Carmina et gracia et / elegantia; cum ceteris eius opusculis quae subiciuntur—De scientia et eo quod scitur contra Academicos / De triplici anima vegetabili: sensili: et rationali / De vera pasche inveniendi ratione Quam*

ex Isaac / Arguro greco excepisse apparet De Rhetorica De / arte et inertia / De sensu et sensili De moribus / De philosophia / De incarnationis misterio Erotemata. "This title is misleading as the volume contains only the *Carmina* and not the *cetera opuscula,*" J. IJsewijn, "Alexander Hegius + 1498, *Invectiva in modos significandi,*" in I. D. McFarlane, ed., *Renaissance Studies: Six Essays* (Edinburgh and London, 1972), 1–20. The second volume did contain the *opuscula* (IJsewijn, 3). Faber's prefatory letter explains that the title is deliberate: "I have deliberately decided to issue [Hegius's poems] in advance of his other productions, even though the latter were far more accomplished, for I shall thereby come to know what reception they can expect. When I perceive that they have won approval . . . I shall then be more ready, without suffering the printer's importunate insistence as I do now, to send his other works to the press to be printed," *Correspondence of Erasmus letters 142 to 297, 1501 to 1514, Collected Works of Erasmus* 2 (Toronto, 1977), 65–69 (letter 174); 68. Here, already, we have an early editor (and printer) constructing a story for their readers, while twentieth-century scholarship discards the "tale" in favor of hard-print "facts."

14. P. S. Allen, *Opus Epistolarum Des. Erasmi Roterodami* I, 384–88 (letter 174); 385–86. See Appendix 1.

15. As we have already seen, prefatory letters customarily "tell" the reader pertinent things. We shall see that a good number of prefatory letters to minor works in what I shall call the Erasmus "circle" advertise connections between that work and forthcoming or promised, doctrinally or intellectually related works.

16. So that we keep the facts straight: Hegius became headmaster of the Deventer school in 1483; he taught the top class. Erasmus was at the Deventer school until sometime in 1484, when he was withdrawn because of an outbreak of plague; he had not reached the top class. In my view the best account by far of Erasmus's life and intellectual influences during the Deventer and Steyn periods is to be found in C. Reedijk, *The Poems of Desiderius Erasmus with Introduction and Notes* (Leiden, 1956), ch. III, "His Brethren in Apollo" (42–86). Faber was at the school sometime later (but before Hegius's death in 1498), and stayed on as a master.

17. Sixteenth-century editors seem to have been in the habit of pointing out to fellow editors their failure adequately to acknowledge the author they themselves championed. When Gabriel Harvey published his *Ciceronianus* in 1577, Thomas Hatcher, who had recently published the collected works of Walter Haddon, wrote to Harvey expressing surprise at the omission of Haddon from Harvey's list of great Cambridge Ciceronian orators (see V. Stern, *Gabriel Harvey*). If the account I give here of how such epistolary exchanges were orchestrated is correct, Hatcher (a friend of Harvey's) may well have expected such a letter to provide a prefatory epistle for a second edition of Harvey's *Ciceronianus,* which would then serve simultaneously as an additional embellishment for the Harvey work, a connecting thread between Harvey's work and other contemporary English scholars, and a "puff" for Hatcher's own publication.

18. Ibid., 68–69.

19. Apparently Erasmus's Libanius did not in fact reach print until Thierry Martens published it in 1519, although the prefatory letter to Nicholas Ruistre is dated 1503 (Allen I, 390–93 [letter 177]). Allen suggests that this was because Mar-

tens was not yet in a position to set Greek type in 1503 (Allen I, 390). On printers of Greek manuals see A. T. Grafton and L. Jardine, *From Humanism to the Humanities: Education and the Liberal Arts in Fifteenth- and Sixteenth-Century Europe* (London and Cambridge, Mass., 1986), ch. 5.

20. I am coining the term "purposive" for documents in which authors affirm one thing, but use the occasion to make further connections which give the document a further purpose.

21. On the connection between the Paffraet publishing house and the Deventer school see Reedijk, 25; P. C. van der Meersch, *Recherches sur la vie et les travaux des imprimeurs néerlandais* (Gand, 1856).

22. Huisman, 4.

23. See Appendix 1 for the full text of the 1508 "Quid cani et balneo" adage.

24. Margaret Mann Phillips, tr., *Adages* I.i.1–I.v.100, *Collected Works of Erasmus* 31 (Toronto, 1982), 348–51, esp. 351.

25. W. A. Copinger, *Supplement to Hain's Repertorium Bibliographicum*, 3 vols. (Milan, 1950), items 2430, 2431.

26. There were also editions by Johannes de Westfalia, Louvain, 1483; and edited by Jacopus Canter, published by Peter von Friedberg, Mainz, about 1495 (Cop. 4768, 4767).

27. Cop. 3328.

28. For an account of early Agricola publishing history as I have so far been able to piece it together, see Appendix 2.

29. "Quod petis, ut Luciani Mycillum, quem Latinum feci, tibi mittam, dedicemq́[ue] tuo illum nomini, utrunq[ue] si non petisses etiam, facturus era[m]: sed uereor ne tam celeriter illum tibi mittere queam, nondum recognoui, aut ë prima schaeda illum repurgaui, adeo ne respexi quidem, postea quäm traduxi." Letter to Hegius, reprinted in Alardus, ed., *Rodolphi Agricolae Lucubrationes* (Cologne, 1539; repr. Nieuwkoop, 1967), 185. Nevertheless, it is quite possible that these Lucian fragments will turn up in an early edition (particularly since in the Alardus edition the "De non facile credendis delationibus" has a prefatory letter by Agricola).

30. "Accedunt, praeter Latina & Graeca, quae mihi quocunq[ue] possum modo, tuenda sunt, quanquäm & no[n]nihil damni in eis me facere intelligo. Sed accedu[n]t ad haec (ut dico) studia Hebraicarum literarum, quae mihi nouum & plenum molestiae negocium exhibent. . . . destinaui senectutem meam (si modo me manet senectus) studio sacrarum literarum" (185–86).

31. Nauwelaerts, 165.

32. Huisman, item 3. This may be the first printed edition of the important eight-page letter, "De formando studio," but I am not even confident of that. Everything else in the volume I believe to have appeared elsewhere. This is, nevertheless, an important publishing event for our story, because Faber's prefatory letter to the volume contains a crucial reference to a manuscript of the missing *De inventione dialectica*, and is therefore vital for the story of the retrieval of that work. See Alardus, *Lucubrationes*, 203, and see especially above, pages 52–55.

33. Huisman, 3: *Rhodolfi Agricole. parae / nesis siue admonitio qua / ratione studia sunt tractanda. et qui auctores sunt / euoluendi vna cum epistola eiusdem ad Alexandrum / hegium gymnasiarcham dauentriensem. et parae- / nesis Isocratis ad demonicum Rho-*

dolfo agrico / la interprete e greco traducta / & Hermolai barbari patriarchae Aquileiensis / versus in sepulcrum Rodolphi Agricolae grunningensis / Inuidia [sic Huisman] clauserunt hoc marmore fata Rhodolfum / Agricolam frisij spemque decusque soli / Scilicet hoc viuo meruit Germania laudis / Quicquid habet latium graecia quicquid habet.

34. "Lucubrationes Rodolphi Agricolae, hominis vere diuini, iamdudum expectamus; cuius ego scripta quoties lego, toties pectus illud sacrum ac coeleste mecum adoro atque exosculor" (*De copia*, fol. 2ʳ, reprinted in P. S. Allen, *Opus Epistolarum Des. Erasmi Roterodami*, 12 vols. (Oxford, 1906–58), II, 32 [letter 311]).

35. Allen, "Letters of Rudolph Agricola," 305. Beatus Rhenanus worked first as corrector for the printer Stephanus in Paris, then did editorial and prefatory work for Schürer, moving to Strasburg in 1508–1509 "to take a more active part in Schürer's undertakings." From 1511 he lived and worked in Basel, with the printing house of Amerbach-Froben (Allen, *Opus epistolarum* II, 60). See J. D'Amico, *Theory and Practice in Renaissance Textual Criticism: Beatus Rhenanus between Conjecture and History* (Los Angeles, 1988), ch. 2, "The Novice Critic."

36. Erasmus and Rhenanus later became close friends; they met in 1515, when Rhenanus was working for the Froben press and assisted Erasmus in his edition of Seneca's *Lucubrationes* (D'Amico, *Beatus Rhenanus*, 63–65).

37. "Salutat te . . . Matthias Schurerius, qui plurimum rogat B. Rhenanum vt aliquando manus Rodolpho adhibeat; nam si castigatus esset, non diutius editionem eius moraretur" (Allen, *Opus epistolarum* II, 121).

38. Allen, *Opus epistolarum* III, 19 (letter 606).

39. Allen, *Opus epistolarum* III, 55 (letter 633).

40. Allen, *Opus epistolarum* III, 30 (letter 612).

41. And what was the relationship between that first prefatory announcement by Rhenanus and Schürer's (his employer's) printing aspirations in relation to Erasmus?

42. Huisman 266: *Opuscula aliquot Erasmo / Roterodamo castigatore & interprete: quibus / primae aetati nihil prelegi potest; Neque vtilius neque / elegantius. / & Libellus elegantissimus, qui vulgo Cato in- / scribitur, complectens sanctiss. vitae communis / praecepta. & Mimi Publiani. / & Septem sapientum celebria dicta. / & Institutur [sic] Christiani hominis carmine [sic] pro pueris. / ab Erasmo compositum. / & Parenesis Isocratis Rodolpho Agricola inter / prete, castigatore Martino Dorpio. / Cum gratia et priuilegio. / A. Maximi. Aug. & Car. Aust. / Prostant louanij in edibus Theodorici Martini Alustensis e regione Scholae / Iuris ciuilis.* On this volume see Reedijk, 304–6 (introduction to the poem "Christiani hominis institutum," which was published for the first time in this volume). Note that Dorp, who corrected the Agricola, in fact saw the entire volume through the press, since he too corrected proof for Thierry Martens: "Catonem abs te castigatum mihique creditum castigate impressit, me erratorum vindice. Eam operam magistro Ioanni Neuio [to whom the *Cato* was dedicated], Lilianorum gymnasiarchae, vti iussisti, dicaui; qui te ob hoc beneficium ita complectitur, vt qum redieris, sis profusissime sensurus" (letter from Dorp to Erasmus [1514], Allen, *Opus epistolarum* II, 10–16 [letter 304]).

43. Huisman, 3.

44. Huisman, 4. On Martens see C. Reedijk, "Erasme, Thierry Martens et le *Julius Exclusus*," in J. Coppens, ed., *Scrinium Erasmianum*, 2 vols. (Leiden, 1969),

II, 351–78 (particularly as specifying a group centered on the Martens printing house, which included Gilles, Dorp, Goclenius, and Alardus, as well as Erasmus [357]); A. F. van Iseghem, *Biographie de Thierry Martens d'Alost, premier imprimeur de la Belgique* (Malines, Alost, 1852); P. C. van der Meersch, *Recherches sur la vie et les travaux des imprimeurs belges et Néerlandais* (Gand, 1856). "He was a devoted friend and admirer of Erasmus (cf. Ep. 304 and Lond.v.25, LB. 357); for whom he published nearly sixty volumes" (Allen, *Opus epistolarum* I, 514). The Gilles Agricola collection was reprinted several times, first by Martens and then by Schürer. The *Cato* volume has a very similar publishing history to the Agricola *Opuscula*: two editions by Martens, followed by one by Schürer (Reedijk, 304–6, 372), further suggesting that Erasmus is "ghosting" the publishing history of Agricola. In 1515 P. Quentell published an edition of the *Cato* collection in Cologne, drawing explicitly to an Agricola connection on its title page: . . . *Parenesis Isocratis Rodolpho Agricola interprete. castigatore / Martino dorpio. / Epigramma Gerardi Nouiomagi. in laudem D. Erasmi / Roterodami Theologi eloquentissimi / Attica se claram iactat Demosthene tellus / Facundus colitur Tullius Ausonijs / Agricolam Phrysius celebrat Germanus Erasmum / Mellifluum laudet. cantet. ad astra ferat. / Cuius ab ore fluit melliti gurgitis vnda / Oblectat mentes que Cicerone magis / Nam docet ingenuos animos sermone polito / Et recte sapere. & verba diserta loqui* (Huisman 267; Reedijk, 304–6, 372). This volume also went through a number of editions over the following years. From 1522 Agricola disappears from the title page, and the Isocrates is implicitly attributed to Erasmus (Huisman, 282). This may have contributed to the "slur" of 1523, in which Erasmus was accused of appropriating an Agricola translation of a Euripides play as his own.

45. Allen, *Opus epistolarum* III, 98.

46. *Opus epistolarum III*, 100 (letter 677); *Correspondence* 5, 139.

47. *Correspondence* 5, 139.

48. Allen, *Opus epistolarum* I, 413–14. Gilles was another proof corrector in Thierry Martens's publishing house, whom Erasmus had probably met and befriended around 1504, when he was seeing his *Panegyric* and his *Lucubratiunculae* through the Martens press.

49. Huisman, 4. The configuration is, again: scholarly proof corrector associated with Erasmus's printed works; printing house associated with Erasmus's current print output; editor/printer of (derivative) Agricola volume. I am suggesting that this must lead us to the conclusion that Erasmus is "ghosting" (at the very least by some kind of patronage) Agricola's emergence in print in the volumes edited by Faber, Gilles, and Dorp (see below).

50. "Petrus Egidius Anuerpianus, Martino Dor- / pio Theologo, Amico iucundissimo. S. D. (Anuerpie pridie Idus decembris.)." Erasmus apparently did not meet Thierry Martens until September 1515 (Reedijk, 336–37) in Antwerp, so one assumes his visits to the Martens shop in Louvain postdate 1515. Erasmus's later estrangement from Dorp over Dorp's criticisms of some of his published works need not concern us here.

51. At least, I have not so far been able to track down an incunabulum printing of this oration.

52. Huisman, 124: *De recta latini grae- / cique sermonis pronunciatione Des. Era-*

/ smi Roterodami Dialogus. Eivsdem Dialogus cui titulus, Cice- / ronianus, siue De op-
timo genere di / cendi. / Cum alijs nonnullis quorum ni- / hil non est nouum. / [printer's
mark] / AN. M.D.XXVIII / Cum gratia & priuilegio Caesareo.

53. LB I 1013D–1014A. Hegius and Goclenius (among other Netherlanders)
also figure. So the same roll call that caused such offense for slighting French scholars is extremely careful in its mention of "German" humanists who provide Erasmus with his own immediate pedigree. See Reedijk, 74–83.

54. The more I look at the exchange between Faber and Erasmus, the more
convinced I become that they are the product of collaboration and not simply of
Erasmus's responding to Faber's published letter. There is a long poem by Cornelius Gerard (Cornelius Aurelius) which survives in manuscript at Deventer, composed between 1494 and 1497 and dedicated to Jacobus Faber (then a teacher at the
Deventer school). In the preface Gerard writes that "Iam enim prime decadis libris
absolutis mihi prae animi pusillanimitate in tanto opere pene labenti piae exhorta-
tionis manum porrexit quidam canonicus regularis, Herasmus nomine, etate flori-
dus, religione compositus et omnium facile nostri evi tam prosa quam metro
praestantissimus," as further evidence of a continuing Faber-Erasmus connection
(A. Hyma, The Youth of Erasmus [Ann Arbor, 1930], 207; see the whole chapter
"Poems and orations" [205–19]). If I am right about the neo-Latin poetry connection in the 1489–90 letter to Cornelius Gerard (see below), that would also support the link (and see Reedijk, ch. 3, passim).

55. The letter, indeed, including the adage, is in Alardus's Lucubrationes,
205–11. Alardus's commentary (212) quotes the Greek from Erasmus's Adages.
Hegius had, in fact, been Agricola's pupil only briefly, around 1474, to learn Greek.

56. Allen, Opus epistolarum I, 580–83.

57. R. A. B. Mynors and D. F. S. Thompson, trs., The Correspondence of Erasmus letters 1 to 141, 1484 to 1500 (Toronto, 1974). "Miror autem maiorem in modum
cum hunc solum dixeris qui 'veterum vestigia seruet.' Nam, vt te praeteream, innu-
meros videre mihi videor nostra hac tempestate literatissimos qui ad veterum elo-
quentiam non parum accedunt. Ecce occurrit imprimis Alexandri mei praeceptoris
quondam praeceptor, Rodolphus Agricola, vir cum omnium liberalium artium
egregie eruditus, tum oratoriae atque poeticae peritissimus. Denique et Graecam
linguam non minus quam Latinam calluit. Accedit huic Alexander ipse, tanti ma-
gistri non degener discipulus; qui tanta elegantia veterum exprimit dicendi stylum,
vt si desit carmini titulus, in autore facile erraueris: sed ne hic quidem Graecarum
literarum omnino ignarus est" (Allen, Opus epistolarum I, 105–6 [letter 23]).

58. On the connecting thread of neo-Latin poetry writing among northern
humanists see Reedijk, ch. 3. In another letter to Gerard written around 1489, Erasmus indicates that he is enclosing some of his own poems but that he has sent
others to his old teacher Hegius for his approval: "Porro aliud quod ad te darem,
ad manum habui nihil; quidquid enim reliquum erat, partim ad Alexandrum
Hegium, ludi litterarii magistrum, quondam praeceptorem meum, et Bartholo-
maeum Coloniensem traductum est" (Allen, Opus epistolarum I [letter 28], cit. Reedijk, 48). My surmise is supported by the neat fact that the only clear piece of
evidence of direct influence of Agricola on Erasmus's own literary production is
poetic: in the final ten lines of Erasmus's poem in praise of St. Anne (1489),
"Rhythmus iambicus in laudem Annae, auiae Iesu Christi" (Reedijk, poem 22, op.

cit., 201–5), Reedijk suggests there is direct influence of Agricola's "Anna mater" (44–45). For evidence that Erasmus knew the Agricola "Anna mater," see the 1501 letter to Anna van Borssele (Allen, *Opus epistolarum* I, 342 [letter 145]).

59. "Agricola's letter of 1. Nov. ‹1482›, probably as printed in Agricola's translation of Plato's *Axiochus,* Louvain, John of Westphalia, c. 1483 (Campbell, 1420, Copinger, 4768)." Allen *Opus epistolarum* I, 581.

60. In just the same way, Jacobus Faber's account of the intimacy between Agricola and Hegius turns out to be patched together (Bolgar's humanistic "bricolage") out of textual fragments pillaged from the letters of the two men themselves. I have traced enough of these to be confident that every phrase in Faber's affecting account can be found somewhere in their surviving correspondence. Compare, e.g., Faber: "Quanti autem is ipse nostrum fecerit, hinc profecto clarum; siquidem nostrum sibi persuasit pro eius summo studiorum amore proque eius candore animi (qualem sibi exoptabat) studiorum fuisse acerrimum et exactorem et stimulum et socium, quocum communicaret gratissimum fuit quicquid cogitando inuenerat, quicquid scribendo effecerat, quicquid legendo didicerat, quicquid vel laude vel acriori dignum iudicio annotauerat; que in eius aures ipse, vt itidem in suas ille, deposuit. Semper vel ingerebat aliquid vel contabatur vel dubitabat vel disceptabat, nunc negligentiam liberiori reprehensione castigabat, nunc conatum benigniori prouehebat laude, verum et dicere et audire qui et sciuit et voluit. Itaque quocum etatem vna degere hoc nostro maluerit habuit neminem; id quod per res vtriusque non licuisse tulit egerrime;" and Agricola to Hegius (1480) (Alardus, *Lucubrationes,* 187–88): "deest enim acerrimus mihi studioru[m] stimulus, exactor eoru[m] & socius, quo cu[m] co[m]munice[m], in cuius aures ego, ut itide[m] in meas ille deponat q[ui]quid cogita[n]do inuenerit, scribe[n]do effecerit, lege[n]do didicerit, & uel laude dignu[m], uel acriori iudicio annotarit, quiq[ue] semp[er] ingerat aliquid, perco[n]tetur, dubitet, disceptet, modo neglige[n]tiu[m] liberiori reprehe[n]sio[n]e co[n]stringet, modo conatu[m] benigniori prouehat laude, utq[ue] semel syncere omne[m] inter studia beneuole[n]tiae fructu[m] co[m]plectar, q[ui] dicere ueru[m], quiq[ue] audire sciat et uelit, eu[m] quu[m] te mihi esse persuadea[m]. pro summo tuo studioru[m] amore, proq[ue] candore animi tui, nihil est omniu[m] quod malim, q[uam] posse unä nos aetate[m] degere" [echoed passages underlined].

61. The passage in the *Compendium vitae* was "Rodolphus Agricola primus omnium aurulam quandam melioris literaturae nobis inuexit ex Italia; quem mihi puero ferme duodecim annos nato ‹Dauentriae› videre contigit, nec aliud contigit" (Allen, *Opus epistolarum* I, 2). For the Melanchthon "Vita Agricolae," see C. G. Bretschneider, ed., *Melanthonis opera quae supersunt omnia, Corpus reformatorum* XI (Halle-Brunswick, 1843), cols. 438–46, where Melanchthon, unlike Erasmus, is quite unselfconscious about the derivative nature of his biographical material: "Nos pauca collegimus, sumpta partim ex ipsius scriptis, partim ab iis qui meminerunt sermones senum, quibus in Academia Heydelbergensi cum Rodolpho familiaritas fuit" (439). For the "Oratio de Erasmi," see *Melanthonis opera . . . omnia* XII (Halle-Brunswick, 1844), cols. 264–71. He attributes the anecdote to Erasmus himself: "Literas Latinas et Graecas Dauentriae didicit in Schola Alexandri Hegii, qui familiaris fuit Rodolpho Agricolae. Ac solitus est ipse Erasmus narrare praesagium Rodolphi Agricolae de adolescentis studio. Forte ostenderat Hegius hospiti

Rodolphi in scholam ingresso, adolescentum scripta. Cumque tyrocinium illud probaret, et gratularetur studiis, praetulit tamen Erasmiacum scriptum caeteris, propter inventionis acumen, orationis puritatem, et figuras, apte ceu flosculos interspersos. Eoque scripto adeo delectatus est, ut ex lineamentis quoque, de indole coniecturam sumere cuperet. Iubet igitur vocari Erasmum, quem cum pauca sciscitatus esset, contemplans figuram capitis, et charopos oculos, hortatur ad discendum, inquiens: Tu eris olim magnus" (266). Melanchthon has a prefatory letter in Alardus, ed., Agricola, *Lucubrationes*.

62. Hyma, 48.

63. Allen, *Opus epistolarum* I, 581. The evidence for the 1484 visit is contained in a letter to Antonius Liberus, printed in Alardus, *Lucubrationes*, 176–77. The letter starts out: "Annam matrem imprimendam dedi." It is therefore interesting to juxtapose Allen's hopeful hypothesis of a meeting between Agricola and Erasmus on this occasion with the following (based presumably on the preface to the *Anna mater* as published in 1484 by Richard Praffaert): "On 7 April 1484 Richard Paffraet and his wife Stine were honoured by a visit to their home by the great man Agricola. In his luggage the humanist had a panegyric to St. Anne, the mother of the Virgin Mary. Paffraet hastened to his workshop and returned with Agricola's *Anna Mater* in ten pages of print. Agricola, in a hurry to continue his journey, had to overlook the printing errors" (H. D. L. Vervleit, *Post-Incunabula and Their Publishers in the Low Countries: A Selection Based on Wouter Nijhoff's L'art typographique Published in Commemoration of the 125th Anniversary of Martinus Nijhoff on January 1, 1978* (The Hague, 1978), 118. This does not suggest that any such meeting with a young pupil of Hegius's was leisurely. I am inclined to follow a suggestive remark in Reedijk and think that Erasmus "saw" Agricola on some such occasion, but that Agricola never, as it were, met him. It is, however, possible that Hegius did show Agricola an early Erasmus poem, for instance, the "carmen bucolicum" (Reedijk, 131–39).

64. "Apud Dauentriam primum posuit in literis tyrocinium, vtriusque linguae rudimentis imbibitis sub Alexandro Hegio Vuestphalo, qui cum Rudolpho Agricola recens ex Italia reuerso amicitiam contraxerat et ab eodem Graece docebatur; nam huius literaturae peritiam ille primus in Germaniam importauit" (Beatus Rhenanus to Hermann of Wied, Allen, *Opus epistolarum* I, 53 [letter III]). For a continuation of this tradition among scholars of Dutch humanism see E. H. Waterbolk, "Rodolphus Agricola, Desiderius Erasmus en Viglius van Aytta. Een Leuvens triumviraat," in J. Coppens, ed., *Scrinium Erasmianum*, 2 vols. (Leiden, 1969), I, 129–50.

65. There are a number of references in the secondary literature to copies of the *De inventione dialectica* circulating in manuscript, or to individuals possessing copies of the manuscript (e.g., Allen, "Letters of Agricola," 304), but I can find no evidence to support this, or a single reference to anyone's reading the *De inventione dialectica* before it appears in print. We do know that Agricola's personal friends, the von Pleningen brothers, owned a complete codex (transcribed by themselves), but, as far as we know, they did nothing at all with it. On the important relationship between Agricola and Dietrich von Pleningen (c. 1453–1520), for whom the *De inventione dialectica* was written and to whom it was dedicated, see F. G. Adelmann, "Dr. Dietrich von Plieningen zu Schaubeck," *Ludwigsburger Geschichtsblät-*

ter 28 (1976), 9–139. Adelmann writes (personal communication, 1977): "In the Cod. poet. et phil. 4036 Dietrich and his brother state clearly that the contents are collected to be published later on."

66. I should emphasize how difficult it is, however, to excavate problems out of Erasmus's letters, in particular, because of the care Erasmus himself took in cosmetically tidying up exchanges for publication (as I am stressing throughout this story, Erasmus's self-conscious command of print communication is an important feature of the narrative). See, for instance, the letter to Budé of October 1516, published in the *Epistolae elegantes,* edited by Gilles and published by Martens in 1517 (Allen, *Opus epistolarum* II, 362–70 [letter 480]), where Erasmus writes: "After [the *De copia*] was published I discovered a certain amount in Rudolphus Agricola." I take this to be an "instruction to the reader" (of both Erasmus and Agricola), rather than a fact (it is indeed the link Erasmus's loyal "castigatores" make in their scholia to the Agricola). See the suggestive article by L.-E. Halkin, "Erasme éditeur de sa correspondance: le cas de *l'Auctarium,*" *Bibliothèque d'Humanisme et Renaissance* 40 (1978), 239–47.

67. On Alardus see above all A. J. Kölker, *Alardus Aemstelredamus en Cornelius Crocus: Twee Amsterdamse Priester-Humanisten, Hun leven, werken en theologische opvattingen* (Nijmegen-Utrecht, 1963). See also B. de Graaf, *Alardus Amstelredeamus (1491–1544) His Life and Works with a Bibliography* (Amsterdam, 1958); and entry in P. G. Bietenholz and T. B. Deutscher, *Contemporaries of Erasmus,* 3 vols. (Toronto, 1985–87), I, 15–17. Much as in the case of Faber, almost everything we know about Alardus is derived from his relationship either with publishing Agricola's works or with Erasmus, or both. Alardus's own prefaces and title pages regularly introduce both. See, e.g., de Graaf, bib. 22 (page 52): *D. Erasmi / Roterodami Bvcolicon, Le / ctu digniss. cum scholijs Alardi Aemstelre- / dami, cuius studio nunc primum & re / pertum & aeditum est. / Locus communis de uitando pernitioso aspectu, eo- / dem pertinens. / Sacerdotum coelibatus. / Mulier iuxta omneis Inuentionis Dialectic(a)e locos ex- / plicata per Alardum Aemstelredamum* (Cologne, 1539).

68. Kölker, 21: "Toch uit andere gegevens weten we zeker, dat Alardus reeds in 1514 te Leuvan was. We hebben nl. een hele serie werken, uitgegeven bij Theodoor Martens te Leuven, die door Alardus voorzien zijn van een inleidend gedichtje. Het eerste dateert van November 1514. Heruit zouden we mogen opmaken, dat Alardus zeker van af die tijd bij deze uitgever, een van de eerste belgische drukkers, minstens af en toe heeft gewerkt, mogelijk als corrector." Fol. 15ᵛ of Erasmus's *De constructione octo partium orationis libellus* (Martens, Louvain, November 1514) has: "Alardi Amstelredami in Erasmianam syntaxin ad puerum Dimetrum" (Kölker, 21).

69. See Allen, *Opus epistolarum* II, 1 (letter 298), dated 1 August 1514, Louvain, in which he indicates renewed contact with Dorp—also a corrector at Martens (lines 42–43).

70. De Graaf, *Alardus,* 22. In 1518 Alardus contributed a long Latin poem to Erasmus's *Ratio seu methodus,* celebrating Erasmus's *ordo ac ratio* (Kölker, 22, 34–35).

71. All the sources for Agricola studies that I cited in note 9 accept Alardus's version of the story entirely at face value.

72. Allen, "Letters of Agricola," says the letter "was presumably in some

book edited by Faber; but I have not been able to trace it" (304). I mention this only because this is the only case in this entire piece of work where, when I had painstakingly reconstructed the provenance and location of a crucial piece of evidence, I did not find that Allen had correctly identified it.

73. "Quod si quis latius ista et per omnes locos dialecticos fuderit, quatenus cuiusque natura capax eorum est, inge[n]s utiq[ue] copia & ad dicendum, & ad inueniendum se praebebit. quod quomodo faciendum sit, maius est, quäm ut epistola id capiat, & copiose est ä me ea de re in tribus libris eis, quos de inuentio[n]e dialectica scripsi disputatum" (Alardus, *Lucubrationes* [Cologne, 1539], 199).

74. Alardus's lurid account of the consequences for himself of this announcement are contained in a textual note to this very passage in the "De formando studio" (Alardus, *Lucubrationes* [Cologne, 1539], 203). Alardus says this copy had belonged to Hegius (it seems eminently plausible that Faber, editing Hegius's works, had found the lost work there). See Alardus, *De inventione dialectica*, 11–12.

75. It also suggests that he had insufficient understanding of the material it contained. Without going too far into technicalities at this point: it might appear that a work advertised as containing three books "de inventione dialectica" required a matching "twin" in the form of three books "de iudicio."

76. Alardus claims that it was the reference to six books that drew him to Deventer, implying that this was not the only copy of the work he had access to, but I am inclined to doubt this and to think that this was the first surfacing of any trace of the lost work.

77. Huisman, 11. *Rodolphi Agricole Phrisij Dialectica / Dorpius Studiosis / vt rectis studiis co[n]sulatur studiosi, excusa sunt vobis haec Agricola [sic] dia / lectica: q[ui]bus nihil ce[n]seo vtilius futuru[m] iis: q[ui] vera[m] secta[n]tur arte[m] diserte eloquenterq[ue] dice[n] / di: q[ui]q[ue] no[n] verbis t[a]m[en] inanibus: sed vberi reru[m] copia studeant summa cu[m] admiratione p[er] / suadere: atq[ue] de re qualibet ex p(ro)babilibus apposite: dece[n]terq[ue] ratiocinari: quod noster / ille munus esse dialecticu[m] testatur: hic itaq[ue] garrula sophistar(um) delirame[n]ti ne expectetis: / veru[m] ea expectate: quae a multis- sci[enti]arum limites co[n]funde[n]tibus: rhetoric[a]e tributa: p(ro)pria / t[ame]n sunt dialectic[a]e: quaeq[ue] in Aristotelis Ciceronisq[ue] libris desidera[n]tur: q[ui]bus certe hic li / ber nihilo est inferior: siue elegantiam filumq[ue] dictionis spectemus: siue doctrine prae- / ceptorumq[ue] traditionum.* Dorp had already been the addressee of the prefatory letter to Gilles's 1511 volume of Agricola *Opuscula*.

78. Alardus (and subsequent re-tellers of the story like Allen) embellishes his account with tales of dangerous journeys, failed rendezvous, Faber's deception and reluctance to show him the manuscript, and subsequent headaches trying to decipher and transcribe the text. See Allen, "Letters of Rudolph Agricola," 304–5.

79. For evidence of the unsatisfactory state of this manuscript see Matthaeus Phrissemius's graphic description in his commentary on *De inventione dialectica* II, 16 (Cologne, 1528 ed., 282–83); also Alardus, *Lucubrationes,* sig. *4ʳ⁻ᵛ. On the handwriting see Adelmann, "Dietrich von Plieningen." Adelmann writes (personal communication, 1977): "When Alardus Amstelredamus finally published his Cologne edition in 1539 as 'ad autographi fidem,' according to Alardus himself rumours were running around in Cologne that he did not possess Agricola's own signed

manuscript. Since Dietrich copied it in 1479 because Agricola's manuscript was *il-legible,* I wonder if Alardus really had Agricola's own manuscript." See Allen, "Letters of Agricola," 312, Ep. 18 ‹1479›, to Adolphus Occo: "The *Dialectica* is just finished and is being copied by Theodoric of Plenningen."

80. It is striking how many works from the Martens press around this date are corrected and/or prefaced by Dorp. See van Iseghem, *Biographie de Thierry Martens.*

81. On Dorp see Allen, *Opus epistolarum* II, 11. On his technical competence as a logician see, e.g., R. Guerlac's treatment of the More-Dorp correspondence in her edition of Juan Luis Vives's *In Pseudodialecticos* (Leiden, 1979).

82. Huisman, item 16. Matthaeus Phrissemius's corrected version of the text alone (based on the 1515 printed version, which was full of typographical errors, curious choices of punctuation, and obvious errors of transcription) appeared in Cologne in 1520 (Huisman, item 12) and his commented edition in 1523 (Huisman, item 14). The supposedly further revised text is substituted in Phrissemius's commented edition in 1528, but this is not signaled on the title page until 1535. Huisman, item 27: *Rodolphi / Agricolae Phrisii de inven- / tione dialectica libri tres, cu[m] scholijs Iohan / nis Matthaei Phrissemij: & marginalibus / annotationibus nunc auctis passim ac reco / gnitis, sublatis etiam multis erroribus, qui / cum Rodolpho ipso, tum etiam in scho- / lijs hactenus animaduersi non fuere* (Cologne, 1535). In 1529 (a year after the better text of the *De inventione dialectica* had been retrieved by Alardus and apparently worked through for publication by Alardus and Phrissemius together), Phrissemius offered to help get it published (Allen, "Letters of Agricola" and Alardus, *Lucubrationes,* sig. + 2ᵛ).

83. On the history of the retrieval see Allen, "Letters of Agricola"; Jardine, "Distinctive Discipline."

84. "Pompeius . . . quicquid habuit Rodolphi Agricolae ab auunculo suo Adolpho Occone Sigismundi Archiducis Austriae medico celebratissimo, non tam legitimo Rodolphi Agric[olae] haerede, qua[m] assiduo eiusde[m] studii collega (neq[ue] enim est sanctius sanguinis uinculo co[n]iungo qu[am] studiis sacris-q[ue] iisde[m] initiari) relictu[m]" (Alardus, *Lucubrationes,* sig. +1ᵛ), also Pro-tucius's elegy to Agricola, sig. *3ʳ.

85. We saw in the case of the similarly vivid and compelling account of the pursuit of Faber's copy that Alardus's version of events is at the very least highly colored.

86. On Alardus's extended publishing relationship with Pompeius Occo, of which the publication of the Agricola *Opera* forms only a part, see Kölker, *Alardus,* and F. J. Dubiez, *Op de Grens van Humanisme en Hervorming: de Betekenis van de Boekdrukkunst te Amsterdam in een Bewogen Tijd 1506–1578* ('s-Gravenhage, 1962).

87. Allen, "Letters of Rudolph Agricola," 308–9. In the end the *Opera* came out after Erasmus's death.

88. Let alone "christian humanism," which will surely now have to enter the story. I note here that while many of Erasmus's works went on to the index, Agri-cola's *De inventione dialectica* (in spite of its strenuously Erasmian scholia) not only did not, but was specified as an acceptable pedagogic text in dialectic, at least in Louvain and Paris (whose index lists I have looked at).

89. "Gerardus [pater] Romam se contulit. Illic scribendo, nam tum nondum erat ars typographorum, rem affatim parauit. Erat autem manu felicissima. Et vixit iuueniliter. Mox applicauit animum ad honesta studia. Graece et Latine pulchre calluit. Quin et in iuris peritia non vulgariter profecerat. Nam Roma tunc doctis viris mire floruit. Audiuit Guarinum. Omnes auctores sua manu descripserat" (*Compendium vitae Erasmi*, Allen, *Opus epistolarum* I, 47–48). On the authenticity of this biographical sketch see Allen, *Opus epistolarum* I, appendix I, 575–78.

90. "Praeerat illic ludo literario tum Alexander Hegius Vestphalus, homo bonarum literarum minime expers et Graecarum nonnihil peritus, Rudolpho Agricola communicante; cuius amicitia familiariter vtebatur nuper ex Italia reuersi, vbi Guarinum Veronensem Ferrariae profitentem et alios aliquot eruditione celebres audiuerat. Ingenium Erasmi mox eluxit, quum statim quae docebatur perciperet et fideliter retineret, aequales suos omnes superans" (Beatus Rhenanus to Charles V, prefatory letter to *Erasmi omnia opera* [1540]; Allen, *Opus epistolarum* I, 57).

91. "Deinde Daventriam deductus, Alexandrum Hegium, Rodolphi Agricolae, et Guarini Veronensis Discipulum, Virum sanctum, facundum aeque ac eruditum, gloriae humanae contemptorem audiuimus, nullo coaetaneorum, aut soldalium [sic] inferior in percipiendis aut retinendis praelectis. . . . Haec fuerunt Viri optimi, infantiae nostrae institutiones, his ficta est Praeceptoribus, huiusmodi Puellus sum imbutus rationibus" ("Pages 'Autobiographiques' de Philopseudes, 139–152" [LB. VIII.636F-640E.], in M. Mann Phillips, "Une vie d'Erasme," *Bibliothèque d'Humanisme et Renaissance* 34 (1972), 229–37, esp. 233).

92. Talon/Ramus, 1569. "Hanc differentiam Rodolphus Agricola docuit 1. lib. de Inventione, quam P. Ramus sequutus est, sic ut aemulatus in hac arte in primis industriam illius viri, quem in studio logico, post antiquam illam Socraticorum Logicorum scholam (in qua non minus usus artis, quam scientia tractabatur) omnibus postea natis Logicis anteponere solitus est, dicereque palam ab uno Agricola verum germanae Logicae studium in Germania primum, tum per ejus sectatores et aemulos, toto terrarum orbe excitatum esse." Petrus Ramus, *Dialectica A. Talaei praelectionibus illustrata* (Basel, 1569), 95; cit. N. Bruyère, *Méthode et Dialectique dans l'Oeuvre de La Ramée* (Paris, 1984), 305–306. As Bruyère points out, this edition of Talon's commentary on Ramus's *Dialectica*, revised well after Talon's death by Ramus himself during his stay at Basel, undoubtedly reproduces Ramus's own views on his works and their intellectual origins. See also J. W. Ong, *Ramus and Talon Inventory* (Cambridge, Mass., 1958), 190–91.

93. See J. D. Tracy, "Erasmus Becomes a German," *Renaissance Quarterly* 21 (1968), 281–88; C. Reedijk, "What Is Typically Dutch in Erasmus," *Delta* (1969), 73–82 [not seen].

94. The figure of humane learning "crossing the Alps" is a humanist trope. It is worth noting that one of Beatus Rhenanus's early editing tasks had been to see through the Froben press Battista Guarino's *De modo et ordine docendi ac discendi* (1514)—this work is the printed source for all *Guariniana* (see D'Amico, *Beatus Rhenanus*, 62).

95. The vagueness has a point to it. Hyma cites the following assessments of Erasmus's birth, which assume that Erasmus's father was in holy orders at the time of his birth: "Et deinde, licet defectum natalum patiatur, ex illicito et, ut timet,

incesto damnatoque coitu genitus" (Pope Leo X); "Nunc populares tui, aliquot etiam vicini, viri boni, nobilis, te aiunt ex incesto natus concubitu, sordibus parentibus, altero sacrificulo, altera prostituta" (J. C. Scaliger, *Epistola* 15) (Hyma, op. cit., 53, 57). I do not think it matters for my argument whether the *Compendium vitae Erasmi* is by Erasmus himself or compiled out of his works and letters—that is, it does not matter for the "life" who transfers the Italian and Guarinian discipleship from Agricola to Gerardus.

96. It is worth pointing out here that Rudolph Agricola was also the illegitimate son of a priest: his father was appointed abbot of the Benedictine House at Selwert on the very day he was born. See P. G. Bietenholz and T. B. Deutscher, *Contemporaries of Erasmus*, 3 vols. (Toronto, 1985–87), 1, 15.

97. "Rudolph Agricola's Life of Petrarch," in Eugene F. Rice, Jr., ed., *Theodor E. Mommsen: Medieval and Renaissance Studies* (Ithaca, 1959), 236–61, esp. 249.

98. "Ac primis annis iuris civilis auditor fuit magisque id agebat, ut suorum obsequeretur voluntati quam quod eo delectaretur studio. Fuit namque in homine animus excelsior atque generosior quam ut ad levia illa exiguaque rerum momenta, quibus magna ex parte, ut ipsius verbis utar, ius civile constat, abjici posset neque passus est se ad ipsum alligari, precipue cum putaret vix constanti fide ac integritate a quoquam posse tractari. Relicto itaque iuris studio ad maiora eluctans, litteris pollicioribus et artibus, quas humanitatis vocant . . . animum applicuit" (ibid).

99. "Non potest dici quam sit insignis artifex Aphthonius Sophista, ut qui lectorem alliciat, inescetq[ue] commoda breuitate. luce. ordine, aliisq[ue] id genus epitomis: quiq[ue] non minore diligentia, quam fide discentis agit negotium, non id statim captans, ut ipse doctus appareat, sed ut lectorem doctum reddat. In hisce progymnasmatis, quam scito compe[n]dio, quam miro ordine, qua simplicitate rhetorices summam co[m]plexus est, ceu simulacro quodam nobis deliniato?" (*Lucubrationes,* sig. A2ʳ) [echoed phrases underlined, see next note].

100. Surely the passage just quoted should also have "illecebrae" in place of "epitomae"?

101. ". . . quos allici inescariq́[ue] potius oportuit commoda breuitate, luce, ordine, alijsq́[ue] id genus illecebris. At unus omnium Agricola uir ubique sui similis, in quauis materia insignis artifex non minori iudicio quäm fide discentis agit negotium, non id statim captans, ut ipse doctus appareat, sed ut lectorem doctum reddat" (Alardus, *De inventione dialectica,* sig. a3ʳ) [echoed phrases underlined].

102. In a stimulating article, A. Hayum suggests that Erasmus recognized that there was a particular art to using the comparatively new medium of print as a means of communication and that his admiration for Dürer (as expressed in the *De pronuntiatione*) is for his command of the equivalent "mass" communication form of engraving (A. Hayum, "Dürer's Portrait of Erasmus and the ars typographorum," *Renaissance Quarterly* 38 [1985], 650–87) ("Durerus, quanquam et alias admirandus in monochromatis, hoc est nigris lineis, quid non exprimit?").

103. "Rodolpho Agricolo et Alexandro Hegio, quibus ego sane minimum debebam, nonne plenam laudem tribuo?" (*Spongia adversus aspergines Hutteni* [Basel, 1523], ed. C. Augustijn, *Opera omnia Desiderii Erasmi Roterodami* 9.1 [Amsterdam and Oxford, 1982], 196). See C. Reedijk, *The Poems of Desiderius Erasmus* (Leiden,

1956), 42. As Reedijk points out, this recantation is confirmed by the phrase "nec aliud contigit" in Erasmus's *Compendium vitae*, where he states that Agricola visited his school: ". . . quem mihi puero ferme duodecim annos nato ‹Daventriae› videre contigit, nec aliud contigit" (Allen, *Opus epistolarum* I, 2).

104. P. S. Allen, *Opus Epistolarum Des. Erasmi Roterodami* I, 384−88 (letter 174).

105. *The Correspondence of Erasmus Letters 142 to 297, 1501 to 1514*, tr. R. A. B. Mynors and D. F. S. Thomson, *Collected Works of Erasmus* 4 (Toronto, 1977), 65−69 (letter 174).

106. 1508−23. Altered in 1526 edition to: "There were lying hidden in some people's possession his treatises on dialectic, and they have recently appeared, but in a mutilated state."

107. LB II 166A−167D; Margaret Mann Phillips, tr., *Adages* I.i.1−I.v.100, *Collected Works of Erasmus* 31 (Toronto, 1982), 348−51.

108. H. D. L. Vervleit, *Post-Incunabula and Their Publishers in the Low Countries: A Selection Based on Wouter Nijhoff's L'art typographique Published in Commemoration of the 125th Anniversary of Martinus Nijhoff on January 1, 1978* (The Hague, 1978), 118. Presumably based on a prefatory letter, which I have yet to see.

109. The problem in straightening out the publishing history of Agricola's works seems, indeed, to stem almost entirely from the complete separation of bibliographies of incunabula printing (pre-1500) from bibliographies of post-1500 printing. Agricola's works crucially straddle the 1500 dividing line in a bibliographically inconvenient way.

110. It is worth noting that Hain items 15921 and 15922 are further editions of this work by de Breda and Paffraet, respectively (who frequently exchanged sheets, publishing the same works in the same or consecutive years). 15921 (undated) runs: "Vita divi Antonii. F.Ia: Vita divi Antonii ad sanctissimum Eugenium papam quartum: per Mapheum Vegium laudensem. Incipit una cum dialogo quodam de nativitate Christi a magistro Sandero Hegio Schole Daventriensis olim rectore composito et edito . . . Impressum Daventriae per me Iacobum de Breda." The 15922 entry runs: "Vita divi Antonii. F.Ia. tit: Vita diui Antonij ad Sanctissimum dnm Eugeni\\um papa[m] quartu[m]. p[er] Mapheu[m] vegium laudensem . . . Impressum Dauentriae. In platea episcopi Anno d[omin]i. Mcccc.yc. . . . 11ff. (Rich. Paffroed.)" It seems to me entirely likely that both these editions contain the Agricola "Anna mater" as well as the Hegius dialogue as part of the customary padding with what Paffraet and de Breda had at hand.

111. Allen, "Letters of Rudolph Agricola," 310 (letters 3 and 4).

112. *Incunabula in Dutch Libraries* 375, items 2514, 2515.

113. *The Correspondence of Erasmus Letters 594 to 841, 1517 to 1518, Collected Works of Erasmus* 5 (Toronto, 1979), 137.

114. Iseghem, item 62 (231): "C'est la traduction faite par Agricola de trois opuscules grecs, à savoir: *Isocrates de Regnô; Luciani libellus de non credendis delationibus; Luciani micyllus sive gallus.*"

Inga Clendinnen

3. Cortés, Signs, and the Conquest of Mexico

Models of the Conquest

The conquest of Mexico [1] mattered to the men of the sixteenth century because it provided Spaniards and other Europeans with their first great paradigm for European encounters with an organized native state and, in the person and strategy of Cortés, a model not only for other and lesser conquistadores, but, through the swift publication in several European languages of his dispatches to his king, for a much wider audience. It matters to us because it poses a painful question: how was it that a motley bunch of Spanish adventurers, never numbering more than four hundred or so, were able to defeat an Amerindian military power on its home ground within two years, and what was it about Spaniards, or about Indians, that made so awesomely implausible a victory possible? The question has not lost its potency through time and, as the consequences of the victory continue to unfold, has gained in poignancy. I will not seek to answer that question directly but rather to pursue the implications of one kind of answer often given to it.

The Mexican conquest was reanimated for the English-speaking world through the marvelously dramatic history written by W. H. Prescott in the early 1840s, a best-seller in those glorious days when History still taught lessons. The lesson that great history taught was that Europeans will triumph over natives, however formidable the apparent odds, because of cultural superiority, manifesting itself visibly in equipment, but residing much more powerfully in mental and moral qualities. Prescott presents Spanish victory as flowing directly out of the contrast and the relationship between the two leaders: the Mexican ruler Moctezuma, despotic, effete, and rendered fatally indecisive by the "withering taint" of an irrational religion, and his infinitely resourceful adversary, Hernando Cortés. Prescott found in the person of the Spanish commander the model of European man: ruthless, pragmatic, single-minded, and (the unfortunate excesses of

Spanish Catholicism aside) superbly rational in his capacity to decide a course of action and to persist in it.[2]

The general contours of the Prescottian fable are still clearly discernible in the most recent and certainly the most intellectually sophisticated account of the conquest, Tzvetan Todorov's *The Conquest of America,* published in French in 1982, in English translation in 1984. Todorov's Mexicans suffer decisive defects: faced with the European challenge they are other in ways which doom them. Dependent as they are on the rote-learnt wisdom of the past, that "submission of the present to the past,"— together with their cyclical understanding of time, "where the singular event is merely the realization of omens always and already present,"— paralyzes effective response to the unique event of the Spanish invasion. Although "masters in the art of ritual discourse," they are "inadequate in a situation requiring improvisation, and this is precisely the situation of the conquest": "their verbal [oral] education favors paradigm over syntagm, code over context, conformity-to-order over efficacity-of-the-moment, the past over the present" (87). Signs for the Indians necessarily proceed from the world they designate, rather than being a weapon intended to manipulate the other. Their "characteristic interrogation" is not (as among the Spanish conquistadores) "praxeological, 'what's to be done?,'" but epistemological: 'how are we to know?'" (69). Throughout the crisis Moctezuma is incapable of producing "appropriate and effective messages": "intentional messages do not communicate what their authors have hoped" (89); for example, Moctezuma's sending gold "to convince his visitors to leave the country" (87), while damaging unintentional messages fail to be suppressed: "the war cry the Indians invariably utter when they do battle, whose whole purpose is to alarm the enemy, actually reveals their presence and permits the Spaniards to orient themselves more effectively" (89). Meanwhile, the Spaniards are "specialists in human communication" (97): "what Cortés wants from the first is not to capture but to comprehend; it is signs which chiefly interest him, not their referents" (99). Faced with novel challenges he moves freely and effectively, "not only constantly practicing the art of adaptation and improvisation, but also being aware of it and claiming it as the very principle of his conduct" (87).

So for Todorov, Cortés ensured his control over the Mexican empire (in a conquest he sees as "easy") through "his mastery of signs" (87). Note that this is not an idiosyncratic individual talent, but a European cultural capacity grounded in "literacy," where writing is considered "not as a tool, but as an index of the evolution of mental structures": it is that evolution which liberates the manipulative intelligence, strategic flexibility, and semiotic sophistication through which Cortés and his men triumph.[3]

I want to examine some of those claims about the nature of the contrast between European and Indian modes of thinking and action as demonstrated during the conquest encounter. First, for an overview of the action. Analysts and participants alike agree the conquest falls into two phases. The first begins with the Spanish landfall in April of 1519, and Cortés's assumption of independent command in defiance of the governor of Cuba, the patron of the expedition; the Spaniards' march inland, in the company of coastal Indians recently conquered by the Mexica, and marked first by bloody battles and then by alliance with the independent province of Tlaxcala; their entry into the rich city of Cholula, and their unprovoked attack on its people; their welcome into the Mexican imperial city Tenochtitlan, a city of perhaps 200,000 or more inhabitants, built on a lake, and linked to the land by three great causeways; the Spaniards' seizing of the "Great Speaker" Moctezuma, and their uneasy rule through him for six months; the arrival on the coast of another and much larger Spanish force charged with the arrest of Cortés, its defeat and incorporation into Cortés's own force; a native "uprising" in Tenochtitlan, triggered in Cortés's absence by the Spaniards' massacre of unarmed warriors dancing in a temple festival; the expulsion of the Spanish forces, with great losses, in mid-1520, and Moctezuma's death, probably at Spanish hands, immediately before that expulsion. End of the first phase. The second phase is much briefer in the telling, although about the same span in the living, a little over a year. The Spaniards retreated to friendly Tlaxcala to recover health and morale. They then renewed the attack, reducing the lesser lakeside cities, recruiting allies, not all of them voluntary, and placing Tenochtitlan under siege in May of 1521. The city fell to the combined forces of Cortés and an assortment of Indian "allies" in mid-August 1521. End of the second phase.

Prescott and Todorov, like most analysts of the conquest, have concentrated on the first phase, drawn by the promising whiff of exoticism in Moctezuma's responses—allowing the Spaniards into his city, his docility in captivity—and by the sense that final outcomes were somehow immanent in that response, despite Moctezuma's removal from the stage in the midst of a Spanish rout a good year before the fall of the city, and despite the Spaniards' miserable situation in the darkest days before that fall, trapped out on the causeways, bereft of shelter and support, with the unreduced Mexica before and their "allies," potential wolves, behind. This dispiriting consensus as to Spanish invincibility and Indian vulnerability springs from the too eager acceptance of key documents, primarily Spanish but also Indian, as directly and adequately descriptive of actuality, rather than as the mythic constructs they largely are. Both the letters of Hernando Cortés and the main Indian account of the defeat of their city owe as much to the ordering impulse of imagination as to the devoted inscription of events as they occurred.

The messy series of events that began with the landfall (Fig. 3.1) on the eastern coast has been shaped into an unforgettable success story largely out of the gripping narratives of Hernando Cortés and Bernal Díaz, who were part of the action; that superb irresistible forward movement which so captivated Prescott, a selection and sequence imposed by men practiced in the European narrative tradition, and writing, for all their artfully concealed knowledge of outcomes, when outcomes were known. The foot soldier Bernal Díaz, finally completing his "True History" of the conquest in old age, can make our palms sweat with his account of yet another Indian attack, but at eighty-four he knew he was bequeathing his grandchildren a "true and remarkable story" about the triumph of the brave. The commander Hernando Cortés, writing his reports to the Spanish king in the thick of the events, had repudiated the authority of his patron and superior, the governor of Cuba, and so was formally in rebellion against the royal authority. He was therefore desperate to establish his credentials. His letters are splendid fictions, marked by politic elisions, omissions, inventions, and a transparent desire to impress the king with his own indispensability. One of the multiple delights in their reading is to watch the creation of something of a Horatio figure, an exemplary soldier and simple-hearted loyalist unreflectively obedient to his king and the letter of the law: all attributes implicitly denied by the beautiful control and calculation of the literary construction itself.

The elegance of Cortés's literary craft is nicely indicated by his handling of a daunting problem of presentation. In his "Second Letter," written in late October 1520 on the eve of the second thrust against Tenochtitlan, he had somehow to inform the king of the Spaniards' first awareness of the splendor of the great city, the early coups, the period of perilous authority, the inflow of gold, the accumulation of magnificent riches—and the spectacular debacle of the expulsion, with the flounderings in the water, the panic, the loss of gold, horses, artillery, reputation, and altogether too many Spanish lives. Cortés's solution was a most devoted commitment to

Figure 3.1. Collapsing time: the Spaniards are sighted (upper right); disembark (lower left); Doña Marina interprets for Cortés (lower right). Florentine Codex, Book 12, Plate I. Courtesy of Biblioteca Medicea-Laurenziana.

a strict narrative unfolding of events, so the city is wondered at; the dead Moctezuma speaks, frowns; the marketplace throbs and hums; laden canoes glide through the canals; and so on to the dark denouement. And through all continues the construction of his persona as leader: endlessly flexible, yet unthinkingly loyal; endlessly resourceful, yet fastidious in legal niceties; magnificently daring in strategy and performance, yet imbued with a fine caution in calculating costs. It is unsurprising that along the way Cortés should claim "the art of adaptation and improvisation" as "the very principle of his conduct"; and that we, like his critical royal audience, should be impressed by his magisterial mastery of men and events; dominating and duping Moctezuma, neutralizing Spanish disaffection by appeals to duty, law, and faith; managing Indians with kind words, stern justice, and contrived displays of the superiority of Spanish arms and the priority of the Spanish god.

. The notion of fatal Indian passivity is powerfully introduced by Cortés's extended and circumstantial account of his relationship with the captive Moctezuma during the initial six-month stay in the city. Cortés insisted on the voluntarism of Moctezuma's submission, presenting his reception of the Spaniards as an explicit abdication in favor of a legitimate ruler returned. (His seizing and imprisonment, unintelligible given that account of things, is therefore presented as no more than a precaution, prompted by the farsighted Cortés's anxiety that the Great Speaker's perfect docility might be ruptured by some inadvertent Spanish roughness.[4]) Cortés went on to describe his administration of the affairs of what he represented as a thriving colony which had never needed conquering, "seeing to the things which I thought were required in the service of Your Sacred Majesty and subduing and persuading to Your service many provinces and lands, discovering mines and finding out many of the secrets of Moctezuma's lands and of those which bordered on them and those of which he had knowledge. . . . All of which was done with such good will and delight on the part of Moctezuma and all the natives of the aforementioned lands that it seemed as if *ab initio* they had known Your Sacred Majesty to be their king and rightful lord; and with no less good will have they done all that I, in Your Royal name, have commanded them." Then came the fatal Spanish expedition under Narváez, inspired by the malice and envy of the Cuban governor; the tranquil, productive order was disrupted, and all, despite Cortés's heroic endeavors, was lost.[5]

And so to the rest of the story as Cortés chose to tell it. J. H. Elliott and Anthony Pagden have traced the filaments of Cortés's web of fictions back to particular strands of Spanish political culture, and to his particular and acute predicament within it, and have explained the "legitimate inheritors returning" theme by demonstrating its functional necessity in Cortés's legalistic strategy, which pivoted on Moctezuma's voluntary cession of his empire and his authority to Charles of Spain—a splendidly implausible notion, save that so many have believed it.[6]

Bernal Díaz is a rather different case. He is not quite Prescott's "untutored child of nature" dedicated to an I-am-a-camera verisimilitude or the "honest eyewitness" he promises us in his prologue. He recycles what he had been told or gleaned at the time, came to believe in the years between experience and writing, or was teased into "remembering" in reaction to the competing "History" written by Cortés's chaplain, which lay at his elbow as he wrote. Nonetheless, despite the lapse of years, despite the occasional disarming efforts at self-promotion, he is invaluable: one of those rare observers so in love with the extraordinariness of what he sees as to be content to describe it, without too much elaboration or interpretation.[7] But along with that marvelous facticity went a delight in presenting "the natives" as gullible. He makes much of naive Indians' marvelings at the great Spanish dogs, the ferocious horses which chased down Indians on command, the cannon which spoke out of iron mouths, and, above all, of the fact that the native term for the Spaniards, "teule" in the Spanish hearing of it, for the Nahuatl "teotl," meant "god."[8] This identification has been made to bear massive import, as with Todorov, who presents "the paralyzing belief that the Spaniards [were] gods" as crucial: "the Indians' mistake did not last long . . . but just long enough for the battle to be definitively lost and America subject to Europe" (77).

Díaz's kind of running on about the quaint notions of the natives, however therapeutic for nervous incomers, finds its ground in the distortions of radically thinned translation. For example, the word "teotl" does indeed have the meaning of "god." It was also used to convey the notion of "a thing consummate in good or in evil": that is, powerful or extreme in character, or, as we might say, "weird." It is a European preference to claim it as a recognition of divinity. Díaz himself "knew" this: it was, he said, only after Cortés had dared to urge violence against Mexican tax gatherers who had entered the coastal tributary town of Cempoalla that the local lords "said that no human beings would dare to do such things, and that it was the work of Teules, for so they call the idols which they worship, and for this reason from that time forth, they called us Teules, which is as much as to say that we were either gods or demons." But he was not attentive to it, and so "gods" the Spaniards became. His gleeful dwellings on manipulative mystifications pandered then as they do now to a familiar "smart Europeans bamboozle innocent natives" notion, powerfully gratifying in its reduction of the Other to patsy.[9]

It is true that the most elaborate Indian account of the conquest, the twelfth book of Fray Bernardino de Sahagún's Florentine Codex, compiled from the recollections of surviving native informants, introduces a Moctezuma paralyzed first by omens, and then by the conviction that Cortés was the god Quetzalcoatl, Precious-Feather Serpent, returned. (Quetzalcoatl-Topiltzin, ruler of the mythic "Tollan," or Tula, the previous great imperial power in the valley before he withdrew to the east in some shadowy former time, was ambiguously associated with Quetzalcoatl-Ehecatl, the Wind God.) We are given vivid descriptions of Moctezuma's vacillations, tremulous decisions, collapses of will, panic, as he awaits the Spaniards' coming, and then of his supine acquiescence in their depredations, while his lords abandon him in disgust.

That is a very late-dawning story, making its first appearance thirty and more years after the conquest. Its acceptance requires that Sahagún's informants had been privy to Moctezuma's responses to the first news of the Spanish landfalls, as to the activities of the inner court of Tenochtitlan. In actuality very few men in the closed politics of the city would have had access to Moctezuma's person, and fewer still to his thoughts. Sahagún's informants, young and inconsequential men in 1519, would not have been among those few. In that first phase they can report on certain events (the entry of the Spaniards into the city, the massacre of the warrior dancers) which were public knowledge, and to which they were perhaps witness, with some degree of "accuracy," although even their reporting, it is worth remembering, will be framed in accordance with Mexica notions of significance. But the dramatic description of the disintegration of Moctezuma bears the hallmarks of a post-conquest scapegoating of a leader who had indeed admitted the Spaniards to his city in life, and so was made to bear the weight of the unforeseeable consequences in death.[10]

What the informants offer for most of the first phase of the conquest is unabashed mythic history, a telling of what ought to have happened along with a little of what did in a satisfying mix of collapsing time, eliding episodes, and dramatized encounters as they came to be understood in the bitter years after the conquest. With the fine economy of myth, Moctezuma is represented as being made the Spaniards' prisoner at their initial meeting, thenceforth to be their helpless toy, leading them to his treasures, "each holding him, each grasping him," as they looted and pillaged at will.[11] In the Dominican Diego Durán's account, built in part from painted native chronicles unknown to us, in part from conquistador recollections, this process of distillation to essential "truth" is carried even further, with Moctezuma pictured as emerging from his first meeting with Cortés with his feet shackled.[12] It is likely here that Durán made a literal interpretation of a symbolic representation: in retrospective native understanding, Moctezuma was captive to the Spaniards, a shackled icon, from the first moments.

Todorov has found "something emblematic in Moctezuma's repeated refusal to communicate with the intruders," and something pathetic about his incapacity to convey the intended message when he did (for example, the gold sent to persuade the Spaniards to go away). The message exchanges were public events reported in both Spanish and Indian accounts, and so perhaps will bear some analysis. The problem here is too narrow a definition of "communication" as primarily verbal.[13] Moctezuma communicated at least as much by the splendor and status of his emissaries, by their gestures and their gifts, as by the nuances of their most conventionalized speech. None of the nonverbal messages could Cortés read, nor is it clear that his chief Nahuatl interpreter Marina, as a woman and a slave, would or could inform him of the protocols in which they were framed: these were the high and public affairs of men. The first "gifts" he interpreted variously as gestures of submission or as naive attempts at bribery, and this despite the fluency of his own language of gifts, sending as his first prestations to Moctezuma a crimson cap decorated with a St. George medallion and a carved chair along with the usual glass beads, with the request that the Mexica ruler should welcome him into Tenochtitlan sitting on his Spanish chair with his Spanish cap on his head.[14] From what we know of Amerindian cultures, Moctezuma's "gifts" were statements of dominance, superb gestures of wealth and liberality made the more glorious by the arrogant humility of their giving: statements to which the Spaniards lacked both the wit and the means to reply. (To the next flourish of gifts, carried by more than a hundred porters and including the famous "cartwheels" of gold and silver, Cortés's riposte was a cup of Florentine glass and three holland shirts.[15])

As indicated by the "teotl" example, the verbal exchanges for all of the first phase are not much easier to retrieve. We glimpse some moments of communication of raw sense, but not of intended meaning: for example, Cortés's attempt to convey innocent curiosity, straightforwardness, and flattery by his expressed desire "to look upon Moctezuma's face." That ambition, conveyed to a ruler whose mana was such that his face could not be looked upon save by a special few must have seemed marvelously threatening, and could suffice to explain Moctezuma's purported determination that the Spaniards should not come to his city.

While Anthony Pagden has persuasively demonstrated how many of its formulations echoed Spanish and European usages, and most precisely met Cortés's specific political needs, the famous "abdication" speech of Moctezuma as reported by Cortés need not have been a complete fiction. It is possible that Moctezuma used some "my house is your house" formula—such expressions were current in Nahuatl, as they were and are in many tongues—but being told to make yourself at home is not usually interpreted as an invitation to sell the furniture. And despite those reassuring inverted commas of direct reportage, all of those so-fluent speeches passed through a complicated chain of interpreters, with each step a struggle for some approximation of unfamiliar concepts. Such discourse presents in acute form the classic problems of "translation" and of mangled messages. We cannot know at what point the shift from the Indian notion of "he who pays tribute" to the Spanish one of "vassal" was made, but we know the shift to be momentous. Throughout all of that first phase verbal communication remained rudimentary. For the six months the Spaniards spent in the city, Cortés was sufficiently starved for information to be grateful for the gleanings of the Spanish lad Orteguilla, page to Moctezuma, who, having picked up some Nahuatl, made what sense he could of the conversations overheard in the course of his duties.

In part our puzzlement over the peaceful entry into Tenochtitlan is self-inflicted, and springs from our knowledge of Cortés's brisk statement of his program in his second letter to his king: to "take him [Moctezuma] alive in chains or make him subject to Your Majesty's Royal Crown." He continued: "With that purpose I set out from the town of Cempoal, which I renamed Sevilla, on the sixteenth of August with fifteen horsemen and three hundred foot soldiers, as well equipped for war as the conditions permitted me to make them."[16] There we have it: warlike intentions clear, native cities renamed as possessions in a new polity, an army on the move. Inured to the duplicitous language of diplomacy, we take Cortés's persistent swearing of friendship and the innocence of his intentions as transparent deceptions. Cortés's own confusion deepens our confidence in our reading, as he aggressively sought to collect what he called "vassals" along the way, with no demur from Moctezuma. For example, the lord "Pánuco" sent gifts and freely offered to supply certain Spaniards in his region whom he took to be members of Cortés's party with food.[17] These were almost certainly not gestures of political subordination but the normal courtesies—the provision of supplies and, if necessary, warmth and shelter—extended to official travelers within the more effectively subdued Mexica territories. Where Cortés made the condition of "vassal" more explicit by requesting not food or carriers but gold, the request was as directly denied.

The Tlaxcalans, with hostiles on their frontiers, fought the Spaniards because they had breached their symbolic wall. No such wall guarded the imperial city of Tenochtitlan, open as it had to be to trade, tribute, and legitimate travelers (Fig. 3.2). Even had Moctezuma somehow divined the

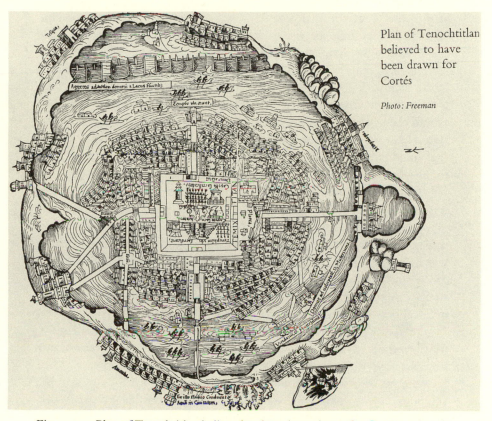

Plan of Tenochtitlan
believed to have
been drawn for
Cortés

Photo: Freeman

Figure 3.2. Plan of Tenochtitlan believed to have been drawn for Cortés; printed with the Latin edition of his "Second Letter" (Nuremberg, 1524). Courtesy of the British Library.

Spaniards' hostile intent, to attack without formal warning was not an option for a ruler of his magnificence. Cortés declared he came as an ambassador, and as an ambassador he appears to have been received. The lodging of the Spaniards in a royal palace is not especially remarkable, visiting rulers and ranking ambassadors being routinely luxuriously housed and feted, in the not unfamiliar determination to impress potentially troublesome visitors while keeping an eye on them.[18]

Nonetheless, there is much that is puzzling in Moctezuma's conduct. The acts of Spanish terror against particular towns, like the killings in the tribute city of Cholula, need have carried no clear message of hostility against the Mexica: in that polity of discrete political units the Cholulans, apart from their quite precise tribute obligations, were autonomous. But the Tlaxcalan involvement in those killings is a different case: they ought to have been punished. Even more disquieting is Moctezuma's admission of the enemy Tlaxcalans into his city. In the Florentine Codex account they enter in battle array and making their war cries, which strains credulity. Durán claims their entry was questioned by Moctezuma, and that Cortés stated he was bringing them in not as soldiers, but carriers. Just possibly that could be accepted, if the Tlaxcalans stayed close to the Spaniards at all times—but only if they were not "in battle array." [19]

One factor clearly distinguished Moctezuma from his own and other lesser lords, as it distinguished the Mexica from the non-Mexica. The Mexica insisted—with some plausibility, given the grandeur of their achievements, exemplified in the grandeur of their city—that Mexica tribal history was implicated in the sacred; that they were a chosen people predestined to dominate, standing in special relationship to the gods; that their own tutelary deity Huitzilopochtli was identified with the sun, and their own political dominance with cosmic necessity.

In face of the visible might and magnificence of Tenochtitlan, no other Central Mexican people could plausibly present a counterclaim, however little they might have been persuaded, however obstinate their own dreams of glory. Nor could those other peoples, whose time was not yet, be as directly threatened by an untoward intrusion. The Maya of Yucatan also held vague notions of a self-exiled culture hero who might one day return. Yet they had no epistemological doubts when faced with Spaniards: they killed or enslaved those unlucky enough to be shipwrecked on their shores, and met more deliberate landfalls briskly, identifying these strangers as equivalent to earlier invaders, fighting them with determination, and only when very thoroughly defeated acquiescing—for the moment—in the Spaniards' political domination.

The Yucatecan cognitive situation was simpler than that of the Mexica: invasion was a familiar story, not a crisis potentially marking the end of a great imperial system. [20] Most of the Indian peoples of the mainland seem to have responded as pragmatically as the Maya, attacking, exploiting, or cooperating with the intruders as the situation allowed. It was the peculiar responsibility, and therefore the vulnerability of the Mexica, or more precisely he among the Mexica who happened to be responsible for such matters at the time of the encounter, to define and diagnose in cosmic terms the significance of the Spaniards: who they were; what their coming meant. For others—those readily aggressive Tlaxcalans, even those lofty

Mexica tax gatherers—the question of identification was not pressing. For Moctezuma, emblem and representative of the Mexica and of the Mexica empire in its external dealings, it was primary. It would have been remarkable if the "departed ruler returned" hypothesis had not been considered, however briefly (we have a similar rumor in general circulation, which would probably at least be entertained in similar circumstances), but there is no clear indication on the evidence when carefully assayed that it long influenced his mind.

Here I think a heroic act of renunciation is required. Historians are the camp followers of the imperialists: as always in this European and native kind of history, part of our problem is the disruption of "normal" practice effected by the breach through which we have entered. For Cortés, the acute deference shown Moctezuma's person established him as the supreme authority and executive of the empire. In fact we know neither the nature nor the extent of the Great Speaker's normal authority within and beyond Tenochtitlan, nor (given the exuberant discrepancies between the Cortés and Díaz accounts) the actual degree of coercion and physical control imposed on him during his captivity. The apparently smooth functioning of the city throughout his imprisonment, during which time he was permitted to receive ambassadors and foreign lords, perhaps suggests that the official titled Cihuacoatl, "Woman Snake," was indeed in charge of internal "administration," if that is not too active a notion for the smooth, routinized system of rotated obligations by which the city seems to have lived. From the fugitive glimpses we get of the attitudes of some of the other valley rulers, and of his own advisers, we can infer something of the complicated politics of the metropolis and the surrounding city-states, but we see too little to decode the character of Moctezuma's authority, much less its particular fluctuations under the stress of foreign intrusion. Nor, against this uncertain ground, can we hope to catch the flickering indicators of possible individual idiosyncrasy. We must resign ourselves to allowing much of his conduct to remain enigmatic. We cannot know how he categorized the newcomers, or what he intended by his apparently determined and certainly unpopular cooperation with his captors: whether to save his empire, his city, his position, or merely his own skin.

Strategies

Of Cortés we know much more, which presents its own problems of categorization and assessment. He was not remarkable as a combat leader:

personally brave, an indispensable quality in one who would lead Spaniards, he lacked the panache of an Alvarado, the solidity and coolness of a Sandoval. He preferred talk to force with Spaniards or Indians, a preference no doubt designed to preserve numbers, but also indicative of a personal style. He knew who to pay in flattery, who in gold, and the men he bought usually stayed bought. He knew how to stage a theatrical event for maximum effect, as in the plays concocted to terrify Moctezuma's envoys—a stallion, plunging uncontrollably as he scented a mare in estrus— a cannon fired to blast a tree. When he did use force he had a flair for doing so theatrically, amplifying the effect; cutting off the hands of fifty or more Tlaxcalan emissaries freely admitted into the Spanish camp, then mutilated as "spies"; the mass killings at Cholula; the shackling of Moctezuma while "rebellious" chiefs were burnt before his palace in Tenochtitlan. He was a man careful to count every Spanish life, yet capable of conceiving heroic strategies—to lay siege to a lake-girt city, the prefabrication of thirteen brigantines on the far side of the mountains, eight thousand carriers to transport the pieces, their reassembly in Texcoco, the digging of a canal and the deepening of the lake for their successful launching. And he was capable not only of the grand design but of the construction and maintenance of the steepling alliances, intimidations, and promised rewards necessary to implement it (Fig. 3.3). In that extraordinary capacity to sustain a complex vision through the constant scanning and assessment of unstable factors, as in his passion and talent for control of self and others, Cortés was incomparable. (The concern for control might explain his inadequacies in combat: in the radically uncontrolled and uncontrollable environment of battle, he had a tendency to lose his head.)

None of this undoubted flair makes Cortés the model of calculation and rationality he is so often taken to be. His situation was paradoxically made easier by his status as rebel. That saved him from the agonizing assessment of different courses of action: once gone from Cuba, in defiance of the governor, he could not turn back, save to certain dishonor and probable death. So we have the gambler's advance, with no secured lines back to the coast, no supplies, no reinforcements, the ships deliberately disabled on the beach to release the sailors for soldiering service and to persuade the fainthearted against retreat, and behind him in Cuba an implacable enemy. The relentless march on Mexico impresses, until one asks just what Cortés intended once he'd got there. We have the drive to the city, the seizing of Moctezuma—and then the agonizing wait by this unlikely Micawber for something to turn up, as the Spaniards, uncertainly toler-

Figure 3.3. The siege in place. Lienzo de Tlaxcala, Plate 42. Courtesy of the Bodleian Library, Oxford.

ated guests, sat in the city, clutching the diminishing resource of Moctezuma's prestige as their only weapon. That something proved to be the Spanish punitive expedition, a couple of providential ships carrying gunpowder and a few reinforcements and so a perilous way out of the impasse. Perhaps Cortés had had in mind a giant confidence trick: a slow process of securing and fortifying posts along the road to Vera Cruz and then, with enough gold amassed, to send to the authorities in Hispaniola (bypassing Velázquez and Cuba) for ships, horses, and arms, which is the strategy he in fact followed after the retreat from Tenochtitlan.[21] It is nonetheless difficult (save in Cortés's magisterial telling of it) to read the performance as rational. As John Elliott has observed: "it is hard to think of a crazier strategy."[22]

His genius lay in his capacity to coax, bully, and bribe his men, dream-led, dream-fed, into making the same gambler's throw; to participate in his own desperate personal destiny. Bernal Díaz recorded one of Cortés's speeches at a singularly low point in the Tlaxcalan campaign. With numbers already dangerously depleted, the remaining men wounded, cold, frightened, the natives ferocious, Cortés is reported as promising his men not wealth, not salvation, but deathless historical fame.[23] Again and again we see Cortés dare to cheat his followers in the distribution of loot and of "good-looking Indian women," but he never discounted the glory of their endeavors. He lured them to acknowledge their own most extreme fantasies; then he persuaded them, by his own enactment of them, that the fantasies were realizable.[24]

A brilliant leader—of Spaniards. How effective was he in encounter with Indians, in this first phase? The acts of terror were possibly useful: after the "spies" episode, the Tlaxcalans sued for peace and alliance.[25] But, as I will argue, routine acts of war in the European style were probably significantly more destructive of Indian confidence in their ability to predict Spanish behavior. His mystification maneuvers were minimally effective, however dear they were to Spanish self-esteem. The Cempoallan chief tricked into doing what he so much wanted to do (seizing Moctezuma's tax gatherers) remained notably more afraid of Moctezuma in his far palace than of the hairy Spaniards at his elbow.[26] Nor was manipulation all on the Spanish side: the chief tricked into defiance of Moctezuma immediately tricked Cortés into leading four hundred Spaniards on a hot and futile march of more than fifteen miles in pursuit of phantom Mexica warriors, in his own pursuit of a private feud, but that is notably less remarked on.[27] There are other indications (of Tlaxcalan involvement in provoking the Cholula massacre, for example) which hint at extensive native manipulations, guile being admired among Indians as it was among Spaniards, and Spanish dependence on Indian informants and translators being total, but they are indications only, given the relative opacity and ignorance of the Spanish sources on what the Indians were up to. Here I am not concerned to demonstrate the natives to have been as great deceivers as the Spaniards, but simply to suggest we have no serious grounds for claiming they were not.

As for his sensitivity to signs: in Cempoalla Cortés destroyed the existing idols, whitewashed the existing shrine, washed the existing attendants and cut their hair, dressed them in white, and taught these hastily renovated priests to offer flowers and candles before an image of the Virgin; an intriguing economy of effort. The pagan attendants might have been clad suitably clerically, in long black robes like soutanes, with some hooded "like Dominicans," but they also had waist-long hair clotted with human blood, and stank of decaying human flesh. Nonetheless, they were "read" as "priests," and therefore fit to be entrusted with the Virgin's shrine.[28] All this was achieved at the sword's point, despite Cempoalla being the town on whose goodwill the little fort of Vera Cruz was most dependent. Cortés was not to be so impolitic again, but his later excursions into the religious zone were marked more by vigor than curiosity as to how the natives might interpret his interventions.[29]

A more consequential opacity lay at the center of his crucial first-phase strategy. In the thick of the Mexica "uprising," Cortés forced Moctezuma out on to the roof of the Spanish quarters to calm his people, despite Moctezuma's insistence that they were his people no longer, having found a new lord. As Cortés heard the cries of anger and saw the shower of stones, he must at last have known that his puppet had broken in his hands. It is unlikely that he realized how much he had to do with the breaking. He had taken Moctezuma to be absolute ruler over an empire and over Tenochtitlan. That conviction rested on his own notions of imperial power, with the Spanish emperor Charles as model, and on the extreme deference offered Moctezuma's person: approached closely only by kinsmen; walking in gold while lords went barefoot and humble. Díaz had noted how at the first formal entry of the Spaniards into the imperial city, "none of these lords thought of looking Moctezuma in the face, but kept their eyes lowered with much reverence, except for those kinsmen, his nephews, who were supporting him," and that when Cortés moved to embrace him, he was prevented by the attendant lords, "for they considered it an indignity."[30] Nonetheless, he was persuaded that Moctezuma was "delighted" with the courtesies he was offered in the Spanish quarters, for "whenever we came before him we all of us, even Cortés, doffed our caps and helmets."[31]

"Even Cortés." Cortés can have had no sense of how inadequate such gestures were to preserve the authority of the Great Speaker. (He reported as no more than a quaint detail of exotic protocol that "certain of [the] chiefs reproved the Spaniards, saying that when they spoke to me they did so openly without hiding their faces, which seemed to them disrespectful and lacking in modesty.") His simple pragmatism at first "worked": Moctezuma could be seized in his own palace by armed Spaniards precisely because such an action was unthinkable. But the authority through which

Cortés sought to rule had begun to bleed away from the initial encounter with Spanish unmannerliness, as they gazed and gabbled at the sacred ruler.[32] It bled faster as they seized his person. Then Cortés, intent on achieving personal psychological domination, had Moctezuma shackled as his chiefs died in the flames of Spanish fires, from which novel treatment, he complacently reported, "he received no small fright."[33] Moctezuma's authority could not survive such casual manhandling. Diego Durán's account of Moctezuma pictured as emerging shackled from his first meeting with Cortés is "objectively" wrong, but from the Indian political perspective right: the Great Speaker in the power of outsiders, casually and brutally handled, was the Great Speaker no longer. His replacement probably came when Cortés (now in his conciliatory mode) released Moctezuma's formidable brother Cuitlahuac, lord of Ixtapalapa, to assuage Indian anger: immediately the attack took on a new coherence. As Moctezuma stepped out on to the roof, he knew he could effect nothing; that his desacralization had been accomplished, first and unwittingly by Cortés, then, presumably, by a ritual action masked from us, and that a new Great Speaker had been chosen: a step unprecedented to my knowledge in Mexica history. There can be no doubt of Cortés's determination to master and to manipulate, but it is difficult to see much "mastery of signs" in all this.[34]

Battle

Analysts, save for military historians, have overwhelmingly concentrated on the first phase of the conquest, assuming that from that point the consummation of the Spanish victory was merely a matter of applying a technological superiority: horsemen against pedestrian warriors, steel swords against wooden clubs; muskets and crossbows against bows, arrows, and lances; cannon against ferocious courage. I would argue that the final conquest was a very close-run thing; a view with which, as it happens, the combatants on both sides would agree. After the Spanish ejection from Tenochtitlan the Mexica remained heavily favored in things material, most particularly manpower, which more than redressed any imbalance in equipment. Spanish technology had its problems: the miseries of slithering or cold-cramped or foundering horses, wet powder, the brutal weight of the cannon. A great smallpox epidemic had come and gone, but its ravages had presumably affected committed "allies" of the Spaniards and of the Mexica equally. The sides were approximately matched in knowledge: if

Cortés was to profit from his familiarity with the fortifications and functioning of the lake city, the Mexica at last knew the Spaniards as enemies, and were under the direction of a ruler liberated from the ambiguities which appear to have bedeviled Moctezuma.

We tend to have a "Lord of the Flies" view of battle: that in deadly combat the veils of "culture" are ripped away, and natural man confronts himself. But if combat is not quite as cultural as cricket, its brutalities are nonetheless rule-bound. Like cricket, it requires a sustained act of cooperation, of an admittedly peculiar kind, with each side constructing the conditions in which both will operate, and so, where the struggle is between strangers, obliging a mutual "transmission of culture" of the shotgun variety. And because of its high intensities, it promises to expose how one's own and other ways of acting and meaning are understood and responded to in crisis conditions, and what lessons about the other and oneself can be learned in that intimate, involuntary, and most consequential communication.

The sources for the second phase are comparatively solid. Since it is cultural assumptions we are after, equivocation in recollection and recording matter little. Cortés edits his debacle on the Tacuba causeway, where more than fifty Spaniards were taken alive through his own impetuosity, into a triumph of leadership in crisis; Díaz marvels at Spanish bravery under the tireless onslaughts of savages: both are agreed as to the vocabulary through which they understand, assess and record battle behavior. Sahagún's informants, able to report only bitter hearsay and received myth on the obscure political struggles of the first phase, move to confident detail in their accounts of the struggle for the city, in which at least some of them appear to have fought, naming precise locations and particular warrior feats; revealing in the structure of their accounts as much as in their rich detail their principles of battle. The challenge is to assess how effective each group was as innovators, and how well they "read" each other.

War, at least war as fought among the dominant peoples of Central Mexico, and at least ideally, was a sacred contest, the outcome unknown but preordained, revealing which city (and which local deity) would rightfully dominate another. Something like equal terms were therefore required: to prevail by mere numbers or by some piece of treachery would vitiate the significance of the contest. So important was this notion of fair testing that food and weapons were sent to the selected target as part of the challenge, there being no virtue in defeating a weakened enemy.[35]

The warriors typically met outside the city of the defenders. Should the attacking side prevail, they swept into the city to fire the temple where the local deity had its place. That action marked victory in occurrence and record; the formal sign for conquest in the painted histories was a burning temple.

Free pillage continued until the terms of tribute were set: then the victors withdrew to their home city with their booty and their captives, including not only the warriors taken in the formal battle, but "civilians" seized during the period of plunder, and (if the victors were Mexica and imbued with Mexica pretensions) with the image of the defeated deity the most significant captive, to be held in the "god captive house" in Tenochtitlan. Defeat was bitter because it was a statement and judgment of inferiority, on individuals and on the group, a judgment the victorious warriors were only too ready to reinforce by savage mockery, and which was institutionalized by the imposition of tribute.[36] The duration of the decision was always problematical. Defeated towns paid their tribute as a regular decision against further hostilities, but remained independent, and usually notably disaffected, despite the conquering city's conviction of the legitimacy of its supremacy. Many towns in the valley, allied or defeated or intimidated by the Mexica, paid their token tribute, fought alongside the Mexica in Mexica campaigns, and shared in the spoils, but they remained mindful of their humiliation and unreconciled to their subordination. The monolithic "Aztec empire" is a European hallucination: in this atomistic polity, the units were held together by the tension of mutual repulsion. (Therefore the ease with which Cortés could recruit "allies," too often taken as a tribute to his silver tongue, and therefore the deep confusion attending his constant use of the word "vassal" to describe the relationship of subject towns first to Tenochtitlan, and later to the Spanish Crown.)

If war was ideally a sacred duel between peoples (and so between the gods of those peoples), battle was ideally a sacred duel between matched warriors, a contest in which the taking of a fitting captive for presentation to one's own deity was a precise measure of one's own valor, and one's own fate. One prepared for this individual combat by song, and the ritual decking with the sacred war regalia. (To go "always prepared for battle" in the Spanish style was unintelligible: a man carrying arms was only potentially a warrior.) The great warrior, scarred, painted, plumed, wearing the record of his victories in his regalia, screaming his war cry, erupting from concealment or looming suddenly through the rising dust, could make lesser men flee by the pure terror of his presence: warriors were practiced in projecting ferocity. There were maneuverings to "surprise" the enemy, and a fascination with ambush, but only as a device to confront more dramatically: to strike from hiding was unthinkable. Indian weaponry, with its dearth of effective projectile weapons and its emphasis on the obsidian-studded war club, signaled warrior combat aims: the seizing of captives for presentation before the tutelary deity.

In the desperation of the last stages of the battle for Tenochtitlan, Mexica inhibition against battleground killing was somewhat reduced: Indian "allies" died and Spaniards who could not be quickly subdued were killed, most often, as the Mexica were careful to specify, and for reasons which will become clear, by having the backs of their heads beaten in. But the priority on the individual seizing of preferably important captives remained. In other regards the Mexica responded with flexibility to the challenges of siege warfare. They read Spanish tactics reasonably accurately: a Spanish assault on the freshwater aqueduct at Chapultepec was foreseen, and furiously, if fruitlessly, resisted. The brigantines, irresistible at their first appearance on the lake, were later lured into a carefully conceived ambush in which two were trapped. The horses' vulnerability to uneven ground, to attack from below, their panic under hails of missiles, were all exploited effectively. The Mexica borrowed Spanish weapons: Spanish swords lashed to poles or Spanish lances to disembowel or hamstring the horses; even Spanish crossbows, after captive crossbowmen had been forced to show them how the machines worked.[37] It was Indian invention and tenacity which forced Cortés to the desperate remedy of leveling structures along the causeways and into the city to provide the Spaniards with the secure ground they needed to deploy their horses and cannon effectively. And they were alert to the possibilities of psychological warfare, capitalizing on the Spaniards' peculiar dread of death by sacrifice and of the cannibalizing of the corpse. On much they could be flexible. But on that most basic measure of man's worth they could not compromise.

The passion for captives meant that the moment when the opponent's nerve broke was helplessly compelling, an enemy in flight an irresistible lure. The pursuit reflex was sometimes exploited by native opponents as a slightly shabby trick. It was to provide Cortés with a standard tactic for a quick and sure crop of kills. Incurious as to the reason, he nonetheless noted and exploited Mexica unteachability:

Sometimes, as we were thus withdrawing and they pursued us so eagerly, the horsemen would pretend to be fleeing, and then suddenly would turn on them; we always took a dozen or so of the boldest. By these means and by the ambushes which we set for them, they were always much hurt; and certainly it was a remarkable sight for even when they well knew the harm they would receive from us as we withdrew, they still pursued us until we had left the city.[38]

The passion could not be relinquished merely because it had become fatal.

That commitment bore heavily on outcomes. Had Indians been as uninhibited as the Spaniards in their killing, the small Spanish group, with no secured source of replenishment, would soon have been whittled away to nothing. In battle after battle the Spaniards report the deaths of many Indians, while their own men suffer not fatalities but wounds, and fast-healing wounds at that: those flint and obsidian blades sliced clean. It preserved the life of Cortés: time and again the Spanish leader struggled in Indian hands, the prize in a disorderly tug of war, with men dying on each side in the furious struggle for possession, and each time the Spaniards prevailed. Were Cortés in our hands, we would knife him. Mexica warriors could not kill the enemy leader so casually: were he to die, it would be in the temple of Huitzilopochtli.[39]

If the measurable consequences were obvious and damaging, there were others less obvious, but perhaps more significant. We have already noted the Spanish predilection for ambush as part of a wider preference for killing at least risk. Spaniards valued their crossbows and muskets for their capacity to pick off selected enemies well behind the line of engagement: as snipers, as we would say. The psychological demoralization attending those sudden, trivializing deaths of great men painted for war, but not yet engaged in combat, must have been formidable. (Were the victim actively engaged in battle, the matter was different. Then he died nobly; although pierced by a bolt from a distance, his blood flowed forth to feed the earth as a warrior's should.) But more than Indian deaths and demoralization was effected through these transactions: to inflict such deaths—at a distance, without putting one's own life in play—also developed a Mexica reading of the character of the Spanish warrior.[40]

Consider this one episode, told by a one-time conquistador. Two Indian champions, stepping out from the mass of warriors, offered their formal challenge before a Spanish force. Cortés responded by ordering two horsemen to charge, their lances poised. One of the warriors, against all odds, contrived to sever a horse's hooves, and then, as it crashed to the ground, slashed its neck. Cortés, seeing the risk to the unhorsed rider, had a cannon fired so that "all the indians in the front ranks were killed and the others scattered." The two Spaniards recovered themselves and scuttled back to safety under the covering fire of muskets, crossbows, and cannon.[41]

For Cortés the individual challenge had been a histrionic preliminary flourish: he then proceeded to the serious work of using firepower to kill warriors, and to control more territory, which was what he took war to be about. Throughout, Spaniards measured success in terms of body counts, territory controlled, and evidence of decay in the morale of the "enemy," which included all warriors, actively engaged in battle or not, and all "civilians" too. Cortés casually informed the king of his dawn raids into sleeping villages and the slaughter of the inhabitants, men, women, and children, as they stumbled into the streets: these were necessary and conventional steps in the progressive control of terrain, and the progressive demoralization of opposition. To an Indian warrior, Cortés's riposte to the challenge was shameful, with only the horses, putting themselves within reach of the Indian champions' weapons, emerging with any credit. Cortés's descents on villages are reported in tones breathing incredulity: on the Spanish retreat from Tenochtitlan they "quickly slew the people of Calacoaya . . . [they] did not provoke them; without notice were they slain."[42]

There is in the Florentine Codex an exquisitely painful, detailed description of the Spaniards' attack on the unarmed warrior dancers at the temple festival, which triggered the Mexica "uprising." The first victim was a drummer: his hands were severed, then his neck. It continues: "of some they slashed open their backs: then their entrails gushed out. Of some they cut their heads to pieces. . . . Some they struck on the shoulder; they split openings; they broke openings in their bodies." And so it goes on. How ought we interpret this? This was not, I think, recorded as a horror story, or only as a horror story. The account is sufficiently careful as to precise detail and sequence to suggest its construction close after the event, in an attempt to identify the pattern and so to discover the sense in the Spaniards' cuttings and slashings, the Mexica having very precise rules about violent assaults on the body, and the notion of a "preemptive massacre" of warriors not being in their vocabulary.[43]

Such baffling actions, much more than any deliberately riddling policy, kept Indians off balance. To return to that early celebrated bit of mystification by Cortés, the display of the cannon to impress the Mexican envoys on the coast with the killing power of Spanish weapons. The men who carried the tale back reported the thunderous sound, the smoke, the fire, the foul smell—and that the shot had "dissolved" a mountain, and "pulverized" a tree.[44] It is highly doubtful that they took the point of this early display; that this was a demonstration of a weapon of war for use against human flesh. It was not a conceivable weapon for use by warriors. So it must have appeared (as it is reported) as a gratuitous assault upon nature: a scrambled lesson indeed. Mexica warriors learned, with experience, not to leap and shout and display but to weave and duck when faced with cannon fire and crossbows, as the shield canoes learned to weave and zigzag to avoid the cannon shot from the brigantines, so that the carnage was less.[45] But they also learned contempt for men who were prepared to kill indiscriminately, combatants and noncombatants alike, and from a secure distance, without putting their own lives in play.

About Spanish horses, that other key element in Cortés's mystification program, Indian warriors seem to have felt rather differently. We have clear evidence of swift and effective warrior response to the horses, and of a fine experimental attitude to verifying their nature. A small group of Tlaxcalan warriors having their first sight of horses and horsemen managed to kill two horses and to wound three others before the Spaniards got the upper hand.[46] In the next engagement a squad of Indians made a concerted and clearly deliberate attack on a horse, allowing the rider, although badly wounded, to escape, while they killed his mount and carted the body from the field. Bernal Díaz later recorded that the carcass was cut into pieces and distributed through the towns of Tlaxcala, presumably to demonstrate the horse's carnal nature. (They reserved the horseshoes, as he sourly recalled, to offer to their idols, along with "the Flemish hat, and the two letters we had sent them offering peace."[47])

Indians were in no doubt that horses were animals. But that did not reduce them, as it did for Spaniards, to brute beasts: unwitting, unthinking servants of the lords of creation. Indians had a different understanding of how animals signified. It was no vague aesthetic inclination which led the greatest warrior orders to mimic the eagle and the jaguar in regalia and conduct: those were creatures of power, exemplary of the purest warrior spirit. The eagle, slowly turning close to the sun, then the scream, the stoop, the strike; the jaguar, announcing its presence with the coughing rumble of thunder, erupting from the dappled darkness to make its kill: these provided unmatchable models for human emulation. That horses should appear ready to kill men was unremarkable. The ferocity and courage of these creatures, who raced into the close zone of combat, facing the clubs and swords; who plunged and screamed, whose eyes rolled, whose saliva flew (for the Mexica saliva signified anger) marked them as agents in the battle action. (Remember the charge of the two horses against the two Indian challengers.) In the Mexica lexicon of battle, the horses excelled their masters. They were not equal in value as offerings—captured Spanish swords lashed to long poles were typically used against horses to disembowel or hamstring them, but not against their riders, judged too valuable to damage so deeply—but their valor was recognized. When the besieged Mexica won their major victory over Cortés's men on the Tacuba causeway, they displayed the heads of the sacrificed Spaniards on the skull rack in the usual way, and below them they skewered the heads of the four horses taken in the same melee.[48]

There is one small moment in which we see these contrary understandings held in counterpoise. During a skirmish in the city some Spanish horsemen emerging from an unsprung ambush collided, a Spaniard falling from his mare. Panicky, the riderless horse "rushed straight at the enemy, who shot at and wounded her with arrows; whereupon, seeing how badly she was being treated, she returned to us," Cortés reported, but "so badly wounded that she died that night." He continued: "Although we were much grieved by her loss, for our lives were dependent on the horses, we were pleased she had not perished at the hands of the enemy, for their joy at having captured her would have exceeded the grief caused by the death of their companions."[49]

For Cortés the mare was an animal, responding as an animal: disoriented, then fleeing from pain. Her fate had symbolic importance only through her association with the Spaniards. For the Indians the mare breaking out from the knot of Spaniards, rushing directly and alone toward enemy warriors—white-eyed, ferocity incarnate—was accorded the warrior's reception of a flight of arrows. Her reversal, her flight back to her friends, probably signaled a small Indian victory, as her capture and death among enemies would have signaled to the Spaniards, at a more remote level, a small Spanish defeat. That doomed mare wheeling and turning in the desperate margin between different armies and different systems of understanding provides a sufficiently poignant metaphor for the themes I have been pursuing.

Spanish "difference" found its clearest expression in their final strategy for the reduction of the imperial city. Cortés had hoped to intimidate the Mexica sufficiently by his steady reduction of the towns around the lake, by his histrionic acts of violence, and by the exemplary cruelty with which resistance was punished, to bring them to treat.[50] Example-at-a-distance in that mosaic of rival cities could have no relevance for the Mexica—if all others quailed, they would not—so the Spaniards resorted, as Díaz put it, to "a new kind of warfare." Siege was the quintessential European strategy: an economical design to exert maximum pressure on whole populations without active engagement, to secure control over people and place. If Cortés's own precarious position led him to increase that pressure by military sorties, his crucial weapon was want.

For the Mexica, siege was the antithesis of war. They knew of encircling cities to persuade unwilling warriors to come out, and of destroying them, too, when insult required it. They had sought to burn the Spaniards out of their quarters in Tenochtitlan, to force them to fight after their attack on the warrior dancers.[51] But the deliberate and systematic weakening of opposition before engagement, and the deliberate implication of non-combatants in the contest, had no part in their experience.

As the siege continued, the signs of Mexica contempt multiplied. The warriors continued to seek face-to-face combat with these most unsatisfactory opponents, who skulked and refused battle, clung together in tight bands behind their cannon, and fled without shame. When the greatest warriors, swept in by canoe, at last had the chance to engage the Spaniards closely, the Spaniards "turned their backs, they fled," with the Mexica in pursuit (Fig. 3.4). They abandoned a cannon in one of their pell-mell flights, positioned with unconscious irony on the gladiatorial stone on which the greatest captured warriors gave their final display of fighting prowess; the Mexica worried and dragged it along to the canal and dropped it into the water.[52] Indian warriors were careful, when they had to kill rather than capture Spaniards in battle, to deny them an honorable warrior's death, dispatching them by beating in the back of their heads, the death reserved for criminals in Tenochtitlan.[53] And the Spaniards captured after the debacle on the Tacuba causeway were stripped of all their battle equipment, their armor, their clothing: only then, when they were naked, and reduced to "slaves," did the Mexica kill them.[54]

What does it matter, in the long run, that Mexica warriors admired Spanish horses and despised Spanish warriors? To discover how it mattered we need to look briefly into Indian notions of fate and time. To begin with a comparison of the structure of the Indian and Spanish accounts of the final battles. The Spanish versions present the long struggles along the causeways, the narrow victories, the coups, the strokes of luck, the acts of daring on each side. Through the tracing of an intricate sequence of action we follow the movement of the advantage, first one way, then the other. God is at the Spaniards' shoulders, but only to lend power to their strong right arms, or to tip an already tilting balance. Through selection and sequence of significant events we have the familiar, powerful, cumulative explanation through the narrative form.

The Indian accounts are, superficially, similar. There are episodes, and

Figure 3.4. Killing at a distance. Florentine Codex, Book 12, Plate 121. Courtesy of Biblioteca Medicea-Laurenziana.

they are offered serially: descriptions of group or individual feats, of contemptible Spanish actions. But these are discrete events, moments to be memorialized, with time no more than the thread on which they are strung: there is no cumulative effect, no significance in sequence. Nor is there any implication that the human actions described bore on outcomes. The fact that defeat was suffered declares it to have been inevitable.

In this sense Todorov is right to say that the Indians "interrogated the world" rather than human action. But just as those anomalous events noted before the Spanish advent could be categorized as "omens" and their portent identified only retrospectively, this "interrogation" was very much an after-the-event diagnosis, not an anterior (and paralyzing) certitude. Events were problematical in their experiencing, and innovation and desperate effort were neither precluded nor inhibited. Altogether too much has been made of the Mexica concern for "day signs," the determining authority of the auguries associated with one's day of birth over the individual's *tonalli,* or destiny. It is true that in some passages of the Florentine Codex—the only source with the kind of "spread" to make this sort of concept-mapping viable—the individual is presented as quite mastered by his or her "fate." That clarity blurs on broader acquaintance, emerging as part of the characteristic stylistic movement of much of the codex between firm statements of the ideal and the necessary qualifications of actuality. Day signs had about as much determining power as horoscopes do now for the moderate believer. They mattered, but more as intimations or as post-hoc diagnoses (and even then, one suspects, not by the individuals concerned) than as iron determinants of action.[55]

However, some few signs were recognized as unequivocal. An example: at a place called Otumba, the Spaniards, limping away from Tenochtitlan after their expulsion, were confronted by a sea of Mexica warriors; a sea which evaporated when Cortés and his horsemen drove through to strike down the battle leader and to seize his fallen banner. The Spanish accounts identify the striking down of the commander as decisive, but while the fall of a leader was ominous (and attack on a leader not actively engaged in combat disreputable) it was the taking of the banner which signified. Our initial temptation is to elide this with the familiar emotional attachment of a body of fighting men to its colors: to recall the desperate struggles over shreds of silk at Waterloo; the dour passion of a Roman legion in pursuit of its lost Eagle and honor.[56] There might have been some of this in the Indian case. But the taking of a banner was to Indians less a blow to collective pride than a statement: a sign that the battle was to go, indeed had gone, against them.[57]

By the second phase of the conquest, while Spanish banner carriers remained special targets, being subjected to such ferocious attack that "a new one was needed every day," the Mexica had come to pay less heed to signs, because they had discovered that Spaniards ignored them. The essential mutuality was lacking.[58] In the course of the causeway victory a major Spanish banner had been taken: "the warriors from Tlatelolco captured it in the place known today as San Martín." But while the warrior who had taken the banner was carefully memorialized, "they were scornful

Figure 3.5. Attack on the main temple precinct. Lienzo de Tlaxcala, Plate 46. Courtesy of the Bodleian Library, Oxford.

of their prize and considered it of little importance." Sahagún's informants flatly record that the Spaniards "just kept on fighting."[59]

Unresponsive to signs of defeat, Spaniards were equally careless of signs of victory. When Spaniards fired the temple in Tlatelolco the "common people began to wail, expecting the looting to begin" (Fig. 3.5). Warriors had no such expectation. They knew the fighting would go on: these enemies were as blind to signs as they were deaf to decency. When a Spanish contingent penetrated the marketplace of Tlatelolco, where the Mexica had taken their last refuge, they managed to fight their way to the top of the main pyramid, to set the shrines on fire and to plant their banners there before they were forced to withdraw. The next day from his own encampment Cortés was puzzled to see the fires left unquenched, the banners still in place. The Mexica would respect the signs and leave them to stand, even if the barbarians did not, even if they had lost their efficacy, even if the rules of war were in abeyance.[60]

John Keegan has characterized battles as "essentially a moral conflict [requiring] a mutual and sustained act of will between two contending parties, and, if it is to result in a decision, the moral collapse of one of them."[61] Paradoxically, that mutuality is most essential at the point of disengagement. To "surrender," to acquiesce in defeat and concede victory, is a complex business, at once a redefinition of self and one's range of effective action, and a redefinition of one's relationship with the erstwhile enemy. Those redefinitions have somehow to be acknowledged by the opponent. Where the indicators which by marking defeat allow "moral collapse" and the redefinitions to occur are not recognized or acknowledged, neither victory nor defeat is possible, and we approach a sinister zone in which there can be no resolution save death.[62]

That, I think, came to be the case in Mexico. The Mexicans on good evidence had concluded their opponents were cowardly opportunists impossible to trust. The Spaniards had also unwittingly denied them the way to acquiesce in their own defeat.[63] So the Mexica, lacking alternatives, continued to resist. The chronicles record the stories of heroic deeds; of warriors scattering the Spaniards before them, of the great victory over Cortés's troop, with terrified Spaniards reeling "like drunken men," and fifty-three taken for sacrifice.[64] Spanish accounts tell us that the victory which had given so many captives to the Mexican war god was taken at the time to indicate the likelihood of a final Mexica victory, hopefully prophesied by the priests as coming within eight days. (The Indian records do not waste time on false inferences, misunderstood omens.) Cortés's allies, respectful of signs, accordingly removed themselves for the duration. But the days passed, the decisive victory did not come, and the macabre dance continued.[65]

And all the while, as individual warriors found their individual glory, the city was dying: starving, thirsting, choking on its own dead. This slow strangling is referred to as if quite separate from the battle, as in the Mexican mind it presumably was. Another brief glory, when eagle and ocelot warriors, men from the two highest military orders, were silently poled in disguised canoes to where they could leap among looting native allies, spreading lethal panic among them. But still the remorseless pressure: "they indeed wound all around us, they were wrapped around us, no one could go anywhere. . . . Indeed many died in the press."[66]

So the Mexicans made their end-game play. Here the augury component, always present in combat, is manifest. Quautémoc, who had replaced the dead Cuitlahuac as Great Speaker, and his leading advisers selected a seasoned warrior, clad him in the array of Quetzal Owl, the combat regalia of Ahuitzotl, the ruler before the despised Moctezuma, and armed him with the flint-tipped darts of Huitzilopochtli; so he became, as they said, "one of the number of the Mexicans' rulers." He was sent forth to cast his darts against the enemy: should the darts twice strike their mark, the Mexica would prevail. Magnificent in his spreading quetzal plumes, with his four attendants, Quetzal Owl entered the battle.[67] For a time they could follow his movements among the enemy, reclaiming stolen gold and quetzal plumes, taking three captives, or so they thought. Then he dropped from a terrace, and out of sight. The Spaniards record nothing of this exemplary combat.

After that ambiguous sign, another day passed with no action.[68] On the next evening a great "bloodstone," a blazing coal of light, flared through the heavens, to whirl around the devastated city, then to vanish in the middle of the lake. No Spaniards saw the comet of fire which marked the end of imperial Tenochtitlan. Perhaps no Indian saw it either. But they knew great events must be attended by signs, and that there must have been a sign. In the morning Quautémoc, having taken council with his lords, abandoned Tenochtitlan. He was captured in the course of his escape, to be brought before Cortés. Only then did the Mexicans leave their ruined city (Fig. 3.6).[69]

So the Mexica submitted to their fate, when that fate was manifest. A certain arrangement of things had been declared terminated: the period of Mexica domination and the primacy of Tenochtitlan was over. A section of the *Anales de Tlatelolco* is often cited to demonstrate the completeness of the obliteration of a way of life and a way of thought. It runs:

Broken spears lie in the roads;
we have torn our hair in our grief.
The houses are roofless now, and their walls
are red with blood.

Worms are swarming in the streets and plazas,
and the walls are splattered with gore.
The water has turned red, as if it were dyed,
and when we drink it,
it has the taste of brine.
We have pounded our hands in despair
against the adobe walls,
for our inheritance, our city, is lost and dead.
The shields of our warriors were its defence,
but they could not save it.[70]

Figure 3.6. The surrender of Quautémoc. Lienzo de Tlaxcala, Plate 48. Courtesy of the Bodleian Library, Oxford.

And so it continues. But what is notable here (apart from the poetic power) is that the "lament" was a traditional form, maintaining itself after the defeat, and so locating that defeat and rendering it intelligible by assaying it in the traditional mode. If the Mexican vision of empire was finished, the people, and their sense of distinctiveness as a people, were not. The great idols in the temples were somehow smuggled out of the city by their traditional custodians before its fall, and sent towards Tula: a retracing of their earlier route. A cyclical view of time has its comforts. And if the "Quetzalcoatl returned" story as presented in the Florentine Codex is indeed a post-conquest imposition, as is likely, and if indeed it does move away from traditional native understandings of human action in the world—Moctezuma's conduct described in order to explain the outcome of defeat, not merely to memorialize his shame—its fabrication points to an interest in the construction of a viable and satisfying public history for the conquered, an emollient myth, generated in part from within the European epistemological system to explain the catastrophe of Mexica defeat.

Consequences

There is something appealing to our sense of irony in the notion that the Spaniards' heroic deeds, as they saw them, were judged shameful by the Mexica warriors. But attitudes of losers have little historical resonance. Attitudes of victors do. Here I want to pursue an impression. Anyone who has worked on the history of Mexico—I suspect the case is the same for much of Latin America, but I cannot speak for that—is painfully impressed by the apparent incorrigibility of the division between the aboriginal inhabitants and the incomers, despite the domestic proximity of their lives, and by the chronic durability, whatever the form of government, whatever its public rhetoric, of systemic social injustice grounded in that division. In Mexico I am persuaded the terms of the relationship between the incoming and the indigenous peoples were set very early. A line of reforming sixteenth-century missionaries and upright judges were baffled as much as outraged by what they saw as the wantonness of Spanish maltreatment of Indians; cruelties indulged in face of self-interest. Spaniards had been notoriously brutal in the Caribbean islands, where the indigenes were at too simple a level of social organization to survive Spanish endeavors to exploit them, and in Tierra Firme. Yet in their first encounters with the peoples of Mexico they declared themselves profoundly impressed. Cortés's co-venture with the Tlaxcalans seems to have involved genuine cooperation, a reasonably developed notion of mutuality, and (not to be sentimental) some affection between individuals.[71]

Then something happened, a crucial break of sympathy. It is always difficult to argue that things could have been other than they turn out to be, especially in the political maelstrom of post-conquest Mexico. But I have a sense of Cortés relinquishing both his control over the shaping of Spanish-Indian relations and his naturally conservationist policies—a conservationism based in pragmatism rather than humanity, but effective for all that—earlier and more easily than his previous conduct would have us expect. I think that shift had to do with that obstinate and, to Spanish eyes, profoundly "irrational," refusal or incapacity to submit.

Cortés was sensitive to the physical beauty and social complexity of the great city of Tenochtitlan. It was the dream of the city which had fired his ambition and provided the focus for all his actions. We must remember that Tenochtitlan was a marvel, eclipsing all other cities in Mesoamerica in size, elegance, order, and magnificence of spectacle. Cortés had contrived the complex, difficult strategy of the blockade and pursued the mammoth task of implementing it, to preserve the city in its physical and social structures by demonstrating the futility of resistance. Then he watched the slow struggle back and forth along the causeways, as the defenders, careless of their own lives, took back by night what had been so painfully won by day. So he moved his men on to the causeways, into physical misery and constant danger. Then he undertook the systematic destruction of the structures along the causeways to secure the yards won, a perilous prolongation of a task already long enough.[72]

So, with patience, access to the city was gained, and the noose of famine tightened. From that point victory was in Spanish (and our) terms inevitable. Yet still the resistance continued, taking advantage of every corner and rooftop. So the work of demolition went on. At last, from the top of a great pyramid, Cortés could see that the Spaniards had won seven-eighths of what had once been the city, with the survivors crammed into a corner where the houses were built out over the water. Starvation was so extreme that even roots and bark had been gnawed, with the survivors tottering shadows, but shadows who still resisted.[73] Cortés's frustration, forced to destroy the city he had so much wanted to capture intact, is manifest, as is his bewilderment at the tenacity of so futile a resistance:

As we had entered the city from our camp two or three days in succession, besides the three or four previous attacks, and had always been victorious, killing with crossbows, harquebus and field gun an infinite number of the enemy, we each day expected to see them sue for peace, which we desired as much as our own salvation; but nothing we could do could induce them to it . . . we could not but be saddened by their determination to die.[74]

He had no stomach to attack again. Instead he made a final resort to terror. Not to the terror of mass killings: that weapon had long lost its efficacy. He constructed a war engine, an intimidatory piece of European technology: the marvelous catapult. It was a matter of some labor over three or four days, of lime and stone and wood, then the great cords, and the stones big as demijohns. It was aimed, as a native account bleakly recorded, to "stone the common folk." It failed to work, the stone dribbling feebly from the sling, so still the labor of forcing surrender remained.[75]

Four days of patient waiting, four days further into starvation, and the Spaniards entered the city again. Again they encountered ghostly figures, of women and gaunt children, and saw the warriors still stationed on the remaining rooftops, but silent now, and unarmed, close-wrapped in their cloaks. And still the fruitless pretense at negotiation, the dumb, obdurate resistance.

Cortés attacked, killing "more than twelve thousand," as he estimated. Another meeting with some of the lords, and again they refused any terms save a swift death. Cortés exhausted his famous eloquence: "I said many things to persuade them to surrender but all to no avail, although we showed them more signs of peace than have ever been shown to a vanquished people for we, by the grace of our Lord, were now the victors."[76] He released a captured noble, charging him to urge surrender: the only response was a sudden, desperate attack, and more Indians dead. He had a platform set up in the market square of Tlatelolco, ready for the ceremony of submission, with food prepared for the feast which should mark such a moment: still he clung to the European fiction of two rulers meeting in shared understanding for the transference of an empire. There was no response.

Two days more, and Cortés unleashed the allies. There followed a massacre, of men who no longer had arrows, javelins, or stones; of women and children stumbling and falling on the bodies of their own dead. Cortés thought forty thousand might have died or been taken on that day. The next day he had three heavy guns taken into the city. As he explained to his distant king, the enemy, being now "so massed together that they had no room to turn around, might crush us as we attacked, without actually fighting. I wished, therefore, to do them some harm with the guns, and so induce them to come out to meet us."[77] He had also posted the brigantines to penetrate between the houses to the interior lake where the last of the Mexican canoes were clustered. With the firing of the guns the final action began. The city was now a stinking desolation; of heaped and rotting bodies; of starving men, women, and children crawling among them, struggling in the water. Quautémoc was taken in his canoe, and at last brought before Cortés to make his request for death, and the survivors began to file out, these once-immaculate people "so thin, sallow, dirty and stinking that it was pitiful to see them."[78]

Cortés had invoked one pragmatic reason for holding his hand in the taking of Tenochtitlan: if the Spaniards attempted to storm the city the Mexica would throw all their riches into the water, or would be plundered by the allies. His perturbation went, I think, very much deeper. His earlier battle narratives exemplify those splendid Caesarian simplicities identified by John Keegan; disjunctive movement, uniformity of behavior, simplified characterization, and simplified motivation.[79] That style of high control, of magisterial grasp, falters when he must justify his own defeat on the causeway, which cost so many Spanish lives. It then recovers itself briefly, to fracture, finally and permanently, for the last stages of his account of the battle for Tenochtitlan. The soldierly narrative loses its fine onward drive as he deploys more and more detail to demonstrate the purposefulness of his own action, and as he frets more and more over fathoming native mood and intentions.[80]

Cortés had proceeded in the world by treating all men, Indians and Spaniards alike, as manipulable: that sturdy denial of the problem of otherness, usually so profitable, had here been proved bankrupt. He had also been forced into parodying his earlier, once successful, strategies. His use of European equipment to terrify had produced the elaborate threat of the catapult, then its farcical failure. "Standard" battle procedures—terror-raiding of sleeping villages, exemplary massacres—took on an unfamiliar aspect when the end those means were designed to effect proved phantasmal; when killing did not lead to panic and pleas for terms, but a silent pressing on to death. Even the matter of firing a cannon must have taken on a new significance: to use cannon to clear a contended street or causeway or to disperse massed warriors was one thing; to use cannon to break up a huddled mass of exhausted human misery was very much another. It is possible that as he ran through his degraded routine of stratagems in those last days, Cortés was brought to glimpse something of the Indian view of the nature and quality of the Spanish warrior.

His privilege as victor was to survey the surreal devastation of the city which had been the glittering prize and magnificent justification for his insubordination, and for the desperate struggles and sufferings of the last two years, now reduced by perverse, obdurate resistance to befouled rubble, its once-magnificent lords, its whole splendid hierarchy, to undifferentiated human wreckage. That resistance had been at once "irrational," yet chillingly deliberate.[81]

He had seen, too, the phobic cruelty of the "allies," most especially the Tlaxcalans.[82] He had known that cruelty before, and had used and profited from it. But on that last day of killing they had killed and killed amid a wailing of women and children so terrible "that there was not one man amongst us whose heart did not bleed at the sound."

Writing later of that day and what he saw then, Cortés was brought to make one of his very rare general statements: "no race, however savage, has ever practiced such fierce and unnatural cruelty as the natives of these parts."[83] "Unnatural" cruelty. Against nature: a heavily freighted term in early sixteenth-century Spain. He had described Moctezuma as a "barbarian lord" in his earlier letter, but he had done so in the course of an elaborate description of the Mexica city and its complex workings which demonstrated the Mexica ruler was a "barbarian" of a most rare and civilized kind. I think his view was changed by the experience of the siege. "Fierce and unnatural cruelty," an unnatural indifference to suffering, an unnatural indifference to death: conduct in violation of "nature." A terrifying, terminal demonstration of "otherness," and its practical and cognitive unmanageability. Todorov has called Cortés a master in human communication. Here the master had found his limits.[84]

In what was to follow, the Spaniards expressed their own cruelties. There was a phobic edge in some of the things done, especially against those men most obviously the custodians of the indigenous culture.[85] I do not suggest that any special explanation is required for Spanish or any other conquerors' brutalities. All I would claim at the end is that in the long and terrible conversation of war, despite the apparent mutual intelligibility of move and countermove, as in the trap and ambush game built around the brigantines, that final nontranslatability of the vocabulary of battle and its modes of termination divided Spaniards from Indians in new and decisive ways. If for Indian warriors the lesson that Spaniards were barbarians was learned early, for Spaniards, and for Cortés, that lesson was learned most deeply only in the final stages, where the Indians revealed themselves as unamenable to "natural" reason, and so unamenable to the routines of management of one's fellow men. Once that sense of unassuageable otherness has been established, the outlook is bleak indeed.

I owe particular thanks to my colleague at the Institute for Advanced Study, William Taylor, whose acute reading of an earlier draft did much to clarify my thinking.

Notes

1. I call the people of the imperial city of Tenochtitlan-Tlatelolco, commonly known as the "Aztecs," the "Mexica," in part because that is what they called themselves, in part to free them from the freight that "Aztec" has come to bear. (I shall

distinguish between "Tenocha" and the "Tlatelolca" only as necessary.) Life and language being imperfect, I shall call the peoples of Central Mexico "Indians," which is a purely European term. The Nahuatl sounds of the name of the Mexica ruler known as "Montezuma" are probably best facsimilated by "Motecuhzoma," but that is to carry linguistic piety too far: I shall name him "Moctezuma."

2. Anthony Pagden notes several editions of the letters in five languages between 1522 and 1525. Anthony Pagden, *The Fall of Natural Man: The American Indian and the Origins of Comparative Ethnology* (Cambridge, 1982), 58. He also comments on the use made of the conquest as early as the 1540s by Juan Ginés de Sepúlveda, the emperor's chaplain and official chronicler, in his "Democrates secundus sive de justis causis belli apud Indos," which Pagden describes as "the most virulent and uncompromising argument for the inferiority of the American Indian ever written." Sepúlveda has his Democrates recite "the history of the fall of Mexico, contrasting a noble, valiant Cortés with a timorous, cowardly Montezuma, whose people by their iniquitous desertion of their natural leader demonstrated clearly their indifference to the good of the commonwealth." Pagden, *The Fall of Natural Man,* 109, 117. For Prescott, see the fine study by David Levin, *History as Romantic Art* (New York, 1963).

3. Tzvetan Todorov, *The Conquest of America: The Question of the Other,* tr. Richard Howard (New York, 1984; first published in Paris, 1982), passim. For the quotations, 69–70, 87–89. For an illuminating discussion of very much earlier European views of the definitive importance of a system of writing, see Pagden, *The Fall of Natural Man,* chapters 6 and 7. For the central importance of language and so communication in the definition of the truly human, see 20–22.

4. *Hernán Cortés: Letters from Mexico,* tr. and ed. Anthony Pagden, with an introduction by J. H. Elliott (New Haven and London, 1986), Second Letter, 88. Hereafter cited as Pagden.

5. Pagden, Second Letter, 112–13, 119, 127.

6. It is possible, with the Pagden translation and commentary on the Cortés Letters once again available, that the "god-ruler returned" story as a factor in the conquest might lose its luster. Possible, but unlikely, those gullible natives paralyzed by their own preposterous imaginings being altogether too attractive to Western sensibilities.

7. On self-promotion: Díaz claims the four Spanish heads tossed into Cortés's camp after the great Mexica victory on the causeway, in a Mexica variant of psychological warfare, were named as belonging to Alvarado, Sandoval, another Spaniard—and Bernal Díaz. B. Díaz del Castillo, *Historia verdadera,* ed. J. Ramírez Cabañas (Mexico, 1966), CLII. He reports with gratification that tears sprang to Cortés's eyes.

8. Díaz, *Historia,* XL; XLV.

9. B. de Sahagún, *The Florentine Codex,* tr. A. J. O. Anderson et al. (Santa Fe, 1950–82), Introductory Vol., 87: Díaz, *Historia,* XXXII; XXI; XXXIV.

10. Initially, Moctezuma is represented as spokesman for the ruling group, who share his alarm, but he is rapidly detached from the other lords, finally being presented as a cowardly and ineffectual individual. For the confusions attending the return of the self-exiled Quetzalcoatl-Topiltzin, legendary ruler of Tollan, see

H. B. Nicholson, "Topiltzin Quetzalcoatl of Tollan: A Problem in Mesoamerican Ethnohistory," Ph.D. diss., Harvard University, 1957.

11. *Florentine Codex,* 12:16:45; 17–18; 48–49.

12. "This I saw in a painting that belonged to an ancient chieftain from the province of Texcoco. Moctezuma was depicted in irons, wrapped in a mantle and carried on the shoulders of his chieftains." Diego Durán, *Historia de las Indias de Nueva España y islas de Tierra Firma,* ed. Ángel María Garibay, 2 vols. (Mexico, 1987), LXXIV, 541–42.

13. Todorov, *Conquest,* 70.

14. Díaz, *Historia,* cap. XXXVIII.

15. Díaz, *Historia,* cap. XXXIX. For the list of gifts, see Pagden, First Letter, 45. Gomara mentions "several books of painted figures which the Mexicans use for writing, folded like kerchiefs." If we knew their contents, much of the mystery could be dissipated. Francisco López de Gómara, *Istoria de la Conquista de Mexico,* cap. 39, p. 86. Moctezuma's earliest prestations perhaps carried a "please identify" message through the inclusion of the regalias of three deities: two of Quetzalcoatl, one of Tezcatlipoca, and Tlaloc. Eduard Seler takes the costumes to be regalias for the four aspects of Quetzalcoatl, or more correctly the four deities dominant in the four quarters of the heavens—Xuitecutli (Fire), Tlaloc (Rain), Tezcatlipoca, and Quetzalcoatl as Wind God, the four being thought of, in his view, as embodiments of Quetzalcoatl. Seler, *Commentary on Vaticanus B.* (London, 1902), 130. As I have indicated elsewhere, I think such firm statements on the hierarchy (and the distinctiveness) of sacred "persons" to be misplaced.

16. Pagden, Second Letter, 50.

17. Pagden, Second Letter, 54. See also the reception offered by "Sienchimalen," ibid.

18. Durán, *Historia,* 2, XLIII. *Florentine Codex,* 12:15:41.

19. Durán, *Historia,* 2, LXXIII. Certainly the Lienzo de Tlaxcala shows them entering as warriors, but that is as we would expect in that self-glorifying document.

20. For a more precise account of the Yucatec Maya, see Inga Clendinnen, *Ambivalent Conquests* (Cambridge, 1987).

21. Díaz, *Historia,* XCV.

22. J. H. Elliott, *New York Review of Books,* 19 July 1984.

23. "Reported" is putting it rather too high: here we have to take the "captain's speech" for the literary convention it is. But it is, at best, close to what Cortés claims he said: at worst, the gist of what Díaz thought a man like Cortés ought to have said on such an occasion. Pagden, Second Letter, 63; Díaz, *Historia,* LXI for "Roman captains" comparison.

24. For a contrary view of the whole conquest phenomenon as very much more pragmatic and routinized, see James Lockhart, *The Men of Cajamarca* (Austin and London, 1972). On the model of Mexico: "[the conquest of] Mexico had no major impact on Peru merely by virtue of some years' precedence . . . Pizarro was certainly not thinking of Cortés and Moctezuma when he seized Atahualpa; he had been capturing *caciques* [chiefs] in Tierra Firme long before Mexico was heard of." James Lockhart and Stuart B. Schwartz, *Early Latin America* (Cambridge, 1983), 84.

25. Pagden, Second Letter, 60–62.

26. The Mexica tax gatherers themselves were unimpressed by the Spaniards and all their doings, if we can believe Díaz's chagrined account of their superb progress through the Cempoallan town, magnificently indifferent to the gazing Spaniards. Díaz, *Historia*, XLVI, XLVII.

27. Díaz, *Historia*, LI.

28. Díaz, *Historia*, XXV, XXVI, LII.

29. Cortés's shifting understanding of his obligations to his God is a marvelously rich theme, but too complex to be explored here.

30. Díaz, *Historia*, LXXXVIII.

31. Pagden, Second Letter, 112; Díaz, *Historia*, XCV.

32. Sahagún's informants exaggerate the physical contact, "recalling" Moctezuma as being prodded and pawed by any and all of the newcomers, although the disgrace of the unabashed glance was as keenly noted: "they caressed Moctezuma with their hands"; they "looked at him; they each looked at him thoroughly. They were continually active on their feet; they continually dismounted in order to look at him." *Florentine Codex*, 12:16:4; 12:17:44–46. Díaz, *Historia*, LXXXVIII.

33. Pagden, Second Letter, 91.

34. It is only one of many painful paradoxes that Cortés's decision to take Moctezuma hostage, a decision based on a mistaken and almost certainly inflated notion of Moctezuma's authority, nonetheless seriously destabilized political relations within the city and within the Mexica-allied valley towns, as Moctezuma's diminishing authority was pressed to new purposes by Spanish misreadings. Cortés reports that as he made his first probes into Tenochtitlan on his second *entrada*, the defenders would ironically pretend to open a way for him, "saying, 'Come in, come in and enjoy yourselves!' or, at other times, 'Do you think there is now another Mutezuma to do what you wish?'" Pagden, Third Letter, 188.

35. Durán, *Historia*, 2, XXXIV.

36. Cf. the deliberate humiliation of the Tlatelolcan warriors, discovered hiding in the rushes after the Mexica victory of 1474, and ordered to quack. "Even today," Durán noted, decades after the debacle, "the Tlatelolca are called 'quackers' and imitators of waterfowl. They are much offended by this name and when they fight the name is always recalled." Durán, *Historia*, 2, XXXIV.

37. Díaz, *Historia*, CLIII; Durán, *Historia*, 2, LXXVII, 315.

38. Pagden, Third Letter, 230.

39. For example, the attack on Cortés in the Xochimilco battle, and the desperate rescue, Cortés sustaining a "bad wound in the head." Díaz, *Historia*, CXLV, 294.

40. Muskets were valued equally with crossbows, a musketeer being allocated the same share of the spoils as a crossbowman, yet, oddly, muskets are mentioned less in Indian accounts, perhaps because the ball could not be followed in flight, while crossbow bolts whirred and sang as they came. *Florentine Codex*, 12:22:62. For a succinct and accessible account of sixteenth-century cannon, in their enormous variety, see Pagden, *Letters*, 507–508. Most of the small guns used in America could fire a ball of twenty pounds over some four hundred meters; n. 59. For a more extended account, Alberto Mario Salas, *Las Armas de la Conquista* (Buenos Aires, 1950).

41. Durán, *Historia,* 2, LXXII.

42. "[The Spaniards] vented their wrath upon them, they took their pleasure with them." *Florentine Codex,* 12:25:73.

43. *Florentine Codex,* 12:20:55. It appears from the funerary rites accorded the fragmented corpses of the warrior dancers that the Mexica somehow decided that the victims had found death in a mode appropriate to warriors, though presumably as offerings rather than combatants.

44. *Florentine Codex,* 12:7:19.

45. *Florentine Codex,* 12:30:86.

46. Pagden, Second Letter, 58.

47. Díaz, *Historia,* LXIII.

48. Note also the offering of the entire skins of five horses, "sewn up and as well tanned as anywhere in the world," in Texcoco. These horses had been taken in a situation where they were riderless at the moment of combat. Pagden, Third Letter, 184.

49. Pagden, Third Letter, 252.

50. Pagden, Third Letter, 192.

51. Díaz recalls them yelling, whistling, and calling the Spaniards "rogues and cowards who did not dare to meet them through a day's battle, and retreated before them." Díaz, *Historia,* CXXVI.

52. *Florentine Codex,* 12:31:89.

53. For example, *Florentine Codex,* 12:35:87.

54. *Florentine Codex,* 12:33:96; 12:34:99.

55. Cf. Todorov: "To know someone's birthday is to know his fate," *Conquest,* 64.

56. John Keegan, *The Face of Battle* (New York, 1977), 184–86.

57. Díaz, *Historia,* CLV.

58. Díaz, *Historia,* CLI.

59. Miguel Léon-Portilla, *The Broken Spears,* 107. The captor was the *Tlapanecatl* Hecatzin—see *Florentine Codex,* 12:35:103, n. 2. For an earlier exploit of the Otomí warrior, see ibid., 101.

60. Spanish attitudes to fate and signs are scanted here. They were, of course, sensitive to signs in their own repertoire, as in their determination to keep flaunting their banner whatever the cost in wounds or worse. In his second letter Cortés represents his men as vulnerable to demoralization through "omens" (as when five horses mysteriously fell on a night expedition, and had to be returned to camp), while he was not: "I continued on my way secure in the belief that God is more powerful than Nature." Pagden, Second Letter, 62–63. Cf. the very different attitude of waiting on God's will, Pagden, Fifth Letter, 422–24. Cortés's vigorous challenge to the religious observances of even friendly natives reflect something that comes close to a contractual notion: God would aid his Spaniards only if they were attentive to His honor. (The installed Christian images also became combatants in the action: war prosecuted by other means.) But the Spaniards appear to be best protected, even from the worst individual and group disasters, by the ample space for misfortune in Christian cosmology: while God is securely in His heaven, all manner of things can be wrong in His world. How Cortés accommodated himself to the continued cannibalism of his Tlaxcalan "friends," and to what I take to

be his lies regarding the toppling of the Mexica idols and their replacement with Christian images, I do not know.

61. John Keegan, *The Face of Battle,* 296.

62. As in the interspecific mayhem described by Konrad Lorenz, where signs of submission are not "understood" in the lethal battle between the turkey and the peacock. Konrad Z. Lorenz, *King Solomon's Ring* (London, 1961), 194–95.

63. Cortés was certainly desperate to treat with Quautémoc in the last days of the siege, but Díaz reports that the ruler would not show himself, despite all reassurances, because he feared he would be killed by guns or crossbows, Cortés having behaved too dishonorably to be trusted. Díaz, *Historia,* CLV, 338.

64. *Florentine Codex,* 12:35:104.

65. Díaz, *Historia,* CLIII; Pagden, Third Letter, 242. Cortés, for his part, deletes any reference to the withdrawal of his Indian "vassals," the admission of such a withdrawal casting altogether too much light on the nature of their commitment to the Spanish cause, and on his authority over them.

66. *Florentine Codex,* 12:38:117.

67. Here we have to remember the power of the sacred garment among Amerindian societies, to protect, and to render formidable. These garments were not only records of personal war biographies, but "memory garments," in Patricia Anawalt's happy phrase, referring to history, and perhaps mimicking a particular tribal group, like the Huasteca. In the case of Quetzal Owl the sacred power invoked was of the warrior Huitzilopochtli himself. How real this kind of power could be is indicated by the fact that some Plains Indians who possess highly efficient shields—a quarter-inch thickness of shrunken rawhide, tough enough to turn a glancing bullet—often chose to ride into battle carrying only the sacred painted shield cover, as protection enough. And so it often proved to be, so great was the awe roused by these death-singers—save, of course, against the U.S. Cavalry.

68. *Florentine Codex,* 12:38:118.

69. *Florentine Codex,* 12:40:123.

70. I offer Léon-Portilla's translation as the version most likely to be familiar. Miguel Léon-Portilla, *The Broken Spears* (Boston, 1962), 137–38. Cf. Leon-Portilla, *Pre-Columbian Literatures of Mexico* (Norman, Oklahoma, 1969), 150–51, and Gordon Brotherston and Ed Dorn, *Image of the New World* (London, 1979), 34–35. For other songs in traditional form to do with the conquest, see John Bierhorst, *Cantares Mexicanos* (Stanford, 1985), esp. 13, pp. 151–53; 60, p. 279 (obscurely); and especially 66, pp. 319–23; 68, for its early stanzas, pp. 327–41; 91, pp. 419–25.

71. It also seems to have involved Cortés in abetting cannibalism: he notes that after a successful ambush led by the Spanish cavalry in the main square of the city "more than five thousand of their bravest and most notable men were lost. That night our allies dined sumptuously, for all those they had killed were sliced up and eaten." Pagden, Third Letter, 251. He had earlier told the king of his allies' jeering at the Mexica, "showing them their countrymen cut to pieces, saying they would dine off them that night and breakfast off them the following morning, which in fact they did." Pagden, Third Letter, 223. Cortés and cannibalism is another major theme neglected.

72. The labor of filling in only one gap cost four days' miserable labor and six Spanish lives. Díaz, *Historia,* CLI.

73. Pagden, Third Letter, 256.

74. Pagden, Third Letter, 232–33.

75. Pagden, Third Letter, 257; Díaz, *Historia*, CLV; *Florentine Codex*, 12 : 38 : 113.

76. Pagden, Third Letter, 258.

77. Pagden, Third Letter, 262.

78. Díaz, *Historia*, CLVI.

79. John Keegan, *The Face of Battle*, 65–66. Which is not to claim any direct classical influence: see Pagden, *Letters*, xlvii, and J. H. Elliott, "The Mental World of Hernán Cortés," *Transactions of the Royal Historical Society*, Fifth Series, 17, 1967, 41–58, for Cortés's slight acquaintance with classical authors.

80. For the control: "While the aguacil-mayor was at Matalcingo, the people of [Tenochtitlan] decided to attack Alvarado's camp by night, and struck shortly before dawn. When the sentries on foot and on horseback heard them they shouted, 'to arms!' Those who were in that place flung themselves upon the enemy, who leapt into the water as soon as they saw the horsemen. . . . Fearing our men might be defeated I ordered my own company to arm themselves and march into the city to weaken the offensive against Alvarado"—and so on. Pagden, Third Letter, 247. For the dislocation: "When we came within sight of the enemy we did not attack but marched through the city thinking that at any moment they would come out to meet us [to surrender]. And to induce it I galloped up to a very strong barricade which they had set up and called out to certain chieftains who were behind and whom I knew, that as they saw how lost they were and knew that if I so desired within an hour not one of them would remain alive why did not Guatmucin [Quautémoc] their lord, come and speak with me. . . . I then used other arguments which moved them to tears, and weeping they replied they well knew their error and their fate, and would go and speak to their lord . . . they went, and returned after a while and told me their lord had not come because it was late, but that he would come on the following day at noon to the marketplace; and so we returned to our camp. . . . On the following day we went to the city and I warned my men to be on the alert lest the enemy betray us and we be taken unawares," and so to more worried guesses and second-guesses. Pagden, Third Letter, 259–60.

81. While Cortés could assert that "I well knew it was only the lord of the city and three or four others of the principal persons who had determined not to surrender; the rest wished only to see themselves out of this pass dead or alive," Mexica actions made all too clear their "evil intention, which was for every one of them to perish." Pagden, Third Letter, 258–59. Throughout the Spanish accounts runs a thread of wonder at the obedience of these people in extremis, coupled with their desperate self-motivated courage. For the allies' killings and Cortés's response, pp. 261–62.

82. The Tlaxcalans seem to have regarded themselves as equal, or perhaps senior, co-venturers in the conquest. They refused to participate in any ventures (like the sortie against Narváez) not in their direct interest; they withdrew at will, taking their loot with them; they required payment for aid given the Spaniards after the expulsion from Tenochtitlan, after discussing and dismissing the utility of killing them. Díaz, *Historia*, XCVIII. Their self-representation as faithful friends and will-

ing servants of the Spaniards (as in the Lienzo de Tlaxcala picturings) came a generation and more after the conquest, in the pursuit of privileges.

83. Pagden, Third Letter, 262.

84. Those limits were to be drawn more narrowly through the shaking experience of the Honduran expedition. The Cortés who early in the Mexican campaign could dismiss "omens" in the confidence that "God is more powerful than Nature" learned in Honduras how helpless men are when Nature, not men, opposes them, and where God seems far away. There he learned that God is bound by no contract, and that he, like all men, must wait upon His will. The Fifth Letter reads like a mournful antiphon to the sanguine assurance of Cortés's early conquest accounts.

85. *Anales de Tlatelolco: Unos Anales Historicos de la Nación Mexicana*, prepared by Heinrich Berlin (Mexico, 1948), 371–89, pp. 74–76.

Donald R. Kelley

4. "Second Nature": The Idea of Custom in European Law, Society, and Culture

For use almost can change the stamp of nature.

Hamlet, III, iv, 167

Altera Natura

"Custom is second nature" (*consuetudo altera natura*).[1] This has been a commonplace, though a debatable commonplace, at least since Aristotle. Primary Nature has been worshiped in many ways—has been matrified as well as deified—but Custom has enjoyed no such conceptual respect. While there have been countless historical and philosophical discussions of the "idea of nature," no serious effort has been made, so far as I know, to study the "idea of custom" in a comprehensive and critical fashion—nothing comparable, say, to R. G. Collingwood's *Idea of Nature* or to Robert Lenoble's *Idée de la nature*.[2] Yet as the virtual twin, or shadow, of nature, the idea of custom has run through the length and breadth, the height and depth, of Western thought and culture.

The contrast between nature and custom is evident in Western thought and linguistic usage going back to the pre-Socratics.[3] The story begins most explicitly with the crucial distinction between nature (*physis*) and law (*nomos,* in the sense of man-made rules), a duality that also invaded the fields of language, art, literature, and especially law.[4] Aristotle was the first to formulate the distinction between a primary and a second nature in philosophical terms. In his essay on memory, custom (*ethos*) seems to approach or take the place of nature, just as recalled experiences are gathered into general thoughts.[5] An analogous movement from the particular to the general can also be seen in the *Rhetoric*.[6] Here, defining pleasure as a movement of the soul to a natural state, Aristotle remarks that "that which has become habitual becomes as it were natural; for the distance between 'often' [*pollakis*] and 'always' [*aion*] is not great, and nature belongs to the idea of 'always,' custom to that of 'often.'" From the beginning the notion that repetition over time establishes a permanent pattern has been essential to the idea of custom.

"Custom" played a prominent role in ancient Roman rhetoric.[7] The term *consuetudo* was employed by both Cicero and Quintilian in the sense of a norm of the speech community as well as a form of human law.[8] Cicero contrasted everyday, customary life (*vitae consuetudo*) with the philosophical idealizations of Plato's *Republic*. These attitudes were preserved in the medieval *trivium* and various ways expanded by Renaissance humanists. Following the lead of Quintilian, Lorenzo Valla insisted on the primacy of custom (*consuetudo, usus,* or *consensus*) in language and denounced the technical jargon of scholasticism (in law and theology as well as philosophy) because it substituted a false "reason" for ordinary usage and "convention."[9] Language itself, according to Valla, was the product not of nature but of human custom (*hominum usus, qui verborum est autor,* and Quintilian's formula, *consuetudo vero certissima loquendi magistra*); and its principles were to be found not in formal philosophy but in the discipline of rhetoric in particular and the liberal and perhaps fine arts in general, especially since "art" itself was commonly distinguished from, or even regarded as a secondary and derivative form of, "nature."

In all of these contexts, over twenty-five centuries or more, one common theme has persisted, and that is the association of the idea and term "custom" and its semantic neighbors with law, rhetoric, grammar, and the European humanist tradition, and in modern times with philosophical and later empirical "anthropology." From the ancient Greek "custom is king" (*nomos basileus; despotes nomos*)[10] to Bagehot's "cake of custom" and modern ethnographic study of folkways and "norms," "custom" has usually signified forms of what Clifford Geertz has called "local knowledge" and internalist approaches to cultural understanding, often in contrast to the transcendent aspirations of theology, natural philosophy, and most mainstream social science.

It is hardly surprising that, philosophically, the idea of custom has commanded little respect—and the notion that it resembled nature was still less acceptable. Rather, for Cicero and Seneca, custom was contrary to nature, and Christian authors inclined to a similar opinion. Both Augustine and Jerome took the idea of "second nature" as a surrender to the corruption both of human nature and of human law and as further alienation from the divine; Clement of Alexandria spoke of "thrusting away custom as some deadly drug"; and Thomas Aquinas identified "second nature" with the bad habits (*malitia*) produced by the animal side of human nature.[11] Emblematic of this deep-seated prejudice was the reminder of Cyprian, often repeated (by Luther among others) and preserved in canon law, that Christ had represented himself not as the "custom" but rather as the "truth," referring to John 14:6, "Sed Dominus noster Christus veritatem se non consuetudinem cognominavit."[12]

Yet canon law, while drawing sustenance from patristic authority, increasingly had to come to terms with the limitations of the human condition and in effect with human history and customs, which indeed were conscripted into canonist service. Thus Gratian's *Decretum* opens with the fundamental proposition that "the human race is ruled in two ways, either by natural law or by unwritten customs"—either by nature or by second nature.[13] This has been a premise of Western social thought which not only antedated but also outlasted the medieval Christian formulation.

This brings us to the major premise in the story of "custom," which is that, between ancient Greco-Roman and modern anthropological conceptions, the major formulations have arisen within the world of Western jurisprudence—an intellectual and professional continuum that begins with the earliest stages of the Roman art of law and ends with the earliest stages of modern social science (which was itself in various ways endebted to the study of law).[14] From Gaius to Max Weber these theorists of custom and law—practitioners of "civil science" (*civilis scientia* or *civilis sapientia,* in the words of the Accursian Gloss)—form a "community of interpretation" which, ideological differences aside, has preserved a remarkable continuity of language, method, and conceptualization across many centuries and cultural frontiers. It is in large part out of this hermeneutical and honoratorial (judicial-scholastic-humanistic-scientific) tradition that the idea of custom has taken its modern shape, and this is the elusive target of the present study.

Custom and Law

"Custom" was not included among the classical sources of Roman law, except implicitly in the famous distinction between written and unwritten law (*ius scriptum, ius non scriptum*); but from the late third century jurists began to recognize custom—"local" and "long" or "longest" custom—in a more formal sense than mere "manners" (*mores*) or "usage" (*usus*) or even "prescription."[15] This conventional notion of custom as a product of popular and "tacit" consent (*consensus populi*) was developed in postclassical jurisprudence, found a permanent home in the Digest, became standard fare in university instruction, and thence passed into the mainstream of European legal, social, political, and cultural thought.

The standard definition of custom is attributed to the last of the classical jurists, Hermogenianus, writing in the fourth century: "But also those rules which have been established by ancient custom and observed, like a tacit agreement, are to be followed no less than the rules that are written." [16] Here in a nutshell, with certain other supporting texts, are the essential ingredients of the Western idea of custom, including those developed by the social and cultural sciences: the origins in social behavior, the popular and parochial base, the parity with law, and the element of time.

To this locus classicus, however, were added a large number of medieval and modern "extensions," produced by efforts to accommodate Roman ideas to European society. Beginning especially with Azo in civil law and Hostiensis in canon law, theories of *consuetudo* gave definition, intelligible form, relevance, and a kind of legitimacy to the feudal and urban institutions of late medieval Europe, and from there moved into various national traditions. The conceptual umbrella of *consuetudo* has given shelter to the massive materials gathered in the French *coutumiers,* in German *Gewohnheitsrecht,* and in the Spanish *usos* and *fueros,* as well as in the endless commentaries on all of these accumulations. English common law, according to Bracton, was wholly a product of *consuetudo,* and it illustrated marvelously the Aristotelian principle of pleasure, or "love" (quoted in this connection by Sir John Fortescue in the later fifteenth century), that "use becomes another nature" (*usus alteram facit naturam*)—and specifically that English use was altogether "natural" and "reasonable." [17]

In general, medieval discussions of custom were framed by the twin legal concepts of natural law (*ius naturale*) and the law of nations (*ius gentium*)—a legalistic version of the distinction between *physis* and *nomos.* Another way of stating this fundamental duality was to distinguish between a "primary law of nature" (*ius naturale primarium* or *primaevum*) based on reason and a "secondary law of nature" (*ius naturale secondarium*) based on convention and utility and equivalent to custom. [18] By definition, in any case, "custom" belonged to the realm neither of civil (that is, Roman) law nor of natural law but to the secondary realm of the "law of nations" (*ius gentium* or *ius naturale gentium*), including the societies of the New as well as the Old World; and it is in this fundamental legal sense that *consuetudo* expresses "second nature."

What jurists recognized as "customary," of course, was not random human behavior but more regular social patterns. At the very least, according to a medieval adage which simplified the Aristotelian formula, "Twice makes a custom."[19] Beyond this minimum requirement and despite scholastic complications, the European idea of custom preserved the attributes of its classical prototype—the contingent origin, the popular base, the temporal element, and especially the parity with written law.

Custom filled the gap left by the cessation of Carolingian legislation. Though its primary arena was the family, custom became increasingly identified with the usages of feudal society and, attached to the "fief," shifted from a personal to a territorial base. It was given its most concrete expression in the long-enduring institution of the cultivated field (*campagne*), which Gaston Roupnel called "the characteristic creation of the West . . . , the nature and spirit of its civilization."[20] In this and other forms European customs made their appearance in local settings and in terms of particular social predicaments for which evidence is scattered in randomly surviving charters, notarial acts, records of inferior jurisdictions, and occasionally oral tradition. As particular *coutumes* were gathered, by literate and lawyerly men, on a higher provincial level and became subject to legal interpretation, they helped to shape the idea of custom.

Over the centuries the idea of custom was commonly associated with various liberties (*libertates et consuetudines*), especially feudal but also provincial, municipal, and ecclesiastical.[21] At first, *consuetudo* reflected mainly the emergence of the feudal domain—seigneurial rights, jurisdiction, and especially taxes and servitudes, which had gained legitimacy in the course of time. All French customs, wrote an eighteenth-century commentator, were only "an expression of the authority of the lord of the fief." It was "custom" in this sense that, from the fourteenth century, was the principal target of peasant revolts. Yet, while capitularies and early charters speak of "new" and "old," of "good" and "bad," customs, *consuetudines* normally referred to accepted local usage. Lords and tenants argued over the application but seldom the meaning of "custom." Even in the peasant uprisings of the seventeenth century, for example, the rebel *croquants,* while protesting recent impositions, recognized the force not only of long-standing custom but also "new" customs sanctioned by a meeting of the three estates.[22]

More formally, the European idea of custom took shape as a reconceptualization of the old Roman idea of *consuetudo,* which gave local usages intelligibility and a certain borrowed legitimacy. The primary issue was always the relationship between custom and law (*jus*), and about this "the doctors disagreed," as indeed they have done ever since. A famous summary of this debate appears in a thirteenth-century collection entitled

Dissensiones Dominorum, in which the contradictions in the classical and postclassical texts are elaborated and exacerbated by modern "interpreters of ancient Roman law"—that is, pre-Accursian glossators.[23] "Some say that no custom, whether special or general, contrary to law abrogates or derogates from [civil] law. . . . They say that written law abrogates a custom contrary to law. . . . But others say that a custom which can be confirmed by express consent should be observed, for custom is nothing else than a tacit agreement, according to the Digest. Others say that a good but not a bad custom prevails over a law."

Here we can see the idea of custom situated at the very storm center of modern political and constitutional debates. Imperial, royal, and papal ideologists tended normally to argue that law, which was the exclusive monopoly of the sovereign, always superseded custom; but judicial doctrine inclined to the opposite view, which was that, according to the authoritative Accursian Gloss, "Custom abolishes law" (*Consuetudo vincit legem*), or in the words of Baldus, "Later custom annuls earlier law."[24] Politically, the suggestion was to place the *populus* above the *princeps* as a source of law, but the more practical purpose was to reinforce the professional judicial monopoly over legal interpretation.

Custom "represents the will of the people," Bartolus wrote (*consuetudo repraesentat mentem populi*); and so, ultimately, according to the common Aristotelian formula, the people were regarded as the "efficient cause of law" (*efficiens causa legis erat olim populus*).[25] Or as Bartolus alternatively put it, the four causes included "the natural cause, from [what was] frequently done or performed; the formal, from the consensus [of the people]; the efficient, from the time; and the final, from the rationale, the utility of the custom." In any case, the *populus* was the alpha and omega of *consuetudo*. But what was a "people"? The term and concept of *populus*, which had been transferred from ancient Rome to the Christian faith (*populus christianus* was a common expression of Augustine and Jerome), might be applied from communities ranging from an empire or nation to a village, a monastic community, a guild, or even smaller groups ("ten makes a people," was another medieval adage; *decem faciunt populum*); but it was normally defined by adherence to a particular "custom," whether general, provincial, local, or even familial.[26]

The most difficult question, debated for centuries by jurists and historians alike, was the origin of customary law. The first answer given by scholastic commentators was that custom emerged from social practice— "law arises from fact" (*lex ex facto oritur*) was the often-repeated formula.[27] Custom arose from usage and manners (*ab usu et moribus*), as Baldus put it.[28] For centuries this temporalized form of the commonplace distinction between de facto and de jure suggested the pattern of legal development, and it was reinforced by the Augustinian notion that human dominion, public as well as private, was based on force. Not only did law originate, humanly and historically, in custom but, by inference, right originated in might.

The element of time remained central to the idea of custom, and so was the notion of historical change. For if custom, representing a process in time, was continually being created, it was also and concomitantly becoming obsolete: *consuetudo* was ever counterbalanced by *desuetudo,* counterpart of the dual Aristotelian process of generation and corruption. In many ways, Odofredus observed, "custom today has changed" (*mutata est hodie consuetudo*).[29] In the sixteenth century Philippe Bugnyon devoted a whole treatise to laws which, "today" (*hodie*) had fallen "out of usage" (*ab usu longe recessit; hors d'usage*) through contradictions, confusion, and (in a modern sense) "abuse."[30]

Customs were tied to geographical as well as historical conditions. Technically, the rule was that "place determines act" (*locus regit actus,* or *formam actus*), but the more general premise was that both laws and judgments had to be in accord with the character and environment of a people. "The customs of a region must be followed," wrote Azo (*consuetudines regionis servandae sunt*); and local custom, according to the fourteenth-century *Somme Rurale* of Jean Bouteiller, was to be in accord with the "situation of a place" as determined by the local inhabitants.[31] Local customs should be followed, wrote Beaumanoir, "because we ought to remember what since childhood we have seen in use and judged in our province better than in others of which we do not know the customs and usages."[32] Such assumptions—that "local knowledge" had to be joined to high theory and general norms—furnished a sort of geohistorical base for philosophical and "scientific" as well as practical jurisprudence, and for less professional forms of social and cultural thought.

From Memory to Written Record

For historians as well as jurists, the essential question is how, concretely, custom was promoted from a social to a legal and even political level, how it came not only to "represent" but also to regulate the behavior of people. Here we confront a fundamental problem much discussed in recent years, which is the link between oral and scribal or literate culture.[33] How did custom pass from unrecorded, collective memory to authoritative written form? How, more technically, was *consuetudo* transformed into *jus consuetudinarium*? How, more specifically, did French *coutumes* become *droit civil,* German *Gewohnheit* become *allgemeines Recht,* and English customs become "common law"?

In theory, the answer came from simple social inquiry and judgment. As the English civilian John Cowell wrote, "It is enough for the profe of a custom by witness in the common lawe (as I have credibly heard), if two or more can agree, that they have heard their fathers say, that it was a custome all their time and that their fathers heard their fathers also say, that it was likewise a custome in their time." [34] This definition was equivalent to the "immemorial custom" celebrated by common lawyers like Cowell's nemesis Edward Coke and Matthew Hale (though it emphasized human testimony as well as judicial intuition), but it also held for continental customs, which were likewise authenticated transcriptions of popular memory.

The essential problem was one of "proof" or "approval," and it could be resolved in several ways. In primitive or preliterate societies no proof was called for; or rather the members of that society were themselves "living proof" of their customs. In more complex cultures a certain level of expertise was required, and in medieval Europe this meant first law-finders or lay "sayers of the law" (*sapientes, diseurs de droit, Gesetzsprecher*), who consulted their own memories or consciences, and then of more formally trained jurists, who claimed special expertise, or rather who received it from higher authority. [35]

From the twelfth century or earlier, "proof" implied the "redaction" of customs into written form, and to begin with this was a matter of private recording, exemplified by the *Libri Feudorum* assembled by Obertus de Orto and Girardus Niger, the anonymous *Establissements de Saint-Louis,* the *coutumes* of Beauvaisis by Philippe de Beaumanoir, the *Sachsenspiegel* by Eike von Repgow, the *Siete Partidas* of Alfonso the Wise, and perhaps the treatises of Glanvil and Bracton, which all gained authority only in retrospect. These collections represented not only a shift "from memory to written record" (in the words of M. T. Clanchy) but also the outcome of what Eugen Ehrlich called a "universalizing process," by which local customs were formulated and expanded geographically by judicial decisions and precedents. [36] This process was intensified by the introduction of more formal "Romano-canonical" procedures and by the teaching of civil and canon law in the universities.

Yet the institutions of popular approval were ostensibly retained. According to the fourteenth-century *Grand Coustumier de France* by Jacques d'Ableiges, custom was to be "proved by a meeting of ten men worthy of faith" (*prouvés en turbe par dix hommes dignes de foy*); and a little later Jean Bouteiller, in his *Somme rurale,* declared that custom was to be proved "by twelve of the wisest and oldest men of the place" (*douze hommes les plus sages et anciens du lieu*).[37] As Gilles Fortin wrote three centuries later of the *coutume* of Paris, "This customary law was for a long time observed without being written or engraved anywhere except on the hearts of the citizens who keep it; and if in doubt, the proof was not in books but in the assemblies [*turbes*] of those who knew the practice and ordinary usage"[38] (Fig. 4.1).

In France the development of custom from unwritten usages to learned doctrine, from fact to law, and from jurisprudence to legal philosophy, can be followed with some precision. The story begins in the thirteenth century when the central government began to take a serious interest in local customs, bound up as they were with the rival interests of feudal, seigneurial, and urban courts. By an ordinance of 1270 St. Louis instituted the device of the collective inquest (*inquisitio per turbam, enquête par turbe*), or rather adapted the old Carolingian inquest, designed originally to establish facts in criminal cases, to the authentication of local customs.[39] According to this ordinance, the royal commissioners (*enquêteurs*) convoked a certain number of sworn "wise men" representing the three estates, then proposed a series of customs for their consideration, and wrote down the customs mutually agreed upon.

This dramatic confrontation between king and people is a model of the aforesaid transition "from memory to written record." The assembled *turbiers* not only affirmed the existence—and more specifically the common and acknowledged "notoriety"—of each *coutume,* but they were also required to demonstrate the most minute "local knowledge." According to one thirteenth-century formulary, the members of the *turbe* were asked if they had ever "seen judgment by the said custom, and how many times, and by what judges, and between which persons, and at what time . . . and if all or the better part of the people agreed to introduce this custom."[40] Then, after unanimous agreement about the wording, the royal *enquêteurs* set the custom down in writing, leaving the delegates of the people to speak then or forever hold their peace. As for the organization of topics, sometimes the text followed Roman order, (persons, things, actions), sometimes feudal order (that is, beginning with "fief" or feudal jurisdiction and going on to questions of manorial rights, kinship, marriage, succession, and so forth).

In this process of "redaction" first the old "wise men" and later the

LA
COVSTVME
DE
PARIS,
CONFEREE
AVEC LES AVTRES COVSTVMES DE FRANCE.
ET

EXPLIQVE'E PAR LES NOTES DE
M.ᶜ CHARLES DV MOLIN *fur les mefmes Couftumes , les Arrefts de la Cour, & diuerfes autres Remarques.*

Enfemble vne recherche d'Autheurs, pour l'intelligence de la Couftume de Paris , & des autres Couftumes.

Commencée par M. G. FORTIN *Aduocat en Parlement.*
ET

Augmentée de plus des deux tiers par M.ʳ R. *auffi Aduocat en la Cour.*

AVEC VNE TABLE DES TITRES ET ARTICLES dans laquelle font rapportez les Edicts , & Ordonnances de nos Roys , & tous les Arrefts de la Cour de Parlement.

A PARIS,
Chez ⎰ IEAN GVIGNARD le fils, dans la grand'Salle , à l'Image S.Iean.
⎰ *Et en la boutique de Langelier ;*
⎱ RENE' GVIGNARD, au premier pillier de la grand'Salle, au au Palais, Sacrifice d'Abel.

M. DC. LXVI.
AVEC PRIVILEGE DV ROT.

Figure 4.1. Title page of a seventeenth-century edition of *La coustume de Paris* with the notes of Charles Dumoulin, as compiled in part by Giles Fortin. Source: Charles Dumoulin, *La coustume de Paris* (Paris, 1666). Courtesy of Princeton University Library.

lawyers played out, in the context of feudal relations and the institution of the royal inquest, the formation of a fundamental "social contract." Not only metaphorically but also in a technical legal sense, French customs were contractual ("sur le consentement des peuples des trois ordres," as Guy Coquille wrote in his sixteenth-century commentary on the *coutume* of Nivernais, "elles obligent *quasi ex contractu*").[41] In the eighteenth century another commentator celebrated the Bourbon *coutume* as "a public convention which one is obliged to execute and to observe in all good conscience."[42]

The introduction of writing changed the medium but not the spirit and intention of customary law, and indeed in the ritual of endorsement (*lecture et publication*), the reading retained parity with the process of writing and dissemination.[43] The formalism of the written word did not displace, it only reinforced the formalism of the spoken word. In oral procedure a man was still only as good as his word, and the words spoken by persons in a judicial proceeding could neither be changed nor withdrawn "under peril of their souls." So it was with French custom, for its recitation was almost a life-and-death matter to the subjects involved, concerning as it did their "liberties" and "honor," which was to say their property; and the texts of these usages were gone over with rabbinical care. In general custom was transformed into "customary law" (*droit coutumier*) "not in order to declare new law," as Pierre d'Angleberme put it, "but in order to preserve its memory" (*memoriae causa*).[44]

What complicates the idea of custom in social context is the fact that it cannot quite be fixed by legal formulation. In part this is because of the process of *desuetudo*, practical and theoretical obverse of *consuetudo*, in part because many customs, as Marc Bloch has shown in his extraordinary study of French rural history, have "no force apart from the wills of the inhabitants" and are preserved only in oral culture, where "human memory is the sole arbiter."[45] As Eusèbe Laurière observed in the seventeenth century, only "where the crops are showing" could customary law protect possession. In practice cultivated land was "subject to the law of nations and the common property of all." "How true it is," adds Bloch, "that all rural customs take their origin from an attitude of mind."

Redaction, of course, was intended to change all that. Endorsed by the crown in the famous ordinance of 1453, it was a process that clearly represented a political intrusion into the sphere of custom; and it was succeeded by a still more serious threat, which was the sixteenth-century movement to "reform" French customs. According to the official view, the

ordinance of 1453 had created the authority "not only to publish the ancient customs but also to reform, to abrogate, and to adjust new articles
and new customs, and to interpret and to revise them, with the advice of
those in attendance, or the majority thereof."[46] This was the policy of
Christofle de Thou, premier président of the parlement of Paris, leading
figure in the reformation movement, and champion of legal uniformity.

Like redaction, "reformation" can be seen as a ceremonial reenact-
ment of the original social compact, though admittedly under some du-
ress. In conventional fashion, representatives of all three estates were in
attendance, and especially those whose liberties, that is, interests, were at
issue. The written record (*procès-verbal*) established by the royal officers
was the very spirit of the custom (*l'âme de la coutume*); it began with a
hierarchical listing of members of the nobles, churchmen, and bourgeois,
and included an article-by-article account of the discussions of the unre-
formed custom—"in order to show how the redaction was conducted,"
wrote Simon Marion about the "first project" of the reformation of the
Parisian custom, "and what disputes and difficulties were presented."[47]
The fiction of popular approval was maintained by the view, which René
Choppin expressed in his commentary on the *coutume* of Anjou, that the
"new" custom, which was represented by some jurists as just "interpretation" of the old, went into force not with official publication but "from the
moment when it was established in the assembly of estates, for the abolition or acceptance depends on the decision of the people."[48]

During the discussions objections were often raised that particular
liberties were being neglected, or particular exemptions not recognized;
and more than once complaints were lodged against de Thou for exceed-
ing his authority.[49] In the reformation of the Parisian custom, for example,
the bishop of Paris protested against infringement of the ancient liberties
of St. Denis; and, speaking for the count, more recently duke, of Es-
tampes, Marion argued that this *bailliage* was exempt because it "in no
way recognized the custom of the *prévôté* of Paris." The social drama of
"the reformation of customs" turned in reality on the struggle between
local "liberties" and a larger conception of royal authority and national
unity pursued by the lawyers of the last Valois.

In the long run the result was that political "approval" came to out-
weigh popular "consent" and the institutions through which it had been
expressed. The seminal Ordinance of Montils-les-Tours of 1453 defined the
procedures of royal visitation and redaction; but while the principle of
consent by representatives of the three estates was preserved, this law also

"prohibited any of the advocates of our realm from alleging or proposing other customs, usages and styles except those written down, agreed upon, and ordered."[50] Except in marginal cases where written rules were ambiguous or lacking, the *turbe,* too, became obsolete, and in 1667 it was officially abolished by an ordinance of Louis XIV. In matters of "proof," popular memory was established by written "certificates of usage" and "acts of notoriety"; and provincial custom was added to the canon of official legislation to be itself "interpreted."

Montesquieu summed up the process in this way: "These customs were preserved in the memories of old men, but insensibly laws or written customs were formed." Montesquieu was also aware of the political implications, for as he added, "Thus our customs were characterized in a threefold manner: they were committed to writing, they were made more general, and they received the stamp of royal authority." However imperfectly, "custom" was joined to royal jurisdiction—"private" to "public" law—as social base to governmental superstructure and so subjected, at least potentially, to official interpretation and control. In this way "custom" was given a political dimension lacking in the classical definition. Though still immune from legislative change, custom became, as Laurent Bouchel wrote in the early seventeenth century, "a civil law approved and received by the Estates of the province, under the authority of the king."[51]

The French School

If the idea of custom was given substance through judicial practice and political intrusion, it received theoretical form by academic jurists (Fig. 4.2). One of the best illustrations of the early modern idea of custom as an object of social and historical thinking is to be found in the commentaries on civil law by François Connan, published posthumously in 1553.[52] For Connan *ius civile* referred not merely to the particular tradition of Rome but more generally to the customs and laws of modern nations—to what Baldus had called the modern law of nations (*ius novissimum gentium*); and of course "custom," too, belonged to this modern law of nations. According to Connan, *consuetudo,* along with its darker sibling *desuetudo,* originated in the mores of particular peoples (*ius ex facto oritur*), those of the New as well as the Old World; was the product of willful human acts over a period of time; had the force of law (*pro lege*) and interpreted it (*consuetudo legem interpretatur*); and ceased to be valid—became *desuetudo*—

Figure 4.2. Scene at the Palais de Justice—a crier in the sixteenth century. Source:
Henri Stein, *Le Palais de Justice et la Sainte-Chapelle* (Paris, 1912), facing p. 36.
Courtesy of Princeton University Library.

not only through a natural process of "antiquation" but also through neglect and considerations of "equity," which for Connan was the true aim of "civil law."

Connan also spoke of custom as "second nature" (*altera natura*), but he did so in order to emphasize that *consuetudo* was indeed "other" than *natura*, and indeed marked a fundamental break with the natural world (*deflexit de via naturae*). In his view custom arose not from necessity or even instinct but rather from moral virtue and will (*virtutes hae non vocantur naturales, sed morales et voluntariae, quae non sunt naturae sed voluntatis*). Custom, in short, was the ruler of civil society, and could not be identified with natural instinct or with universal reason; nor could it be investigated and understood in such naturalistic and super- or subhuman terms. For Connan—invoking here Pindar's celebrated *nomos basileus*—this is exactly what the Greeks meant when they declared that custom or law was "king."

The study of law can be general and philosophical; the study of custom had to be carried on at least in part in an empirical, historical, and comparative way. In the sixteenth century Eguinarie Baron was the most prominent exemplar of this method.[53] In his own commentaries on "civil law" Baron declared the independence of French customs according to the old "pro lege" rule, that custom was the equivalent of law (*sola consuetudo, sine iudicio, pro Iure, id est Iure scripto servatur*), and, moreover, that judicial decisions had to follow accepted custom (*res iudicata non servatur sine consuetudine*). More generally, Baron tried to give local meaning to civil law by "accommodating it to the customs of the French and the royal laws" (*accommodata ad mores Galliarum et leges Regias* was his formula). Baron's work was in effect one of the first systematic efforts of comparative jurisprudence, a discipline which itself was conspicuously nourished by the idea of custom down to the time of Henry Sumner Maine.

The new methods of early modern French jurists reinforced another significant dimension of late medieval jurisprudence, which was the insistence on the practical rather than the theoretical character of law. If law originated in custom, it was given expression most fundamentally not by legislative "action" but by judicial decisions (*res judicatae*)—for these decisions, according to an old Roman maxim, were to be accepted as truth (*res iudicata pro veritate accipitur*), while judicial decisions were themselves not valid unless they were in conformity with custom (*res iudicata non servatur sine consuetudine*, in the words of Baron). What this signified for jurists like Ayrault, who compiled a new Digest based on *res judicatae*, was that the major part of law consisted in such judgments. The study and application of law and custom was a *prudentia* even more than a *scientia*—a *phronesis* even more than an *episteme* in currently fashionable terms—and based fundamentally not on theoretical rules but on "local" knowledge, which is to say knowledge not just of principle and its application but also of "people" and its environment, culture, and history.[54] In a manner of speaking it was the jurists who were the experts in the "second nature" of a people and in this sense in an early form of human science.

It is also clear that the idea of custom encouraged a historical interpretation of society and culture long before the historical schools of the nineteenth century. According to the formula cited by François Connan in the sixteenth century, "Manners should precede custom" (*mos praecedat consuetudinem*), just as custom itself preceded written law; and "written law confirms [custom] by the course of times" (*confirmat ab historia temporum*). In later ages this became a historiographical commonplace. As Jacques Godefroy put it in the seventeenth century, referring to the Roman as well as vernacular traditions, "If one thinks back to the origin of laws, one must recognize that customs preceded them, and indeed form the first part of positive law, though placed at the end."[55]

"Custom Is the Best Interpreter of Law"

In many respects *consuetudo* was absorbed by the culture of literacy and even transformed by it. Yet the break with oral culture was not complete. Invocation of "custom" was preserved not only in the oral pleading of lawyers but also, and more controversially, in the practice and theory of judicial discretion and "interpretation." The most generous view had been expressed by Odofredus in this way: "The power of custom is three-fold: it is the founder of law, the interpreter of law, and the abrogator of law" (*potestas consuetudinis est legum conditrix, est legum interpretatrix, est legum arrogatrix*).[56] This set of topoi was itself an extension of a late classical formula attributed to Paulus, that custom was the best interpreter of law (*optima enim est legum interpres consuetudo*), and it continued to be "extended" with abandon by modern jurists, theorists as well as practitioners. From the sixteenth century in particular there was a flood of treatises on interpretation, and *consuetudo* almost invariably figured as an aid to judicial interpretation, a supplement to "equity," and a limitation on political authority.[57] In this hermeneutical form, and in the growing rivalries between judiciary and legislature, the idea of custom persisted and even flourished into modern times, reinforcing the conception of custom as a fundamental category of judicial and social thought antecedent and superior to the law.

In France the idea of custom was given shape and substance in the context of a massive and continuous legal canon centering on the provincial *coutumiers,* some three hundred of them eventually, which were written aggregations of many more local collections that have largely disappeared from the horizons of historical research.[58] These surviving customals accumulated a vast amount of commentary, not only legal and practical but also historical, philosophical, and literary, including verse renditions of the *coutumes* of Normandy and Paris (as later the Napoleonic Code), composed in part for mnemonic purposes. The customs also produced an indigenous theory of interpretation (*ars hermeneutica,* as it was called from the seventeenth century). "In order not to be slaves, imitators, and worshippers of foreigners," wrote Coquille, "let us not involve the interpretation of our customs with the confusing rules of statutes" (referring to the opinions of the civilians of the Bartolist school).[59] According to Paul Challine's *Method for the Understanding of French Customs* of 1666, the *coutumes* had to be interpreted in their own terms (*se doivent expliquer par elles-mesmes*), should be abolished by nonusage, and, especially, should be related to "common law" (*droit commun*) and to social context.[60] When particular customs were defective, application might be made not only to royal ordinances and to "the reason of Roman law" but also to unwritten usages, neighboring customs, and "the general spirit of French custom," especially that of Paris.

From the time of Beaumanoir down to that of Marc Bloch it has been clear that French social customs need to be studied in particular geohistorical context. The test of local character was often the degree of "liberty" enjoyed by all the social orders, especially in contrast to the Roman tradition of tyranny and "paternal power" (*patria potestas; puissance paternelle*). "For in France it is liberty that is ancient," Coquille remarked, "and despotism that is modern."[61] In his province of Nivernais, for example, the old maxim of the feudal domination of land did not hold: not "nulle terre sans seigneur" but "nul seigneur sans titre." In Burgundy—in sharp contrast to Normandy—virtually all land without title was allodial. More generally, Le Roy Ladurie has pointed out the emergence of "anti-paternal" and "egalitarian" patterns of succession in Normandy and, from the new *coutume* published in 1510, in the Paris-Orléans area.[62] These features were emphasized and elaborated by later commentators, who tried to give legal and literary form to local traditions.

Increasingly, commentators tried to place their *coutumes* in historical perspective, employing for this purpose documents (including charters, the *procès-verbaux,* inscriptions, and monographic studies of feudal origins). In his commentary on the custom of Auxerre in the late seventeenth century, Edme Billon quoted Baldus to the effect that the original Gallic inhabitants, "though dominated by the Roman Empire and its constitutions, could not force themselves to follow them, and that this People (jealous of their liberties and regarding these laws as a servitude) formed in their own way particular customs in each province, which they guarded inviolably against the said constitutions made for everyone in general."[63] And the spirit of the original custom was presumably preserved throughout the processes of redaction, reformation, and interpretation.

The survival of some customs, at least in a general form, can be seen in the persistence of maxims, which reflected folk wisdom as well as legal experience. One of the most fundamental questions has been that of boundaries, which sometimes had a religious dimension (symbolized more famously by the Roman god Terminus) and which involved issues of time and locale. In French custom the setting of boundaries (*bornage*) was first a matter of private, then of feudal agreement. "All parties who require *bonnage* [sic] should have it," declared Beaumanoir, "and if they agree, they may set boundaries without legal process [*bonner sans justice*], but this is not the case in many seigneuries . . . , where [the custom is that] the tenant may not set boundaries without appealing to the lord."[64] The principle that was most widely recognized, however, was that "boundaries must be set under judicial authority" (*bornes se mettent par auctorité de justice*). This was the maxim that appeared in the medieval *coutumes* of Anjou and Maine, in Antoine Loisel's *Institutes coutumiers* in the early seventeenth century, and in the Civil Code of 1804. After the Revolution *bornage* could still be accomplished *amiablement* as well as *judiciairement,* but this implied a modern contractual agreement which could always be contested. By then, however, most boundary disputes were in fact settled in terms not of "property" but of "possession," which is to say in terms of the old customary law of *saisine* and under the jurisdiction of the newly instituted justices of the peace. Thus a customary rule was preserved over many centuries and legal and social transformations, accommodating popular will but inclining as usual toward expert legal judgment.

This exemplifies the life cycle of one particular usage. To illustrate the canon formation and deformation of a whole complex of customs, consider the long career of the *coutume* of Burgundy, which was a hybrid of Roman law and the old *Leges Burgundionum* established in the fifth century by King Gundobad "for the good and tranquillity of our people."[65] In the later Middle Ages the Burgundian customs emerged from conditions of what Marc Bloch characterized as "primitive communism," surviving at least in part until the seventeenth century. They preceded, and outlasted, both the old kingdom and the modern duchy of Burgundy; and they were applied and were interpreted over generations of social turmoil and hardship, including the disappearance of villages and last-ditch efforts to reaffirm seigneurial rights.

The Burgundian *coutume* was redacted in 1459 by Duke Philip the Good, responding to complaints and petitions from the three estates, which were assembled in Dijon in traditional fashion. The representatives were "interrogated concerning the fact of the customs," article by article, documentary sources were examined, and after corrections and many altercations, the text of the custom was established, following the arrangement of Roman law. In 1575 it was "reformed" according to the same inquisitional procedure and with the inevitable controversies between the estates and the royal commissioners. All of this was set down in the published *procès-verbal*—in order, as one witness put it, "to know how the redaction was conducted and what disputes and difficulties were presented."[66] A second reformation in the eighteenth century was judged to be unnecessary, though it was still "incomplete," as Professor Dunod admitted in 1756, and needed to be "a little more developed."

The *Coutumes générales de Bourgogne* was the first book published in Dijon (in 1490), and it was reissued at least seventy-five times down to the Revolution. Not to mention many manuscript sources, pre-redaction versions, and glosses, it was interpreted by at least eighteen jurists, from Barthélemy de Chasseneux (whose Latin commentary appeared in 1517 and was reprinted at least twenty times before the end of the seventeenth century) down to Jean Bouhier, president of the parlement of Burgundy (whose French commentary was published for the last time between 1787 and 1789). To complicate this scholastic and humanistic tradition further, Bouhier wrote a "history of the commentators on the custom of Burgundy," in which he upheld the Roman provenance and "spirit" of French customs against the rival "party" of customary law—and indeed the authority of Roman law as "common law" (*droit commun*) in Burgundy.[67]

In general the Burgundian custom was not only accommodated to civilian and canonist tradition but it was overlaid with scholastic apparatus, classical adornments, historical scholarship, comparisons with civil law and other customs, rational analysis according to the "enlightened" norms of modern natural law, and the debates over the proper way to unify French law. It was interpreted in terms of what might be regarded as rudimentary "rules of sociological method"—considerations of geography, the culture and "humors" of the people, historical tradition, social structure, and other aspects of "local knowledge" essential to the legal science of the old regime. In these and other ways the Burgundian custom enjoyed an extraordinary intellectual odyssey, especially under the leadership of the jurists, before disappearing, along with the other provincial customs, in the revolutionary maelstrom which took legal form on the famous night of 4 August—only to emerge again in the antiquarian labors of modern French scholars.

Custom and Codification

In Bouhier's time the major issue of the legal tradition was that of legal unification, or codification; and judicial opinion was sharply divided between two "parties"—that of Roman law, defended by Bouhier, and that of customary law, based on the Franco-Germanic interpretations of Parisian commentators and historians, who dreamed of a law "peculiar to the French nation" (*peculier à la Nation françoise*).[68] The division is illustrated by the old anecdote, told by Coquille in the sixteenth century and repeated later by Bouhier, about the controversy between the "two great personnages of that time, who were successively presidents of the Parlement of Paris."[69] The first, "Pierre Lizet held that Roman law was our common law [*droit commun*] and accommodated to it as best he could our French law, which he thought invalid when contrary to Roman law." Contradicting this view, Christofle de Thou regarded French customs and laws as "our common law." This cultural dialectic was highlighted also by the competing reputations of the two greatest scholars of the day, the Romanizing Jacques Cujas and the Germanizing Charles Dumoulin.

The division between Germanists and Romanists continued into the eighteenth century and was duly noted by Montesquieu. Among the Germanic peoples, he wrote, everyone was "tried by the established customs of his own nation"; and the feudist tradition retained this principle of personality.[70] On the other hand, the foreign doctrines of Roman law were received only as "written reason" (*ratio scripta; raison écrite*)—and had no other claim to authority.

The idea of a racially pure French custom (*consuetudo Franciae* or *con-*

suetudo gallicana), applying at least to the territory between the Loire and the Rhine and distinguished both from Roman law and from the *coutumes* of other provinces, can be traced back to the thirteenth century; and by the sixteenth century it was firmly established in professional tradition.[71] In de Thou's time the best expression of the ideal of a national custom was that of the great feudist Charles Dumoulin, who commented on all of the French *coutumes* as well as the *stilus* of the parlement of Paris and monuments of French law. Dumoulin rejected the authority of Roman law in favor of the native feudal law of France; and indeed it was his program, which he expressed as "the concord and union of the customs of France," that in effect served as the theoretical basis for the reformation of French customs led by Dumoulin's colleague de Thou.[72] For Dumoulin the *coutume* of Paris was dominant in France (*caput huius regni etiam Gallicae et Belgicae consuetudines*), and this thesis was defended by many of his followers down to the Revolution—and, indeed, in legal as well as scholarly terms, long afterwards. In the next generation, Louis Le Caron, himself a commentator on the Parisian custom as well as an editor of the *Grand Coustumier de France,* celebrated a generalized "French law" (*Droit françois*) based on the custom of Paris.[73] So, a century later, did Dumoulin's disciple and biographer Julien Brodeau, who argued that Paris was not only "the ordinary residence of the kings and their court" but also "the center of the state" (*le centre de l'Estat*).[74] And a century after that François Bourjon was celebrating the "common law" of France as "the exact explication of [Parisian] custom."[75]

The scholarly investigation of French legal tradition, beginning especially with Dumoulin, reinforced this royalist thesis through imaginative as well as historical reconstruction. In his *Institutes coustumières* Antoine Loisel sought the heritage of native French law and folk wisdom in a variety of medieval sources, literary and proverbial as well as legal; and his work, like Dumoulin's, had a considerable following (Fig. 4.3).[76] One successor was François de Launay, whose commentary on Loisel's work emphasized the extreme antiquity of this heritage. "Charlemagne himself did not distinguish laws from customs," Launay wrote; and, further, "It is certain that the ancient custom of which we hear in the capitularies was a general rule for the whole kingdom, a law universally observed in all of France."[77] In the eighteenth century Pierre Groseley went on to claim that French customs could be traced back "to the ancient inhabitants of Frankish Gaul."[78]

What these juridico-historical scholars were seeking was nothing less

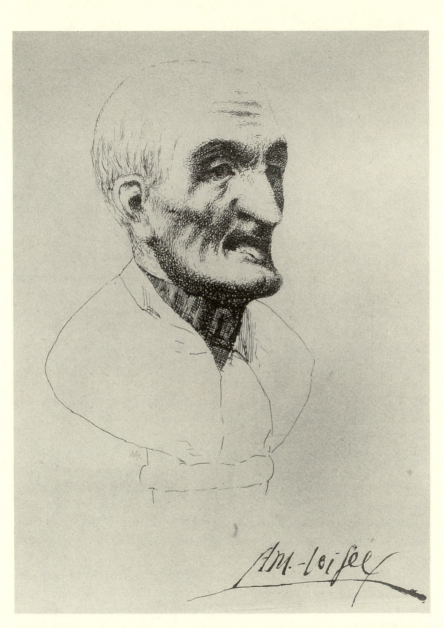

Figure 4.3. Antoine Loisel (1536–1617), from a wax bust. Source: Ernest Charvet, *Les dernières années d'Antoine Loisel* (Beauvais, 1880). Courtesy of Princeton University Library.

than the "common law" or "spirit of the law" of France—an imaginative legal fiction akin to the "immemorial custom" imagined by Edward Coke. In civil law the "spirit" of law (*mens legum, esprit des lois*) referred to its true meaning or its "reason" (*ratio legis*); and so jurists like Domat and Montesquieu employed the phrase. Groseley, a friend of Montesquieu, was careful to distinguish his researches into the "spirit" of French law (*l'esprit particulier de nostre Droit coutumier actuel* was his phrase) from the project of his more distinguished colleague. For Groseley the "spirit" of the law resided not in nature in the sense of universal reason but rather in the "second nature" of the French people—in Challine's words, "the general spirit of all the customs of France" (*l'esprit général de toutes les Coutumes de France*).[79] According to Claude de Ferrière, writing in the later seventeenth century, French custom "was formed by nature and reason" and it was generally opposed to the abstract "reason" supposedly possessed by Roman law. "People are most naturally inclined to follow what conforms most closely with their state and their manners and what concerns their common interest," he continued; and further, "the common inclinations of peoples come from the diversity of social orders and environments and may be called 'civil reason' [*la raison civile*], which is the foundation of customs and laws."[80]

Just a few years before the Revolution, P. G. Michaux celebrated custom as a reflection of the ancient state of things—"social laws" (*loix sociales,* or *loix fondamentales*) as distinguished from the "political" and "administrative" creations of Roman law and modern legislators. "Customs were not the work of the French monarchy and . . . not the work of the Roman domination," Michaux argued. On the contrary, "customs are the true monuments of the nations of Europe . . . and the creation of these nations as a body" (*le propre ouvrage de ces nations en corps*). As for the French people, he concluded, "We emerged into a social and political order . . . not as imagined by Pufendorf and other [social-contract] theorists but rather as revealed in our customs."[81] One can hardly imagine a less fashionable position to take in 1783.

Natural Law

It was over the life cycle of a legal genre—the texts and critical commentaries on *droit coutumier*—that the modern idea of custom took its form and content. There was, however, another school of legal thought and practice which gave further definition to the old regime conception of custom (and further impetus to the codification movement, which was aimed in effect at superseding custom). What Gierke called the "antique-modern" doctrines of natural law revived the old distinction between "primary" and "secondary natural law," and, of course, it was to this second, derivative class that custom was consigned.

"There are two kinds of law used in all nations of the world," wrote Jean Domat in the later seventeenth century. "One is natural law and the other the laws proper to each nation, such as customs authorized by long usage." [82] Thus Domat paraphrased and "naturalized" the famous observation of Gaius, that "all peoples observe in part their own special law and in part a law common to all men"; and he accommodated not only a universal law based on reason but also a localized custom based in effect on the accidents of history and on human will. As God created nature or indeed was Himself nature (*Deus, id est Natura* was the medieval formula)—so man created a "second nature," which was custom.

Natural law of course dominated the social thought of the Enlightenment, especially that of "jusnaturalists" like Leibniz, Pufendorf, and Domat, who hoped to bring reason and "natural order" to the wilderness of European customs. One of Domat's contemporaries, Louis Boullenois, had gone so far as to propose a sort of Cartesian jurisprudence that would dispense with conventional scholarship and practical judgment and, in his words, deliver itself over to "meditation." [83] In practice this meant isolating and ordering the economic interests of men in a rational way that amounted to the juridical equivalent of Physiocracy. By thus joining the "passions and the interests"—in effect, by isolating and ordering the economic nature of men—Boullenois hoped "to lead French customs to unanimity" and so "to reduce a great kingdom to the same law."

The same impulse to rationalism can be seen in practical jurisprudence. French jurists like François Bourjon and Pierre de Merville tried to reduce the customs of Paris, Normandy, and others to natural "principles" or "maxims"; and P. C. L. Gin, following Domat, published a "reasoned analysis" of French law by comparing Roman law with the *coutume* of Paris (a work which, from the first edition of 1782, evolved directly and with little change of substance into his commentary on the Napoleonic Code in 1803). [84] Montesquieu made his own contribution by piecing together a "theory of feudal laws" and disengaging the tradition of customary law from the errors of Romanist interpretation. [85]

French custom itself also tended to incorporate notions which legal theorists attributed, belatedly, to "jusnaturalism." Principles of self-defense (the formula *vi vim repellere*) and especially the "natural liberty" of men were not discoveries of modern philosophy but rather part of the legacy of customary law as the "common law of France," which also had access to principles of natural law. As Nicolas Bohier had written of the *coutumier* of Bourges, for example, "This custom shows by natural law that all men are born free."[86] And as François Bourjon wrote over two centuries later, the principle that "every person is free if there is no contrary law or judgment" is part of the "common law of France and the custom of Paris."[87]

The French Revolution was a paradigmatic battleground for the clash between the ideals of natural law and the inertial forces of custom—which by then seemed not an expression but the very antithesis of the *Volonté Générale*. On the question of codification in particular, philosophes, Jacobins, and Bonapartists seemed united in their common devotion to natural law, to legislative solutions for social problems, and to the idea that pure reason would prevail. "Do you want new laws?" Voltaire had asked: "Burn yours and make new ones." Such indeed was the apparent result of the Revolution. The major target of the provincial uprisings of July 1789, beyond the chateaux and feudal titles, was "custom" and all that it stood for. Subsequent revolutionary legislation put an end not only to the feudal and corporate society of the old regime (as well as many of its written records) but also to the provincial customs accumulated over the centuries. In the spirit of the provincial *cahiers* and the extraordinary "sacrifices" made by the French nobility on the famous night of 4 August, the National Assembly "entirely destroyed the feudal regime" (the *complexum feudale* is the phrase of Dumoulin quoted in the assembly sessions of 4 September) and with it the accumulated customs, local and general, of many centuries.[88]

The next step was a "new judicial order," and one of the first items on the agenda was the construction of a code, although this was accomplished only after a decade of war, political extremism, social upheaval, and the legal confusion of *le droit intermédiaire*. As J. J. R. Cambacérès declared in his first "project" of 1793, the aims were first to destroy existing laws and customs and then, by a "perfect legislation," "to establish forever the empire of liberty and the destiny of France."[89] In the preliminary discussions of the code, which were the modern and authoritarian counterpart to the *procès-verbaux* of the old customs, the citizen redactors (and sometimes the first consul himself) denounced the old customs, paradoxically, as derogations from the national will. Still more dangerous was the attendant notion of judicial "interpretation," warned one of the Bonapartist redactors, for this old form of corruption represented a loophole through which all the abuses of the old regime would return.[90]

These fears were not imaginary, for in fact much of the substance of the Civil Code was drawn from old regime customs, especially that of Paris, and the attendant jurisprudence. The institution of private property itself, though theoretically following the "absolute" definition drawn from civil law, was in fact based on the old customary distinction, preserved in the Burgundian as well as Parisian *coutume,* between feudal and usufructuary domain (*domaine direct* and *domaine utile*).[91] Not surprisingly, since the "Committee on Feudalism" was headed by Merlin de Douai, a distinguished jurist and editor of a massive *Répertoire de jurisprudence* appearing almost continuously between 1784 and 1830. Conservative attitudes also infected the Committee of Redaction, on which Cambacérès was opposed by J. E. M. Portalis, who celebrated custom as "the wisdom of our fathers which formed our national character" (*la sagesse de nos pères, qui ont formé le caractère national*), and he did not scruple to cite Dumoulin and other feudists in this connection. Regarding the Civil Code as a "bridge between the old and the new law," Portalis argued that "we should preserve what we do not have to destroy."[92]

Moreover, if the Revolution aroused the codifiers, it also awakened the People, who were the source of custom and law and who, infused with a new "bourgeois" spirit, continued themselves in their actions to "interpret"—to modify, extend, and abrogate—the legislation which Jacobins and Bonapartists had imposed on the French nation. They continued, that is to say, to produce their own customs according to changing needs and pressures; and as always the jurists followed—when they did not guide—this new spirit by producing a corresponding jurisprudence and social philosophy and by contributing to what Philippe Sagnac called a "return to custom."[93]

Over succeeding generations the highly abstract law assembled in the Napoleonic Code was in many ways applied and interpreted in the light of customary law and the habits and mentality of the old legal profession (which Napoleon was shortly to restore). During the restoration the credit of the idea of custom—and the idea that "custom is the best interpreter of law"—continued to rise. In the interpretations of conservative jurists, in the theories of the Historical School of Law, and in Romantic historiography, the canon of customary law was given new life, along with many of its premises, prejudices, and (in some cases) political inclinations. In short, like Talleyrand, French customs also "survived"; they survived through social habits and persisting mentalities as well as judicial decisions and legal and historical reconstructions.[94]

Custom and Social Science

The idea of custom was present at the birth of modern social science, first as a threat and then as a central problem in the understanding of social structure and change. "Social science" was associated in particular with the great enterprise of codification designed to complete Napoleon's neo-Roman imperial edifice. The fashionable term "Science sociale" was used precisely in this connection not only by latter-day philosophes and Ideologues, whom Napoleon despised, but also by the redactors of his code. In a *Discours sur la science sociale* delivered at the Institut National in 1798, Cambacérès had celebrated legislation, political economy, and moral philosophy, and their common goal, which was nothing less than the "perfecting of social relations" and the fulfilling of "civilization."[95] In effect French "social science" arose as an expression of a kind of internal imperialism in which customs would be subjected to the Bonapartist effort of social engineering.

In another discourse presented to the institute at this time, A. L. Jussieu was even more specific about the connections between *la science sociale* and the understanding of customs and laws.[96] "Social science studies the various colonies emerging from the Roman Republic," Jussieu declared;

it examines elsewhere the customary laws and codes of the ancients, the laws favoring marriage, the perhaps too limited rights of mothers over children, the negotiations of the Athenian people to form and especially to abolish their laws; and it always seeks lessons for this generation in the experience of earlier centuries. It concentrates especially on the early period of the French monarchy; it reflects on national sovereignty, the liberty of suffrages and individual liberty, on moral elements, the nature and effects of public opinion, on the way to shape public spirit and to determine the level of prosperity of modern peoples.

The fundamental problem of this new conception of social science was first and best expressed in the exchanges between Cambacérès and Portalis—reflecting and often invoking the spirits of Rousseau and Montesquieu, respectively. Portalis rejected Cambacérès's plan to "perfect everything" and to "foresee everything." "How can one control the action of time?" asked Portalis.[97] "How oppose the course of events or the imperceptible force of manners? How know and calculate what experience alone can reveal to us?" In the context of the new "social science," in other words, the old contest between custom and law, debated so often by the doctors of law, was once more recapitulated, this time in connection with the methodology of modern social science.

This was the issue taken up in a more scholarly fashion by another post-revolutionary product, the Historical School of Law, which had branches in France as well as Germany. Savigny, the leading figure of this school, took the French debates over the Code Napoléon as the point of departure and the principal source of documentation for his famous manifesto "On the Vocation of this Age for Legislation and Jurisprudence."[98] To the notion of a perfect society created by modern legislation, the Historical School opposed the model of customary law, along with its natural accumulation of jurisprudence. The old notion that custom reflects the spirit of the people was revived by Romantic scholars—Herder's and Savigny's *Volksgeist* being the equivalent of Bartolus's *mens populi* and the feudists' *esprit du droit coutumier*, the "spirit of a people" as determined by learned jurists. For Savigny, custom was scientific not through its efforts of legislation but rather through its understanding of the continuing force of custom—"first," in Savigny's words, "as part of the aggregate experience of a community, and second [as] a distinct branch of knowledge in the hands of the jurists." For Savigny, too, "custom" located the battle between the legislative and judicial forces—and the local knowledge essential to the understanding of custom was the mark of the scientific expert.

The Philosophical School of Law, deriving its strength from Hegel, engaged Savigny's Historical School in mortal combat; but despite methodological differences, there was remarkable agreement about the source, if not the role, of custom: it was the product of nature and of human "spirit" and will. "The basis of right is, in general, mind [*das Geistige*]," declared Hegel; "its precise place and point of origin in the will [*der Wille*]. The will is free, so that freedom is both the substance of right and its goal, while the system of right [*Rechtssystem*, that is, system of law] is the realm of freedom made actual, the world of mind [*Geist*] brought forth out of itself like a second nature [*eine zweite Natur*]."[99] Characteristically (though at the same time quite in keeping with the old legal tradition), Hegel reconciled primary and secondary nature by historicizing them.

The founding fathers of modern social science, especially anthropology and sociology, carried on the assumptions and attitudes developed by the old jurisprudence and its epigones in the Historical and Philosophical schools. The exception was France, where Comte's positivist model of "Sociology" superseded Savigny's and Hegel's small followings. In England the key figure was Henry Sumner Maine, who took comparative jurisprudence as the high road to social understanding. In legal terms his work was hardly as influential as that of the arch-codifier Bentham or John Austin, whose *bête noire* was the idea of popular custom (which he dismissed as "only a moral rule until enforced by the tribunals"); but then law and social science long remained estranged in England.[100] In Germany Ferdinand Tönnies—reacting to the naturalist approach of Hobbes—proclaimed custom to be the most direct expression of the *Volksgeist*. "Custom is social will itself," he wrote "distilled from habit, usage, and practice."[101] And in support of his position he summed up the view of Savigny, that "law grows in a manner which common usage terms customary law [*Gewohnheitsrecht*], that is to say, it originates in customs and popular beliefs first, in jurisprudence next; everywhere, then, by forces quietly doing their work, and nowhere by the arbitrary fiat of a legislator."

When Albion Small, one of the founders of sociology in the United States, wrote the history of his discipline, he too found it necessary to take as his point of departure the debate over custom and codification which Savigny had publicized a century before. Small was quite aware of the contributions of legal science to social science, and in particular to the ethnographic and anthropological conceptions of "custom" and the collective behavior of so-called primitive peoples in general.[102] In this transmuted, modernized form, "custom" retained many of its former traits, including its popular character, its cultural specificity and historicity, and its estrangement from nature. "Custom," according to the *Encyclopedia of the Social Sciences,* applies "to the totality of behavior patterns which are carried by tradition and lodged in the group. It is not properly applicable to those aspects of communal activity which are obviously determined by biological considerations."[103]

In this entry Edward Sapir recognized, at least in a general way, the heritage of the term "custom" as "a common sense concept which has served as the matrix for the development of the more refined and technical and anthropological concept of culture." In the new, ostentatiously more "scientific" *International Encyclopedia of the Social Sciences,* this article has been replaced by one on "norms" (which, with unconscious irony and historical innocence, remarks that the old *Encyclopedia* "did not even mention the term 'norms.'"[104] Here the question of origins is posed, but in purely abstract, behavioralist, causal, and explanatory terms; and while custom is acknowledged "tacitly to be supported by social approval," in general the term (and by implication the older literature on the subject) has been consigned to the antiquarian, and so presumably irrelevant, stages of social science. And no doubt the old questions posed by Portalis, Savigny, and indeed Albion Small (who was virtually disowned by his successors in the Chicago school) have been deposited in the same dust bin by the new— legislative as well as "scientific"—experts.

Custom in Perspective

This is only a part of the story of "custom," for as I have suggested there are also literary, psychological, religious, and especially philosophical dimensions that invite exploration. By definition, of course, "custom" fell short of perfection. In the early modern period it was denounced by religious doctrinaires like Luther and Calvin, for whom it was a "public pestilence." More secular-minded persons, however, tried to come to terms with the idea of custom and even, like Montaigne, came to identify it, in effect, with the human condition. "After at first rejecting custom," Jean Starobinski has concluded, "Montaigne for want of anything better ultimately reconciled himself to it: since the present is the only place in which men can dwell, it is unwise to shake its foundation." [105] For Montaigne custom was indeed second nature (*l'accoutumance est une seconde Nature*) and, in his rendering of Pindar, "empress and queen of the world"—"another powerful and imperious mistress," as Pierre Charron put it, or in the words of Bacon, "the principal magistrate of man's life." [106]

Renaissance moral thought, drawing on classical and Christian sources, displayed a striking ambivalence toward the idea of custom. Though born in nature, custom went its own way and became the most oppressive of tyrants. "Who would believe how great and imperious is the authority of custom?" Charron asked. "Those who call it another nature have not gone far enough, for it does more than this; it struggles against nature." [107] For Montaigne's friend and soul mate Etienne de la Boétie, it was custom above all that subjugated man to tradition and undermined his natural freedom. "Custom," he concluded, "is the first cause of voluntary servitude" (*la premiere raison de la servitude volontaire, c'est la coustume*).[108] Pascal, beset by religious anxieties as well as concern for the human condition, carried the argument another step. Custom is not only second nature, he concluded, but a "second nature that destroys the former"; and "as custom is a second nature, so nature itself is only a first custom."[109] This humanizing critique of philosophy was brought to its logical and epistemological extreme by Hume, for whom "custom" replaced the imputation of natural "causes" through reason, whose natural sovereignty he came, on the most conventional grounds, to reject. "Custom then," he concluded, alluding again to the Pindarean formula, "is the great guide of human life"—and, indeed, by extension, of philosophy.[110]

But the efforts of philosophers, rhetoricians, and jurists have not succeeded in preserving the conceptual status of the idea of custom. From the seventeenth century custom was more thoroughly eclipsed than ever by nature, and the science thereof; and political considerations contributed further to its decline. For custom was undeniably fashioned at least as much by social experience as by the discourse of the learned, as much by the moved and the shaken as by the movers and the shakers.

"Custom," then, the concept as well as the term, seems to have returned to its hiding places in ordinary language, and it is for the most part left to historians to reconstruct its extraordinary adventures as companion and rival of primary nature. Following the fortunes of "second nature" gives us access to various levels of Western historical experience. It leads us, for example, into the prehistorical and metahistorical labyrinth of Western languages, into the technical recesses of the Western legal tradition, into the little explored area of preliterate culture, into the upper layers of social history and the lower reaches of political theory, into the transcultural career of an enduring intellectual and professional canon, into the ideological context of revolutionary action and counterrevolutionary reaction, and into the prehistory of the modern sciences of society, culture, and politics. It also reminds us that these disciplines, as well as the study of history broadly conceived, have a richer heritage than the prevalence of "scientific" styles of research and rhetoric might suggest; but I leave the moral of this story for another occasion.

Notes

1. Azo, *In Ius civile summa* (Lyon, 1564), 233 v: "Dicitur consuetudo, quasi communis assuetudo: et alias dicitur consuetudo, et in alia significatione, altera natura," one of many statements of this conventional view. Cf. Walter Ullmann, *The Medieval Idea of Law as Represented by Lucas de Penna* (London, 1946), 62; also, more generally, Hans Kelsen, *Society and Nature* (Chicago, 1943).

2. The exception is Gerhardt Funke, *Gewohnheit* (Bonn, 1958), and his entry

in the *Geschichtliche Grundbegriffe,* ed. O. Brunner et al. (Stuttgart, 1972–); also *Historisches Wörterbuch der Philosophie,* although these treat the psychological rather than the social aspect of custom (i.e., "habit").

3. Charles H. Kahn, *The Art and Thought of Heraclitus: An Edition of the Fragments with Translation and Commentary* (Cambridge, 1979), 260–61, 335, on fragment #119, "character is fate" (*ethos anthropoi daimon*).

4. See, e.g., W. K. C. Guthrie, *A History of Greek Philosophy,* III (Cambridge, 1969), 55ff.; Felix Heinemann, *Nomos und Physis* (Basel, 1945); Martin Ostwald, *Nomos and the Beginnings of Athenian Democracy* (Oxford, 1969); Clarence J. Glocken, *Traces on the Rhodian Shore: Nature and Culture in Western Thought from Ancient Times to the End of the Eighteenth Century* (Berkeley, 1967), 116.

5. *On the Soul,* tr. W. S. Hett (Cambridge, Mass., 1975), "On Memory and Recollection," 304; cf. Richard Sorabji, *Aristotle on Memory* (London, 1972), 56. Though dealing with psychology, these classical texts were also extended to "custom" in a social and collective sense.

6. *Rhetoric,* tr. J. Freese (Cambridge, Mass., 1967), 1370a5.

7. I refrain from reproducing all the references, but besides modern dictionaries, see H. Estienne, *Thesaurus linguae graecae* and *Thesaurus linguae latinae; Suidae lexicon;* Thomas Cooper, *Thesaurus linguae Romanae et Britannicae;* Du-Cange; and lexicons of jurisprudence (e.g., Calvinus, Ragueau) and of philosophy (Chauvin).

8. For example, Cicero, *De Finibus,* V, 74; Quintilian, *Inst. orat.,* I, 1. Also cf. Varro, *De Lingua latina,* VIII, 27; Aulus Gellius, *Noctes atticae* XII, 13, 29; and Sextus Empiricus, *Outlines of Pyrrhonism,* I, 146, tr. in J. Annas and J. Barnes, *The Modes of Skepticism* (Cambridge, 1985).

9. *In eundem Poggium libellus primus,* "Praefatio," in *Opera omnia,* ed. E. Garin (Turin, 1962), I, 386. See Lawrence Manley, *Convention 1500–1750* (Cambridge, Mass., 1980), 90ff.; Salvatore Camporeale, *Lorenzo Valla. Umanesimo e teologia* (Florence, 1972); Sarah Stever Gravelle, "The Latin-Vernacular Question and Humanism: Theory of Language and Culture," *Journal of the History of Ideas* 49 (1988), 367–86.

10. Pindar, *Nemean Odes,* IV, 10; Herodotus, *History,* VII, 104; and see Marcello Gigante, *NOMOS BASILEUS* (Naples, 1956).

11. Augustine, *Contra Julianum Pelagium* (*Patrologia Latina,* XLIV, 816), and *Doctrina christiana,* II, 19–27; Jerome, *Epistolae,* XCVIII, 3; Clement, *Exhortation to the Greeks,* x; Thomas, *Summa Theologiae,* Ia, 63, 5; II, i, Q. 95–97. On "second" and other grades of natural law in theologians as well as jurists, see Reginaldo Pizzorini, *Il Diritto naturale dalle origini a S. Tommaso d'Aquino* (Rome, 1978), 203.

12. *Epistolae,* lxxiv (Gratian, *Decretum* I, D. VIII, ii, c. 5); also Tertullian, *De Virginibus celandis,* c. 1; and cf. Gerhard Ladner, *The Idea of Reform* (Cambridge, Mass., 1959), 137.

13. *Etymologiae,* V, 2, cited by Gratian, *Decretum,* I, d. 1. In general, Hostiensis, *In primum librum Decretalium commentaria,* 1, "Quid est consuetudo. . . . Usus rationabilis competente tempore confirmatus"; Rufinus, *Summa Decretalium,* D. 1, "Mores autem isti partim sunt redacti in scriptis et vocantur ius constitutum; partim absque scripto utentium placito reservantur, et dicitur simpliciter consuetudo."

See also *Corpus juris canonici, per regulas naturali ordine digestas* (Cologne, 1738), I, 79ff., offering twelve definitions of *consuetudo;* René Wehrle, *De la Coutume dans le droit canonique* (Paris, 1928), 40ff.; and the article in *Dictionnaire du droit canonique*.

14. The best guide to the massive literature on the European legal tradition is Helmut Coing, ed., *Handbuch der Quellen und Literatur der neueren europäischen Privatrechtsgeschichte* (Munich, 1976–); also, the recent surveys (especially Franz Wieacker and Adriano Cavanna); and cf. my various essays in *History, Law and the Human Sciences* (London, 1984). A recent book of major importance is L. Waelkens, *La Théorie de la coutume chez Jacques de Révigny* (Leiden, 1984), with edition of various manuscript texts.

15. Digest, I, 1, 6 (Ulpianus), "Hoc igitur ius [civile] nostrum constat aut ex scripto aut sine scripto, ut apud Graecos: *ton nomon oi men eggraphoi oi de agraphoi*"; and I, 3, 32.2 (Julianus), "Inveterata consuetudo pro lege non immerito custoditur, et hoc est ius quod dicitur moribus constitutum." On customary law in general see Siegfried Brie, *Die Lehre vom Gewohnheitsrecht* (Breslau, 1899), Francesco Calasso, *Medio evo del diritto,* I (Milan, 1954), Auguste Lebrun, *La Coutume* (Paris, 1932), Eugen Ehrlich, *Fundamental Principles of the Sociology of Law,* tr. W. Moll (Cambridge, Mass., 1936), 436ff., Filippo Gallo, *Interpretazione e formazione consuetudinaria del diritto* (Turin, 1971); Paul Ourliac, *Etudes d'histoire du droit médiéval* (Paris, 1979), I; and R. W. and A. J. Carlyle, *A History of Medieval Political Thought in the West* (New York, 1903–36), II, 50–67; III, 41–51; IV, 45–50; VI, 17–25, 150–53.

16. Digest, I, 3, 35 (Hermogenianus), "et ea, quae longa consuetudine comprobata si per annos plurimos observata, velut tacita conventio non minus quam ea quae scripta sui servantur"; Code, VIII, 52 ("Quae sit longa consuetudo"), 2, "Consuetudinis ususque longaevi non vilis auctoritas est, verum non usque adeo sui valitura momento, ut aut rationem vincat aut legem"; and in general Burkhard Schmiedel, *Consuetudo im klassischen und nachklassischen römischen Recht* (Graz, 1966).

17. Bracton, I, 1, 2, "Cum autem fere in omnibus regionibus utatur legibus et iure scripto sola Anglia usa est in suis finibus iure non scripto et consuetudine. In ea quidem ex non scripto venit, quod usus comprobavit." Fortescue, *De Laudibus Legum Anglie,* ed. S. B. Chrimes (Cambridge, 1949), 5. I omit here the various "customs" produced by guilds and monastic communities.

18. See, e.g., François Connan, *Commentariorum juris civilis libri X* (Paris, 1553), fol. 18v, and Hugues Doneau, *Opera omnia* (Lucca, 1762), I, 48; cf. Ennio Cortese, *La Norma giuridica* (Milan, 1962–64), I, 55–56, and Gierke, *Natural Law and the Theory of Society, 1500–1800,* tr. Ernest Barker (Cambridge, 1934), 38, with many later references; also the critical discussion in Samuel Rachel, *Dissertations on the Law of Nature and of Nations* [1676], tr. J. P. Bate (Washington, 1916), 23.

19. Pierre de Fontaines, *Le Conseil à un ami,* ed. A. J. Marnier (Paris, 1846), 492.

20. *Histoire de la campagne française* (Paris, 1932), 20; also Kassius Hallinger, "Consuetudo, Begriff, Formen, Forschungsgeschichte, Inhalt," *Untersuchungen zu Kloster und Schrift,* ed. Max Planck Institut für Geschichte (Göttingen, 1980), 140–66; *Revue historique du droit français et étranger* [hereafter *RHDFE*] 65 (1987); and *Droit: Revue française de théorie juridique* 3 (1986), various articles.

21. See, e.g., Isambert et al., eds., *Recueil général des anciennes lois françaises*, IX (Tours, 1458), 390, confirming the Norman custom. Cf. the essential work of François Olivier-Martin, *Histoire de la Coutume de la Prévôté et Vicomté de Paris* (Paris, 1922), I, 25ff.; Robert Besmier, *La Coutume de Normandie* (Paris, 1935); Olivier Guillot, "Consuetudines, Consuetudo: Quelques remarques sur l'apparition de certains termes dans les sources françaises des premiers temps capétiens (à l'exception du Midi)," *Mémoires de la Société pour l'histoire du droit et des institutions des anciens pays bourguignons, comtois et romands* [hereafter *MSHDB*], XL (1983), 21–48; K. J. Hollyman, *Le Développement du vocabulaire féodal en France pendant le haut moyen age* (Paris, 1957), and Robert Latouche, *The Birth of Western Economy*, tr. E. Wilkinson (New York, 1961). Cf. René de la Bigotière, *Commentaires sur la Coutume de Bretagne* (2d ed.; Rennes, 1702), "avertissement."

22. Roland Mousnier, *Fureurs paysannes* (Paris, 1967), 71.

23. *Dissensiones Dominorum sive Controversiae veterum iuris romani interpretum qui glossatores vocantur*, ed. G. Haenel (Leipzig, 1834), 151–52 (#46); cf. John P. Dawson, *The Oracles of the Law* (Ann Arbor, 1968), 129–30. For a later summary, see Pietro Tommasi (+1508), *De Consuetudine*, in *Tractatus Universi Juris* (Venice, 1584), fols. 381r–90v.

24. Accursius, Gloss ad D. I, 3, 32, "Consuetudo vincit legem, sicut una lex vincit aliam"; and Baldus, *In primam veteris [Digesti] partem Commentarius* (Orléans, 1574), fols. 20r and 21r. The locus classicus is *Digest*, I, 3, 33 (Ulpian), "Diuturna consuetudo pro iure et lege in his qui non ex scripto descendunt observari solet." Cf. Odofredus, *Lectura super Digesto veteri* (Lyon, 1550), fol. 14v, "Consuetudo inveterata servatur pro lege, nam consuetudo est jus non scriptum"; *Lex Salica*, prologue; *Leges Visigothorum*, V, xii, and virtually the same wording in a capitulary of Charlemagne (cited by Calasso, *Medio Evo*, 196), "Longa consuetudo, quae utilitatibus publicis non impedit, pro lege servabitur [servetur]"; and *Petri Exceptiones*, iv, 3, "Et enim, ut in Digestis loquitur, longi temporis usu approbata, non habet minorem authoritaten quam lex scripta." François Connan, *Commentarii*, fol. 40v, "Inveterata enim consuetudo pro lege non immerito observatur"; and Pierre d'Angleberme, *Commentarius in Aurelianas consuetudines* (Paris, 1517 [1509]), fol. clxxxvi, "Hoc ius *agraphon* Graeci vocant, id est non scriptum, quas patrias leges (inquit Plato) cognomento vocitant. Sunt enim diuturni mores utentium animis comprobati, et pro legibus observati."

25. *Commentarii*, fol. 17v; also *Super Digesto veteri* (n.p., 1535), fol. 21r (ad D. I, 3, 32), "consuetudinis sunt quattuor cause, [viz.] naturalis, ut frequens factum sive actus, formalis ut consensus, efficiens ut tempus, finalis ut ratio, ut utilitas consuetudinis"; and see now Joseph Canning, *The Political Thought of Baldus de Ubaldis* (Cambridge, 1987). Cf. Jean Coras, *In titulum Pandectarum de Iustitia et Iure* (Lyon, 1568), 247; and Andrea de Isernia, *In Usus feudorum commentaria* (Frankfurt, 1598), 4; A. London Fell, *Origins of Legislative Sovereignty and the Legislative State* (1984—), on Coras and the "four causes"; and cf. Hermann Kantorowicz, *Studies in the Glossators of the Roman Law* (Cambridge, 1938), 37.

26. Jeremy Duquesnay Adams, *The Populus of Augustine and Jerome* (New Haven, 1971); and cf. George Boas, *Vox Populi* (Baltimore, 1969). A. Esmein, "Decem faciunt populum," *Mélanges P. F. Girard* (Paris, 1913), I, 457–73, citing, among other sources, the *coutumes* of Brittany, Bourges, and Nivernais.

27. Antoine Favre, *Jurisprudentiae Papinianae Scientiae* (Lyon, 1667), 12, "ex facto enim, ut vulgo aiunt, ius oritur" (Code II, 4, 15), and Ulrich Zasius, *Operum omnium* (Lyon, 1550), IV, col. 16, and III, col. 101; and see Luigi Prosdocimi, "Ex facto ius oritur," *Studi senesi*, LXVI–VII (1954–55), 808–19, and Cortese, *La Norma giuridica*, II, 150.

28. Baldus, *Commentaria*, fol. 20r, and cf. Bartolus, *Omnia opera* (Venice, 1590), col. 18r, "Dicit Pet. usus et mores sonant factum, ex quo descendunt con-suetudo. . . . Consuetudo quando declaret legem, quando illam corroborat, quando illam imitatur, quando tollit, et quando per legem tollatur." And see Walter Ullmann, "Bartolus on Customary Law," *Jurisprudence in the Middle Ages* (London, 1980).

29. Odofredus, *Lectura super Codice* (Lyon, 1552), fol. 3r; cf. Connan, *Commentarii*, fol. 42r (see below, at n. 52), and François Le Douaren, *In primam partem Pandectarum . . . enarratio*, in *Opera omnia* (Lucca, 1765), I, 14, "quia non sufficit usus populi, nisi longus, et inveteratus sit."

30. *Traicté des lois abrogées et enusitées en toutes les cours du royaume* (Lyon, 1563). Cf. François Connan, *Commentarii*, fol. 42r, "Antiquitatur autem lex non solum quae nimia vetustate consenescit, sed et quae recens et nuper nata aut non observatur, aut sane non ad longum tempus."

31. Azo, *Summa* (Venice, 1561), col. 123; and *Somme rurale* (Paris, 1603), 5: "Coustume locale selon les anciens est un establissement tenu et gardé au pays et par les anciens sages à ce d'accord et enfermez estre et demeurer ainsi selon la situa-tion du lieu, où ce est fait tel: et par si long temps que a coustume prescrite et confermée peut et doit suffire."

32. Philippe de Beaumanoir, *Coutumes de Beauvaisis*, ed. A. Salmon (Paris, 1899), 3 ("C'est li prologues"); and cf. 5, "Et bien i pert a ce que les coustumes sont si diverses que l'en ne pourroit pas trouver ou roiaume de France deus chasteleries qui de tous cas usassent d'une meisme coustume."

33. Especially Jack Goody, *The Logic of Writing and the Organization of Society* (Cambridge, 1986), Brian Stock, *The Implications of Literacy, Written Language and Models of Interpretation in the Eleventh and Twelfth Centuries* (Princeton, 1983), and Jan Vansina, *Oral Tradition* (Chicago, 1965); and more specifically Th. Buhler-Reimann, "La Ritualisation comme moyen de maintenir vivante une coutume orale," *MSHDB* 49 (1983), 103–10, Louis Ligeron and Michel Petitjean, "La Cou-tume en rites: Quelques exemples de symbolisme juridique," *MSHDB* 40 (1983), 283–93, and Paul Guilhiermoz, "La Persistance du caractère oral dans la procédure civile française," *Nouvelle revue de droit française et étranger* 13 (1889), 21–65.

34. *The Interpreter, Digested into the Method of the Civil or Imperiall Institutions* (Cambridge, 1607). And cf. M. T. Clanchy, *From Memory to Written Record: En-gland 1066–1307* (London, 1979).

35. Beaumanoir, *Coutumes de Beauvaisis*, I, 346 (683): "Coustume si est ap-prouvee par l'une des .II. voies, dont l'une des voies si est quant ele est generaus par toute le contée et maintenue de si lonc tans comme il puet souvenir a homme sans debat. . . . Et l'autre voie que l'en doit connoistre et tenir pour coustume si est quant debas en a esté et l'une des parties se vout aidier de coustune et fu aprouvee par jugement si comme il est avenu mout de fois en parties d'oirs et en autres

quereles." In general see *La Preuve, Recueils de la Société Jean Bodin pour l'histoire comparative des institutions* (Brussels, 1963–65), esp. vol. II.

36. Clanchy, op. cit.; Ehrlich, *Fundamental Principles of the Sociology of Law,* tr. W. Moll (Cambridge, Mass., 1936); and cf. J. P. Dawson, *A History of Lay Judges* (Cambridge, Mass., 1960). The most authoritative source for feudal custom was the *Libri Feudorum;* on which E. M. Meijers, "Les glossateurs et le droit féodal," in *Etudes d'histoire du droit,* ed. R. Feenstra and H. Fischer (Leiden, 1956–66), III, 261–70, the still valuable work of Savigny's student E. A. Laspeyres, *Libri Feudorum* (Berlin, 1830), and D. R. Kelley "De Origine Feudorum: The Beginnings of a Historical Problem," in *History, Law, and the Human Sciences.* Many commentaries on the *Libri Feudorum* are collected in *Tractatus Universi Juris,* X (1).

37. Jacques d'Ableiges, *Le Grand Coutumier de France,* ed. Louis Le Caron (Paris, 1598), 102, "Coutume est un raisonable establissement non escript, nécessaire et profitable pour aucun humain besoign, et pour le commun profit, mis au pays, et par le peuple gardé et approuvé, notoirement par le cours de 40 ans"; and Bouteiller, *Somme rurale,* 6 (see above, n. 31); also *Las Siete Partidas,* ed. G. Lopez (Paris, 1851), 24, "costumbre es derecho o fuero que non es scripto, el qual han usado los homes, luengo tiempo, ayudandose del en las cosas et en razones sobre que lo usaron." And cf. Georges Duby, *The Three Orders: Feudal Society Imagined,* tr. A. Goldhammer (Chicago, 1980).

38. *Conference de la Coustume de Paris, avec les autres coustumes de France* (Paris, 1605), "Epitre."

39. Hippolyte Pissard, *Essai sur la connaissance et la preuve des coutumes* (Paris, 1910), Yvonne Bongert, *Recherches sur les cours laïques du Xe au XIIIe siècle* (Paris, 1949), Piero Craveri, *Ricerche sulla formazione del diritto consuetudinario in Francia (sec. XIII–XVI)* (Varesi, 1969); J. P. Dawson, *Oracles of the Law,* Henri Beaune, *Introduction à l'étude historique du Droit coutumier français* (Paris, 1880), and Henri Klimrath's pioneering *Travaux sur l'histoire du droit français,* ed. L. Warnkoenig (Paris, 1843).

40. Document (Echevinage de Rheims, 1253) cited by Aubépin, "De l'Influence de Dumoulin sur la législation française," *Revue critique de législation et de jurisprudence* 6 (1855), 77.

41. Coquille, *Commentaires sur les coustumes de Nivernois,* in *Les Oeuvres* (Paris, 1646), 2.

42. *Coutumes générales et locales . . . de Bourbonnais,* ed. M. A. des Pommiers (Paris, 1732), iii, "La Coutume étant un contrat et une convention publique, on est obligé de l'exécuter et observer, meme en conscience."

43. Heinrich Brunner, *Wort und Form im altfranzösischen Process* (Vienna, 1868), 661.

44. *Commentarius in Aurelianas [Orleans] consuetudines,* fol. clxxxvi v: "ut consuetudo in scripturam redigatur: potest redigi memoriae causa, non ut novum ius dicatur, nam scriptura non inventa est: sed ad probandum."

45. *French Rural History,* tr. J. Sondheimer (Berkeley, 1966), 46, 70, 59. "And so," Bloch concludes his learned but romantic essay, which strives to reach beyond written sources, "the past continues to dominate the present."

46. René Filhol, *Le Premier Président Christofle de Thou et la réformation des*

coutumes (Paris, 1937), 115, and J. P. Dawson, "The Codification of the French Customs," *Michigan Law Review* 38 (1940), 765–800.

47. Bibliothèque Nationale MS Fr. 5281, "Premier project de la nouvelle Coustume de Paris," fol. 1v; and cf. MS Fr. 5282, "Second project," and MS Fr. 5254, Marion's "Observations." In 1580 Marion was spokesman for the nobility, Antoine for the clergy, two lesser known lawyers for the third estate.

48. *Commentaires sur la Coustume d'Aniou* (Paris, 1662), 3.

49. *Procès-verbal,* published by Louis Le Caron, *Nouveaux commentaires sur la Coustume de . . . Paris* (Paris, 1613), 234r.

50. Isambert, IX, 253. In its legal development the idea of custom was distinguished from simple "usage," curial "style," and statutory forms. See Barthélemy de Chasseneux, *Consuetudines ducatus Burgundiae* (Frankfurt, 1574), col. 1–3, "Primo quaeritur, quid sit consuetudo. . . . Et dicitur consuetudo a con, quod est simul et suetudo usus: quasi communis usus. . . . Et differt consuetudo ab usu, stylo et statuto: nam ab usu differt tanquam causa, a suo effectu: quia consuetudo per usus inducitur: et usus proprie dicit factum, consuetudo ius. . . . A Stylo differt, quia stylus proprie dicitur circa illa quae tangunt modum ordinandi acta, et sententias et aliae quae scribuntur stylo quo scribitur. consensu introducitur: consuetudo vero tacito. . . . Sed tamen finaliter concludit, quod consuetudo potest esse scripta." Cf. Pissard, *Essai,* 167.

51. *De l'Esprit des Lois,* Bk. XXVII, ch. 45. Laurent Bouchel, *Les coustumes générales des bailliages de Senlis* (Paris, 1631), 1, "Coutume" is a "loy civile approuvée et reçue par les Estats du pais, sous l'authorité du Roy." Cf. Jean Viguier, commentary on *Les Coustumes du pais et duché d'Angoumois* (Paris, 1650), 2.

52. *Commentarii Iuris Civilis Libri X* (Paris, 1553), I, x (fol. 39v–44v, passim), fol. 41r, "Quae consuetudo tantum gerit naturae similitudinem, ut altera natura esse videatur, cum tamen non sit. Idcirco virtutes hae non vocantur naturales, sed morales, et voluntariae, quia non sint naturae, sed voluntatis, a qua nascuntur, et natae perficiuntur. . . . Eadem ratione factum arbitror, ut populorum mores appellantur ea, quae ipsis tacito assensu quodam, nullo certo authore communis vitae consuetudo attulisset. . . . Morem, inquit [Vergil, iii, 5], praecessisse dicit, quem secutus est cultus moris, id est consuetudo. . . . Consuetudo ususque longaevi non levis authoritas est, verum non usque adeo sui valitura momento, ut aut rationem vincat, aut legem. . . . At vero civitates, corpora etiam et collegia civitatum, quin et eiusdem quasi gentis et agnationis populi sibi consuetudinis authores sunt. . . . At desuetudo, ut volunt, nil aliud est quam consuetudo contraria, antecedenti consuetudine vel legi, quod si ita est, ut consuetudo, sic et desuetudo non sola patientia vel negligentia inducetur, sed contrariis factis et rebus . . . ," etc.

53. *Opera omnia,* ed. F. Baudouin (Paris, 1562), 67 (on Digest 1, 1, 3): "Consuetudo absoluta et inveterata, et longa, et diuturna, et Ius moribus vel consuetudine introductum, et mos maiorum, et interpretatio prudentium, a Iureconsultis in iis rebus, quae non ex scripto descendunt, et observantur, dici solet. Est autem consuetudo, communis usus iubens quae facienda sunt, et prohibens contraria: non dico verbis, sed rebus ipsis, atque factis. . . . Sicut enim leges scriptae firmantur consuetudine utentium, ita consuetudo iudicatis rebus firmatur, ut cum longa consuetudo, quasi civium conventio, nos teneat, tum maxime si secundum morem ali-

quando etiam iudicatum sit. Nam et sola consuetudo sine iudicio, pro Iure, id est, Iure scripto servatur: res iudicata non servatur sine consuetudine nisi perpetuo similiter iudicatum sit." And cf. Kelley, "Civil Science in the Renaissance: Jurisprudence in the French Manner," in *History, Law and the Human Sciences*.

54. *Rerum ab omni antiquitate iudicatarum Pandectae* [1573] (Geneva, 1677), on Digest 50, 17, 207; Baron, loc. cit., and Connan, *Commentarii*, fol. 43r, "Consuetudo legem interpretatur"; "Res iudicatae consuetudinem confirmant."

55. Jacques Godefroy, *Commentaires sur la coustume réformée du pays et duché de Normandie* (Rouen, 1626), 1: "Si on veut retrograder à l'origine, on sera contrainct de reconnoistre que les Coustumes ont précédé, et partant font la première partie du droict positif, quoy qu'on les mette les derniers." Cf. Connan, *Commentarii*, fol. 40r.

56. *Lectura super Digesto veteri* (Lyon, 1550), fol. 14v; cf. Azo, *In Ius civile summa*, 233v, "Et quidem videtur quod consuetudo sit conditrix legis, et abrogatrix, et interpretatrix," and many other references, all following Digest, I, 3, 37 (Paulus), "Si de interpretatione legis quaeritur, in primis inspiciendum est, quod iure civitatis retro in eiusmodi casibus usa fuisset: optima enim est legum interpres."

57. More on this question in D. R. Kelley, "Civil Science in the Renaissance: The Problem of Interpretation" (above, n. 14), with further references.

58. References here are minimal; in general see André Gouron and Odile Terrin, *Bibliographie des coutumes de France* (Geneva, 1975), and Jean Caswell and Ivan Sipkov, *The Coutumes of France in the Library of Congress* (Washington, D.C., 1977); also C. A. Bourdot de Richebourg, *Nouveau coutumier général*, 4 vols. (Paris, 1724), and Charles Berroyer and Eusèbe de Laurière, *Bibliothèque des Coutumes* (Paris, 1699). And see Olivier-Martin, *La Coutume de Paris*, Paul Viollet, "Les Coutumes de Normandie," *Histoire littéraire de France*, XXXIII (Paris, 1906), 41–190, and [Garnier], *La Coutume de Paris, mise en vers* (Paris, 1768). The major repository of research on French customs is *RHDFE*, published from 1855 to the present.

59. *Commentaires*, 1, "Et noue afin de ne nous rendre serfs imitateurs et admirateurs des estrangers, ferons bien de n'infrasquer et embrouiller l'intelligence de nos coustumes selon les reigles perplexes des statuts"—for which the civilian rules of "interpretation" were much more rigorous.

60. *Méthode générale pour l'intelligence des coustumes de France* (Paris, 1666), règle no. 1. Cf. *Coutume de la prévosté et vicomté de Paris, commentée par Julien Brodeau* (Paris, 1669), and Choppin, *Commentaires sur la Coustume d'Aniou*, which also discuss problems of method and interpretation. The massive literature on "interpretation" (especially the work of Woldemar Engelmann, Vincenzo Piano Mortari, and Enno Cortese) is limited almost entirely to Roman and canon law.

61. *La Coutume de Nivernais*, ed. A. Dupin (Paris, 1864), 57.

62. *The French Peasantry 1450–1660*, tr. A. Sheridan (Berkeley, 1987), 136; and Jean Yver, "Les caractères originaux du groupe des coutumes de l'Ouest de la France," *RHDFE* 30 (1952), 18–79.

63. *Coutume du Comté et Bailliage d'Auxerre* (Paris, 1693), preface: "Balde, et plusieurs autres Docteurs disent que, quoique les Gaulois, soumis à la domination de l'Empire Romain et ses Constitutions; ils ne pouvoient cependant s'assujeter à les suivre, et que ce Peuple (jaloux qu'il estoit de conserver sa liberté, prenant lesdites loix pour une servitude) se fit à la fantaisie des Coutumes particulières en

chaque Province, qu'il garda inviolablement contra lesdites Constitutions qui estoient faites pour tous en general."

64. *Coutumes de Beauvaisis*, I, 436 (851): "Toutes gens qui requierent bonnage le doivent avoir et bien pueent les parties, s'eles s'acordent, bonner sans justice, mes que ce ne soit en divers seignourages ou il ait pluseurs seigneurs; car en devise de pluseurs seigneurs li tenant ne pueent bonner sans les seigneurs apeler," adding "et pour ce se convient il garder en chascune vile selone la coustume." See also Loisel, *Institutes coustumières* (Paris, 1607), 46 (241), and Henri Roland and Laurent Boyer, *Locutions latines et adages du droit français contemporain* (Lyon, 1978), I, 118.

65. *Leges Burgundiorum*, in *Monumenta Germaniae Historica, Leges,* ed. L. R. Salis (Hannover, 1892), 29.

66. Bourdot de Richebourg, II (ii), 1169ff. In general see Guillot (see n. 21) Emile Champeau, "Coutumes de Bourgogne et coutumes du duché de Bourgogne," *MSHDB* 2 (1935), 47–76, and E. Champeau, ed., *Les Ordonnances des ducs de Bourgogne* (Paris, 1908); Josette Metman and Michel Petitjean, "Le Coutumier bourguignon glosé," *MSHDB* 40 (1983), 103–110; Petitjean, "La Coutume de Bourgogne. Des coutumiers officieux à la coutume officielle," *MSHDB* 42 (1985), 13–20; J. Bart, "Coutume et droit romain dans la doctrine bouguignonne du XVIIIe siècle," *MSHDB* 28 (1967), 141–72, and "Les tentatives de réformation de la coutume du duché de Bourgogne," *MSHDB* 42 (1985), 91–100; A. B. Poulalier, *Essai sur l'histoire de la dévolution héréditaire dans les successions ab intestat en Bourgogne* (Dijon, 1912); Pierre Bodineau, "Les rédacteurs 'inconnus' de la coutume de Bourgogne de 1459," *MSHDB* 40 (1953), 111–25; P. de Saint-Jacob, *Les Paysans de la Bourgogne du Nord au dernier siècle de l'ancien régime* (Paris, 1960), and Marcel Bouchard, *De l'Humanisme à l'Encyclopédie: L'Esprit public en Bourgogne sous l'ancien régime* (Paris, 1930). And cf. F. I. Dunod de Charnage, *Observations sur les titres des droits de justice, des fiefs, des cens, des gens mariés et des successions de la coutume du Comté de Bourgogne* (Besançon, 1756), "avertissement."

67. Bouhier, *Oeuvres de jurisprudence* (Paris, 1787), I, 353, "Observations sur la coutume du duché de Bourgogne"; *Histoire des commentateurs de la Coutume du duché de Bourgogne* (Dijon, 1742); and J. Bart, "Les préoccupations du président Bouhier pendant les dernières années de sa vie," *MSHDB* 28 (1967), 141–72. Bouhier (*Oeuvres de jurisprudence,* I, 190–200) also published the local usages of Dijon, which had been set down from oral testimony ("Il est coutume de Dijon que," etc.).

68. Bouhier, *Oeuvres de jurisprudence,* 359. See A. J. Arnaud, *Les Origines doctrinales du code civil français* (Paris, 1969), G. Tarello, *Le Ideologie della codificazione nel secolo XVIII* (Genoa, 1971), and *Storia della cultura giuridica moderna*, I, *Assolutismo e codificazione del diritto* (Bologna, 1976), and J. Q. C. Mackrell, *The Attack on Feudalism in Eighteenth-Century France* (London, 1973).

69. Bouhier, op. cit., 396, and Coquille, *Les Oeuvres,* 2.

70. *De l'Esprit des lois,* bk. XXVIII.

71. Olivier-Martin, *Coutume de Paris,* I, 25ff.

72. *Oratio de concordia et unione consuetudinum Franciae* (Paris, 1546), and *Pars prima commentariorum in Consuetudines Parisienses* (Paris, 1539); and see Kelley, "Charles Dumoulin and the Gallican View of History," *Traditio* 22 (1966), 347–402.

73. See Kelley, "Louis Le Caron Philosophe," in *History, Law and the Human Sciences*.

74. *Commentaire*, 3. On academic aspects of this controversy, beginning with Louis XIV's founding of chairs in French customary law to rival the old professorships in civil law, see Alfred de Curzon, *L'Enseignement du droit français dans les universités de France aux XVIIe et XVIIIe siècles* (Paris, 1920), and Christiane Chêne, *L'Enseignement du droit français en pays du droit écrit (1679–1793)* (Paris, 1982).

75. *Le Droit commun de la France et la coutume de Paris réduits en principes* (Paris, 1747), I; and see Renée Martinage, *Bourjon et le Code Civil* (Paris, 1971).

76. See above, n. 64; also Michel Reulos, *Etude sur l'esprit, les sources et la méthode des Institutes coutumières d'Antoine Loisel* (Paris, 1935). Cf. Klaus Luig, "Institutionen-Lehrbücher des nationalen Rechts im 17. und 18. Jahrhunderts," *Ius Commune*, III (1970), 64–97.

77. *Commentaire sur les Institutes Coutumières de Mr. Antoine Loisel* (Paris, 1688), xxxiii. "il y avoit une ancienne Coutume en France; car Charlemagne lui-meme n'auroit pas distingué les Loix d'avec les Coutumes. . . . Or il est certain que l'ancienne Coutume dont entendent ces Capitulaires estoit une règle générale de tout le Royaume, une Loi universellement observée dans toute la France."

78. *Recherches pour servir à l'histoire du droit françois* (Paris, 1752), 122ff., and see Kelley, "Ancient Verses on New Ideas," *History and Theory* 26 (1987), 319–38.

79. *Méthode*, 134, citing Loisel (whose *Institutes coustumières* he edited in 1656).

80. *Nouvelles Institutions coutumières* (Paris, 1692), t. 1, "Du Droit coutumier en général coutume ou usage n'est autre chose qu'un Droit non écrit, qui s'est introduit par un tacite consentement du Souverain et du Peuple, pour avoir esté observé pendant un temps considérable"; and t. 5, "Les inclinations communes des peuples viennent de la diversité du gouvernement et des climats; nous les pouvons appeler la raison civile, qui doit estre le fondement des Coustumes et des Loix."

81. *Les Coutumes considérées comme loix de la nation dans son origine et dans son état actuel* (Paris, 1783), 30, 97.

82. *Les Loix civiles dans leur ordre naturel* (Luxembourg, 1702), preface: "Pour les loix de ces deux sortes de matières [public and private], il y en a de deux sortes dont on a l'usage dans toutes les Nations du monde. L'une est de celles qui sont de Droit naturel, et l'autre est des Loix propres à chacque Nation, telles que sont les Coutumes qu'un long usage a autorisées." And cf. Vico, *Diritto universale*, ed. P. Cristofolini (Florence, 1974), 93 (I, 91), "'Ius naturae prius' et 'posterius' interpretum eadem quae 'prima natura' et 'naturae consequentia' stoicorum."

83. *Dissertations sur des questions qui naissent de la contrariété des loix et des coutumes* (Paris, 1732).

84. D. R. Kelley, *Historians and the Law in Postrevolutionary France* (Princeton, 1984), and the literature there cited.

85. *De l'Esprit des lois*, bk. XXX. Cf. Antoine Le Conte, *Methodus de Feudis*, printed with G. Fornerius, *De Feudis tractatus* (Hanover, 1599), and Hervé, *Théorie des matières féodales et censuelles* (Paris, 1785), 1, "le système féodal," and 386, "la Doctrine féodale."

86. *Consuetudines Bituricenses* [Bourges] (Paris, 1543), fol. 1: "Haec consuetudo comprobatur iure naturali quo omnes homines nascuntur liberi"; and cf. *Les Notes de Maistre Charles Dumoulin sur les coutumes de France* (Paris, 1715), 29.

87. *Le droit commun de France et la Coutume de Paris* (Paris, 1742), ch. 1; Argou, *Institutions du droit françois* (Paris, 1771), 5 (all born free except for "nègres" in the French colonies); Jean d'Arrerac, *Pandectes ou Digestes du droict romain et françois* (Bordeaux, 1601), 67, "Ceste loi permet de repousser la force et l'injure par une contraire force." Cf. Q. Skinner, *Foundations of Modern Political Thought* (Cambridge, 1979), I.

88. *Archives Parlementaires* (Paris, 1862), VIII, 574. See also Marcel Garaud, *La Révolution et la propriété foncière* (Paris, 1959), and Xavier Martin, "L'Unité du droit français à la veille de 1789: une aspiration modérée?" *Il Pensiero politico* 19 (1986), 319–28.

89. P. A. Fenet, ed., *Recueil complet des travaux préparatoires du Code Civil* (Paris, 1927), I, 1; and see François Papillard, *Cambacérès* (Paris, 1961).

90. Fenet, *Recueil*, II, 169.

91. E. Meynial, "Notes sur la formation de la théorie du domaine divisé (domaine direct et domaine utile) du XIIe au XIVe siècles dans les romanistes," *Mélanges Fitting* (Montpellier, 1908), II, 409–61.

92. F. Portalis, ed., *Discours, rapports et travaux inédits* (Paris, 1844), I, 19, 90ff. Cf. II, 263, citing Dumoulin on the first title of the Parisian custom, "Et illae consuetudines erant jus peculiare et commune Francorum et Gallorum."

93. *La Législation civile de la révolution française* (Paris, 1898), 387; also Edmond Seligman, *La Justice en France pendant la révolution (1789–1792)* (Paris, 1901), A. Mater, *L'Histoire juridique de la révolution* (Besançon, 1919), P. P. Viard, *Histoire générale du droit privé français (1789–1830)* (Paris, 1931), and D. R. Kelley and Bonnie Smith, "What Was Property? Legal Dimensions of the Social Question in France (1789–1848)," *Proceedings of the American Philosophical Society* 128 (1984), 200–230, with further references.

94. See Soboul, "Persistence of 'Feudalism' in the Rural Society of Nineteenth-Century France," *Rural Society in France,* ed. R. Forster and O. Ranum (Baltimore, 1977), and Valette, *De la Durée persistante de l'ensemble du droit civil français pendant et depuis la révolution de 1789* (Paris, 1872).

95. Fenet, *Recueil,* I, 11. On Cambacérès's famous address see Georges Gusdorf, *Les Sciences humaines et la pensée occidentale,* IX, *La Conscience révolutionnaire. Les Idéologues* (Paris, 1978), 746, and especially Sergio Moravia, *Il Pensiero degli Idéologues. Scienze e filosofia in Francia (1780–1815)* (Florence, 1974), 746. This is an aspect not discussed by Keith Baker, "The Early History of the Term 'Social Science,'" *Annals of Science* 20 (1964), 211–26, or by B. W. Head, *Ideology and Social Science* (The Hague, 1985), 109ff.

96. *Discours. Corps Législatif. Conseil des Cinq-cents.* (Paris, An 7; BN Le.43.3603), 3: "La science sociale étudie l'organisation des colonies diverses émanées de la République Romaine; elle examine ailleurs les droits coutumiers, les codes des anciens, les lois favorables à l'union conjugale, les droits peut-être trop restreints des mères sur les enfans, le marché mesuré du peuple athénien pour former et surtout pour abroger ses lois, et toujours elle cherche à tirer l'expérience des siècles précédens des leçons pour la génération actuelle."

97. Fenet, *Recueil,* I, 469; and see Arnaud, *Les Juristes face à la société du XIXe siècle à nos jours* (Paris, 1975), 31.

98. *Vom Beruf unsrer Zeit für Gesetzgebung und Rechtswissenschaft* (Heidel-

berg, 1814), 28, with an appendix publishing some of the preliminary discussions, pro and con, of the French courts concerning the Civil Code; and *System des heutigen römischen Rechts* (Berlin, 1940), I, 116; also "Su Federico Carlo di Savigny," *Quaderni fiorentini per la storia del pensiero giuridico moderno* 9 (1980), and Peter Stein, *Legal Evolution: The Story of an Idea* (Cambridge, 1980). On custom the major work from the Historical School is G. F. Puchta, *Gewohnheitsrecht* (Erlangen, 1828). Of Savigny's and Puchta's discussion of *Volksrecht,* Georges Gurvitch observed (*L'Idée du droit social* [Paris, 1932], 476), "C'est précisément le dernier fondement de la réhabilitation de la coutume par l'école historique."

99. *Philosophy of Right,* tr. T. M. Knox (Oxford, 1942), 20. Knox's rendering of "Recht" exclusively as "right" tends to individualize and desocialize Hegel's usage and obscure its connections with the tradition of law.

100. Maine, *Ancient Law* (London, 1861), 7ff., and Austin, *Lectures on Jurisprudence* (London, 1873), II, 553.

101. *Custom: An Essay on Social Codes,* tr. A. Borenstein (New York, 1961), 131, citing Savigny; *Community and Association,* tr. C. Loomis (London, 1955), 240, and *On Social Ideas and Ideologies,* tr. E. Jacoby (New York, 1974), 129, on the historical school. See also Paolo Grossi, *"Un altro modo di possedere"* (Milan, 1977), on the debates over "primitive communism," which cut across the frontiers between law and early social science, and Henri Lévy-Bruhl, "Rapports du droit et de la sociologie," *Archives de philosophie du droit* III–IV (1937), 21–25.

102. *Origins of Sociology* (Chicago, 1924). Later surveys of the history of anthropology and sociology make little of this legal connection. See Ernst Becker, *The Lost Science of Man* (New York, 1971), and D. R. Kelley, "The Prehistory of Sociology," in *History, Law and the Human Sciences.*

103. *Encyclopedia of the Social Sciences,* ed. Edwin Seligman (New York, 1930–35).

104. *International Encyclopedia of the Social Sciences,* ed. David L. Sills (New York, 1968–79).

105. *Montaigne in Movement,* tr. A. Goldhammer (Chicago, 1958), 293.

106. *Les Essais,* I, xxiii, "De la Coustume et de ne pas changer aisement une loi reçüe"; see also III, x. Bacon, *Essays,* xxxix, "Of Custom and Education," devising his own provenance for the Aristotelian topos: "[Machiavelli's] rule holdeth still, that nature, nor the engagement of words, are not so forcible as custom." Charron, *De la Sagesse,* ed. A. Duval (Paris, 1820), II, 191.

107. Ibid., 201.

108. *De la Servitude volontaire,* ed. Malcolm Smith (Geneva, 1987), 51.

109. *Pensées,* nos. 325, 440, 426, 93, 144.

110. *An Enquiry Concerning Human Understanding,* III, vi; and cf. *A Treatise of Human Nature,* II, iii: "It is that principle alone which renders our experience useful to us, and makes us expect, for the future, a similar train of events with those which have appeared in the past."

Lucette Valensi

5. The Making of a Political Paradigm: The Ottoman State and Oriental Despotism

Of the present king, who as a young man of fourteen years became the ruler of this large empire after his uncle Mustafa's deposition . . . , such a good opinion was conceived that it produced in everybody's heart a deep expectation of his success. It was universally thought that he would become the best prince the Ottoman house ever had. But in a matter of a few years, he showed how human judgment fails to anticipate future events. For just as one cannot be sure of the serenity of the day from the splendor of a fine morning, since the contrary so often occurs; and just as the more placid the tranquility of the sea appears at the beginning of a journey, the greater the chance and more obvious the danger once it is stirred up by powerful winds, so too this prince emerged as totally different from what was expected. He allowed his mother and his ministers to govern for some time, and suffered with as much bitterness as fear the offenses of the militia who forced him to give up the heads of his chief ministers and of his greatest favorites in the seraglio, and who, not content with that, murdered the Prime Vizier Cafis, his brother-in-law, [who was standing] so close to him that the blood fell on his clothes, an event he witnessed with such horror and terror that for two full days he remained in a stupor as if he were out of his mind. Having then been comforted by Bostangi Bassi (who was once Achmet Bassa of Cairo), and by Cussein Effendi Mufti (both were shortly thereafter strangled on his very own orders) who advised him to show courage and to inflict chastisement, he turned all his thoughts to revenge. Immersed in vengeance, as if seduced and soothed by it, moved by indignation and prompted by anger, he became fierce and cruel to the most extreme degree. On a day in which he took no one's life, he would not call himself happy and would show no sign of true elation. On the other hand, when many were killed in his presence as was more often the case, he would appear joyful and consoled. That is why those close to him would wait for such circumstances to seek some grace or favor. To curry favor, his ministers would present him with heads when they could not offer him gold and silver. And when he stayed far from the city, they would obtain from those in charge the delivery of those people sentenced to death in order to console his spirit with their large numbers and to advance in his good graces. It was quite remarkable that in his most ostentatious and pompous entries, he ordered that beheaded corpses be exposed on the streets through which he would pass. Where on similar occasions other princes would grant pardon, free prisoners and remit sentences, to win the people's love and affection, he preferred the streets enameled with blood rather than decorated with roses and chose to exhibit his severity with utmost rigor rather than have his clemency shine forth with some act of mercy.[1]

This is how Pietro Foscarini portrayed the Ottoman emperor Murad IV in 1637.

*   *   *

Words possess their history. They emerge and float and shape our perceptions and modes of thought. They find space on our intellectual maps before being submerged by waves of new notions. The terms *despote, despotique,* and *despotisme* first appeared in a French dictionary in 1720.[2] The latter concept seems to have been created at the end of the seventeenth century and designated a political system combining the servitude of the subjects with the absolute authority of the monarch. Later on, the concept was firmly fixed in European political thought by Montesquieu in his *L'Esprit des Lois* of 1748. Yet, one century earlier Pietro Foscarini, in portraying Murad IV, had already characterized his government as "the most immoderate, the most extravagant ever," an "absolute and despotic power."

How did the extravagant character of the despot emerge? When did the Sublime Porte become the place where a political form found the most suitable climate to produce a modality of "oriental despotism"? In this paper I ask these questions of Pietro Foscarini who, as the Venetian ambassador, had spent more than three years in Istanbul between 1633 and 1636. I also ask them of his peers, the other representatives of the Serenissima who, like all other ambassadors sent from Venice to major capitals, had to deliver public, detailed accounts about the states in which they had just served upon their return home.

A Class of Humanists, Politicians, and Observers

With remarkable rationalistic exactness and regularity, Venice was able to keep a precise record of the forces, resources, institutions, and circumstances of the strategically significant kingdoms and states of the period. In the case of the Ottoman Empire, Venice maintained in Constantinople (Fig. 5.1) a permanent ambassador, the *bailo,* who for two years would be responsible for defending the persons and property of individual Venetian citizens, as well as the interests of the republic. Venice also dispatched special envoys to greet a new sultan upon his accession to the throne, to offer

Figure 5.1. A fifteenth-century depiction of Constantinople. Source: Hartmann Schedel, *Liber Chronicarum* (Nuremberg, 1493), f. 257r. Courtesy of Princeton University Library.

congratulations on a military success, or to negotiate a new treaty. These *oratori,* like the ambassadors, were required to deliver to the senate full reports on the countries they had visited. Although not all of these accounts have been preserved, more than fifty emanating from the sixteenth and seventeenth centuries were collected and published in the nineteenth century.[3]

Venetian envoys worked at the intersection of three different domains: humanism, political action, and empirical observation. They were part of the most highly educated elite, and many of them had studied in the schools of Padua and the academies of Venice. As is well known, Venetian education had emphasized politics and civil science since the fifteenth century. In 1546, the Florentine exile Antonio Bruciolo published the first translation of Aristotle's *Politics* into the Italian vernacular[4] and the text became compulsory reading in the schools of Padua shortly thereafter. Members of the educated elite remained immersed in humanistic culture throughout their lives. Several Venetian ambassadors to Istanbul held the title of Reformers of the Schools in Padua, and were themselves artists, bibliophiles, and art collectors.

Yet although Venetian culture paid special attention to the teaching of political philosophy, it did not encourage theoretical speculation. Unlike Florence and other Italian cities, Venice produced no influential work in this field. After Gasparo Contarini wrote his *De Magistratibus et Republica Venetorum* in the 1520s, the Venetian political ideal was left unchallenged for several generations.[5]

Instead of launching its young patricians into the adventures of imaginative creation, Venice put them to work in the service of the republic. A perfect state, Venice had realized social concord and civil peace; a city without walls, Venice was protected by the excellence of its laws and institutions. Once this ideal picture had been accepted by the Venetian patriciate, it fell to its members to maintain the political system. Thus, by the age of twenty-five every patrician had embarked upon a career in politics and, after being admitted as a member of the Grand Council, became a servant of his country. Embassies—ordinary as well as extraordinary—were part of the *cursus honorum*,[6] among which the position of *bailo* in Istanbul was the most prestigious and most important that a patrician could hope for. Feeling as at ease in the realm of ideas as in the realm of action, Venetian ambassadors were in a favorable position to appreciate Ottoman realities. They stayed long enough and made enough contacts in the capital city to be able to collect personally the most accurate data on the most powerful empire of the times.

The ambivalent attitude of the Venetian republic toward the Ottoman Empire is well known and needs no elaboration here. Venice was, to use Braudel's term, the courtesan city. I can find no better metaphor for her oriental policy than *Juditha Triumphans*, Vivaldi's *oratorio militare*—even though the work was composed in the eighteenth century.[7] Venice seems to have taken some pleasure in being embraced by Holofernes before slaying him in his sleep. At least Venice was not fanatically obsessed with the organization of a Christian crusade against the Infidel—Venice knew better. Indeed, what Venice knew she owed to the quality of the dispatches and letters her ambassadors sent during their long sojourns in Istanbul and, more comprehensively, to the final reports they presented on the state of the empire.

This knowledge was the basis of her policy. At the same time, the ambassadors' reports were the most formal expression of Venetian political discourse. Although the shared political culture permeated the entire life of the city and expressed itself in public rituals as well as in art, popular literature, and history books, her ambassadors' reports constituted the most articulate elaboration of the values, principles, and categories of Venetian thought.[8]

Shaping the political consciousness of Venetian citizens, these reports themselves also became a kind of literary genre. The same structure and headings were expected regardless of the vantage point of the observer. Even non-ambassadors who traveled abroad returned from their journeys with reports organized along the same lines as those of the ambassadors. After reading their reports in public sessions of the senate, they were then required to deliver written versions of their texts. Copies of these circulated in the city and were acquired by collectors both in Venice and in other cities as far away as Rome and Oxford. Beginning in 1589, some reports enjoyed a wider distribution, since they were printed in the *Tesoro Politico,* a compendium of "reports, instructions, and various ambassadors' speeches appropriate for the knowledge and understanding of the state, interests and dependencies of the main princes in the world." A few reports on Istanbul were included in this collection. First published in Italian, the *Tesoro* went through numerous editions and translations. These texts formed a kind of political science textbook for the education of political elites, and although they were originally aimed at the Venetian patriciate, ambassadors' reports reached a much wider circle of European readers, contributing in turn to the shaping of their political vision.[9]

Why did these texts enjoy such great success? Precisely because of the realistic, pragmatic precision of the analysis they provided. As a literary genre, as an early form of political anthropology, the Venetian ambassadors' reports can therefore be read as reliable indicators of change both in the political discourse of that part of Europe and in the perceptions of the Ottoman state between the sixteenth and seventeenth centuries.

Rationalistic as they were, Venetian ambassadors nevertheless intended to convey effects as much as facts. Because all reports had to fit the same framework with the same sequential order, the result could have been utterly dull. It has been repeatedly argued that Venetian ambassadors had invented statistics—a claim that contains more than a grain of truth[10]— but they did it with art, that is to say, with words rather than with figures and tables. What becomes significant to us, then, is less the content of their observations than the manner in which they were arranged; less the repetitive subtitles of the reports—size and limits of the state, material and human resources, army, navy, form of government, character of the ruler and those close to him, alliances and conflicts with other powers, and so forth—than their contrasts. Differentiating elements are to be found in the rhetorical devices, the choices of images, the combinations of words, the arrangements of motives and lexical shifts, as much as in the evidence of "hard facts" about the Ottoman Empire.

"Il Maggior Signor del Mondo"

In the collection of accounts covering the Ottoman Empire, a first homogeneous series emerges corresponding to the reigns of Bayezid II, Selim I, Suleyman the Magnificent, Selim II, and part of the reign of Murad III. Spanning over three-quarters of the sixteenth century, they display significant similarities. One can discern in these reports several ingredients of the mixture that Montesquieu would later label as "despotism." These were not only descriptive features, or what Montesquieu called "choses d'accident," that might disappear with changing circumstances or the coronation of a new prince. They were what he considered "distinctive properties": components both permanent to a specific regime and basically alien to the values and principles of European minds. Yet to isolate these ingredients would impose a teleological bias on the texts. In the sixteenth century, these distinctive features did not constitute a system, but remained associated with other structural characteristics of the Ottoman state.

This first group of accounts displays a constant ambiguity. The formidable empire inspired a fascination that combined admiration and aversion. Neither sympathy nor acceptance was ever expressed, since the sultan was seen as the major enemy of Christendom. There would always be something unacceptable in the power of an Infidel whose colossal force was used to weaken the Christians. There would always remain an obscure paradox in the repeated demonstration that God tolerated, even supported, the Infidel's success over His own flock. This disturbing thought was exacerbated by the knowledge that the indignities inflicted upon the Christians were precisely the work of coreligionists who had been uprooted from the true faith and converted to Islam. In 1573, two years after Lepanto, a victory obtained, at long last, by the coalition of Christian navies, the *bailo* Marcantonio Barbaro formulated once again the paradox of this usurpation: "It is a matter deserving consideration that the wealth, strength and government, in short the entire state of the Ottoman Empire be based on and put into the hands of people all born in Christ's faith, who by different means have been made slaves and transferred to the Mahometan sect" (315). In most accounts, however, the authors leave it to God to solve this enigma and proceed to give detailed descriptions of the Ottoman system.

Fascination resulted in the first instance from the extraordinary power of the Turkish "Lord." His regular title of Great Lord, or Great Turk, was not sufficient; the superlative mode was used to convey an even more exalted status. The earliest report, dating from 1503, declared that the Great Lord was the major prince on earth, reigning over the most beautiful city in the world, and owning a treasure larger than those of all Christian princes combined. In 1522, Marco Minio began his report with a statement on the "grandissima potenzia di questo signor" (71). "This Great Lord is the most powerful," Barbarigo wrote in 1564. The sultan's power was first described as territorial. While some reports simply gave a list of the provinces and kingdoms annexed by the empire, the flood of geographical names (which became more and more exotic when they designated eastern provinces) produced the impression of immeasurable greatness. Most reports, however, evoked more emphatically the vastness of the empire. At times, they used the superlative mode ("vastissimo impero dei Turchi," anonymous, 1582, 439), or they insisted on the comprehensiveness of every single part of the whole: the empire included "all of Greece," "all of Asia Minor," "all the coasts of Africa in the Mediterranean," "all the borders of Venetian dominions," and so forth. They also measured the considerable distances between the different parts. Or, by making a list of all the countries that shared a border with the empire—from Spain to Abyssinia, and from Moscovia to the empire of Prester John—they raised the Ottoman Empire to mythical proportions. At times, a simple, declarative statement was sufficiently eloquent: this empire covered "the three parts of the world" (Garzoni 1573, 428); "Domina il Gransignor nell'Asia, nell'Africa e sull'Europa" (Erizzo 1557, 127); "The Sultan is the master of a great part of the world" (Navagero 1553; Barbarigo 1564). As late as 1583 Paolo Contarini, to avoid repeating in his account things that he suggested could be found in many books, simply indicated "that a large part of Africa, the major part of

Europe and a very large part of Asia find themselves today under the obedience of this Empire."

What was implied in this emphasis on the size of the empire was made clear by Barbaro, who wrote in 1573, two years after Lepanto: "Since the fall of the Roman empire, no prince ever brought under his rule as many provinces and kingdoms as the Ottoman did today by the force of their armies" (302). Here, a new paradox surfaced. The Ottoman Empire had inherited the power of the Romans; neither the Church nor a Christian prince had been able to resume the Roman conquest and unify the entire world. What was at stake in Venetian minds was to anticipate who would establish a universal monarchy. A vision of world history inspired by the prophecy of Daniel was then still popular in Europe. The four pagan monarchies—Babylonian, Persian, Greek, and Roman—were to be followed by the establishment of the fifth empire. Were this prophecy to be realized, the Muslim ruler would obviously succeed where all Christian monarchs had failed.[11]

"E potente di entrata, di gente e di obbedienza," wrote Minio in 1522. Reformulated in a variety of ways, this statement would be elaborated in most subsequent reports. The financial resources of the Ottoman state would receive a chapter in every account. Again, the flood of items, the evaluation of each of them, the use of the superlatives and many other rhetorical devices served to demonstrate that Ottoman resources knew no limits. With a single exception, all the reports suggested that the Great Turk's receipts always exceeded his expenses, and that these, in turn, were considerable, a further evidence of the sultan's power. Endless descriptions of costumes, textiles, and jewels served to underscore the infinite opulence of the sultan's palace.

Measured by the extent of his territories, his income, and his expenses, the sultan's power was also evaluated by the extent of his human and material resources, and in this respect as well, he was more than amply endowed. The sultan could draw indefinitely on the large populations he controlled and on the products they provided to meet the needs of his capital city, his army, and his navy. Human resources meant not only products and taxes, but also, and more important, an unlimited supply of soldiers. Venetian ambassadors repeatedly underlined the immense advantage the sultan enjoyed over Christian powers, Venice included, who had to rely for their defense on mercenaries more eager to make money than to fight.

For obvious reasons, the chapter on maritime and land forces was the focus of the ambassadors' careful attention. Detailed descriptions of the institutions, hierarchy, equipment, mode of recruitment, training, and promotion were provided, although occasionally deficiencies were also noted; for example, the arsenal was inadequate, the naval leadership was deemed mediocre, or their arms inferior. But it was as if the Ottoman army could readily correct its imperfections and reestablish its gigantic strength either by borrowing techniques from its enemies or by exploiting the extraordinary power of recuperation made possible by the availability of any desired resources. After the battle of Lepanto, when the Ottoman navy had been destroyed, Garzoni again described at great length the newly reorganized army and navy by means of which the Turk would again be in a position to torture all of Christendom, "travagliare la christianita tutta" (1573, 419).

Besides, the Ottoman superiority was not only a matter of numbers. It was rather a matter of virtue, of experience, and of the understanding of warfare by its officers and its rank and file. "All the best conditions which are sought for in an army, all, in my opinion, are displayed by this Lord's soldiers," Dandolo wrote in 1563 (166). These conditions were courage, endurance, frugality, and the impeccable order of the army when on the battlefield, a unity that enabled soldiers to act as "of one single will." In the minds of Renaissance Venetians, this was not to be taken lightly. "Unanimitas"—acting as of one single will for the commonwealth—was one of the major values of Venetian humanism, as was the "obedience," which was described in most reports and epitomized the perfect organization of the army, the soldiers' discipline. Above all other virtues was their wholehearted devotion to the emperor. We shall return to this notion later.

A Perfect Organization

As a consequence of the enormous power of the empire and its army, Marco Minio wrote in 1521 after the fall of Belgrade that the Great Turk "holds in his hands the keys to all of Christendom in such a way that he could easily enter the Christians' entrails" (75). "From now on," the same ambassador explained, "all of Christendom should fear a wide extermination" (71). A threatening, frightening, and invincible power: this fear became the leitmotif of all subsequent reports. "The Turks are the greatest fighters in the world," wrote Cavalli in 1560; "one should not fight them but fear them" (280). In 1564, Barbarigo wrote that he believed that the Grand Signor disposed of so many territories, so much money, and such an abundance of obedient men, that "these three elements alone make him invincible" (33). As mentioned earlier, two years after Lepanto, Barbaro was still wondering whether the Ottoman Empire would not appropriate the entire world and transform itself into a universal monarchy. This apprehension was not merely a rhetorical device placed as an introduction to his account. On the contrary, he demonstrated at length why Venice would then be the first target of Turkish expansion. A few years later, Tiepolo reiterated this analysis of the balance of power: there was good reason to think that Murad III could threaten the entire world; not only Venice, but also the Germanic Empire. He concluded his assessment with these words: "the fall of such an empire [i.e., the Ottomans] by the hands of men is therefore the vainest thing to think of" (1576, 173).

This Ottoman Empire, which, as Contarini put it as late as 1583, could provoke "terror among all the princes on earth, especially bordering Christians," was not built only on sheer strength. It rested on a political order, and it was precisely this aspect that most fascinated Venetian observers. They saw a system in which all the parts were connected to the center by relationships of balanced tension. They saw a structure in which all the levels in the hierarchy were interdependent, and all depended on the top. Even when they searched for signs of erosion or malfunction in any cog in this vast machinery, even as they emphasized how remote every Ottoman institution was from their own, they contemplated the Ottoman system as an imposing construct, subject to a single logic that accounted for its material strength as well as its continuous territorial expansion. They saw the same logic at work when they described the council's sessions, the court ceremonial, or the organization of the seraglio—a logic that could achieve a perfect orchestration together with a complete mobilization of all energies in the service of the sultan's mightiness.

When they detailed the facts of life in the four seraglios, they portrayed them as schools where the most handsome and talented youths from all over the empire were brought together to receive the best training in mind and body. The Venetians perceived their activities as a permanent celebration of the imperial order in which gestures, sounds, voices, and costumes were as carefully planned as were those in a ballet. This institution prepared its young students for single-minded devotion to their prince's service. There was no need to coerce them with his orders, for they obeyed him of their own volition; they became the true architects of his might. They could be viewed as friars, equal brothers in the service of the father and trained to respect order, silence, chastity, and religious law, the equivalent of monks in a Christian monastery.

Was there anything more noble Venetian ambassadors could propose

Figure 5.2. Turks in battle. Bernhard von Breydenbach, *Peregrinationes* (Mainz, 1486), f. 137. Courtesy of R. H. Taylor Collection.

to the admiration of their colleagues? The same perfect organization based on the same principles could be observed in the army or in the four weekly meetings of the Porte. At the court as on the battlefield, the display of huge numbers of actors would take place without confusion in the glistening of the uniforms, the shimmering of feathers on the soldiers' caps, the glittering of their arms, and their absolute silence (Fig. 5.2). The driving force of this majestic grandeur was precisely that the men involved had their share in it. There were two correlated aspects to the whole system. One was the total submission of the subjects from the bottom to the top of the social ladder, and the other was the absolute authority of the ruler. A recurrent theme of Venetian reports was that the populations were directly subject to the sultan's authority because there was no lord other than the sultan himself; no aristocracy or intermediate body stood between the ruler and his subjects. In the eighteenth century, Montesquieu wrote critically: "No nobility, no monarch, and you have a despot." But it was not so in the sixteenth century. In fact, Venetian ambassadors insisted that the absence of aristocratic families reduced the dangers of political upheavals. "It is not a minor profit," wrote Barbaro in 1573, "nor a minor security not to allow the families of great men to remain successively in the government" (328).

"Obedience, which everybody considers as the most solid foundation of all empires, certainly supports this one," Erizzo wrote in 1557 (131). In the sixteenth century no one challenged the notion of obedience, but would rather understand how it was obtained. In the Ottoman case, people were obedient because they were slaves, because of the fear that the exercise of force inspired in them. But the other side of the coin was that because of the absence of a hereditary aristocracy, the ruler could easily promote any of his subjects. Any individual could enjoy a dazzling ascent solely through the will of the ruler and, more generally, through the process of selection and training that operated in the army and the palace. Absolute devotion to the sultan was the condition for their success, and this included, of course, a readiness to sacrifice their lives. Indeed, if the sultan so decreed, they would accept their sentence and offer their heads without even trying to flee.

From the point of view of the ruler, absolute submission to his will meant that he enjoyed equally absolute authority, including the power of life and death over all of his subjects regardless of their social position. Was this power arbitrary? By no means, since wisdom and a sense of justice were qualities repeatedly found in most sultans of this period. Venetian ambassadors, who had been educated within the humanistic tradition, attributed both of these qualities to the sultans' education and knowledge of literature. In 1518, Mocenigo wrote that the Sultan Selim I was considered a "just man" who, nurtured by *The Life of Alexander,* wished to imitate his feats and become the master of Asia, Africa, and Europe. "This Lord is just," wrote Marco Minio in 1527, speaking of Suleyman; "he dedicates much time to study, he is considered to be a philosopher and has a good knowledge of his law" (116). In the course of his long reign (1520–66), Suleyman the Magnificent was portrayed as a man of his word who would do no harm when he was well informed; as a true believer who observed his faith and his law; as a reader of Alexander's exploits and of the history of Persia who devoured glorious examples of the past. His wisdom showed on his face, which "displayed a wonderful grandeur together with a sweetness that made him lovable to anybody who would see him" (Navagero 1553, 72).

After the reign of Selim II (1566–74), which has generally been depicted in rather somber tones, the succession of Murad III seemed to reestablish royal justice. Dedicated to "the study of law and history, he is greatly inclined to govern with justice" (Tiepolo 1576, 166).

The first prince described as just was Selim I, who was suspected of having poisoned his father to take power. "No," Mocenigo wrote, "the rumor had no ground" (1518, 59), and while it is true that he had Janus Pasha and his own son-in-law Mustazi Pasha killed, he had three good reasons to justify his severity. As for Suleyman, he continued to be called "very wise and very just" by the ambassadors even after he had assassinated his best friend, confidant, and prime vizier, Ibrahim Pasha, in 1536, and then ordered the assassination of his universally loved eldest son, Prince Mustafa, the presumptive heir to the throne. Only Donini observed in 1562 that Suleyman, renowned as the wisest prince, deserved "the title of the most cruel, most impious father, who stained his hands with his own blood by having his older son Mustafa killed," then his son Mehemet, and finally Bayezid and his four sons who had found refuge in Persia (176). But even after this strong indictment, unperturbed ambassadors would reassert the infinite wisdom of this major sultan. When he decided on these people's deaths, it was because they had challenged his authority; since they had infringed upon the accepted order, they received the expected punishment.

More than natural qualities and a knowledge of the literary works of the past, what made a prince just and wise was his strict enforcement of the law. Venetian ambassadors kept emphasizing the existence of a law in the Ottoman state, namely Islam. *Legge* and *fede* were two interchangeable notions. Within the framework of a system of nonsecular thought, religion remained the basis of law for the Venetian ambassadors. While Islam as a religion did not appeal to them, they still admitted that religious law provided the monarch and his subjects with an unquestioned ethos. A man of faith was a man of honor. Suleyman was thus a just, merciful prince because he was a "perfect Turk"—that is, a perfect Muslim (Minio 1521, 74); "extremely religious in his law" (Barbarigo 1558, 148); or "utterly observant of his law" (Dandolo 1562, 164). Conversely, when other princes were described as cruel and bloody, it was, as in Selim I's case, because he governed "alone and of his sole head," without reference to the law, and in Selim II's case, because as a man of no faith, he constantly transgressed the prohibitions of his religion.

An ordered, centralized system, the Ottoman regime nonetheless harbored tensions that the Venetian ambassadors were eager to uncover and to take advantage of, with or without the help of other Christian princes. One was the subjection of Christian populations within the empire, who would be potential allies should external forces attempt to subvert the Great Turk's domination (that proved unrealistic, but the ambassadors kept nurturing this hope). Other threats to the sultan's power emanated from the center of the system, since it could be corroded by the corruption of its very operators. Venetian ambassadors noticed that the amount of respect an individual enjoyed and his significance could be measured by the quantity of gifts that would flow in, a practice that undermined righteousness and virtue. Everything could be bought: justice, ranks in the army, the pashas' favors in any negotiation. Since any service required payment, decisions were often unpredictable; since promotions were bought with money, one could never guess who would be the next chosen, and the best policy was "to favor everybody, including the *marioli*,[12] because a perpetual wheel of fortune would raise and debase everyone, depending on the gyration of the Signor's caprice" (Erizzo 1557, 136). Under such circumstances, the regulation of the entire system rested not on respect of the law, but on the devotion to the ruler's greatness and on fear of his punishment. One further paradox of Ottoman life was that in all aspects of public life, everyone was obliged to serve at his best as long as the master himself exercised his authority fairly, but whenever he failed, the whole system was affected.

The sultan failed to behave as the just ruler when he moved away from religious law. By deviating from the law, he would cease to be a man of his word and a man of honor and fall prey to every form of vice (lust, homosexuality, hypersexuality, and drunkenness being the most frequently observed). Since the system did not allow for any "natural," blood-transmitted nobility, there could be no social bounds to temper the ruler's corruption. Instead, Ottoman sultans preferred the company of the most abject people: eunuchs, dwarfs, mutes, buffoons, and women—all the vilest people in a community of slaves.

The last cause of tension and possible weakening of the Ottoman Empire was found in the uncertainties of the succession to the throne and in the inevitable competition among surviving sons following every sultan's death, with all the existing factions in the seraglio and the army taking this opportunity to exhibit their rivalries.

Up to this point, however, the abstract categories used by Venetian ambassadors to describe the Turkish political system were all neutral designations—*imperio, dominio, governo, regno,* and so forth—that were used equally to describe other systems. While the Ottoman Empire exhibited fracture lines along which Venice hoped to intervene, and while some of its specific features were considered contrary to Venetian values and traditions, it nonetheless reflected an implacable logic that accounted for its repeated military victories and its continuous expansion. The system was not only powerfully efficient, it was legitimate, and even though it might degenerate, it still belonged to the accepted forms of political organization. Indeed, more than any other existing power, it might fulfill the ultimate goal of every monarchy by succeeding in establishing a universal monarchy, a mirror image in this world of God's kingdom.

"Never on Earth Was a Larger Tyranny Conceived" [13]

By the last quarter of the sixteenth century, the image of the Ottoman Empire in Venetian ambassadors' reports had become clouded, the ruler's portrait had become disfigured, and every component of the tableau was deformed. Some ambassadors even added new chapters to their reports about the continuing changes in the empire of which Venice might be able to take advantage (for example, Bernardo 1592, 324–25). From that point on, the ambassadors' diagnoses of the strength of the empire were very different from those encountered earlier in the century. It remained the largest territory ever and was steadily gaining new provinces from Persia. Indeed, in a kind of Braudelian formula, Nani could still write in 1600 that the empire was "more a world than a state" (32). It continued to constitute the most formidable challenge to Venetian strategy. Bernardo, for example, wrote in 1592: "The Turk has entered the gates of our Italy, garden of the world and center of Christendom" (350); the Turk aspires to a "monarchy over this world" (401).

Of course, Venetian ambassadors stuck to the themes of the unlimited abundance of human and material resources of the empire, the exceptional position of its capital city, and the proven qualities of its army, but at the same time, they described a process of corruption in the entire system in all of its parts. While the word *ordine*—a term that at times referred to the ruler's authority, at times to the perfect organization of civil and military bodies—was constantly used by earlier ambassadors, the reports after 1575 repeatedly pinpointed every sign of dysfunction. "Al presente," Bernardo argued in 1592, "tutto questo ordine si va alterando e corrompendo" (332).

In a long report that circulated widely and gained notoriety, Bernardo proceeded to explain that while janissaries had never been defeated in their entire history, they were, however, "cascati"—they had fallen from their former worth. While the navy remained fearsome to any prince on earth, it was "diminished" in number, skill, and quality, and besides, it was badly paid.

More important, the three pillars on which the Turks had built their power in such a short time—religion, frugality, and obedience—were now shattered. Turks had lost their religious unity, their manly frugality, and their fierce ardor. "Obedience was the third source of the great power of the Turkish empire. In the old days obedience made them united, union made them strong, and strength rendered their armies invincible."[14] By Bernardo's time, however, disunity and disobedience had permeated civil and military bodies. But Bernardo did not yet speak of an irresistible decline. He stressed that the empire "had never lost a single palm of the land it conquered," but he could detect several principles of "declinazione," among which he mentioned the slow internal corruption resulting from changes in the ruler himself. From a victorious prince he had turned into a man of the palace, while his expanding empire had turned into an amorphous mechanism. Constant references to the model of the Roman Empire underscored Bernardo's entire analysis, including the idea that empires, like all living organisms, experience youth, maturity, and decline. As in Rome after the Trajans, the advent of idle princes would irresistibly dissipate all the glory accumulated by previous conquering emperors. After Bernardo, other reports repeatedly announced the impending decline of the Ottoman Empire.

At the same time that they announced and discussed the deterioration of the system, Venetian ambassadors began stressing its complete incompatibility with their own. The Ottoman Empire belonged to a different horizon. At the very beginning of their reports many ambassadors immediately pointed to the absolute antinomy separating the two orders.[15]

Reports from earlier in the century all contained implicit or explicit comparisons between Ottoman institutions and those of Venice or, more broadly, of Christian countries. On many items, the comparisons turned to the advantage and superiority of the former. The ratio was reversed after 1575, even when some Ottoman practices were still offered as examples to be emulated by Christian states. The appraisal of the Turks highlighted what was lacking in the Ottoman system; all the adjectives used in evaluating them became pejorative. Most of the statements about their manners and actions were set in a negative form. Rather than providing a systematic description of their institutions and resources, Venetian reports became a hodgepodge of critical remarks about most Turkish habits. As a people, the Turks lacked civility in human relations, in table manners, and in their architecture and city planning. They lacked skills in arts and technology and training in abstract reasoning. "In all their customs, they do the opposite of what Christians do, as if their legislator had that in mind when he ordered their ceremonies. . . . In all their deeds they do the opposite of what we do. Few Turks understand anything in mechanical matters, they do not till the soil, do not practice any significant exercise, do not enjoy any kind of virtue. . . . They know of no other pastime than archery" (Morosini 1585, 269; see also anonymous, 1582, 250; Venier 1582, 460, 467–68). Turks were thus unfit for both action and inaction, work and leisure.

While observations in the earliest part of the century seemed to be made from a distance and calibrated to achieve an exact appreciation of an external reality, denunciation became the general mode in later reports. Sharp criticisms of all social practices, condemnations of a false religion, and diatribes against the form and style of government combined for a total rejection of the Ottoman sociopolitical order. Here a dividing line was clearly drawn between the Venetians and the Turks. On the one hand, the Venetian order was characterized by the freedom of all the inhabitants—therefore all citizens—by the presence of a blood nobility that translated into the nobility of the souls and characters, and by stable institutions based on accepted laws.

On the other hand, in the Ottoman system the extirpation of the nobility from all the annexed lands and the reduction of its inhabitants into servitude led to the debasement of all values and the lowering of all men to the vilest level. "This is," Morosini wrote in 1585, "the government or republic of slaves" (267). Slaves exalted to power would act only with slaves' minds; without any observance of faith and word, they could only govern by the use of violence. Here another element was found to anticipate the decline of the empire: as its expansion slowed down, its preservation became more dependent on the quality of its institutions. When the benefits drawn from the annexation of new territories decreased, then those of a just government had to make up for them. The Ottoman Empire had obviously not achieved such a capability.

Bad government bore a name: tyranny. A predicate to any aspect of Ottoman life, the word was used as a noun, a verb, an adjective, and in connection with other notions that made its meaning more explicit. "Their proper state is tyranny, violence, and usurpation," Bernardo wrote in 1592 (398). Indeed, the idea of tyranny was first linked to the notion of usurpation. This nonlegitimate power was acquired by force rather than through regular inheritance or through the state's inhabitants' free assent (Zane 1594, 386). According to Morosini in 1595, "The form of this government is based on force" (255). Acquired by force, such a power was also maintained by the constant exercise of force.

Violence, not a common reference to law and regular institutions, was the normal style of relations between the ruler and his subjects. Such a power was then an "irragionavole governo," a government without reason, whose immoderation manifested itself in continuous extortions and exactions. Extortion was a natural action of a tyrannical government, oppression the natural condition of its subjects. Tyranny rested on an absurd logic: since it destroyed nobility to promote slaves, it then destroyed the very countries and people by whom it was fed, and then could only devour itself. A sea swallowing all rivers that flooded in (Nani 1604, 35), an uninterrupted chain of thieves robbing everything from those beneath them, then robbed of everything by those above (Moro 1590, 337): Venetian ambassadors did not lack metaphors to describe the circle of violence and death. Tyranny "eats to the bone" its oppressed subjects, depopulates the countries it conquers, turns into deserts the paradises that fall into its power, and brings death wherever it reaches. This was tyranny. In such a government, the prince had "no other reason than his own will" (Bernardo 1592, 381), which amounted to no reason at all. Having grown up secluded from the real world and being a prisoner of his seraglio, he had no notion of law or wisdom. Neither would he welcome good advice from wise men, since he had destroyed the nobility and become estranged from his slaves themselves.

A theme already present in earlier reports recurred regularly in later ones, that of the menagerie of monsters and infrahuman beings surrounding the sultan (Bernardo 1592, 364, 373; Moro 1590, 328). Another theme was the transfer of the absolute authority—*assoluto dominio*—from the tyrant to his prime vizier whose choice was due not to his virtue but to the ever-changing mood of the ruler (Venier 1582, 439, 440). The country has "no other ear" than the vizier's to listen to the voices from the empire, "no other mouth" to decide, order, allocate, or condemn; "no other head" to manage such a huge state. The master of an illegitimate state, the tyrant in turn gave away his authority to an illegitimate minister. Then, subject to just one man's will, authority could only turn into violence and arbitrariness (Bernardo 1592, 351). Again following an absurd logic, the tyrant not only could decide the deaths of any of his subjects and make them go willingly to their deaths, but also could destroy his own blood (Morosini 1585, 279). From the bottom to the top, the empire worked like a formidable homicidal machine.

The word "tyranny" had already emerged in a few reports before 1575, first in Navagero's text in 1553 in which he twice evoked the tyranny exercised upon the subjects by the emperor's agents (40, 41), and then by Cavalli in 1560 while speaking of a pasha (295). In the early 1570s, Garzoni mentioned more specifically how Turks of all conditions inflicted tyranny upon the Christians in the empire (396), and Barbaro spoke of provinces "tyrannicized" and countries destroyed (307). He already had a formulation Montesquieu could have endorsed: "Subornation, violence, and tyranny are natural conditions" (351). These remarks, however, remained isolated in the series of relations of that period as well as in the texts in which they are found. They denounced practices observed more at the periphery than at the center of the empire and a deformation of the system rather than the system itself. After 1575, the entire construct was perceived as the largest tyranny in history.

A twenty-two-year break interrupts the series of Venetian reports after 1616. Only when Giovanni Cappello returned from Istanbul did a new picture of the Ottoman Empire emerge. In this later series of reports from the seventeenth century, tyranny continued to be the comprehensive notion that characterized the system and maintained the same content as in earlier reports. The monstrous quality of this form of government was further accentuated and illustrated by the description of sultans such as that of Murad IV which introduces this paper. Some changes in the vocabulary can be observed. Terms that had neutral meanings in the sixteenth century, or which simply designated a strong government, were now introduced to indicate immoderation, excess, extravagance, and a generally corrupt form of government. Now, for example, the word *dominio* was contrasted with other forms: in 1616 Valier wrote that "one should call [this empire] more properly *dominio* than principality or empire" (278). *Dominio,* by the seventeenth century, comes closer to domination than to domain. Something similar occurred with *assoluto,* an amply used adjective in the sixteenth century. By the seventeenth century, it was associated with *dominio,* or *autorità,* to stigmatize an abusive form of government. A new noun, *monarco,* came to designate the ruler, together with former titles such as prince, king, emperor, sultan, Great Turk, or Grand Signor. The more abstract term "monarch" obviously referred to a specific type of government and emphasized more than other words the concentration of authority in the hands of a single ruler.

Finally, a new word came to characterize the Grand Turk's government: *despotico*. The term made its first hesitant appearance in a text attributed to Venier and dated between 1579 and 1582. It then disappeared for more than half a century and was revived by Capello in 1634. It was associated with *governo, dominio,* and *authorità,* a connection that recurred in subsequent reports, including the Foscarini report which began this paper. The verb *despotizzare* was also invented, but thus far the abstract notion of despotism had not been forged, nor had *despotico* replaced the words that sprang from the root "tyrant." Both "tyrannical" and "despotic" would travel together throughout the seventeenth century.

Why Did a Normal Body Grow into a Monster?

What accounts for this change in the picture, for this reversal of the image? Three sets of hypotheses can be proposed. The first, centered on the Porte, belongs to the realm of *histoire événementielle* and to objective data: changes in the perception and description of the Ottoman Empire were reflections of real problems being faced by the Ottoman political system. Among them, recent scholarship mentions those due to internal contradictions of an empire based on continuous expansion. As frontiers were extended, the enemies increased in number and campaign costs became excessive. The benefits of later conquests did not meet expenses, and the size of the empire made administration more and more difficult.

There was also degeneration at the center. The poor quality of later sultans in turn increased the influence of women in the palace. As a matter of fact, Murad III (1574–95) killed his five brothers on the very day of his accession to the throne and kept forty-odd concubines who gave him more than one hundred sons. As for Mehmed III (1595–1603), he had his nineteen brothers and twenty sisters killed by his deaf-mute servants when he came to power and four of his sons assassinated during his reign. So much for the *événementiel.*

On a more profound level, historians of the Ottoman Empire date the beginning of its decline from the end of the sixteenth century, an analysis that corresponds exactly to the change observed in Venetian reports. One major factor was the shift in world trade from the Mediterranean to the

Atlantic and the negative effects of the Atlantic trade on the Ottoman economy (an influx of gold and silver, sharp price increases that affected fixed incomes). Changes in the methods of government and administration encouraged the spread of violence, bribery, and other abuses all over the empire. Some voices in the empire spoke of tyranny, like our Venetian ambassadors, and asked for a return to traditional institutions and modes of government. Others waited for the millennium, since the year 1591–92 corresponded to the thousandth anniversary of the Muslim calendar. Others still rebelled against the state between 1595 and 1610.[16] Venetian ambassadors can therefore at least be credited with an immediate awareness of the difficulties being experienced by the Ottomans and of the corruption of their system.

A second interpretation focuses less on the center of the system than on the relationship between Europe and the Turks. Christian countries, having strengthened their position against the sultan, now became more critical of his unprecedented power. The crucial point was, of course, the battle of Lepanto in 1571, which was celebrated as a major victory for the Christians. But one should remember that the Holy League did not last, that Venice had paid an excessively high price for her part in the victory and was the first power to sign a treaty by which she accepted the loss of Cyprus and increased her annual tribute to the Ottomans (1573). As mentioned earlier, the Ottoman Empire was still perceived as threatening. Besides, Christian powers also had their problems. The destruction of the Armada (1588) and religious and civil wars certainly delayed the perception of a shift in the balance of power that occurred during the seventeenth century.[17]

Venetian ambassadors did not anticipate such a shift; they did not claim to. They saw the Ottoman state as a monster, not as the "sick man" it would be called two centuries later. While changes within the empire and in its relations with other powers might explain changes in the picture they conveyed, they do not fully explain the twists in the vocabulary. The very same qualities and phenomena that were characterized earlier as the pillars of the Ottoman power were now transformed into the hallmarks of despotic rule: the absolute authority of the sultan, the terror he inspired, his control over the life and wealth of his subjects, their complete obedience to him, and the force of religion.

Other elements of interpretation are then needed that will take us away from the Porte and closer to Venice. The argument would be that changes occurred in Venetian minds as much as in political realities.

Venetian Ambassadors and the Political Thought of the Sixteenth and Seventeenth Centuries

Let us start with Machiavelli. There is a well-known passage in *The Prince* in which Machiavelli contrasts the French model of government with the Grand Turk's. In a binary mode of argument he uses throughout chapter 4, he distinguishes two forms of states: republics and principalities. Within the latter, he then makes a distinction between hereditary and new principalities. In the same mode, Machiavelli argues that there are two ways principalities are governed. At this point, it is worth quoting the entire passage:

All principalities known to us are governed in one of two different ways: either by one prince with the others as his servants, who, as ministers, through his grace and permission, assist in governing that kingdom; or by a prince and barons who hold that position not because of any grace of their master but because of the nobility of their birth. Such barons as these have their own dominions and subjects who recognize them as masters and are naturally fond of them. Those dominions governed by a prince and his ministers hold their prince in greater authority, for in all his province there is no one that may be recognized as superior to him; and if they do obey any other, they do so as his minister and officer, and they do not harbor any special affection for him.

Examples of these two different kinds of governments in our own times are the Turkish Emperor and the King of France. The entire kingdom of the Turk is ruled by one master; the others are his servants; and dividing his kingdom into parts, he sends various administrators there, and he moves them and changes them as he pleases. But the King of France is placed among a group of established nobles who are recognized in that state by their subjects and who are loved by them; they have their hereditary rights; the King cannot remove them without danger to himself. Anyone, therefore, who considers these two states will find that the difficulty lies in taking possession of the Turkish state, but once it has been conquered, it is very simple to retain it. And therefore, on the contrary, you will find that in some ways it is easier to seize the French state, but it is very difficult to hold on to it.

The reasons for the difficulty in being able to occupy the Turkish kingdom are that it is not possible to be summoned there by the prince of that kingdom, nor to hope to make your enterprise easier with the rebellion of those the ruler has around him. This is because of the reasons mentioned above: since they are all slaves and dependent on the ruler, it is more difficult to corrupt them; and even if they were corrupted, you cannot hope that they will be very useful, not being able to attract followers for the reasons already discussed. Therefore, anyone who attacks the Turks must consider that he will find them completely united, and it is best that he rely more on his own strength than on their lack of unity. But once beaten and broken in battle so that they cannot regroup their troops, there is nothing else to be feared but the family of the prince; once it is extinguished, there remains no one else to be feared, for the others have no credit with the people; and just as the victor before the victory could not place hope in them, so he need not fear them afterward.[18]

While he compares the respective strengths and weaknesses of France and the Ottoman Empire, Machiavelli nonetheless places both regimes in the same category, that of principalities. Not a single word places the Ottoman State among what we would call nonlegitimate or unacceptable forms of government. But that is how this text was most often interpreted. Machiavelli's ideas were thus transformed into the ancestors of Montesquieu's model of despotism.[19] As a matter of fact, it is probably because we know the latter's model that we read it in earlier texts.

In another passage in *The Prince,* he again deals with the Turks. Machiavelli states that a good method to hold a newly conquered country is to settle in it. This, he argues, is what the Turks did in Greece. Finally, in another discussion about political strategy, Machiavelli indicates that princes generally want to satisfy their subjects rather than their soldiers. Not so the Turks.[20]

The *Discourses on the First Decade of Titus Livius* dwell upon the Turks at least three other times. First, in book 1, XIX, he deals with the problem of the continuity of power and argues that a strong kingdom can afford to have one weak, peaceful prince; but the successor ought to be strong. Again, the Turkish state provides an example of such conditions with Bayezid, a weak prince, being succeeded by a glorious one, Suleyman the Magnificent.[21]

In the same book Machiavelli argues that princes who want to avoid living under constant suspicion have to lead military campaigns themselves, "as in the beginning the Roman emperors did, as in our day the Turk does, and as courageous princes both have done and still do." Finally, a passage in book 2 sheds more light on this last statement:

I am persuaded that the world, remaining continually the same, has in it a constant quantity of good and evil; but that this good and this evil shift about from one country to another, as we know that in ancient times empire shifted from one nation to another, according as the manners of these nations changed, the world, as a whole, continuing as before, and the only difference being that, whereas at first Assyria was made the seat of its excellence, this was afterwards placed in Media, then in Persia, until at last it was transferred to Italy and Rome. And although after the Roman Empire, none has followed which has endured, or in which the world has centered its whole excellence, we nevertheless find that excellence diffused among many valiant nations, the kingdom of the Franks, for example, that of the Turks, that of the Soldan, and the States of Germany at the present day.[22]

Once again, the Ottoman system is among the virtuous empires according to Machiavelli's categories and is presented with those which have revived the virtue of ancient Rome. There is no notion of tyranny or arbitrary rule associated with the Ottoman model. The Ottoman Empire does not occupy a separate position in Machiavelli's taxonomies. As far as we are concerned, all these unambiguous statements are consistent with the earlier Venetian ambassadors' reports.

Furthermore, other arguments found in Machiavelli's work would apply to the sultan and fit with the early descriptions by Venetian ambassadors. To give only one example, in *The Prince*, XVII, Machiavelli raises the question of "whether it is better to be loved than to be feared or the contrary." He gives the following answer: "Therefore, a prince must not worry about the reproach of cruelty when it is a matter of keeping his subjects united and loyal" (130).

A similar point was made by Jean Bodin, whom some authors include in the line of philosophers which leads from Machiavelli to Montesquieu (and later, to Marx and his Asiatic mode of production).[23] For his contemporaries, Bodin was the new Aristotle. His models were discussed in Italian circles and reached Venice, where people were all the more interested in knowing his ideas since he challenged the concept of Venice as a "mixt" state. In his *Methodus ad facilem historiarum cognitionem* (1566), which gained him a wide European reputation, then in *The Six Books of the Commonwealth* (1576), Bodin distinguished between three forms of government—monarchy, aristocracy, and democracy—which in turn could evolve into three further forms. Monarchy could be royal, aristocratic, or could become tyrannical. Tyranny occurred when the king did not respect the laws of nature or his subjects and acted abusively toward men and property. To which of the three classes did the Great Turk belong? In Bodin's terms, he belonged to the aristocratic (or "seigneurial") monarchy, as did the kingdom of Muscovy. But these were not tyrannies, he argued, because their empires had been acquired through just wars. Furthermore, while the sultan was the master of men and properties, he governed in a much more courteous manner than the head of a household uses toward his servants (*Six Books*, II).

Elsewhere, Bodin claimed that monarchy was a natural form. In the same way that there was only one sun and one only God, so there ought to be only one king. Bodin illustrated his point by mentioning Sultan Suleyman's assassination of his three sons: the oldest one, Mustafa, deserved to be killed because he had become too popular; the second, because he deplored his brother's death; the youngest, because he tried to flee. Only one son was allowed to live, so that no danger for the royal house would emerge from a division among the princes. "There must be, Suleyman proclaimed, only one God in heaven, and on earth, one sultan, Suleyman,"[24] a claim Bodin strongly supported (*Methodus*, 266).

Other references to the Turks in Bodin's *The Six Books* and *Methodus* belong to the same picture, a picture that remains consistent with the descriptions given by Venetian ambassadors from the beginning of the sixteenth century to the mid-1570s. A major argument is elaborated in the *Methodus*, where Bodin devotes a full chapter to the theory of the four empires inspired by the prophecy of Daniel; it raised the question of who would be able to become the universal monarch. For Bodin, who finally rejects the prophecy, the Turks were, in his time, the most likely to achieve such a goal. It is worth quoting a few passages of his text, which display a striking resemblance to the early ambassadors' argument:

On what ground could the king of Germany compare to the Turks' sultan? Who would have more claims to the title of monarch than the latter? Why argue on an evidence that imposes itself so brilliantly to universal judgment? If indeed there exists somewhere an authority which deserves the name of an authentic empire or monarchy, it is the sultan who holds it in his hands. He occupies the wealthiest countries in Asia, Africa and Europe. His domination extends over the entire Mediterranean, except for a few islands. His military power is sufficient to counterbalance alone that of all other princes. He keeps far from his borders the Persians' and Moscovites' armies, conquers Christian kingdoms and the Byzantine empire, and proceeds to devastate German provinces. . . .

How fair it would be to consider as the successor to the Roman empire the sultan of the Turks who, after having taken over from the Persians the region of Babylon, which is precisely mentioned in Daniel, adding to Rome's provinces all the country beyond the Danube river, up to the banks of the Boristhen which form today most of his territory.

Had we to define monarchy by the power of its armies, the extent of its resources, the fertility of its territory, the list of its victories, the number of its inhabitants, or by its sole etymology, since it applies to Daniel's native country or to the Emperor Babylon, one has to admit that Daniel's prophecy is most meaningful when applied to the Great Turk. (*Methodus*, 289–90)

At this point, we have good reason to argue that there was a coincidence between political philosophers and Venetian ambassadors in the first three-quarters of the sixteenth century. While the notion—and rejection—of tyranny existed, it did not apply to the Ottoman state, which continued to be perceived as a powerful, complex, yet perfect mechanism. By the 1560s, the diffusion of the prophecy of Daniel found an echo in the ambassadors' reports, adding an eschatological dimension to the picture.

By the end of the century, a turning point occurred in Venetian thought. Thanks to the work of W. J. Bouwsma,[25] we know how Venetian identity was then redefined. The theme of tyranny became crucial. As the government of one man, as the state without freedom, where terror and secrecy became the means of control, tyranny was contrasted with a state of liberty resting on the enforcement of the law. From the 1560s on, "tyranny" was applied not to the Ottoman empire but, first of all, to the Medici state.[26] A dichotomy thus structured Venetian thought, opposing the state of liberty to the state of tyranny. After the mid-1570s, the Ottoman state fell into the second category. It was not alone. Florence permanently, and England later and more occasionally, belonged to the same category.[27]

Finally, by the end of the sixteenth century, the word "despotic" had entered the vocabulary, and new taxonomies were forged in Italian political thought. Among other authors, Giovanni Botero appears as a milestone in this evolution with his *Relationi universali,* first published in Venice in 1591. Discussing Bodin's argument, he defined three forms of government: monarchy, democracy, and aristocracy. The three forms could be mixed, "composte," when they combined with other forms. Venice, for example, was a mixture of monarchy and aristocracy,[28] while Athens had combined a principality with a democracy. A corruption of the three governments led monarchy to tyranny, democracy to ochlocracy, and aristocracy to oligarchy. As for the Great Turk (part 2, book 4), he was definitely *despotic.* Botero proceeded to explain why. In the ensuing argument, we can recognize all the features found in the Venetian ambassadors' descriptions. There is no way to establish a direct filiation between Botero and Venetian ambassadors to the Porte—or the direct opposite. I simply mean to suggest that these ideas were "in the air" at the time, as exchanges took place between political philosophers and politicians who shared the same models at the end of the sixteenth century. Here is Botero's text (as an aside, I should mention that the French translation of this text in 1614 did not use the word despotic and preferred "absolute," an indication of the hesitation in the political discourse of the period):

The Ottomans' government is indeed despotic. Because the grand Turk is the master of everything within the limits of his empire [*dominio*], in such a way that the inhabitants are called his slaves, not his subjects. No one is the master of his own person, of the house he lives in, of the land he cultivates, except for a few houses which were granted privileges by Mahomet the Second in Constantinople. There is no person of distinction who is important enough to be sure about his own life, nor about the state in which he finds himself by the Grand Signor's grace. He maintains himself in such an absolute power [*dominio*] by two means: taking the arms from the subjects, and putting everything in the hands of renegades, taken as children as a tithe from his own states. (part 2, book 4)[29]

Conclusion: The Abduction from the Seraglio

In the Venetian ambassadors' reports on Istanbul, we find two stages in the history of their political ideals. In the earlier one, the imperial form of government seemed legitimate, and appeared as a normal development of smaller systems. In such a form of government, authority was expected to be strong, the subjects' submission unchallenged, and religious law working as a hedge against arbitrariness. These were the major elements stressed by Venetian ambassadors when they described the Ottoman state. Tyranny was identified as a political form to which Venetian culture had developed a strong aversion since the fourteenth century, but it was associated with situations found in ancient times, not in the Ottoman Empire.[30]

In a second stage, the Ottoman state, together with other states, fell into the abhorred category of tyranny. Simultaneously, controversies about the different forms of government (which arose in the context of religious and political struggles and the emergence of absolute states in Europe) resulted in a profound renewal of the political vocabulary.

Tracing the origin of Montesquieu's model of oriental despotism, scholars have generally followed two paths. Most have drawn a continuous line connecting philosophers from Machiavelli to Bodin, La Boétie, Hobbes, and finally Montesquieu, as if philosophy floated by itself, independently of other literary forms or other expressions of political aspirations.[31] In his brilliant analysis, Alain Grosrichard found in the travelers' accounts read by Montesquieu all the ingredients of the paradigm he then constructed. These accounts, however, formed only a thin layer of the knowledge available to Montesquieu on the Ottoman state.[32]

I have chosen in this paper to confront political philosophy with the descriptions provided by men who were familiar with both the Ottoman Empire and the intellectual debates of their times, whose reports were known and used by philosophers, and who in turn used the concepts forged by theoreticians.

Another path was followed in the 1950s by R. Koebner.[33] A splendid study in semantics, his article traced the reemergence of Aristotle's category of "despot" in European languages and writing. Reading translations of Aristotle's *Politics* in the Middle Ages, the political thought of the Renaissance, as well as seventeenth-century pamphlets, he showed how reluctantly the word "despot," which would eventually replace the word "tyranny," was reintroduced by French and English writers into the political lexicon of the seventeenth century. Seen from Venice, the Italian case (1) confirms the early synonymy of the terms "tyrannical" and "despotic"; (2) confirms the substitution of "despotic" for "tyrannical" at a later stage; and (3) suggests that Italian thinkers had already reappropriated Aristotle's terminology by the end of the sixteenth century.

Where, then, was the despot until he was rediscovered by European philosophy? Was he living in the seraglio or resting in Aristotle's *Politics*? When Montesquieu opened a new chapter in European taxonomies, was the despot oriental, was he Asiatic? Or was he—as happens so often in the European tradition—a concept produced by Greek philosophy dressed in the costume of an oriental monarch?

This text was first delivered at the Davis Seminar in April 1987. The arguments of this paper were subsequently elaborated in a book-length study, *Venise et la Sublime Porte*, Hachette, 1987. I am grateful to the following for their help and comments: Patricia and Peter Brown, Michael Cook, Charles Issawi, Cemal Kafadar, Lawrence Stone, and Avrom Udovitch of Princeton University, and my graduate students Glenn Robinson and David Waldner at Berkeley.

Notes

1. "Relazioni di Pietro Foscarini," in Nicolo Barozzi and Guglielmo Berchet, *Le Relazioni degli Stati Europei lette al Senato dagli Ambasciatori Veneziani nel Secolo Decimosettimo*, series V, Turchia, one volume (Venice, 1866), 89–90.

2. Alain Grosrichard, *Structure du Sérail. La Fiction du Despotisme Asiatique dans l'Orient Classique* (Paris, 1979).

3. For the sixteenth century, see: Eugenio Albéri, *Relazioni degli Ambasciatori Veneziani al Senato durante il Secolo Decimosesto*, series III, 3 vols. and appendix (Florence, 1840–63). For the seventeenth century, Barozzi and Berchet (see above, n. 1). Since Albéri's volumes do not follow a chronological order, I indicate below where the successive reports are to be found in his collection. In subsequent references, I shall mention only the date of the report and the page in the volume in which it appears.

Andrea Gritti 1503, vol. 3, p. 1; Antonio Giustiniani 1514, vol. 3, p. 45; Alvise Mocenigo 1518, vol. 3, p. 53; Bartolomeo Contarini 1519, vol. 3, p. 56; Marco Minio

1522, vol. 3, p. 69; Pietro Zen 1524, vol. 3, p. 93; Pietro Bragadin 1526, vol. 3, p. 99; Marco Minio 1527, vol. 3, p. 113; Pietro Zen 1530, vol. 3, p. 119; Daniello Ludovisi 1534, vol. 1, p. 1; Bernardo Navagero 1553, vol. 1, p. 33; Anon. 1553, vol. 1, p. 193; Domenico Trevisano 1554, vol. 1, p. 111; Antonio Erizzo 1557, vol. 3, p. 123; Antonio Barbarigo 1558, vol. 3, p. 145; Marino Cavalli 1560, vol. 1, p. 271; Andrea Dandolo 1562, vol. 3, p. 161; Marcantonio Donini 1562, vol. 3, p. 173; Daniele Barbarigo 1564, vol. 2, p. 1; Luigi Bonrizzo 1565, vol. 2, p. 161; Jacopo Ragazzoni 1571, vol. 2, p. 77; Marcantonio Barbaro 1573, vol. 1, p. 299, and appendix, p. 387; Andrea Badoaro 1573, vol. 1, p. 347; Costantino Garzoni 1573, vol. 1, p. 369; Vicenzo Alessandri 1574, vol. 2, p. 103; Anon. 1575, vol. 2, p. 309; Antonio Tiepolo 1576, vol. 2, p. 129; Giacomo Soranzo 1576, vol. 2, p. 193; Maffeo Venier 1579 or 1582, vol. 1, p. 437 (the author was identified in vol. 3, p. 212); Anon. 1582, vol. 2, p. 209; Anon. 1582, vol. 2, p. 427; Paolo Contarini 1583, vol. 3, p. 209; Gianfrancesco Morosini 1585, vol. 3, p. 251; Giovanni Michiel 1587, vol. 2, p. 255; Maffeo Venier 1587, vol. 2, p. 295; Giovanni Moro 1590, vol. 3, p. 323; Lorenzo Bernardo 1592, vol. 2, p. 321; Matteo Zane 1594, vol. 3, p. 381.

All these reports are reproduced in Luigi Firpo, *Relazioni di Ambasciatori Veneti al Senato,* vol. 13, *Costantinopoli 1590–1793* (Turin, 1984). Firpo's volume adds a report to Albéri's collection by Leonardo Dona, 1596, 309–70.

4. Angelo Ventura, *Relazioni degli Ambasciatori Veneti al Senato* (Bari, 1976), p. XIX.

5. Oliver Logan, *Culture and Society in Venice, 1570–1790* (London, 1972). Angelo Ventura, "Scrittori Politici e Scritture di Governo," in *Storia della Cultura Veneta* (hereafter, *SCV*), G. Arnaldi, ed., vol. III, 3 (Vicenza, 1981), 513–63. Franco Gaetta, "Venetia da 'Stato Misto' ad Aristocrazia 'esemplare,'" *SCV,* IV, 2, 436–94.

6. Armand Baschet, *La Diplomatie Vénitienne. Les Princes de l'Europe au XVIIe Siècle d'après les Rapports des Ambassadeurs Vénitiens* (Paris, 1862). On the early association of humanism and politics in Venice, Margaret L. King, *Venetian Humanism in the Age of Patrician Dominance* (Princeton, 1986).

7. On Venetian policy vis-à-vis the Turks, Paolo Preto, *Venetia e i Turchi* (Florence, 1975). F. Braudel, "Bilan d'une Bataille," in Gino Benzoni, *Il Mediterraneo nella Seconda Meta del '500 ala Luce di Lepanto* (Florence, 1974), 109–20. On the theme of Judith, see Eleanor Selfridge-Field, "*Juditha* in Historical Perspective: Scarlatti, Gasparini, Marcello and Vivaldi," in Francesco Degrada, ed., *Vivaldi Veneziano Europeo* (Florence, 1980), 135–53. Denis and Elsie Arnold, *The Oratorio in Venice* (London, Royal Musical Association monographs 2, 1986). Lino Bianchi, *Carissimi Sradella, Scarlatti e l'Oratorio Musicale* (Rome, 1969).

8. Ambassadors' reports as the expression of Venetian political values in Ventura 1981 (see above, n. 5). Also Piero del Negro, "Forme e Istituzioni del Discorso Politico Veneziano," *SCV,* IV, 2, 407–36. On public rituals as a political discourse, see Edward Muir, *Civic Rituals in Renaissance Venice* (Princeton, 1981).

9. On the *Tesoro Politico,* Baschet (see n. 6), Ventura 1976 (see n. 4), 101.

10. Ventura 1981 (see n. 5), 557, who quotes Burckhardt.

11. See Frank E. Manuel, *Shapes of Philosophical History* (Stanford, 1965), 14. For Venice, Giovanni Tarcagnota, *Delle Istorie del mondo* (Venice, 1585). Agostino Ferentilli, *Discorso Universale* (Venice, 1570). There were some authors who thought that the Serenissima could pretend to the Roman heritage and aspire to the gov-

ernment of the entire world: see Sansovino, *Dell'Historia Universale dell'Origine et Imperio de' Turchi* (1564). Also by Sansovino, *Gl'Annali Turcheschi, o vero Ite de'Principi della Casa Othomana* (1571). See also Giuliano Lucchetta, "L'Oriente Mediterraneo nella Cultura di Venezia tra Quattro e Cinquecento," *SCV*, III, 2, 375–432.

12. Common sailors recruited in taverns for the Ottoman navy.

13. Morosini, 1585, 179.

14. Translation taken from James C. Davis, *Pursuit of Power: Venetian Ambassadors' Reports on Turkey, France and Spain in the Age of Philip II, 1560–1600* (New York, 1970), 160.

15. Tiepolo (1576) speaks of a government "differentissimo da ogni altro," 183; also Venier 1579; Moro 1590, 325.

16. Halil Inalcik, *The Ottoman Empire: The Classical Age. 1300–1600,* tr. Norman Itzkowitz and Colin Imber (London, 1973), 41–52. "State, Sovereignty and Law during the Reign of Suleyman," forthcoming in H. Inalcik and H. Lowry, *Suleyman and His Age,* Publication of the Institute of Turkish Studies. Stanford J. Shaw, *The Rise and Decline of the Ottoman Empire,* vol. 1, *Empire of the Gazis, 1280–1808* (Cambridge, 1976), ch. 6, 169. On contemporary analysis within the Ottoman Empire, Bernard Lewis, "Ottoman Observers of Ottoman Decline," *Islamic Studies,* I, 1962, 71–87. Cornell Fleischer, "Royal Authority, Dynastic Cyclism and 'Ibn Khaldunism' in Sixteenth-Century Ottoman Letters," *Journal of Asian and African Studies,* vol. XVIII, 1984, 218–37. Cemal Kafadar, *When Coins Turned into Drops of Dew and Bankers Became Robbers of Shadows: The Boundaries of Ottoman Economic Imagination at the End of the 16th Century,* Ph.D. diss., McGill University, 1986.

17. See Fernand Braudel's beautiful pages on Lepanto in *The Mediterranean World in the Age of Philip II* (New York, 1976), vol. 2, 1088–106.

18. *The Prince,* IV, in *The Portable Machiavelli,* tr. and ed. P. Bondanella and M. Musa (New York, 1979), 88–90.

19. Perry Anderson, *Lineages of the Absolute State* (London, 1974); Paolo Preto 1975 (see n. 7).

20. *Discourse on the First Decade of Titus Livius,* tr. Leslie J. Walker (New Haven, 1950), 281.

21. In fact, Suleyman succeeded Selim I, himself the son of Bayezid.

22. Op. cit., N. Hill Thomson (London, 1883), 189–90.

23. Perry Anderson (n. 19); L. Krader, *The Asiatic Mode of Production: Sources, Development and Critique in the Writings of Karl Marx* (Assen, 1975), ch. 1.

24. Jean Bodin, *La Méthode de l'Histoire,* tr. and ed. Pierre Mesnard (Algiers, 1941). *Les Six Livres de la République* (Paris, 1576).

25. William J. Bouwsma, *Venice and the Defense of Republican Liberty: Renaissance Values in the Age of the Counter Reformation* (Berkeley, 1968; 2d ed., 1984).

26. On Florence, Albéri (n. 3), series II, vol. 1, 325, 327; vol. 2, 76–78, 371.

27. Barozzi and Berchet (n. 1), series IV, *Inghilterra,* 1863, 40–41, on James the First, and p. 422 on Charles the First and Cromwell.

28. Giovanni Botero, *Relationi Universali* (1591). Paolo Preto, "I Turchi e la Cultura Veneta del Seicento," *SCV,* IV, 2, 313–41, argues that Botero found his inspiration in Venetian ambassadors' reports. However, I disagree with Preto's assertion that the Venetian ambassadors had, over the centuries, characterized the

Ottoman government as despotic and absolute (314). There was instead a marked discontinuity in their descriptions.

29. *Les Estats Empires et Principautez du Monde,* followed by *Discours des Estats du Turc,* p. 1275, a French translation of Botero without the author's name, published in 1617.

30. Giorgio Gracco, "La Cultura Giuridico-politica nella Venezia della 'serrata,'" *SCV,* I, 2, 1976, 238–71.

31. Perry Anderson (n. 19); L. Krader (n. 23).

32. Alain Grosrichard (n. 2).

33. R. Koebner, "Despot and Despotism: Vicissitudes of a Political Term," *Journal of the Warburg and Courtauld Institutes,* 14 (1951), 275–302.

6. Civic Chivalry and the English Civil War

> All the time I had from school. . . . I spent in reading these books [of knight errantry], and reading how that Amadis and other knights not knowing their parents, did in time prove to be sons of kings and great personages, I had such a fond and idle opinion, that I might in time prove to be some great person, or at leastwise be squire to some knight.
>
> Francis Kirkman, *The Unlucky Citizen* (1673)

> I rummaged through the propaganda material, picking out one pamphlet whose cover listed every battle the Marines had fought, from Trenton to Inchon. . . . Already I saw myself charging up some distant beachhead, like John Wayne in *Sands of Iwo Jima,* and then coming home a suntanned warrior with medals on my chest.
>
> Philip Caputo, *A Rumor of War* (1977)

Valiant Apprentices

In the fall of 1642, at the outbreak of the English Civil War, a pamphlet appeared in London titled *The Valiant Resolution of the Prentices of London* and purporting to express the sentiments of more than 8,000 London apprentices who were enlisting in the Parliamentary army. The *Resolution* begins by extolling "the famous city of London," which "hath ever been fruitful in noble and heroic spirits, who have performed wonders of magnanimity and valor in foreign parts, for the everlasting honor and glory of their country."[1] Notice the key words in this opening fanfare: "noble," "heroic," "magnanimity," "valor," "honor and glory." These are not the accents of Puritan piety, although historians are quite rightly restoring Puritanism to the center of their explanations of the English Revolution. Instead the rhetoric is emphatically aristocratic; more precisely, it is chivalric.[2]

The apprentices look forward to battle with quasi-sexual anticipation, "marching on as cheerfully as [if] it were their marriage day, and that victory should be their happy bride."[3] Surely there is some confusion here?

As we all know, from *1066 and All That*, it was the Royalists who were "Wrong but Wromantic," while the Parliamentarians were "Right but Repulsive." Yet this erotic excitement at the imminence of danger and violence very closely resembles the mood of the Cavalier poet Richard Lovelace in "To Lucasta, Going to the Wars": "Another mistress I embrace, / The first foe in the field."

The author of *The Valiant Resolution* takes care to distinguish the apprentice volunteers from the mercenary riffraff who filled the armies of early modern Europe. The apprentices are all "servants to honest and sufficient men"; their relatives live "honestly and thriftily." This description accords well with what we know of the social origins of London apprentices in the mid-seventeenth century. Some were, indeed, the younger sons of gentlemen, but in general their parents were scattered more or less evenly across the middle ranks of English society.

But notice the author's next rhetorical move: after establishing the "bourgeois" credentials of these apprentices, the author swiftly reverts to aristocratic terms of eulogy. Their families in the countryside live honestly and thriftily but the apprentices themselves act "as if they [were] all descended of generous blood." They behave, in other words, as born aristocrats: "their minds are so enlarged and their courages so magnanimously advanced that [they] are determined . . . to advance their own fame and bring honor and renown to the City of London."[4]

The *Resolution* declares that the apprentices are also fighting for the "safety and honor" of the king—a king who had allegedly been kidnapped by Papists and evil advisors. It was the embarrassing fact, however, that a large majority of the titled nobility of England, and a good half of the armigerous gentry, were to be found on the Royalist side. To sustain the apprentices' claims to honor it was therefore necessary to impugn the honor of the Royalist nobility and gentry.

The *Resolution* therefore alleges that the civil war was begun by the Papists, in alliance with some "temerarious and rash noblemen" and "the decayed gentry of several counties." These decayed gentry, having squandered their patrimony through "prodigality, excess, riot, and horse-races," now hoped to recoup their fortunes by plundering their countrymen, at the head of "a multitude of drunken and idle people."[5]

In a word, the Royalist aristocracy are traitors. By conspiring with the Papists they have betrayed not only God but the king as well, since popery is fundamentally inimical to the secular power of the Crown. By fomenting civil war they have betrayed their country. And by wasting their inheritances they have betrayed themselves and their own families—their posterity as well as their ancestors.

The Royalist aristocracy are self-attainted; they have derogated from true nobility. And it is interesting to observe that in the case of the "decayed gentry" this loss of honor is attributed to their prodigality and excess: unlike the families of the valiant apprentices, they cannot live "honestly and thriftily." They have lost their nobility through lack of the "bourgeois" virtues.

In the age-old controversy about the nature and source of true honor, the *Resolution* clearly assumes honor to be achieved rather than ascribed: it is the fruit of virtuous action, not a mere accident of birth. The author, and presumably the apprentices themselves, would have agreed with Don Quixote that "every man is the son of his own works."

I have no clues as to authorship of this *Valiant Resolution*. But I am willing to bet that the apprentices found it a most gratifying reflection of their own self-image. Its disorderly fervor and repetitive bombast perfectly capture the accents of adolescent zealotry. If the author himself was not, or had not recently been, a "magnanimous and valiant apprentice" he understood them perfectly.

The Chivalric Tradition

The rhetoric of *The Valiant Resolution* derives unmistakably from the chivalric plays and chapbooks that were so popular with the youth of the seventeenth century. Notice in the very opening sentence the evocation of "wonders performed in foreign parts" by citizens of London. The immediate reference here is to the "knightly" exploits of London citizens in the Crusades and the Hundred Years War, such as those commemorated in the thumping doggerel verse of Richard Johnson's *Nine Worthies of London*.[6] But behind these more or less historical referents, lurking especially in that word "wonders," lies the whole fantastic world of romance and knight-errantry, embodied in the tales of St. George and the Dragon, Guy of Warwick, Bevis of Hampton, Amadis of Gaul, the Knight of the Sun, and dozens more.

This chivalric tradition flourished throughout the seventeenth century in both popular and elite forms. At just about the time these apprentices were marching off to Hull, John Bunyan (as he later regretfully confessed) was eagerly devouring the chapbooks about Bevis of Southampton and St. George. The London bookseller Francis Kirkman, looking back on his youth from the year 1673, recalled spending all his free time reading books of knight errantry. Margaret Spufford's research on seventeenth century chapbooks suggests that Bunyan and Kirkman were typical of young literate commoners.[7] For the illiterate, there were ballad versions of the same stories, and unrecorded fireside storytellings. More polished romances appealed to more refined or mature readers: *Amadis of Gaul,* for example—which Francis Kirkman probably read in a chapbook abridgment—was owned by the third Earl of Essex, the commander of the Parliamentary army that our valiant apprentices were joining.[8]

On a loftier literary plane, there was Sir Philip Sidney's *Arcadia,* its prestige enhanced by its author's reputation as the paradigm of Protestant knighthood, and by his early and heroic death at Zutphen. *The Countess of Pembroke's Arcadia,* regarded as a veritable manual of chivalric ethics, was among the most popular books of the early seventeenth century, going through sixteen printings between 1590 and 1629. Sir Edward Coke, not the most romantic of souls, owned a copy. In 1622 the new edition of *The Arcadia* was purchased by the young Simonds D'Ewes, known to historians as an antiquarian and Parliamentary diarist of dourly Puritan views. D'Ewes read the work "with great delight, the style of it being most sweet and excellent." John Milton also admired it, though with reservations; Charles I, while awaiting his own execution, is said to have drawn comfort from the prayer of Pamela, *Arcadia*'s heroine, during her imprisonment.[9]

Finally, of course, there was that summit of English neo-chivalric literature, the work of Sidney's protégé, Edmund Spenser. *The Faerie Queene* transformed the chivalric conventions of knight-errantry into a combination of religio-philosophic allegory and nationalist epic. The work's complexity and obscurity restricted its readership, but it nevertheless enjoyed a very respectable eight editions between 1590 and 1640, brought out by the same printers and booksellers who handled Sidney's works.

Educated humanists, of the sort who could appreciate *The Arcadia* or *The Faerie Queene* might affect to despise the more vulgar romances from which they derived. But Sidney himself, who defended poetry on the basis of its capacity to foster the aristocratic virtues, was willing to concede this function to the more popular tales as well. "Truly, I have known men," he writes in *The Defence of Poesy,* "that even with reading *Amadis of Gaul,* which God knoweth, wanteth much of a perfect poesy, have found their hearts moved to the exercise of courtesy, liberality, and especially courage."[10]

The social implications of the chivalric mythos are interestingly ambiguous: we have here, I submit, an especially complex and paradoxical case of cultural transmission. The chivalric tradition, by which I mean both the code of knightly honor and the literary genres in which that code was inscribed, resulted from the commingling of classical and Germanic traditions, and first assumed recognizable form amongst the feudal nobility of twelfth-century France. From the next five centuries the ideals of chivalry retained their essentially aristocratic character: chivalric romance exalted the *chevalier sans peur et sans reproche,* whose superiority over lesser mortals was due not only to martial prowess, but to his *courtoisie,* his adherence to the code of courtly behavior.

The central value of the chivalric tradition is honor, a principle that was extended in the high Middle Ages to embrace not only the "heroic" virtues of valor, loyalty, pride, and plain-dealing, but also those of gallantry and self-sacrifice in the defense of endangered innocence and, more particularly, in the service of an idealized mistress. Now honor (as Julio Caro Baroja has stressed) is inevitably comparative and invidious: honor means "*valer mas,*" to be worth more than other men. Hence the chivalric tradition is irrevocably anti-egalitarian. But the tradition is ambiguous about the role of biological heredity in the transmission of honor. Noble ancestry was, of course, esteemed and envied throughout the early modern period: the snobbery of birth is hardly extinct today. And it was frequently alleged that aristocrats at least *tended* to breed true.[11]

Thus the heroes of chivalric fiction are generally well-born, though their ancestry may for long be concealed from the reader, and even from the hero himself. Yet for all that, the popular chivalric romances by and large support the definition of true honor assumed by *The Valiant Resolution:* honor is something achieved through virtuous deeds rather than passively acquired by birth. Noble ancestors, in this fallen world, all too often produce unworthy descendents. It is fatally easy to degenerate from "true nobility," as the Royalist aristocracy is alleged by *The Valiant Resolution* to have done. Sir Philip Sidney says it well and repeatedly in *The Arcadia:* "This man called Pamphilus in birth I must confess is noble," says one character, describing a villain, "but what is that to him, if it shall be a stain to his dead ancestors to have left such an offspring?"[12]

So it is possible, within the chivalric system of values, for men of lowly birth but lofty character to achieve the "true nobility" that is alone worthy of respect. By doing so, they may eclipse, and even supplant, the hereditary but "degenerate" noble. "I value as a gentleman him who is so indeed," declared Oliver Cromwell. He was making the same point as Don Quixote: "Every man is the son of his own works."

The Knight of the Burning Pestle

Every year, throughout the medieval and early modern centuries, hundreds of young males—many of them from provincial towns and villages—were bound apprentice to London craftsmen and merchants. "Mercurius Civicus" speaks in 1643 of mothers who hoped "they might live to see their sons Lord Mayors of London."[13] That prospect cannot have been very heartening to a ten-year-old. How much more consoling it must have been for a lonely and insecure lad in a strange gigantic city to dream like the young Francis Kirkman that he might turn out to be some nobleman's lost heir, "or at leastwise, be squire to some knight."

The tales of knight-errantry provided inspiration as well as distraction and furnished the young with a narrative repertoire through which to articulate their own dreams and projects. Chivalric myth, in other words, fostered self-definition, as do the fairy tales described in Bruno Bettelheim's The Uses of Enchantment.[14] Nor can these dreams have been without consequence for the adult personality. The young John Bunyan, who dreamed about Bevis of Southampton and George on Horseback, was father to the man who created Christian and Great-Heart.

But it was not merely a matter of enchantment and consolation, important as these may be. There were earnest social aspirations involved as well. Adapted for popular tastes and appropriated for its own purposes by the London public, chivalric romance helped to nourish the ideal of citizen honor, the very wellspring of the Londoner's corporate self-esteem. The notion represented an assertion of personal and collective dignity, of a sort that was comparable in kind, if admittedly subordinate in degree, to the hereditary honor of the nobleman.

The portrayal of heroic citizens ennobled by their own valor (as in Johnson's Nine Worthies of London), or of nobly born heroes serving as apprentices (as in Heywood's Foure Prentises of London) did not repudiate social distinctions.[15] But these stories served to reassure the bourgeois public that there was nothing intrinsically "ignoble" about their condition. Popular romance (and romantic popular history) demonstrated that the heroic commoner could rise, as the "son of his own works," to nobility. Equally important was the assertion, by no means uncontested, that the nobly born were undefiled by immersion in the bourgeois world: a matter of some concern to the younger sons of gentry who were packed off to the City to learn a trade.

The bourgeois taste for chivalric literature was amusingly satirized, although with somewhat ambivalent effect, in Francis Beaumont's *Knight of the Burning Pestle,* written between 1607 and 1610.[16] The play, which has a disconcertingly "post-modernist" structure, works through the artful confusion of mimetic planes. At the outset, the players are supposed to be performing a comedy titled *The London Merchant.* But a few lines into the Prologue this performance is interrupted by the Grocer and his Wife, who are represented as spectators seated on the stage—normally the preserve of aristocratic theater-goers (Fig. 6.1).

The Grocer denounces the players for their habitual ridicule of London citizens and demands to see something commendatory of "the honor of the commons of the city." The Wife proposes that a part be found in the play for their apprentice, Rafe, who is among the groundlings in the pit before the stage. Rafe, an amateur ham actor who has gotten by heart whole reams of fustian, is eager to uphold "the honor of grocers" by performing heroic deeds on stage.

After a brief resistance, the players agree to a screwball compromise. Rafe clambers up onto the stage, thus shattering the theatrical frame and simultaneously transgressing the social boundary between common and gentle spectators. The players proceed with their sentimental comedy, an insipid "urban pastoral" about love across class lines. Meanwhile Rafe and his companions intercut this action with mock heroic adventures drawn from popular romances and melodramas, the favorite literary fare of the London apprentices.

The original title is abandoned: *The London Merchant* is rechristened *The Knight of the Burning Pestle,* after the chivalric identity which Rafe has assumed. Rafe's *nom de cheval,* which parodies the title of a popular romance called *The Knight of the Burning Sword,* is doubly apt: the pestle is of course a tool of the grocer's trade, but Rafe, in his knightly incarnation, wields it as a club, the classic weapon of the apprentice riot. (When apprentices assembled to assert their rights or avenge a grievance—usually the encroachment by "strangers," foreign or domestic, on their economic privileges—they rallied to the cry of "Clubs!")

We have here not a "play-within-a-play" but the destructive intrusion of a purportedly "extra-theatrical" reality (itself, of course, fictional) into the expressly artificial realm of the initial plot. The burlesque heroics of

THE
KNIGHT OF
the Burning Peſtle.

—————— ————— ————— *Quod ſi*
Iudicium ſubtile, videndis artibus illud
Ad libros & ad hæc Muſarum dona vocares:
Bœotum in craſſo iurares aëre natum.
Horat. in Epiſt. ad Oct. Aug.

LONDON,
Printed for *Walter Burre*, and are to be ſold at the
ſigne of the Crane in Paules Church-yard.
1613.

Figure 6.1. Title page of *The Knight of the Burning Pestle* (London, 1613). Courtesy of R. H. Taylor Collection.

Rafe and his entourage are never integrated with this ostensible story. The play's unsettling humor springs from the jarring of incongruous worlds. *The Knight of the Burning Pestle* is an exuberant farce, one of the handful of Jacobean comedies that can evoke unforced laughter from a twentieth-century audience. The play's confusion of mimetic planes anticipates the sublimely demented climax of *A Night at the Opera*.

Modern critics, familiar with the poetics of Mikhail Bakhtin, might analyze in depth this polyphonic ambivalence, which represents the collision and interpenetration of cultural galaxies. They might admire the way the work seemingly escapes from the author's control, ascending from social mockery into the euphoric delirium of the carnivalesque. It is Rafe, after all—transformed from satirical butt into Lord of Misrule—who steals the show. The original play gets thoroughly subverted: it now belongs to Rafe, the Knight of the Burning Pestle.

The dramatic climax, quite eclipsing the resolution of the ostensible main plot, is Rafe's death scene, in which he staggers around the stage with a forked arrow through his head (acquired while carelessly strolling through the Finsbury archery fields), bidding bombastic adieu to the joys of apprenticeship, such as pulling down brothels and pelting whores with rotten eggs. He delivers one of the great exit lines of Jacobean drama: "I die; fly, fly, my soul, to Grocers Hall!" Rafe's literal eruption from the pit, his successful invasion of the professional (and aristocratic) space of the stage, bearing his own version of the chivalric myth, symbolizes to the Bakhtinian reader the whole process of cultural appropriation by which the urban citizenry laid claim to its own form of "honor."

But Jacobean Londoners had not, alas, read Bakhtin. The play's first production, sometime between 1607 and 1610, was not only a failure but a scandal. The play did not appear in print until 1613, at least two years after it reached the publisher. Even then Beaumont thought it prudent to conceal his authorship.

The British Library's copy of the first edition bears the following inscription, in a contemporary hand: "Oh how the offended citizens did nestle ["squirm"], / To be abused with Knight of Burning Pestle." This couplet, probably inscribed by the book's first owner, seems to have gone unnoticed by subsequent editors. But it is a precious scrap of evidence on that elusive subject, reader-audience response. Better yet, it is a unique scrap, as far as this play is concerned, and therefore it provides (for the moment) irrefutable support for the *Rezeptionstheorie* which I shall now advance.

Why were the London citizens offended? I suggest it was because they saw in this play an attack not only on the popular chivalric romances, but the whole notion of "civic honor" which these romances helped to sustain. Chivalric myth, as it was appropriated and transformed by the bourgeois audience, had deeply colored the self-imagination of the early modern Londoner. The appropriation by city folk of knightly ideals—a process I shall call "civic chivalry"—was more than a comic plebeian affectation, and more than the stuff of adolescent daydreams. Civic chivalry informed a political movement—which I shall call "urban militarism"—of considerable, and hitherto unrecognized, significance.

This movement has been overlooked because it runs counter to two well-established historiographical clichés. The first of these is the claim that throughout early modern Europe, the military independence of the medieval city was obliterated by the Renaissance and Baroque state. The second is that England in particular experienced a steady and comprehensive "pacification" as a consequence of the long Tudor and Jacobean peace. English society, so the argument goes, was demilitarized from top to bottom: the nobility and gentry forgot how to fight, while the heroic yeoman archers of Crécy and Agincourt degenerated into the drunken yokels of the trained bands.

There is, as usual, a measure of truth in both of these *idées reçues*. But they serve to obscure an important countermovement, originating in London, whose history I wish briefly to trace.

The Artillery Garden

In 1610, right about the time of Beaumont's play, a group of leading citizens determined to revive, "at their own private and particular charge," the weekly military exercises that had been performed during the reign of Elizabeth in the open area adjoining Moorfields known as the Artillery Garden. According to a near contemporary account, these men had been inspired by the fate of cities like Antwerp, sacked by the Spanish in 1576, that in times of peace had neglected their military defense.[17]

The company formed to exercise arms in the Artillery Garden received a royal charter in 1612 and has survived, with occasional intermissions, down to the present day. Despite its name, the Artillery Company has always been a body of infantry; when the company was formed, this French word had not yet caught on in English. In the early seventeenth century, the word "artillery" denoted small arms, including the longbow and crossbow as well as field ordinance. The arms exercised in the Artillery Garden were the pike, the musket, and a lighter firearm, a kind of unwieldy pistol, called a caliver.[18]

The Honourable Artillery Company, as it has been known since the Restoration, today traces its history from the charter granted by Henry VIII in 1537 to a fraternity of archers and handgunners called the Guild of St. George. The guild's members were authorized to train with bows and handguns in the fields of London and its suburbs. They were also endowed by their charter with a number of quasi-aristocratic social privileges. They could, for example, hunt heron and pheasant on royal grounds. Guild members, and their servants, could carry crossbows and handguns in public. They were exempt from jury and inquest duty and from some of the restrictions of the sumptuary laws: unlike other mere citizens, they were permitted to embroider their cloaks with silver thread.[19]

Without scrutinizing the genealogical claim too closely, the Guild of St. George was clearly a forerunner, if not a direct ancestor, of the seventeenth-century institution. But thereafter the guild seems to drop out of sight. (The name of St. George would have disappeared anyway, no doubt, at the time of the Reformation.) In the early 1580s many prominent Londoners belonged to another fraternity of archers, this one calling itself the Knights of Prince Arthur (not King Arthur, for some reason) and indulging in ceremonial role-playing based upon the Arthurian legends. Each member assumed the name of one of the knights of the Round Table, whose number was raised, by the inventive antiquarian poet Richard Robinson, to several score.[20]

Perhaps these Knights of Prince Arthur were the old brethren of St. George, ennobled and desanctified. In any case, they enjoyed great social prestige. In the 1590s their leader—"Prince Arthur" himself—was the immensely wealthy farmer of the royal customs, Thomas "Customer" Smith. Another active member was the famous schoolmaster Richard Mulcaster, who advocated archery in his curriculum for schoolboys. Perhaps it was these Knights of Prince Arthur who in 1583 organized the massive muster of 3,000 London archers, wearing green ribbons and sashes, in Hodgson's Field in Shoreditch.[21]

Both the Guild of St. George and the Knights of Prince Arthur drew their members, by and large, from the London patriciate. But archery itself was a demotic recreation in Elizabethan London. Moreover, it was one of the few popular diversions of which contemporary moralists approved.

Archery was considered not only healthful but patriotic. The English long-bow had mown down the flower of the French nobility at Crécy, Poitiers, and Agincourt, and few Englishmen were prepared to admit that the weapon was now obsolete. The fields of Finsbury and Shoreditch bristled with scores of archery butts bearing colorful ensigns and fanciful names. Archers could trace out a variety of routes between these targets, since like modern golf, sixteenth-century archery was practiced over a course. Rich-ard Mulcaster in his work on education suggested that young lads might combine the hygienic benefits of archery and foot-racing by sprinting be-tween the targets. Looking at contemporary prints of these congested archery grounds, one wonders how many of Mulcaster's young charges met the fate of Rafe in *The Knight of the Burning Pestle*.

The archery fields were common grounds, and the common rights were vigorously defended. In 1514 the parishioners of Shoreditch, Islington, and Hoxton were encroaching on these rights by enclosing gardens from the fields and by snatching and breaking the arrows of trespassers. Popular liberty was redeemed by a crowd said to have numbered in the thousands, who descended on the fields to fill in the new ditches and tear down the hedgerows. The rioters were assembled by a London tanner who ran through the streets dressed as a "Merry Andrew"—a Lord of Misrule—crying "Spades and Shovels!"[22]

The immediate forerunner of the seventeenth-century Artillery Com-pany was the organization formed in 1585, perhaps at the instance of the Knights of Prince Arthur, who had come to realize that the day of the longbow was waning. In that year, John Stowe tells us, amid mounting fears of an all-out war with Spain, "certain gallant, active and forward citi-zens, having had experience at home and abroad," began on their own ini-tiative to train their fellow citizens for war. Two years later the new militia contained nearly three hundred men, whom Stowe terms "merchants and others of like quality." These merchants had not only mastered the arts of war for themselves, but had become "very sufficient and skillful, to train and teach common soldiers the management of their pieces, pikes, and halberts; to march, counter-march and ring."

The company met every Thursday of the year to drill in the field near St. Mary Spital known earlier as the Teasel Ground, where the clothwork-ers had combed up the nap of their broadcloths with teasels, but which was now used as a firing range by the gunners of the Tower, and came to be called the Artillery Garden. Positions of administrative authority in the company were filled by rotation, so that "every man by turns bore orderly office, from the corporal to the captain." In 1587, three hundred members of the company marched with pike, musket, and caliver behind the hearse of the paragon of English chivalry, Sir Philip Sidney. During the crisis of the Spanish Armada, the contingent of Londoners at the Tilbury rendezvous was commanded by members of this company, who were now called "Captains of the Artillery Garden."

As the threat of invasion waned, the exercises in the Artillery Garden appear to have lapsed. One reason for this may be simply that the military zealots among the London citizenry were off serving in Ireland and the Low Countries during these years. (We are told that the "gallant spirits" who resurrected the company in 1610 had acquired military experience through service both "at home and abroad.")[23]

The refounding of the Artillery Company in 1610 reflected the upsurge of martial enthusiasm inspired by the investiture of James's eldest son Henry as Prince of Wales. The Company gave more durable expression to the values represented by the tilts and masques so thoroughly described in Roy Strong's recent biography of the prince.[24] The death of the prince in November 1612 was a terrible blow to the militant Protestant party and to those who shared its aspirations. But the Artillery Garden carried on the martial tradition. An Order in Council issued on 3 July 1612 authorized the citizens of London to exercise arms in the Artillery Garden, provided their number did not exceed 250. Two and a half years later, that number was raised to five hundred, in response to public demand.[25]

The purpose of the Artillery Company was to supply officers for the London trained bands, and it apparently did so throughout the seventeenth century. This fact alone should entitle it to more attention from historians than it has hitherto received. Service in the trained bands was as close as most Londoners could get to military glory during the Jacobean peace. Toward the end of *The Knight of the Burning Pestle,* Rafe—now in his own character as London apprentice rather than knight-errant—reviews a company of these trained bands.[26] Beaumont naturally pokes fun at these artisans and tradesmen in military array, one of whom is described as befouling his britches when the muskets fire. The author's main tactic in this scene, however, is to milk Rafe's drilling orders for sexual double entendres. But Rafe's commands seem, in themselves, to be tolerably professional: this apprentice grocer knows a fair bit about muskets and pikes. Beaumont thus pays backhanded tribute to the military expertise which some Londoners were beginning to acquire.

Beaumont had picked an inopportune time to mock the trained bands. The revival of the Artillery Company in 1610 was welcomed with great enthusiasm on the part of patriotic Londoners. In 1616 Thomas Dekker published a long poem in praise of *The Artillery Garden,* dedicated to "the honour of all those gentlemen who there practice military discipline."[27] A year earlier the popular playwright Thomas Heywood finally put into print his *Foure Prentises of London,* written back in the 1590s, which was probably revived on stage at about this time. Heywood prefaced the text with a dedication to "the honest and high-spirited apprentices, the readers . . . (as whom this play most especially concerns)." The style of the play, Heywood admitted, was somewhat old-fashioned, but the renaissance of civic militarism had restored the topicality of its theme. Thanks to the Artillery Garden, chivalric apprentices were back in style.[28]

In August and September of that same year the Artillery Company staged a spectacular muster, complete with parades and elaborate mock combats. According to the contemporary letter-writer John Chamberlain, 6,000 men took part, "very well armed and furnished in all points."[29] The affair was commemorated at length by the minor poet Richard Niccols in a highly mannered work entitled "London's Artillery." Niccols had sailed, at the age of twelve, on Essex's expedition to Cádiz in 1596, and he continued all his life to support the bellicose Protestant imperialism identified with the ill-fated earl. Like other members of the war party, his hopes had soared as Prince Henry matured into a paragon of martial virtue, only to be dashed by Henry's premature death in 1612. But now Henry's younger brother was beginning to show similar promise. During the muster of 1615, the "soldiers" shouted with joy to see the fifteen-year-old Charles riding out among them: Niccols likened him to the young Alexander mounted on Bucephalus.

Despite his eulogistic intentions, however, Niccols was forced to admit that the troops at this muster were "more rash and turbulent than discreet and well-advised." The firing of the muskets and cannon produced a chaotic scene: clouds of smoke turned the day to night, and spectators in their panic flung themselves on the ground, and upon each other. The confusion even disrupted the hierarchy of the sexes. Niccols reports that thousands of "viragoes" joined the ranks, as if conspiring "through wounds and blood. . . . Bravely to win the britches from the men." It must have been a grand show. And above the confusion, streaming through the acrid smoke of the gunfire, flew banners bearing the ensign of English chivalry—the red cross of St. George. Rafe would have loved it.[30]

Ben Jonson's play *The Devil Is an Ass,* which, like Niccols's poem appeared in 1616, provides further evidence of the Artillery Company's prestige among Londoners. Predictably, Jonson takes a more sardonic view of bourgeois militarism. The play's villain, the swindler Mere-craft, advises a London usurer named Guilt-head to buy his son a captaincy in the company, so that riding down Cheapside and Cornhill festooned with scarves and plumes, he may "draw down a wife, / There from the window, worth ten thousand pounds" and rise to be an alderman.[31] (Guilt-head's son, incidentally, is named Plutarchus, because his father, a devotee of the classics, hopes he may one day write the lives of London's great men.)

Some ten years later Jonson returned to the subject of the Artillery Garden in a poem titled "A Speech According to Horace." To judge by his patronizing but for the most part commendatory account, the men of the company were a good deal better at war games by the mid-1620s than they had been a decade earlier. They reenacted the sieges of Bergen-op-zoom (1622) and of Breda (1624–25) with such skill that Londoners claimed their colonel Sir Hugh Hammersley was a greater general than Tilly.[32]

Among the admiring civilian spectators at the Artillery Garden was the twenty-year-old Sir Simonds D'Ewes, who records watching the exercises on 6 May 1622, and then attending the sermon preached afterward to the company at Merchant Taylors Hall. He mentions attending the Garden again in April of 1624 to see a new invention—a combination pike and bow designed to resurrect the glory of English archery in the age of cannon and musket. D'Ewes was impressed with this technological breakthrough, of which no more is, however, heard.[33]

The example of the London Artillery Garden was widely imitated, first in London and its suburbs, then in the provinces. By the end of 1617 there were companies in Westminster and St. Martin's-in-the-Fields. Cripplegate had one by about 1627, and Southwark by at least 1632.[34] Meanwhile the fame of the Artillery Garden had spread to the provinces. "Many country gentlemen of all shires," we are told, "diligently observed their exercises, which they saw were excellent, and being returned home to their own countries, they practised and used the same with their trained bands."[35]

Companies, most often explicitly modeled on the London Artillery Garden, were formed in Coventry (1617?), Colchester (1621), Bury St. Edmunds (1622), Bristol (1625), Norwich (1625), Chester (1626), Gloucester (1626), Yarmouth (1626), Derby (1627), Ipswich (1629), and Nottingham (1629).[36] These provincial military companies have never been seriously studied. There is reason to suspect, moreover, that they were part of a much broader and deeper cultural movement, one that aimed at nothing less than a thorough remilitarization of English society, in response to Hapsburg victories across the Channel.

The companies listed above were apparently confined to adult house-holders. But their example kindled martial enthusiasm among younger folk. A supplement to Stowe's *Annals of London* describes how

young scholars and other youth, from the age of nine or ten, unto seventeen, of their own warlike dispositions, voluntarily chose themselves captains and lieuten-ants out of their own companies; and with the sound of drum, and other ensigns spread, marched into the field, upon play-days and holidays, and practiced all the points of war which they had seen their elders teach, having got themselves pikes and pieces fit for their handling.[37]

This fascinating description is undated—although it must be earlier than 1631—and frustratingly imprecise. How often did such musters occur? Dekker, in "The Artillery Garden," written in 1615, also describes a "muster made by children."

They stand, move, charge, discharge and fight pell-mell,
No pigmy-battle ever showed so well . . .
Every boy-man in this infantery,
Shewing like Mars in his minority . . .

Dekker tells us that old men wept with joy to see "young spirits far elder to excell," and retold the old stories, heard from their grandfathers, about Henry's conquest of Boulogne. In a sermon preached in 1622, An-thony Jones praises the companies of the Artillery Garden and Military Yard for training not only the city's "valiant men" but also "youths, nay very children in feats of arms," who would have cause to "rise up and bless both parents and preachers and captains for their education."[38]

It is quite possible that one of these martial children training with scaled-down pike and musket during the latter years of James's reign was John Milton, born in 1608. We know that Milton enrolled in the adult Ar-tillery Company in 1635, and his 1649 treatise *On Education* stresses the moral as well as physical value of military exercises for the young. Recent scholarship has suggested that Milton's educational theories owe less to Comenius and Hartlib than had once been thought and more to the edu-cation he himself received at St. Paul's. Richard Mulcaster, who included archery and other sports in his curriculum, was master of St. Paul's when he died, in the year of Milton's birth: Mulcaster's mastership may well have made the school especially receptive to the inspiration of the Artillery Garden.[39]

At any rate we can surely see in these "boy-men," "shewing like Mars in his minority" the forerunners of the "Sons of Mars" of 1642. Nor was this adolescent militarism confined to London. The evidence so far is skimpy, but precisely because it has turned up accidentally in unexpected places, extremely suggestive. Sir John Oglander tells us of a company of youths practicing martial arts on the Isle of Wight in 1627, and again in 1634. There were similar displays at Chichester, where the youngsters successfully petitioned King Charles for a supply of powder to make their maneuvers more realistic.[40]

In the late 1620s, according to Lucy Hutchinson, the town of Lincoln brought a veteran soldier over from the Low Countries to train the scholars of the grammar school. "Instead of childish sports," she tells us, "when they were not at their books, they were exercised in all their military postures, and in assaults and defences." Among these scholars was Lucy Hutchinson's future husband, Thomas, later a prominent commander in the Parliamentary army. Lucy observes that during the civil war, this youthful military training later stood her husband in good stead. By 1639, the free grammar school at Chipping Camden in Gloucestershire also had an arsenal.[41]

How typical were such cases? To be sure, these are only three examples. But they are suggestive because they have turned up unbidden, without any real searching on my part or anyone else's, in scattered and quite ordinary places. Why should Chichester, Chipping Camden, and Lincoln be uniquely militaristic? Should we not rather postulate a more general "militarization" of the English grammar school, a kind of Jacobean ROTC program which simply failed, for understandable reasons, to leave much documentary trace?

However that may be, it is already clear that the urban elites of pre-revolutionary England were a good deal more martial than historians have supposed. This civic militarism was entirely voluntary and owed virtually nothing to the court, at least after the death of Prince Henry. James and Charles were willing to let private citizens build up the country's defenses at their own expense, but they offered little in the way of leadership and nothing, it would appear, in the way of funds.

Arcadia and the Winter Queen

The spread of this military movement coincides with a striking revival of the cult of Philip Sidney. Preaching to the artillery company of Coventry in 1621, Samuel Buggs upheld Sidney as the epitome of the Christian knight, ennobled by his learning as well as his martial prowess. Sidney's *Arcadia* was reprinted no less than nine times between 1613 and 1623 alone. The twenty-year-old Sir Simonds D'Ewes began reading it on 14 March 1622, a few weeks before his first recorded visit to the Artillery Garden.[42]

It is fascinating to speculate how this forty-year-old text would have been "received" amid the terrors and perplexities which beset English Protestants in the 1620s. The plot of the romance revolves around a crisis of royal irresponsibility—a fearful and self-indulgent king, Basileus, has withdrawn from affairs of state, with disastrous consequences for the realm.

It is a matter of debate among literary scholars to what extent *The Arcadia* was intended as veiled critique of Elizabeth's foreign policy. But its political implications must have seemed increasingly salient as the reign of James wore on. As early as 1610, in his "Life" of Sidney, Fulke Greville had stressed the romance's political, and implicitly critical, dimension: according to Greville, the lesson of *The Arcadia* is

that when sovereign princes, to play with their own visions, will put off public action, which is the splendor of majesty, and unactively charge the managing of their greatest affairs upon the second-hand faith and diligence of deputies . . . , they bury themselves and their estates in a cloud of contempt.[43]

For readily understandable reasons, Greville's work remained unpublished during the author's lifetime. It may well have been written for Prince Henry, since the main manuscript was preserved among the family papers of Henry's secretary, Adam Newton.[44] But Henry's death would have made it highly imprudent to put such ideas in print: Greville's literary criticism was radically "deconstructive" of Jacobean prestige.

Prince Henry's one enduring political legacy was the marriage he had helped to arrange between his sister Elizabeth and the leader of Continental Calvinism, Frederick of the Palatinate. In 1619, Frederick rashly accepted the Bohemian crown: an act which marked the real beginning of what turned out to be the Thirty Years War. James was appalled and alarmed by his son-in-law's irresponsibility; zealous Protestants, from Archbishop Abbot down to Simonds D'Ewes and the men of the artillery companies, hailed the venture as the work of divine Providence, opening the way to the swift and final destruction of Antichrist.

Their hopes were soon dashed, and James's misgivings were confirmed. Frederick lost Bohemia to the Hapsburgs and was driven from the Palatinate as well. Thereafter militant Protestants in England clamored for

war with Spain, to recover at least the Palatinate for Frederick and Elizabeth, if not the throne of Bohemia as well. Elizabeth in particular became
the object of intense popular devotion: her supporters persisted in styling
her, to James's displeasure, the Queen of Bohemia.[45]

Read against this background, Sidney's *Arcadia* must have seemed
supernaturally clairvoyant. One could hardly fail to see in the sensual, fearful, and indolent Basileus a prophetic portrait of King James: Basileus's
very name would suggest the title of James's manual of kingship, the *Basili-
kon Doron*. And Elizabeth, known as "the Winter Queen," was the living
incarnation of the damsel in distress, represented in *The Arcadia* by Basileus's daughter Pamela. The twenty-year-old Simonds D'Ewes, who in
1622 was reading *The Arcadia* and at the same time anxiously following the
fortunes of Elizabeth and Frederick, could hardly have failed to liken Elizabeth's misfortunes to those of Sidney's imprisoned heroine.[46]

An anonymous unpublished poem from 1623 movingly expresses this
veneration for the Winter Queen, which was particularly intense, we may
assume, among the volunteer captains of the artillery companies. The poet
laments the failure of James to come to the aid of his daughter and pro-
fesses the eagerness of all true Englishmen and women—shepherds,
ploughmen, "mechanicks" as well as "gentry"—to sacrifice life and live-
lihood in her service.

Of particular interest here is the anguish, attributed to commoners as
well as aristocrats, over the loss of English honor, and the fear of being
shamed in the eyes of posterity. The poet assures Elizabeth that only the
Crown's prohibition prevents her loyal English servants from enlisting in
her cause. He begs Elizabeth to acknowledge these professions of loyalty
so that subsequent generations need not repudiate their ancestors.[47]

Bloody Swords and White Manners

The ideology of civic militarism was provided by the ministers, for the
most part Puritan, or at least aggressively Protestant, who preached to the
Artillery Company and its offspring on the occasion of their annual feasts
and periodic "solemn meetings." These preachers included some of the
most famous Calvinist divines of the age, such as John Davenport, Richard
Sibbes, and William Gouge. Many of these sermons were printed, usually
at the request of the bodies to which they were preached, thereby transmit-
ting these values to a broader audience—especially, no doubt, the military
companies in the provinces.[48]

Let us take as a representative early specimen a sermon by Thomas Adams entitled "The Soldier's Honour," preached before the Artillery Company and published ("on their second request," according to Adams) in 1617. The sermon is dedicated to "the captains and truly generous gentlemen, citizens of London, of the Society of Arms practicing in the Artillery Garden."[49] Notice here the unembarrassed apposition of the terms "gentlemen" and "citizens." Adams, like other "artillery preachers," is at pains to assert the legitimacy of just warfare, and thereby the honorability of the military calling. This encomium of righteous warfare then serves to justify the rhetorical "ennobling" of the preacher's audience, allowing him to address men who were for the most part mere citizens as "truly generous gentlemen."

The *laus belli* of these artillery preachers stressed the essentially conflictual nature of reality. The universe itself was the theater of a cosmic battle between the divine and the demonic, between the legions of Christ and Antichrist, a battle that would end only with the end of Time itself. "We are all soldiers," Thomas Adams told the London company in 1617, "as we are Christians; some more specially as they are men." In the rhetoric of godly warfare, the metaphorical belligerency of all Christians served to validate the literal calling of the terrestrial warrior, assuming, of course, that his cause was just and his character upright.

The soldier in a just war was the type par excellence of the *miles Christi,* the warrior (or knight) of Christ. He was thus a privileged exemplar for all Christians, all of whom were enjoined to serve, according to their calling, in God's army. As Adams expressed it, "You bear both spiritual arms against the enemies of your salvation, and material arms against the enemies of your country: in both you fight under the colors of our great general Jesus Christ."[50]

Preachers of this stripe incessantly warned against the dangers of what they called "security"—by which they meant the complacent neglect of England's defenses, both moral and military. "Security," said Adams in 1617, "[is] a rust grown over our souls in this time of peace." This peace could not be counted on to last forever. "We have not the blessings of God by entail, or by lease" Adams warned, "but held at the good will of our landlord, and that is but during our good behaviour."[51] Divine favor, then, is like true honor—won and maintained by virtue, not owned by right of birth or purchase.

According to Adams, and innumerable other preachers, England's "great iniquities"—pride, avarice, concupiscence, injustice, and so forth—made divine retribution ever more probable. Moreover, England's ingratitude for her miraculous deliverances in the recent past, such as the defeat of the Spanish Armada and the frustration of the Gunpowder Plot, would heighten God's wrath against her. The most likely instruments of that wrath were the Spanish legions, abetted by the expected treachery of England's domestic Papists.

In such an event, Londoners knew what to expect. They had learned from Las Casas and a host of Protestant propagandists about Spanish cruelty in the New World, but there was an even more frightening precedent closer to home. Refugees from Flanders had brought them firsthand accounts of the sack of Antwerp in 1576. At the turn of the century, when Shakespeare's theatrical company produced a gruesome melodrama reenacting Antwerp's tragedy, the play was entitled *A Larum[sic] for London*.[52] The crushing of the Bohemian rebellion and the conquest of the Palatinate added further to the Protestant Black Legend of Hapsburg ferocity.

Adams evoked these horrors in his sermon to the Artillery Garden, conjuring up the spectacle of "our towns and cities burning, our houses rifled, our temples spoiled, our wives ravished, our children bleeding dead on the pavements, or sprawling on the merciless pikes." This catalog of Spanish atrocities, at first largely derived from Aeneas Sylvius Piccolomini's account of the fall of Constantinople but enriched over the next twenty years by the sieges and massacres of the Dutch Revolt and Thirty Years War, became a stock motif in the repertory of militant Puritan preachers for the next two decades.[53]

The godly soldier must combine courage and military prowess with Christian faith and moral rectitude. As Anthony Jones put it in 1622, he must show "zeal for God's glory, with an utter detestation of all lewd company." He must also seek assurance of the justice of his cause. Jones prudently warns against overcritical scrutiny of the mysteries of state: the commands of good rulers are to be obeyed even if their rationale is not fully or immediately apparent. But the moral responsibility of the individual soldier remains: godly soldiers should "use all good means to be thoroughly persuaded of the justice of their cause," so that God, the "mighty defender of the right may stand for them, and they may stand to him with true courage in the field." Soldiers who are indifferent to the justice of war [such as mercenaries] are "ignorant, blockish, and wicked."[54]

This portrait of the godly soldier irresistibly calls to mind the self-image of the soldiers of the New Model Army, or at least of its articulate spokesmen, whose manifestos proudly asserted that they were no "mere mercenary army," but free Englishmen defending liberty and religion. The godly soldier of the artillery sermons has cultural ancestors, however, as well as progeny. He is descended from (among other forebears) the Christian knight of chivalric romance—the seeker of the Grail and Crusader for the Holy Land who had been sung by poets from Chrétien de Troyes down to Tasso and Spenser, as well as by demotic balladeers and storytellers.

For example, Jones insists that "Sion Soldiers," as he calls them, will display true Christian charity (unlike their enemies who follow the "Whore of Whores") even in the midst of slaughtering God's enemies. "Though their banners be red, their manners be white," he assures us: "Though their swords be bloody, their words be gentle and their deeds lovely."[55] Bloody swords and white manners: Jones has perfectly epitomized the chivalric ethos. The word "chivalry" is in fact often used in the commendation of these voluntary companies. In 1622, Anthony Jones praised the companies of the Artillery Garden and Military Yard for "upholding the practice of chivalry."[56] William Gouge's sermon in praise of the Artillery Garden, preached before them in 1626, was titled "The Dignity of Chivalry."

If the Sion Soldier descends from Parsifal and Godfrey of Boulogne, however, he belongs to a very cadet branch. The younger son of a line of younger sons, he represents a limited democratization (the word is inexact, but the alternatives are too ugly) of the chivalric ideal. The justification, if any were needed, for applying knightly rhetoric to an infantry composed of merchants was provided in 1616 by Thomas Adams. The ancient Romans, he declared, had used the same word, *miles,* to describe both knights and common soldiers, since they honored both equally. It was bad philology—overlooking the word *eques* and the semantic shift of *miles* in medieval Latin—but the captains of the Artillery Garden will not have objected.

Thus the moral code of chivalric service has been recast in terms of Protestant eschatology, and the ranks of the warrior elite opened up to men of (relatively) low birth, but lofty character. "Never speak of thy blood," says Adams, "but of thy good: not of thy nobility, . . . but of thy virtue." After all, the titles of nobility themselves derive from military command: "Duke" comes from *dux,* which Adams rather tendentiously translates as "captain."[57]

But while downplaying the contribution of biological ancestry to true honor, the discourse of godly warfare nevertheless retains, indeed accents, the characteristically aristocratic appeal to hereditary obligation—the duty of the living to transmit undiminished to posterity the honor won by the illustrious dead. Anthony Jones commended the Artillery and Military Companies for their "worthy actions concerning matters of chivalry," which would serve as an example not only to the present but "to all posterity." Similarly, Abraham Gibson declared in 1618 that the names of the Artillery Company would be held "in everlasting remembrance; those that are yet unborn shall bless you and bless God for you."[58]

Furthermore, the godly soldier could claim as patrimony the achieved honor of earlier English heroes. "Think with renewed courage of your noble ancestors," Thomas Adams told the Artillery Company, "how their prowess renowned themselves and this whole nation. Shew yourselves legitimate and true born children of such fathers." Here is the key notion: nobility is hereditary after all, but it descends not by blood but by right of merit. Legitimacy in this sense must be proven through deeds.

Caitiffs and Carpet-Knights

Thus the Artillery Company and its fellows came to embody an ideology, elaborated by these Puritan preachers, of "godly gentility" achieved through military service in defense of the true faith, and of the nation conceived as the privileged bastion of the gospel. There was a critical edge to this concept of honor which rendered it potentially subversive—not, to be sure, of aristocracy as such, but of the unworthy tenants of aristocratic status. For the ideal of godly chivalry necessarily entailed the condemnation of those aristocrats—whether Papist or merely degenerate—who shirked their duty to God and country.

Adams rejects the connection of honor with mere wealth, even landed wealth. "Honor should go by the banner, and not by the barn" he tells his "truly generous gentlemen"; reputation should be "valued by valor, not by the acre." He rails against the effete "carpet-knights," who spend their time "dancing levoltos to the lute in a lady's chamber" instead of "marching to the sound of the drum." As a remedy he suggests that ladies, reversing the strategy of Lysistrata, should "forebear their wonted favours" from these "fantastical amorists," until they rediscover "some difference between effeminateness and nobleness," and return to the manly business of killing.[59]

As the sermons make clear, the civic artillery companies were not universally admired. In 1618, John Everard told the men of the St. Martin's Military Yard to expect calumny and abuse; but to remember that "your great general hath called you to follow him in greater conflicts." Everard's own association with the company had made him the victim, as he tells us, of "pale-faced malice, conspiring with most unworthy baseness."[60]

Addressing the Artillery Company in April of the same year, Abraham Gibson acknowledged that "some go about to slander your society and discountenance your undertakings, speaking evil of all because some few miscarry." Preaching to the men of Coventry in 1621, Samuel Buggs exhorted them to "spurn with the heels of contempt the base and faeculent vulgar, whose muddy brains and dull spirits neither can conceive nor dare attempt so high designs." [61]

It is not hard to see why the miltiary movement should have aroused suspicion and hostility, or to guess whence that hostility came. The movement was a direct and deliberate challenge to James's policy of peace abroad and religious toleration at home. This policy, which James pursued with vacillating conviction, was favored by English recusants and the Hispanophile faction at Court. It was violently abhorred by most strong Protestants, who feared domestic subversion by the Catholic minority as much as direct invasion by the Spanish legions.

Hence the artillery companies were warned to be on guard against domestic treason as much as foreign invasion. If "men of place and government" refused to support the Artillery Company, said Abraham Gibson, they were to be accounted "base and ignoble caitiffs . . . , neither good servants of God nor true subjects of the king." Samuel Buggs especially cited "home-bred flatters" among the enemies "to be avenged upon," since traitors were the more dangerous the higher they rose in favor. "If you find a traitor, down with him!" Buggs told the Coventry company, "though he be one of the Twelve." [62] Even Christ's Privy Council had included Judas Iscariot.

John Everard clearly had in mind the Hispanophiles (and homosexuals) of King James's Court when he lashed out against the "wanton, effeminate, base, drunken, coward-like Carpet-knights," engendered by this "rotten and decrepit age." To be sure, Everard purports to be speaking here of the doomed city of Nineveh, but his application was clear enough. No wonder "pale-faced malice" had it in for him. No wonder either that James I repeatedly threw Everard into jail and once threatened to keep him there for good. ("What is this Dr. Ever-out?," James is said to have asked: "His name shall be Dr. Never-Out!") [63]

Everard was admittedly an extreme case, irascible even by the standards of Jacobean divinity. He wound up in the 1640s as an antinomian heresiarch of debatable mental health. But in the prerevolutionary decades he enjoyed the protection of nobles like the earls of Warwick and Holland. When he preached the sermon we have been considering, he was the elected lecturer of the parish of St. Martin's-in-the-Fields, home parish of the Military Yard. He addressed the company at their invitation and published it, so he says, at the request of "many of them." He was not, in 1618, on the lunatic fringe, at least not yet. He was giving especially strident voice to the alarmed outrage felt by many patriotic English Protestants at what they took to be the folly and decadence of the Jacobean regime.

John Everard exhorted the company of St. Martin's to "pluck up again the sunk and drowned honour of our country."[64] The phrase has a familiar ring. Everard is echoing, whether consciously or not, that most eloquent of aristocratic rebels, Shakespeare's Hotspur.

> By heavens, methinks, it were an easy leap
> To pluck bright honor from the pale-faced moon,
> Or dive into the bottom of the sea,
> Where never fathom-line touched any ground,
> And pluck up drowned honor from the lake of hell.

(Is it by chance that in the same sermon, before plucking up drowned honor, Everard had complained against "pale-faced malice?")

The lines quoted above are not, as the casual reader might suppose, taken from *Henry IV, Part I*. They are drawn instead from the Induction to *The Knight of the Burning Pestle,* where Rafe, the apprentice grocer, misquoting only slightly, recites Hotspur's lines by heart. The Tudor state had crushed over-mighty subjects like Harry Percy. Rafe, once fired up by preachers like John Everard, would prove harder to subdue.

Rafe's Revenge

Meanwhile, what of the policy of the Crown toward this extraordinary proliferation of what were, in essence, citizen armies? The simple answer appears to be that there *was* no Crown policy. Hispanophiles on the Privy Council cannot have welcomed the movement, given its ideological coloration, even if they found it prudent to muffle their opposition. Militant Protestants like Conway and Abbot, on the other hand, must have welcomed these initiatives: no doubt they were responsible for the readiness with which petitions to establish military companies were granted. James seems never to have expressed an opinion. Certainly he had little sympathy with the ideals and objectives of belligerent Protestantism. He cannot have been pleased with the Artillery Company's patronage of radical preachers like John Everard. But these companies were effusive in their protestations of loyalty to the Crown and they cost James nothing. He was shrewd enough to have reasoned that it was more prudent to tolerate them than to risk arousing Protestant suspicions by their suppression.

The case of Charles is more complex, and his attitude changed over time. We have seen how he was cheered by the troops in 1615 and hailed by Niccols as a young Alexander. In early manhood Charles did his best to fill the role played by his brother Henry: he became an accomplished horseman and an acceptable performer at the tilt and ring; he read Sidney and Tasso.[65]

The otherwise inexplicable folly of Charles's trip to Spain with Buckingham to court the Infanta makes some limited sense as an effort at chivalric play-acting. The venture was in fact defended in just such terms by some unlikely observers. The sober Calvinist Sir Edward Conway referred to Charles and Buckingham while still abroad as the Knights of the Adventure, and James himself, one of the least chivalric of English kings, said the two "were worthy to be put in a new romance."[66]

During the late 1620s, Charles and Buckingham attempted to conduct the aggressively Protestant foreign policy which the war party had advocated since the days of Leicester and Sidney. In this enterprise, the artillery companies were Charles's natural allies, and they spread most rapidly between the Cádiz expedition in 1625 and the withdrawal from Rhé three years later. During these years no fewer than eight provincial companies were established. But Charles's public image as a Protestant hero was fatally compromised, first by his marriage to the Catholic Henrietta and then by his obdurate loyalty to his father's favorite, the increasingly unpopular duke of Buckingham.

The misgivings aroused by Buckingham and the Queen were aggravated by Charles's promotion of anti-Calvinist churchmen. This loss of public confidence perhaps explains why the spontaneous proliferation of volunteer companies in the late 1620s failed to translate into Parliamentary and financial support for Charles's military campaigns—campaigns which were so ineptly executed as to confirm the already well-established suspicion of treachery in high places.

After Buckingham's death, Charles became convinced that the "Puritans" were to blame for all his political and financial difficulties. He abandoned the policy of Protestant belligerence, which had depended upon Parliamentary support, and withdrew into neutral isolationism, which permitted him to dispense with that troublesome assembly. At the same time he appears to have grown suspicious of the civic military movement. He sought to increase royal control over the selection of officers in the London Artillery Company, with the result that membership in the early 1630s appears to have declined.[67]

English Protestants, losing hope that Charles might assume his brother's mantle, had to look overseas to the Swedish king Gustavus Adolphus for a model of godly chivalry. Gustavus's death in 1632 was deplored by the future regicide John Bradford as the greatest loss suffered by true-hearted Englishmen since the death of Prince Henry. The astounding career of Gustavus Adolphus was likened by several contemporaries to the popular romance of the Knight of the Sun.[68]

Charles no longer sought to manipulate such mythology. The ethos of his court—at least as it was perceived by Protestant militants—was expressed by Thomas Carew in a verse epistle to Aurelian Townsend, explaining his refusal to write an elegy on the Swedish king.

Tourneys, masques, theaters better become
Our halcyon days; what though the German drum
Bellow for freedom and revenge, the noise
Concerns us not, nor should divert our joys;
Nor ought the thunder of their carabins
Drown the sweet airs of our tun'd violins.[69]

An aristocratic milieu that appreciated these sentiments would naturally find the chivalric ideals of common citizens quite ridiculous. Charles's court, therefore, unlike the original London audience, could appreciate the satire of *The Knight of the Burning Pestle*. In 1635 the play came into its own. It was reprinted, and this time not anonymously, but bearing the names of both Beaumont and his frequent collaborator John Fletcher. Queen Henrietta Maria's own company of players produced the play with great success, first on the stage of the fashionable Cockpit Theater in Drury Lane and later at Court. It was revived again in 1639.[70]

One wonders how Charles and his entourage interpreted the work. A more astute ruler, endowed with a finer sense of irony, might have found the play distinctly disquieting, especially those lines, declaimed by an apprentice grocer, about plucking up drowned honor from the lakes of hell. He might even have caught a premonitory echo of the London apprentices' *Valiant Resolution*. In the very year that the play was revived at Court, membership in the Artillery Company expanded dramatically. One of the new members was the twenty-seven-year-old John Milton. In 1637, the

London Artillery Company staged an elaborate masque-like pageant depicting a mock battle between Christian and Saracen armies. The pageant's theme of holy war contrasted starkly with the allegorical masques being staged at Court in praise of an illusory Golden Age. The Artillery Company thus kept alive a tradition of martial Protestantism quite antithetical to the utopian discourse of opulence and fecundity emanating from the Court. William Bariffe, the Artillery Company lieutenant who published an elaborate account of the military pageant of 1637, later served as an officer in John Hampden's Parliamentary regiment.[71]

If later Royalist accounts can be believed, the London Artillery Garden became, in the absence of Parliament, a main vehicle of political puritanism.[72] Virtually no one was yet discussing, or probably even contemplating, insurrection against the Crown itself. But fears of a Catholic coup d'etat were mounting, reviving memories of St. Bartholomew's Day and the sack of Antwerp. Stalwart Protestants were preparing to resist, on their own, if necessary, a mortal peril that their king failed even to perceive. Historians have generally believed that the militant Protestantism of the 1620s was politically paralyzed during the Personal Rule by the suspension of Parliament, to be resuscitated only by the rebellion of the Scots. Further study of the Artillery Company may force a revision of that view.

The English Civil War effectively began at the beginning of 1642, when Charles lost military control of his capital and was forced to withdraw to the north to recruit an army from the more loyal, but less populous and wealthy, hinterland. The London trained bands, whose rebellion precipitated the conflict, were officered by the captains of the Artillery Company, under the command of Philip Skippon, a veteran of the European wars who had been brought over to lead the company in 1639. In the first years of the war the London trained bands were the backbone of the young Parliamentary army.

Under their "Captains of the Artillery Garden," these were the most efficient and dedicated body of foot soldiers in England. Not a large claim, perhaps, given the military state of the realm. But everything is relative, especially in war. Without these relatively effective trained bands, there could have been no civil war, let alone an eventual Parliamentary victory. And when the improvised levies were finally consolidated into a truly professional New Model Army, one of its main architects was Philip Skippon, the former commander of the Artillery Company.[73]

Civic militarism thus made civil war possible. If we knew more about the history of the provincial companies, our sense of the importance of this movement might be enhanced. In the military sense, if in no other, it *was* a "bourgeois" revolution after all. But it was not a revolution in support of the stereotypical bourgeois values. The citizens who joined the various artillery companies had endorsed and appropriated the martial virtues of courage and sacrifice derived from the aristocratic ethos, as mediated by Protestant theology. If it was a "bourgeois" revolution, it was carried out, at least in part, on behalf of "feudal" ideals.

Walter Benjamin believed that it is the memory of enslaved grandparents, rather than the image of liberated grandchildren, that drives people to revolt. Not so in seventeenth-century England. There it was rather the memory of *free* ancestors, and the nightmare of an enslaved posterity, that inspired the Great Rebellion. While Charles seemed indifferent not only to the fate of Continental Protestantism but even to the sufferings of his own sister Elizabeth, Londoners were taking up arms, at least on the drilling ground, in defense of God's cause, England's honor, and their children's liberties.

When the "valiant apprentices" marched off to war in late 1642, they were commanded by two of the greatest nobles in England: Robert Devereux, the third earl of Essex, and his first cousin, Robert Rich, the second earl of Warwick. In the words of Arthur Wilson, who had served as steward to both earls, Essex and Warwick were among those aristocrats who had "upheld the old English honor and would not let it fall to the ground." Essex had fought for Elizabeth of Bohemia in the 1620s, while Warwick had patronized militant Protestant divines and waged his own war against Spain with his squadron of privateers.[74]

Both men had close personal ties to the circle of Sir Philip Sidney, whose political tradition they maintained. Warwick was the son of Penelope Rich, née Devereux, the "Stella" of Sidney's sonnet sequence: she was also the sister of the second earl of Essex, Elizabeth's ill-starred favorite. The elder Essex had been Sir Philip Sidney's best friend: at Zutphen, the dying Sidney had bequeathed to him his widow, along with his favorite sword.

Despite his execution for treason in 1601, this second earl remained, in popular imagination, an exemplar of Protestant chivalry throughout the early Stuart period. (Rumor attributed his downfall to the machinations of enemies like Raleigh and Cecil.) His son and namesake, the future Parliamentary general, unquestionably owed his popularity as much to his parentage as to his personal qualities: he was not only the heir of Elizabeth's Essex, the victor of Cádiz, but also the posthumous stepson (so to speak) of the author of *Arcadia* and martyr of Zutphen. The enormous prestige enjoyed by Warwick and Essex in 1642 demonstrates the enduring potency of the aristocratic ideal in its Protestant-nationalist form. It was against this ideal that Charles and his regime were measured and condemned.

I have suggested that many young lads must have shared Francis Kirkman's fantasy that he "might in time prove to be some great person, or at leastwise be squire to some knight." If so, then it is easy to imagine the feelings on 22 November 1642, of the young Londoners who had enlisted in the Parliamentary army. On that day they heard the great earl of Warwick salute them as equals. He called them "my noble countrymen [who] fight in this just cause to preserve your king's rights, the privilege of Parliament, and the whole kingdom's safety." Their enemies, Warwick reminded them, were "the bloody and inhuman papists" and the "blaspheming and tyrannous Cavaliers" who "keep your dear annointed king from you."

Urging the recruits to behave as "Christian soldiers," avoiding blasphemy, rape, and plunder, Warwick promised his "dear countrymen and fellow soldiers" that together they would swiftly free their king from his seducers and restore him "home to his royal throne." Thirty years earlier, Rafe, the apprentice grocer, had quoted Shakespeare's Hotspur on the redemption of drowned honor: now the earl of Warwick was addressing London apprentices in the rhetoric of *Henry V*. Like King Hal at Agincourt, Warwick was promising them, in effect, that

he today that sheds his blood with me
Shall be my brother. Be he ne'er so vile,
This day shall gentle his condition.[75]

I do not expect that my somewhat whimsical thesis of a "bourgeois" revolution in defense of "feudal" ideals will achieve very wide currency. But I hope I have shown that the ideal of "citizen honor," which Beaumont mocked in *The Knight of the Burning Pestle* played a significant role in the catastrophe of the Stuart monarchy. Moreover, the particular victims of Beaumont's satire were especially energetic in wresting the capital from the king's control.

"Fly, fly my soul, to Grocers Hall," Rafe had cried in his mock death agony. Whatever became of Rafe's soul, it was indeed to Grocers Hall that John Pym and his Parliamentary colleagues flew in earnest in January of 1642, when King Charles was trying to arrest them for treason. Grocers Hall not only provided a refuge for the Five Members, but also served as headquarters for the Militia Committee that secured London for Parliament and took the first steps toward civil war. At the outbreak of the conflict, the Worshipful Company of Grocers contributed more "parliamentary-puritan" activists to the government of the rebellious capital than any other of the city's twelve livery companies.[76] Seven years later, on a scaffold outside the palace of Whitehall, the Knight of the Burning Pestle had his revenge.

Notes

(The place of publication is London unless otherwise indicated.)

1. *The Valiant Resolution of the Prentices of London* (1642), British Library, Thomason Tracts, E. 109 (5), 1.

2. Readers demanding a definition of this term will find an admittedly cursory one on page 208.

3. *Valiant Resolution*, 3.

4. Ibid., 4.

5. Ibid., 6.

6. Richard Johnson, *The Nine Worthies of London* (1592).

7. Margaret Spufford, *Small Books and Pleasant Histories* (Athens, Georgia, 1981), 7; Francis Kirkman, *The Unlucky Citizen* (1673), 10–13.

8. Vernon Snow, *Essex the Rebel* (Lincoln, Nebraska, 1971), 187.

9. Sir Philip Sidney, *The Countess of Pembroke's Arcadia,* ed. Maurice Evans (Harmondsworth, 1977), 9; Charles Mish, "Best Sellers in Seventeenth-Century Fiction," *Papers of the Bibliographical Society of America* 47 (1953), 365; W. O. Hassall, ed., *A Catalogue of the Library of Sir Edward Coke* (New Haven, 1950), 67; Elisabeth Bourcier, ed., *The Diary of Sir Simonds D'Ewes (1622–1624)* (Paris, n.d.), 34, 70; John Milton, *Complete Prose Works* (New Haven, 1953–), vol. I, 371–72, 463; vol. II, 525; vol. III, 362–64.

10. Sir Philip Sidney, *The Defence of Poesy* (Boston, 1909), 24.

11. See Caro Baroja's contribution to Jean G. Peristiany, ed., *Honor and Shame* (1965), 79–137, and Mervyn E. James, *English Politics and the Concept of Honour* (Oxford, 1978), reprinted in *Society, Politics and Culture* (Cambridge, 1986).

12. Sidney, *Arcadia,* 335.

13. *Mercurius Civicus* (1643), 28.

14. Bruno Bettelheim, *The Uses of Enchantment* (New York, 1976).

15. Printed in Robert Dodsley, ed., *A Select Collection of Old Plays* (6 vols., 1825–27), vol. VI, 395–487.

16. The most recent edition is by Sheldon R. Zitner, *The Revels Plays* (Manchester, 1984).

17. John Strype, ed., *A Survey of the Cities of London and Westminster* (1754), vol. II, 572. This is an edition, with many additions by later hands, of John Stowe's classic work.

18. For histories of the Artillery Company, see G. A. Raikes, *History of the Honourable Artillery Company* (2 vols., 1878), and G. Goold Walker, *The Honourable Artillery Company* (1926).

19. Walker, 5.

20. Richard Robinson, *The Ancient Order of Prince Arthur* (1583); see also his amended edition of John Leland, *A Learned and True Assertion of the Life of Prince Arthur* (1582).

21. Richard Mulcaster, *Positions* (1591), 102; Walker, 12.

22. Walker, 10–11.

23. Strype, *Survey,* vol. II, 572.

24. Roy Strong, *Henry Prince of Wales* (1986).

25. *Calendar of State Papers Domestic* [hereafter, *CSPD*] *1611–18,* 137; *Acts of the Privy Council* [hereafter, *APC*] *1613–14,* 667.

26. The scene opens Act V.

27. Thomas Dekker, *The Artillery Garden* (1616). The unique copy of the original edition is in the library of the University of Göttingen in Germany. An edition of some fifty copies was printed by the Bodleian Library, Oxford, in 1952. I have used the copy of this edition at the Beinecke Library of Yale University.

28. Printed in Dodsley, *Old Plays,* vol. VI.

29. Norman McClure, ed., *The Letters of John Chamberlain* (2 vols., Philadelphia, 1939), II, 612.

30. Richard Niccols, *London's Artillery* (1616). Niccols's biography is in the *Dictionary of National Biography* [hereafter, *DNB*].

31. Act III, scene ii.

32. This is poem XLIV of *Underwoods,* printed in Ben Jonson, *The Complete Poems,* ed. George Parfitt (Harmondsworth, 1975), 187–90.

33. D'Ewes, *Diary,* 76, 190.

34. *CSPD 1611–18,* 137, 340, 342; *APC 1613–14,* 667–68; *1616–17,* 415; William Bariffe, *Military Discipline* (1635), dedication; Lindsay Boynton, *The Elizabethan Militia* (1967), 264–65.

35. Strype, *Survey,* II, 573.

36. *APC 1619–21,* 407; *APC 1621–23,* 344; *APC 1623–25,* 482; *APC 1625–26,* 309; *APC 1625–26,* 465, 477–78; *APC 1627–28,* 30; *APC 1628–29,* 407; *APC 1629–30,* 145, 223.

37. Strype, *Survey,* II, 573.

38. Thomas Dekker, *The Artillery Garden* (1616: see n. 27), n.p.; Anthony Jones, *A Spiritual Chaine* (1622), p. A2.

39. See Ernest Sirluck's introduction to volume 2 of the Yale edition of Milton's *Complete Prose Works,* 184–216.

40. *CSPD 1627–28,* 336–37; Francis Bamford, ed., *A Royalist's Notebook* (New York, 1971), 24, 64. Boynton, *Militia,* 264–65.

41. Lucy Hutchinson, *Memoirs of the Life of Colonel Hutchinson,* ed. James Sutherland (Oxford, 1973), 24; on Chipping Camden, William B. Willcox, *Gloucestershire* (New Haven, 1940), 86.

42. Samuel Buggs, *The Midland Soldier* (1622), 37; D'Ewes, *Diary,* 70.

43. Fulke Greville, "A Dedication to Sir Philip Sidney," in *The Prose Works of Fulke Greville, Lord Brooke,* ed. John Gouws (Oxford, 1986), 8.

44. This fact is noted by Gouws, who does not, however, appear to recognize its significance.

45. I discuss these matters at greater length in "Spectral Origins of the English Revolution," in Geoff Eley and William Hunt, eds., *Reviving England's Revolution,* forthcoming from Verso Press, London.

46. D'Ewes, *Diary,* 70.

47. This poem was transcribed, along with many other valuable manuscript poems, by Julian Mitchell, who intended to produce an edition of unpublished political poems from the early Stuart period. Upon abandoning the project, Mitchell deposited his transcripts with Professor Lawrence Stone, to whom I am most grateful for permission to consult them.

48. See John Davenport, *A Royall Edict for Military Exercises* (1629); William Gouge, *The Dignity of Chivalry* (1626); Obediah Sedgwick, *Military Discipline* (1639).

49. Thomas Adams, *The Soldier's Honour* (1617), epistle dedicatory.

50. Ibid.

51. Ibid., 14.

52. Anonymous, *A Larum [sic] for London or, the Siedge [sic] of Antwerp* (1602), STC 16754.

53. Adams, *Soldier's Honour,* 13.

54. Jones, *A Spiritual Chaine,* 18–21.

55. Ibid., 29.

56. Ibid., dedication, sig. A2.

57. Adams, *Soldier's Honour,* 30–31.

58. Jones, *Spiritual Chaine,* dedication, sig. A2; Abraham Gibson, *Christiana-Polemica, of a Preparative to Warre* (1619), 59.

59. Adams, *Soldier's Honour,* epistle dedicatory, sig. B2.

60. John Everard, *The Arriereban* (1618), dedication.

61. Gibson, *Christiana-Polemica,* 27; Buggs, *Midland Soldier,* epistle dedicatory.

62. Gibson, *Christiana-Polemica,* 28; Buggs, *Midland Soldier,* 38.

63. Everard, *Arriereban,* 73; *DNB,* "John Everard, D.D."

64. Everard, *Arriereban,* 103.

65. A translation of a portion of Tasso's *Gerusalemme Liberata* was dedicated to Charles in 1624. The *Eikon Basilike,* which, although written by John Gauden is now generally believed to represent Charles's own sentiments, quotes Pamela's prayer in *The Arcadia.*

66. Roger Lockyer, *Buckingham* (1981), 142; G. P. V. Akrigg, ed., *Letters of King James VI and I* (Berkeley, 1984), 388.

67. For a fuller discussion, see my "Spectral Origins," cited above. On the decline of the Artillery Company in the early 1630s, see *CSPD 1631–32,* 284.

68. On Bradford, see Christopher Hill, *Puritanism and Revolution* (New York, 1964), 129. For the comparison of Gustavus Adolphus to the Knight of the Sun, see Rhodes Dunlap, ed., *The Poems of Thomas Carew* (Oxford, 1949), 75.

69. Dunlap, *The Poems of Thomas Carew,* 77. I should stress that I am dealing here only with contemporary *perceptions,* and hostile ones at that. For the aspirations (and internal conflicts) of Caroline court culture, see R. Malcolm Smuts,

Court Culture and the Origins of a Royalist Tradition (Philadelphia, 1987) and Kevin Sharpe, *Criticism and Complement: The Politics of Literature in the Age of Charles I* (Cambridge, 1987). The forthcoming work by Jerzy Limon on the Caroline court masques will shed important new light on this subject.

70. For the stage history, see Zitner's introduction to his edition of the play, 42–45.

71. Walker, *Artillery Company,* 45; William Bariffe, *Mars His Triumph* (1639); Edward Peacock, ed., *Army Lists of Roundheads and Cavaliers* (1875), 46.

72. *Mercurius Civicus* (1643), 4–5; *Persecutio Undecima,* (1681), 28.

73. *DNB,* "Philip Skippon"; *Mercurius Civicus,* 20; *Persecutio Undecima,* 28.

74. For Essex, see Vernon Snow, *Essex the Rebel* (Lincoln, Nebraska, 1971). For Warwick, see my *The Puritan Moment* (Cambridge, Mass., 1983).

75. Warwick's speech was printed as *A Most Worthy Speech, Spoken by the Right Honourable Robert Earle of Warwick* (1642), British Library, Thomason Tracts, E.128(30). The quotation from King Henry is from *Henry V,* act IV, scene iii, lines 61–63.

76. Valerie Pearl, *London at the Outbreak of the Puritan Revolution* (Oxford, 1961), 174. The term "parliamentary-puritan" is Dr. Pearl's.

7. Theology and Atheism in Early Modern France

In the early decades of the eighteenth century, there appeared in France a philosophical literature of explicit atheism. It claimed, among other things, that no "proofs" of the existence of God were demonstrative or even plausible; that the idea of God was either self-contradictory or otherwise absurd; and that a universe understood without reference to a Supreme Being either was no more or, indeed, was less problematic than a universe understood to stand in some relationship to such a God. This atheism would become a significant current of Enlightenment thought by the late eighteenth century. It first occurred, in written form at least, in a small number of clandestine manuscripts that circulated, more widely than historians first believed, in the world of letters.[1]

Atheism as a concept had a history apart from any actual atheists. Christian and heterodox theists had used the term "atheist" for centuries, either to express outrage at a particular view of the divine, or, most commonly, to identify those who lived "as if" there were no God, the "ungodly" whose behavior seemed to belie their claim to believe in a Supreme Judge.[2] In patristic and later discussions of prior classical philosophy, there were commonplace identifications of the handful of atheists whose existence was deemed the exception to the virtual "universal consent of mankind."[3] Atheistic arguments, one should note, long had been a presence in educated Christian minds. Aristotle's *Topica*, part of a basic philosophical education, had instructed generations of students on the obligation to confront or, if need be, to invent objections to their own claims. True to this formal requirement for "*sed contra*" criticisms of their own demonstrations of God's existence, theologians and philosophers had formulated what they took to be, in theory, the arguments that might be brought to bear against their most fundamental belief, for purposes of reassuring resolution. In a process of no small interest for the history of both the cognitive and the psychological aspects of belief, Christian thinkers in effect had "created" the atheist as an interlocutor in most of the "Book One" sections of their *Summae* and treatises of dogmatic or philosophical theology.[4] Now, however, they faced their imagined archenemy come to life.

The appearance of such atheism occasioned, ostensibly at least, a rather different sort of incredulity within the learned community. Given compelling proofs of God's existence, the resolution of all objections to these, and the utter inexplicability of the world and its phenomena without the role of a Supreme Being, how could anyone be an atheist? How could anyone deny *all* demonstrations of God's being and attribute the world's existence, form, and behavior to the nullity of chance? The theologians, on the whole, claiming that no *mind* could be so blind, looked to the *will*, not the intellect, to explain such a phenomenon. "Atheism" could only be the manifestation in thought of a corrupted soul attempting to justify its corruption and delude itself that there would be no consequences to a depraved, self-serving life. It was dissolution in search of impunity. Modern scholars, who reserve similar explanations largely for each other's views, have looked, more appropriately, to the mentality and thought of that period to seek its atheizing sources or influences.

The emergence of atheism in early modern France is an interesting problem in "the transmission of culture," for it raises the intriguing question of how a civilization generates beliefs antithetical to its own organizing principles of understanding. In attempting to respond to it, historians have worked with a diversity of implicit models: the atheistic or materialistic potential of certain systems of thought, above all, Cartesianism (Fig. 7.1); the long-term transmission of an underground "atheistic" tradition; the particular influence of singular individuals, a Spinoza or Hobbes or Bayle, for example; and, finally, a kind of ideational parthenogenesis, a virgin birth of early modern atheism, generally related to the case of the "isolated" rural priest Jean Meslier, the only author of an atheistic text in this period whom we can identify with near certainty.[5] These all have something to recommend them, but it is what they generally ignore or fail to explain that shall occupy us here.

First, for example, Cartesians relied increasingly on God in their natural and metaphysical philosophy. Who are the atheistic Cartesians? Second, the "batons" are not apparent; texts were read differently in 1677 from 1577, let alone 1277; and compilations of heterodox, primarily ancient philosophy, as in the *Theophrastus Redivivus,* are not reconceptualizations of a world view.[6] Third, Spinoza's *Ethics,* though occasionally reviled, simply was not that widely noted in France; and Hobbes was scarcely discussed as a metaphysician.[7] Finally, the "problem" of the "isolated" priest Jean Meslier ("isolated," of course, from everything that the Catholic world that shaped him stood for) simply assumes that the orthodox culture in which he was educated and lived could not have provided him with the

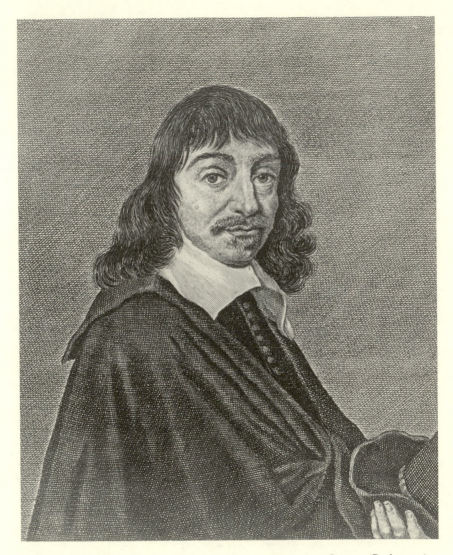

Figure 7.1. René Descartes (1596–1650). Source: Descartes, *Oeuvres* (Paris, 1656), frontispiece. Courtesy of Princeton University Library.

views and criticisms from which he constructed his atheistic system. All of these models presuppose that the dynamics, tensions, and dilemmas of orthodox Catholic thought do not loom large in the emergence of its most fundamental antagonist.

It is this assumption that I wish to challenge here, by examining, in part, the role of the orthodox (as opposed to heterodox) learned world in the genesis of the motifs and content of atheistic thought. What the French atheistic manuscripts reveal, above all, and not surprisingly, is the mental life of the broader, primarily Catholic learned culture that gave birth to them. This is certainly not the whole story, but it is an essential and extremely significant part of it, and (without paradox, I think) allows us to restore even early modern atheistic minds to the richness and contradictions of their culture. Almost all of the individual component motifs of atheistic philosophy first appeared, for quite different purposes, in orthodox culture. It was not any proto-atheistic school that developed refutations of particular proofs of the existence of God in the late seventeenth century, but, rather, intense Christian polemic on the issue of the proper philosophical structure for Christian theology. It was not any seventeenth-century European dissent that obviated in many minds proof from the "universal consent" of all peoples to belief in God, but, rather, the conclusions of Christian historians of thought and, above all, of Christian missionaries and travelers. It was far less any early modern heterodox thought that crafted systems of natural philosophy devoid of the notions of creation and Providence (though the pure Epicurean impulse was there in a few), than the work of orthodox classical scholars and historian-chroniclers of prior philosophy. The polemical impulse to "reduce" to atheism one's opponents' views, fueled by the dramatic combination of passionate concern, institutional struggles, and personal reputations and rivalries, generated a large share of atheistic formulations and, as "theater," assured a large and fascinated audience. The atheists were those who synthesized and embraced all or almost all of the component arguments that emerged.

In a separate work I shall attempt to explicate in detail all of these theses, demonstrate the breadth and representative nature of these phenomena, and integrate this emphasis on the agency of orthodox culture both with more traditional views of the foundations of free thought and with longer-term tendencies of Western philosophy, erudition, and teaching. Here, I shall concentrate on a few examples and modalities of this generation and dissemination of atheistic thought by an orthodox culture for which it was, initially, simply a polemical abstraction and foil.

*   *   *

By the early decades of the seventeenth century, on the surface, French Catholicism had put its house in order. The themes are familiar ones in all historical accounts: the repression of libertinism; the increasing acceptance and diffusion of the reforms and doctrines elaborated by the Council of

Trent; the foundation of schools and seminaries at an unprecedented rate, greatly raising the educational level of the clergy and initiating the serious catechistical instruction of the kingdom; the stemming and reversal of the tide of Huguenot advance; the overcoming of the Ramist, Platonic, and other challenges to the Aristotelianism and Thomism of the universities. So much for the surface. In fact, however, a century of fratricidal or, to judge by the Enlightenment, almost suicidal theological and philosophical struggles within French Catholicism ensued. By mid-century, Aristotelian and Cartesian Catholic thinkers would be at war for the minds of learned France, a phenomenon whose bitterness would be exacerbated by rivalries among monastic and other clerical orders and by competition among schools of thought for control of the institutions of learning. By late century, the same division would be yet further complicated by the subdivision of Cartesianism into its orthodox (that is to say, less altered) and its Malebranchist schools, and, not unrelated to these divisions, by the growth in the number of fideistic theologians skeptical about, if not despairing over, the very role of philosophy in both Christian education and the Christian spiritual life.

These divisions occurred within a church committed to two related positions that elevated philosophy to a central place in the sequence of belief. First, the church generally taught that belief in God was a "preamble to the faith" and not an article of the faith itself. If one examined the sequence as opposed to the act of belief, before one could give faith to Revelation, one had to believe in the existence of the God who revealed.[8] Secondly, the church explicitly had condemned the view that the existence of God or the immortality of the soul was not demonstrable by natural reason, and theologians who had held to such "fideistic" views (Cardinal Pierre d'Ailly in France, for example) were condemned for theological error. It was a matter of faith, if you will, that belief in God was entailed by natural lights.[9] This requisite belief about belief was reinforced by Aristotelian notions of *scientia* and Cartesian criteria of rational assent, and by the growing tendency of the seventeenth-century learned world to distinguish its knowledge from that of the vulgar (as in the case of the assault on witchcraft beliefs and persecutions) by demanding "évidence," either logical or empirical, for beliefs. Further, learned debate was no longer primarily the private activity of the clerics. The spread of university education to the laity, the printing and broader diffusion of books and pamphlets, the success of learned journals and their book reviews, and the concentration of an educated lay public in urban France and, above all, in Paris, meant that contestation among celebrated theologians and philosophers would be followed and discussed by readers with no necessarily primary commitment to theology and church.[10]

*　*　*

If the atheist, even abstractly conceived, were the ultimate enemy of Catholic belief, and if atheism were the ultimate folly, then no philosophical system that could not establish by natural lights the existence of God and his causal relationship to the universe should escape the most serious condemnation and censure. Early modern masters and doctors of philosophy and theology had been raised on exercises in disputation and dialectical analysis that historians, following wits of the time, often caricature, but that indeed made them magisterial and *doctes* in the analysis of arguments. They were forceful, unforgiving critics of each other's works. Certain that their own philosophies proved the cause of matter and motion to be an intelligent God, they often sought to condemn the systems of their equally Catholic rivals by demonstrating how materialistic, atheistic conclusions followed logically from such premises. Two examples:

(1) *Why Cartesians should be atheists.* In 1675, the Oratorian priest and philosopher J.-B. LaGrange, an Aristotelian unpersuaded by the Cartesianism sweeping his congregation, condemned "the new philosophy" in a work dedicated to the Dauphin.[11] The heart of LaGrange's critique was that any consistent Cartesian should be a materialist and atheist. "Unless Descartes denies his principles," the Oratorian wrote, he cannot but agree with the ancient atheists who thought matter to be eternal and capable of forming itself into the world we observe. From Descartes's principle that one cannot negate the idea of extension to form an idea of empty space, "I should conclude that matter existed [of necessity and thus] before the production of the world." If one followed the logic of that conception strictly, he urged, "one should say that matter is eternal and independent of God and that the Creation is impossible." From Descartes's doctrine that this matter, once in motion, could suffice for the production of the world we observe, one should conclude that matter possessed all of the powers that the ancient atheists who had deemed the world formed by chance had assigned to it. All that preserved Cartesians from atheism, LaGrange maintained, was their insistence that God was the cause of motion. However, he argued, they had no right to believe in (let alone insist upon) such a conclusion. In Aristotelian ontology, LaGrange explained, a substance possessed accidental forms that were wholly distinct from itself. Motion

was such an accident. However, in the Cartesians' analysis of being, he noted, there existed in nature only extension and mind, and what Cartesians meant by "modes" or "accidents," he urged, could only derive from the nature of these two substances. In such a system, therefore, motion must be essential to one or the other subject: there was no room for an entity distinct from its subject. Either one preserved the Aristotelian distinction between a subject and its forms, or one concluded logically in a Cartesian ontology for the existence of an eternal matter-in-motion, and there was no need for a God in their philosophy. He acknowledged that no Cartesians believed such a thing, but that merely reflected their inconsistency. From Cartesian premises, atheism was not only "thinkable," but obligatory.[12]

(2) *Why Aristotelians should be atheists*. In the decades that followed, the Benedictine philosopher Dom François Lamy, writing for a broad audience, formulated a Cartesian Catholic apologetic strongly influenced by the Oratorian Malebranche's doctrine of occasional causes.[13] In its common denominator, occasionalism held that the direct causal interaction of mind and body was inconceivable. Rather, actions in one domain were the "occasion" of God's direct causal agency, by which He produced synchronic effects in the other. For example, sense perception in the body was the occasion of God's effecting corresponding awareness of that perception in the soul, rather than the efficient cause of that perception. The two substances shared nothing but a dependence on God, who caused physical events to correspond to the occasion of mental events (and vice versa). The appeal of "occasionalism" was manifold, for it "solved" the mystery of mind-body interaction, prevented the abuse (as in "superstition," for example, witchcraft belief) of confusing the material and spiritual realms and gave deep meaning to God's omnipresence and omnipotence. What we experienced was inexplicable unless there were a God to effect it. François Lamy went further, being one of those later Cartesians for whom divine agency was essential to all "causality": natural events never involved intrinsic causes, but were merely the phenomenal "occasions" of the divine effectuation of other natural events. The alternative, Lamy insisted, was not merely thoughtless natural philosophy, but a metaphysic that would best serve as the foundation for an atheistic world view. The Aristotelians, he argued, invested material substances with "forms" and "virtues" that "explained" the natural behavior of corporeal things. If they were correct, however, there would be no grounds for denying that purposeful, regular activity could result from the essential nature of matter. In the occasion-

alist system of the modern Cartesians, he explained, matter can do nothing of its own nature or forces, and all depended upon the causal role of God. In the Aristotelian system, "if God could give matter these forms and these faculties, capable of acting with such regularity, it is a sign that they are not contrary to the nature of things, and that they have no incompatibility whatsoever with matter. Thus, they also could be eternal and serve for the arrangement of [matter's] parts." The Aristotelians could not fall back on the necessity of a divine cause of motion, for "if matter could receive the motive power from God, there is a natural compatibility between this power and matter." If one allowed Aristotelian powers and forms, then *the* bulwark against atheism, an assurance of matter's impotence to effect motion and order of its own nature, would be fatally breached, and "one can parry this blow only by maintaining, with the Cartesians, that matter is in no way susceptible of force of movement." He conceded that no Aristotelians argued for atheism knowingly, but their "specious and dazzling . . . words" about the role of God in their system were contradicted by their very principles; "the atheists" would have no difficulty with them at all. The "system of occasional causes," thus, constituted the "one and only system appropriate to making the efforts of the atheists useless."

Thus, where historians seem hard-pressed to locate heterodox seventeenth-century "Averroists" drawing atheistic conclusions from Aristotelian premises, or anticipatory La Mettries drawing materialistic conclusions from Descartes, there was no lack of pious and polemical monks, priests, and philosophers, teachers all, doing just that for the opposing school.[14] Having inherited and refurbished "the atheist" in their "objections" to their own proofs and systems, seventeenth-century theologians and philosophers took him along on all fundamental disputes and made their opponents confront him at all turns. The argument that there was no self-contradiction in conceiving of matter as eternal and essentially in motion or as endowed with inherent active forces was foundational in later Enlightenment atheism.[15] It did not first appear in the heterodox manuscripts, however, but in learned polemical works published with theological approbation and ecclesiastical and institutional imprimatur.[16]

✳   ✳   ✳

Historians generally have consigned seventeenth-century Aristotelian scholastics to a marginal place in intellectual history, except as convenient targets of "modern" thought. They look formidable, however, intellectually and institutionally, from the context of their own times. They domi-

Figure 7.2. A view of the Sorbonne in the time of Richelieu. Source: Louis Liard, *L'université de Paris* (Paris, 1909), vol. 1, p. 25. Courtesy of Princeton University Library.

nated the universities and *collèges* of France, wrote the texts from which the educated drew their initial philosophical language and conceptual structures, and successfully summoned royal administrative and papal authority to their assistance. Through the vigorously maintained Aristotelianism of the Jesuits, their cause was supported politically, polemically, and intellectually by that increasingly ascendant clerical *corps*. Accustomed to describing the seventeenth century in terms of the overthrow of Aristotle, we often forget that within Catholicism it was marked dramatically by the increasing prestige of St. Thomas Aquinas, whose Aristotelianism was inseparable from the heart of his work, a process that would continue until in the nineteenth century he had become, in effect, the most privileged "doctor" of the church. Trent had placed Aquinas above all other doctors of the church; the Jesuit *Ratio Studiorum* had given him a privileged place of honor in its curriculum. If Aristotelian scholasticism were dead or dying, someone forgot to inform the publishers, reading public, students, and authorities of France (Fig. 7.2).[17]

This ascendancy was not unchallenged within the church. The theological appeal of Cartesian and Malebranchist philosophies was strongest precisely among institutional rivals of the Jesuits and the universities—Franciscans, Benedictines, and Oratorians, for example (indeed, almost everywhere that Jansenism also appealed). These orders tended to favor, when circumstances allowed,[18] what they took to be those philosophies (natural, moral, and religious) more detached from the senses, more focused by and on inward light, than the philosophy of Aristotle or what they saw as the related ethical and religious teachings of the Jesuits. For many such anti-Aristotelians, Descartes and Malebranche seemed in a line of philosophical theology that included Plato, the neo-Platonists, St. Augustine, St. Anselm, and St. Bonaventure; for them, the anti-Aristotelianism of the condemnation of 1277 had been a correct anticipation of the awful dangers posed by the marriage of Christian spirituality with Aristotelian natural philosophy.[19]

The Aristotelians, on the other hand, believed the new philosophers to offer mere speculations detached from the accumulated *scientia* of the ages. The Cartesians, in their eyes, utterly failed to appreciate how the coherence achieved by a synthesis of Aristotelian method and ontology with Christian revelation allowed us to speak rationally and systematically about the faith. Having manned the ramparts against magicians, radical mystics, alchemists, Pyrrhonists, astrologers, Protestants, and neo-Pythagoreans, their task now, consistent with the preservation of their privileged institutional positions, was to save Catholic thought from its latest deformers. What better way could there be to demonstrate the inanity of Cartesian philosophy than to show its incapacity to prove God to the very creation that reflected Him?

Seventeenth-century disciples *and* critics of Descartes agreed with virtual unanimity that there were two Cartesian "proofs" and that they were both a priori, based upon the mind's understanding detached from the sensible world. For the Cartesians, there was a twofold self-evidence to the idea of God. First, the idea of the most perfect being of which we could conceive entailed actual existence as the predicate of such perfection, just as the idea of a unicorn entailed the predicate of one horn, or the idea of a triangle the predicate of three angles whose sum was 180 degrees. In the same way that a unicorn *must* have one horn, or a triangle three angles, a perfect being *must* have actual existence. The alternative, a perfect being that did not exist, was as much a self-contradiction as a four-sided triangle. Unlike any imperfect entity, which could be or could not be, a perfect being could *not* "not be." God's necessary existence shone with luminous "*évidence*" in our understanding itself. Second, every idea had an object, that is to say, represented something to us, was an idea *of* something, and from the principle that no effect could have more reality than its cause, the cause of the "objective being" of the idea of perfection, representing infinite attributes to infinite degrees, could only be infinite perfection itself. What else could give rise to it? The idea of God could have only God as its "objective cause." The mark of divine authorship and light was on the very idea we had of Him.[20]

The Aristotelians, almost all good Thomists, held firmly to St. Thomas's celebrated "five ways" of proving God: from motion or act; from the series of efficient causes; from the series of contingencies; from degrees of perfection; and from the governance, the guidedness, of the natural world.[21] They deemed these all to be a posteriori proofs, consistent both with Aristotle's dictum that no idea was in the mind except by way of the senses and with St. Paul's own insistence in Romans 1:19–20 that it was the visible things of this world that proved God beyond all forgivable doubt. For the Aristotelians, Cartesians offered risible would-be "proofs" that violated all rules of demonstration and clear understanding. For more than two generations, thus, in every form of theological and philosophical media—courses, formal Latin tomes, serious vernacular treatises, mordant parodies, book reviews in popular journals of the learned world—they scornfully analyzed the flaws of these demonstrations. Cartesians defended these proofs and, we shall see, derided in turn the would-be proofs of the Aristotelian Thomists. There were skilled logicians in both camps, who often from the age of seven had been schooled in and rewarded for the art and science of exposing the fallacies of arguments. They now turned with intellectual passion to the struggle between what they believed to be mutually exclusive philosophies competing for the glory, responsibility, and other benefits of articulating and establishing the *praeambula fidei* and of being the rational voice of Christian faith. Their objections to their own proofs had had to meet the test of strength insisted on by all their peers; straw men were not tolerated. Their refutations of each other's proofs were furious, with no quarter given at all, and would find their way into the literature of French atheism. When the author of an anonymous atheistic manuscript referred to God as "a First Being of whom we have no proof," he was, in one sense, simply agreeing with rival orthodox philosophies about the status of each other's claims.[22]

Let us sample some of the substance and tone of these debates within a French Christianity whose very self-confidence about the inconceivability of admitting atheism would be a contributing factor to the emergence of its "atheistic" foil in real form. These debates make most sense if one understands them *not* as initially or primarily concerned with God per se, but, above all, as focused on the systems of philosophy that were to fulfill the disputational demand to prove Him. Nonetheless, they give substance to the paradox noted by Saint-Evremond in 1662: "We burn a man unfortunate enough not to believe in God, and yet ask publicly in the schools 'if He exists.'"[23]

For the scholastics, Descartes's proof from the necessary existence of a perfect being simply assumed what in fact it was obliged to prove. Descartes's exercise, in the Jesuit Gabriel Daniel's phrase, was "a pure paralogism" in that it began with its would-be conclusion: the possible and actual existence of the object of its proof. Indeed, for Daniel, without "ordinary demonstrations" drawn from "reflection on the [external] things that prove the existence of God," the idea of a supremely perfect being seemed far more chimerical than real.[24] François-Marie Assermet, the leading Cordelier professor of theology, concluded in his *Theologia scholastico-positiva* that the Cartesians, to secure their specious proof, declared their own idea of God to be innate in all mankind. Were this so, he observed, proof would be superfluous. Descartes's disciples, however, need not be taken seriously, for everyone truly learned agreed that God's existence could not be proven a priori.[25] As the scholastic Robert Basselin attempted to explain in his *Dissertation sur l'origine des idées* (subtitled "in which one shows against M. Descartes, [and] Father Malebranche [etc.] . . . that they [ideas] all come from the senses") there could be no natural knowledge of a being imagined apart from sensible experience of its presence or its effects.[26] Perhaps it is not so mysterious that the initial Jesuit response to John Locke was generally sympathetic.[27]

Seventeenth-century philosophers and theologians had all learned as young students the distinction between beings in-the-mind (*a parte intellectus*) and beings in-the-actual-world (*a parte rei*). For Huet's *Censura* of Cartesian philosophy, Descartes had failed to make this elementary distinction, even when it was, in fact, the very issue at stake in his attempted proof. Clarification of an idea, Huet insisted, was *not* deduction of any truth about its supposed object. Thus, *if* God existed in the manner in which we conceived of Him, which would require proof a posteriori, it must be as a being with necessary existence. That was all Descartes had shown.[28] Regnault's textbook on Thomistic philosophy explained that truth did not pertain to "real beings" or "beings of reason" apart from each other, but precisely to a relationship of conformity between the two.[29] As Jean DuHamel, professor of philosophy at the University of Paris, argued, no atheist would ever deny the existence of the *idea* of God as a perfect being existing necessarily; what the atheist denied was what Descartes ignored: the existence of an *actual* perfect being *a parte rei*.[30] J.-N. Colbert, a doctor of the Sorbonne and later archbishop of Rouen, returned in his university textbook to Aquinas's ultimate reply to Anselm's "proof" from the idea of God. Once we knew of God a posteriori, we understood that He existed necessarily of His own essence. God's necessary existence, thus, was always true *for God*. For us, however, who were condemned to the tutelage of the senses in matters of natural knowledge, such truth could only be gained from the external things of the world, and our idea of God, until beatitude, would be "obscure" and "confused."[31]

Critics of the Cartesians proclaimed them hopelessly confused about the nature of ideas, condemning them for equating modifications of the human mind with the objects that it sought to understand. For Michel Morus, principal of the Collège de Navarre and, from 1701, professor of philosophy at the Collège Royal, "the idea of a thing is its definition," and nothing more. The Cartesians consulted not nature, but merely their own definitional terms. Their very use of the term "God" was not a reference to the Supreme Being whose existence was demonstrated by the created world itself but, rather, was an ambiguous name assigned to an assumed being about whom they knew nothing.[32] The Jesuit François Perrin, in his *Manuale Theologicum,* observed that minds often conceived of the existence of "chimerical" beings. What the seeker after knowledge of God required was not an awareness of his own fancies, but judgment a posteriori of God's existence.[33]

For the Aristotelians, this Cartesian confusion revealed itself most pitiably in the alleged proof from the "objective" being of God. They denied the Cartesian *ontological* distinction between an idea considered as a modification of mind (its "formal being") and as a representation of some particular entity (its "objective being"). Given the formal being of an idea, it was a wholly human entity, imperfect, finite, and flawed. An idea of God, thus, could only "represent" perfection imperfectly, which in no way entailed a perfect cause.[34] The very question at issue, then, was whether we knew God to be represented in His infinite perfection by any human idea. Since Cartesians themselves would have to admit that men did not know God "in an infinite and comprehensive manner," DuHamel noted, the question must be resolved in the negative.[35] Pierre-Sylvain Régis, the veritable spokesman of "orthodox" Cartesianism late in the seventeenth century, replied that Descartes's proof was compelling for the existence of "a being in which we know as many perfections as we are capable of know-ing."[36] To this, DuHamel retorted scornfully that the creed did not an-nounce the most perfect being of which we humans could conceive (which could be far from perfect), but "a being in which there are infinite perfec-tions," the divine attributes that the mind of man in no way could con-tain.[37] As Colbert more gently explained, human beings simply could not attain Descartes's desired "clear and distinct idea of God's perfection," and his proof would always be inadequate given not its object, but its subject (the human thinker).[38] For Huet, the only way Cartesians could avoid these criticisms would be by the absurd and blasphemous equation of God and our idea of Him.[39] Perfection, several theologians added, could have no prior "cause," objective or otherwise, beyond its own essence. If the *idea* of God possessed real infinite perfection, it would *be* God, and thus unamenable to proof that categorized it as effect.[40]

Daniel's extremely popular *Voyage au monde de Descartes* put the matter bluntly and ominously: "If there were no other demonstrations of God but these [Cartesian proofs], *there would be none at all*" (emphasis added). Thus, he warned disciples of Descartes and Malebranche against criticiz-ing the common Thomistic proofs: "*For if it were true that the other [proofs] were not more compelling in comparison to these [Cartesian proofs], one would conclude from this principle exceptionally nefarious consequences against the existence of the First Being*" (emphasis added). Either we knew of God's existence a posteriori, or we did not know it at all.[41] The Cartesians, how-ever, would ground demonstration only in a priori argument. The errant senses could not overcome doubt by logical certainty and never could know essences and spiritual beings; from the finite effects and imperfect beings of the world, no infinite and perfect cause conceivably could be in-ferred. They simply reversed Daniel's equation. In 1691, the University of Paris formally condemned as a proposition of Cartesian philosophy that "one must reject all the reasons which theologians and philosophers have used with St. Thomas until this day to demonstrate that there is a God."[42]

The theologian Adrien Baillet's widely read *Vie de Monsieur Des-Cartes* quoted its hero as having noted that many "pious and serious theo-logians have refuted . . . St. Thomas' proofs concerning God's existence." Baillet explained in simple terms Descartes's view that a posteriori argu-ments dependent on sensory knowledge of the world could not establish God. Either we were certain of God's existence a priori, or we were not certain of it at all.[43] Régis went further: since no finite thing could be the cause in us of any notion of the infinite, either the idea of God was innate and essential to the soul and compelled belief both by its very nature and by the necessity of God alone as its author, or there could be no notion of God, let alone of His existence. "The soul," he insisted, "could not form the idea of God without [first] knowing God, and if it knows Him, it has no need to form the idea of Him [from the sensible world]."[44]

For a generation, the journals were filled with mutual refutations in this debate. In the widely circulated *Histoire des Ouvrages des Savans,* for example, a Cartesian theologian explained that the senses simply could not represent to us a necessarily existent perfect being, for they "represented merely material beings, which, unable to be perfect, contain *no necessary existence.* One must listen, thus, to reason alone" (emphasis original). Those who found Descartes's proofs "too metaphysical and too subtle," he urged, had best be silent, for these were the *only* certain proofs.[45] The Benedictine François Lamy agreed: all certainty of God and thus of the faith itself depended absolutely on a priori knowledge of the existence of God.[46] Régis warned the scholastics that St. Thomas's "proofs" were "moral," not "metaphysical," that is to say, that they had a surface plausibility and might be affectively influential, but that they were in no manner logically compelling. The imperfect world to which St. Thomas appealed in a posteriori argument could not possibly give us the idea of God. If the perfection objectively present in the idea of God were not a proof of Him, one "could advance *no* wholly necessary proposition to prove His existence."[47]

Indeed, for the orthodox Cartesians, the scholastic critique of the "objective being" of the idea of God gave fatal weapons to the would-be atheist. If our idea of God were not a clear and distinct idea of an infinitely perfect being, then we had no knowledge of Him. La Coudraye's Cartesian *Traitez de métaphysique* granted that God is "above us," but warned the scholastics "that from wanting to give an exalted notion of Him," they would convince readers that we could not know Him at all. If our idea of God were not innate, not truly representative of His perfection, and not able to surpass what could be represented by the imperfect sensible world, then all we knew were "purely human opinions," or, worse yet, chimeras. God *is* His perfections, and if we cannot know those, we cannot know Him. To say that "God is," a posteriori, is merely to posit the existence of *some* being, without any knowledge of a perfect, infinite, or necessary being. The scholastics "have confused Him with a certain phantom that their imagination has formed from the assemblage of the negations of all that they do know [that is, the imperfect world]."[48] If the Aristotelians truly believed that our idea of God did not clearly represent an infinite and perfect being, Régis asked, then how could they themselves know if any a posteriori proof established the existence of such an entity? (How could you know you had found a unicorn if you did not know clearly and distinctly what "one horn" was?) "One cannot know that a thing exists," in brief, "without knowing in general what it is."[49] The arguments of Enlightenment atheism that no nominal definition of God was amenable to proof of His existence, that no argument from a finite world could prove an infinite being, and that no demonstration of God from an idea of Him could be more than circular were not original. They were commonplace in the learned culture of which the unbelievers were the heirs.

*   *   *

Malebranchism modified these debates in complex ways. It changed their terms, drew dramatic new participants into them, and increased their audience.[50] Malebranche (Fig. 7.3) claimed repeatedly that "Everything proves God,"[51] but his Cartesian rationalism and distrust of the senses led him to a full repudiation of a posteriori proofs. Without self-evident rational certainty of the existence of God, "all the ordinary proofs of the existence and perfections of God drawn from the existence and perfections of His creatures . . . are not convincing." A posteriori arguments proved "that there is some power superior to us," but, he insisted, "they do not fully demonstrate that there is a God or an infinitely perfect being."[52]

Malebranche accepted the Cartesian proof of God's actual existence from His perfection; it was, he wrote, "even more evident than the axiom that the whole is greater than its part."[53] He rejected, however, emphatically, Descartes's proof from the "objective being" of our idea of Him. Ideas, for Malebranche, were not modal attributes or actions of the human mind, but eternal archetypes in the Divine Being. We saw all things in God. The Cartesian (and scholastic) belief that the "formal being of ideas" was a mental mode was incorrect. The scholastic argument that no mental mode could represent the perfection of God, however, was wholly correct. That attempted Cartesian proof was inconceivable for, as he reiterated in work after work, "nothing finite could represent the infinite." In the most widely discussed philosophical work in late seventeenth-century France, the frequently reprinted *Recherche de la vérité* (1674–1675), Malebranche denounced as self-evidently false "the gross error" of "those who support this proposition, that the finite can represent the infinite, and that the modalities of our soul, though finite, are essentially representative of the infinitely perfect being."[54] For the next thirty years, he would debate this issue sharply and frequently with the Cartesian Jansenist Antoine Arnauld

Figure 7.3. Nicolas Malebranche (1638–1715). Source: Yves-Marie André, *La vie du R. P. Malebranche* (Paris, 1886), frontispiece. Courtesy of Princeton University Library.

and with Régis, denouncing this proof as "the most unsupportable opinion that can be imagined, namely, that the modality of his [in this case, Arnauld's] soul is actually representative of God Himself and of infinity."[55] His disciple Henri Lelevel authored a sustained polemic against Régis and the proof from objective being, which he termed unintelligible and question-begging, since "the soul does not have enough reality to contain the Idea of God." If we accepted Régis's principles, Lelevel complained, we must conclude that "the infinite being . . . exists only in the understanding, and, as a consequence, has no objective reality."[56]

For the orthodox Cartesians, Malebranche's criticism obviated his right to accept Descartes's proof from the idea of God as most perfect being and left him without demonstration of God's existence. How could there be an "idea of God" from which to prove Him, if ideas were archetypes in God of that which He created and if, as such, they were particular, finite entities that could not represent infinite perfection to us? In Arnauld's words, Malebranche "had ruined it [Descartes's proof]."[57] Malebranche's reply was an astonishment to many of his readers. Far from weakening Descartes's proof, he insisted, he had both perfected it and shown why it was compelling. In brief, "with regard to the infinite, one knows it by itself, and not by an *idea*, because I know that there is no archetype on which God has been formed, and that nothing can represent God."[58] He correctly reminded Arnauld that he had always maintained this and, indeed, he had argued in the *Recherche* that knowledge of God was "an immediate and direct view" of Him, and that what we termed, for linguistic convenience, the "idea of God," was in fact not an "idea" (since the infinite could not be represented) but an unmediated "vision" [*vue*] of the perfect being.[59] He reiterated this in 1684 both to Arnauld ("this 'idea' will be God Himself") and in his *Entretiens sur la Métaphysique* (God is known "without idea . . . in Himself") and in 1707 was as explicit as he possibly could be: "The idea of God can only be God, since nothing finite can represent the infinite."[60] This formulation quickly found its way into other theological works. Jean-Claude Sommier, professor of theology at the University of Dôle, stated as "axiomatic" that nothing finite "could represent or copy" the infinite and concluded that "when our soul knows and perceives the infinite being, there is nothing between our soul that knows and God who is known."[61] What the scholastics had offered as a reductio ad absurdum of Cartesian thought, the equation of God and our idea of Him, in effect had come to pass.

The Huguenot Cartesian theologian Pierre Poiret began his apostasy from rationalism on just this issue, insisting that "the idea of God . . . is not God Himself," and that "posited in the place of the living God, . . . [it] leaves the soul truly atheistic."[62] The Jesuit Perrin saw this precisely as atheistic too.[63] When the Jesuits threatened one of the two or three overt Malebranchists in their order, Rodolphe Du Tertre, with banishment to unpleasant tasks in unpleasant places unless he recanted, the chastened Jesuit wrote a critique of Malebranchism designed to satisfy his superiors: all the Cartesians, he now concluded, had substituted the idea of God for God Himself and worshiped "a being of [human] logic."[64] For the truly remarkable Jesuit Jean Hardouin and his following, Cartesianism was now revealed, in Descartes, Régis, and Malebranche, as atheism pure and simple. They had deified the idea of God and recognized as divine only "pure chimeras, beings of reason" that our own minds could destroy. Hardouin had refrained from publishing such views, but even before their post-humous edition his public teaching on the subject was legendary among the Jesuits (and, to say the least, among the Cartesians), and a chastened ex-Cartesian under his influence indeed had shared his views in print. The God "proven" by Descartes and Malebranche was "the work of the mind . . . nothing . . . this chimerical God . . . [with] nothing real, that does not exist."[65]

Malebranche, to the contrary, believed that a proper understanding of God, centered on His absolute infinity and omnipresence, reinforced both our reverence and our understanding of why nothing finite could repre-sent Him. God, wrote the most celebrated Catholic philosopher of his time, was not "a particular being . . . a this or a that" but, rather, "the in-finite Being in all senses, in a word, Being." His infinity meant that "He contains in Him . . . all that there is of true reality in all beings created and possible . . . even everything that there is of reality in matter, the least and most imperfect of Beings."[66] Where Régis had insisted that God was a par-ticular spiritual being, since "if God were neither body nor spirit, we would have no idea of Him,"[67] Malebranche's disciple Lelevel replied that since God was "the indeterminate being, in a word, Being," Régis's argu-ment "destroys His existence."[68] The Benedictine philosopher Dom Robert Desgabets, an ardent defender of Malebranche, wrote that we surely all defined God as "Being, purely and simply."[69] Historians look to Spinoza for the "dangers" of such a view, but it was Malebranche (and his critics, who wanted every last implication of such an argument to be apparent) who placed before the broad reading public the formulation that the fun-damental principle of reality could be conceived of not as a particular en-tity, but as "being in general."

Régis and the orthodox Cartesians themselves charged that this reduced God to merely the general idea of universal nature.[70] For the Jesuits, it delivered the Oratorian to them. Reviewing Malebranche, the Jesuit *Journal de Trévoux,* read by an audience far larger than Spinoza would ever have in the eighteenth century, warned that if God were not "a particular being, a this or a that," then our notion of Him could not be distinguished from "the idea of the whole of the universe." Malebranche had advanced "an idea that annihilates the Divinity by reducing it to the totality of the world."[71] For Du Tertre, one could only hope that the Malebranchists did not understand the logical implications of their system, namely, that God was the natural whole of which all particular things were parts.[72] For Hardouin, in lectures given to all within his broad purview, Malebranchists might write that God was immutable, but it was clear that "all they meant by this was that matter acted according to fixed laws of movement." For "the new atheists" of Cartesianism and Malebranchism, "there is no other God but nature," and "the 'will of the Creator' and 'Nature' are the same thing." Hardouin's manuscript of his teaching on "the atheistic new philosophers" stated the argument simply enough, in a phrase historians have reserved for Spinoza or Hobbes: "When the new Philosophy says 'God,' always understand by that the Reality of things, or Truth, or Nature, or the Necessity of the laws of movement, and you will enter into their thought."[73] The atheists did just that.

The toll that this criticism alone took was a striking one. Several disciples of Malebranche himself moved from a commitment to his rationalist proofs to a mystical or fideistic abandonment of all efforts at a natural theology.[74] The young (and later free-thinking) Dortous de Mairan wrote three times to Malebranche, requesting him to distinguish his views from the equation of God with the totality of nature. Malebranche, in three replies, could not satisfy him, and, in one of the last letters of his life, enjoined him to believe on faith.[75]

More broadly, two generations of mutual refutation by Catholic theologians led not only to this confusion within the Cartesian camp, but to the abandonment of particular proofs by many a posteriori theologians as well. Most of these held on to at least one of St. Thomas's proofs as categorically demonstrative, but they held on to different ones, conceding, diversely, the others. The Capuchin Basile de Soissons, for example, in his treatise on the existence of God, wished that the church did not see the need to believe in God by faith alone as "a violence against truth." If, however, one truly insisted on formal proof, he offered, apologizing for the "barbarous" terms of the argument, the demonstration from contingent beings as the only one that compelled assent.[76] Nicolas L'Herminier, professor of theology at the University of Paris, argued that the refutations of a priori proof were unanswerable. He also conceded, however, that the argument that St. Thomas's proofs merely established some first being existing necessarily, which might as well be eternal matter-in-motion as God, was indeed compelling against the first four of St. Thomas's "five ways." The "perfections" of nature central to St. Thomas's fourth way, he conceded, might well be merely beings of reason, that is to say, mere human ideas. Only the argument from governance, he concluded, sufficed to prove an "intelligent" first principle that could not be material.[77] In 1712, the Capuchin theologian Nicolas Anaclet du Havre, in his official textbook for the professors and teachers of his order, informed them that there were now "several theologians" who believed that they could "prove that one cannot demonstrate the existence of God." God, they claimed, could not be proven from the idea of Him: it was not innate; He could never be proven as "effect"; and finite reason could not contain knowledge of the essence of God. He could not be proven a posteriori, they claimed, since no necessity could be inferred from contingency and no infinity from finitude. All one could do, Anaclet du Havre advised his order's teachers and seminarians, was rely on the common consent of the "authorities." He named these: Aquinas *and* Malebranche; Huet *and* François Lamy; the Sorbonne's Denys Petau, *and* the Cartesian Thomassin *and* the fideistic Pascal.[78] In short, he referred them to the very problem itself.

Some fell back upon proof from a "universal consent" that had been eviscerated by generally unchallenged reports by missionaries, and by the German classical scholarship (even then!) that was widely read in France. Certain Christian missionaries made claims for the atheism of many "men of letters" among the Chinese and among the Ottomans. Pious authors proclaimed that whole peoples and nations lived without any belief in or idea of God whatsoever, including the Indians of Brazil, Florida, New France, and Massachusetts; the inhabitants of Siam, of Madagascar, of the Isle de Cayenne, and of the Isle de Maragnan.[79] No one needed Pierre Bayle to argue that a society of atheists was possible; Catholic travelers had made the arguments throughout the century. Nor did they need Bayle to tell them that such a society might be virtuous. The missionary Jean-Baptiste Du Tertre, discussing the black slaves whom he had met in the Antilles, noted that they were not idolators but "worshipped no God, and never had had the slightest thought that there was a God." Nevertheless, he noted, he was moved by "the love they have for one another," and by their "tenderness" and "compassion."[80] This was not an uncommon theme.[81] "What will become," the Jesuit Le Comte asked, "of the arguments that the Holy Fathers, in proving the existence of God, drew from the consent of all peoples?"[82]

Parallel to this, many classical scholars had concluded for the atheism of almost all of the pre-Socratic philosophers and, indeed, for entire movements and major thinkers of Greek philosophy.[83] By the time Buddeus's widely read study of atheism was published in 1717 (later translated from the Latin by the Sorbonne's Louis Philon), its author felt obliged to rescue Plato, Heraclitus, Hippocrates, Plutarch, Cicero, and Pliny from such charges. He agreed, however, that most of the Ionic philosophers, most of the Skeptics, most of the Cynics, most of the Stoics, and the entire "Eleatic Sect" had been properly identified as believing in natural principles alone and not in God. Further, he declared, the case against Aristotle was plausible but not conclusive.[84] He did not heed the warning of several colleagues that it was not edifying to convince the faithful that half the wise men of the world had not believed in God.[85]

While the triumphs of natural science convinced many Catholics and freethinkers that the Providence of God was manifest in the order, regularity, and mechanisms of the natural world (the Enlightenment, of course, would be preponderantly theistic), the theologians were far from unanimous about such an inference. First, of course, all of the Cartesians and Malebranchists were committed to a metaphysic in which one could not infer final causes from the sensible world. For all of the a priori theologians, the governance of the universe by God was only certain when deduced from the rational certainty of His perfection. To make that argument most forcefully, they specifically argued that the last thing one would infer from observing this sorry world, until reason had overcome the impressions of the senses, was its intelligent design or governance. Thus, for example, the Cartesian Carthusian monk Alexis Gaudin insisted that natural inference would lead one to suppose that this imperfect world, with its physical and moral evils, was absolutely incompatible with the being of God as Creator and Providence. Fortunately, however, we knew with certainty from our idea of God that He existed as perfect being, and thus as author and governor of our world.[86] One may not discern the Providence of God in nature, another Cartesian theologian observed, but one may know with rational certainty that it is there.[87]

Consistent, in certain ways, with such a rejection of Aquinas's "fifth way," with Jansenism, and with a deep current of pious teaching, was the commonplace view that the world revealed not God's wisdom to the natural eyes of mankind but the consequences of man's fall, and that submission to the disorders and sufferings of the natural world, in short, submission to Providence, was the very mark of Christian faith. Countless theologians argued that belief in God's governance required Revelation, awareness of sin and its consequences, and the full armor of Christian faith. Only in the light of God's punishments and promises, the formidable Henri-Marie Boudon assured his vast audience, did this natural world make sense.[88] In 1689 and in 1690, the abbé de Gérard reminded his readers of the essential role of faith by noting that Aristotle and Epicurus, both men of "genius," had studied the world solely by natural light and had concluded, respectively, against sublunar Providence and against any Providence at all.[89] Even Lelevel abandoned Malebranche on this issue and insisted that knowledge of God's governance of the natural world was accessible neither through reason nor the senses, but solely by faith.[90]

There were, in fact, a legion of theologians, concerned far more with human humility than with the "order of nature" or niceties of philosophical proof, who at least at times expressed the same belief. We know of God's Providence through Revelation, Bossuet advised, without fathoming His ends, for His design relates solely to eternity.[91] The world is so "badly regulated," the abbés Dangeau and Choisy opined, because suffering is a blessing.[92] The abbé Jean Rousseau's *Traité de Providence* insisted that the seventeenth century's effort to order God's creation was "blind" and "rebellious." Nature was mysterious and terrifying, but the Christian understood Providence under the aspect of eternity, salvation, and damnation, and not in the light of our misleading knowledge of the natural order.[93] The Cartesian Pierre de Villemandy insisted that before Revelation, "almost all the world was in this error, that God had very little part in what occurred in nature."[94] The Benedictine theologian Dom André Roze argued that only Adam could have reasoned by philosophy from nature to the Providence of God. It was "blasphemous," he urged, to speak of the "perfections" and "order" of a world that God made with foreknowledge of our fall. God could have made a "beautiful" world, but chose to create one so punishing that men are able "to convict God, as the impious do, of having lacked wisdom in creating and arranging the world such as we see it."[95] The nature we see, Filleau de La Chaise observed, could not possibly be what a God would have created; only knowledge of the fall could make sense of it.[96] Providence, the great preacher Massillon reminded his Christian auditors, was known to us only in terms of a world *beyond* nature and the present life, for "all the visible world itself is made only for the age to come."[97] In short, natural theology, confident that the exquisite machine of the world proved God and God's governance, was only one seventeenth-century Christian voice. There was another voice, however, of august Christian heritage, that reminded the flock that natural knowledge often led to darkness, and that only supernatural knowledge, revealed and died for on the Cross, made sense of the natural world. The latter voice might be edifying and consoling, but it was not one to be raised in a defense of St. Thomas's fifth demonstration. Indeed, more loudly than Bayle, and long before Hume and Voltaire's *Candide,* such a voice offered evidence and formulations that might be used against natural belief in that Providence it sought to defend.

It is, thus, profoundly ahistorical to think that Bayle, or *Candide,* or Hume was required to create the "problem of Providence," as if it had not always been a theme of Christian thought. While the deists of the Enlightenment detached themselves from the premises and often the very concerns of Catholic thought, the atheists, with the theologians, wrestled with all the dilemmas of orthodox seventeenth-century culture: the demand for compelling proof of God; the mutual assault of a priori and a posteriori schools; the nature of putative knowledge of God's governance. It is not surprising that Meslier was a well-educated priest; it is supremely plausible. He rejected all a priori proofs of the existence of God as question-begging, conceived of the first principle proven a posteriori as Being in general, and obsessed on the conflict between the painful natural order and the idea of a perfect being. What would be mysterious about reaching such conclusions without the intercession of "free thought"?

Consider, thus, two phenomena: the growth of fideism, which surely is the other side of atheism's coin; and the immediate intellectual world of Meslier. If the "évidence" of God's existence could be placed in doubt, there were two primary options for those who felt the effects most deeply: either abandonment of the demand for demonstration, or disbelief. The evidence suggests that the two grew hand in hand as the seventeenth century progressed and turned, with fideism a far more common option than disbelief. There was, of course, the 1670 edition of Pascal's *Pensées:* God had hidden Himself from human sin, allowing plausible doubt about His existence to those who did not know Him through Christ. Neither "by reason" nor "from nature" could one be assured of the being of God.[98] Sixteen theologians offered approbation of the text.[99] The editors conceded that those who wanted "proofs and geometric demonstrations of the existence of God" would be disappointed, but denied the efficacity of empirical, metaphysical, and commonplace proofs. Pascal, they informed the reader, had written elsewhere that "I do not feel myself strong enough" to prove to doubters "the existence of God."[100] The Jansenist Filleau de la Chaise defended Pascal for this, in 1672, quoting him to the effect that one "would seek in vain the traces of God in the dead works of nature," and urging that God be sought by the heart, not the mind.[101] In 1728, the Oratorian librarian Desmolets published the remaining fragments of Pascal's *Pensées,* reminding the reader that neither David nor Solomon, the wisest of our fathers, had sought to "prove" his God.[102] The phenomenon, however, was by no means purely Pascalian.

By the end of his career, Huet had reached conclusions as profoundly fideistic as Pascal's, convinced that natural knowledge a posteriori was as arbitrary as he had deemed natural knowledge a priori to be.[103] Seemingly exhausted by his defense of Malebranche's proof, the Benedictine Desgabets conceded that perhaps the proof only appealed to him because he already knew God, and that perhaps without Revelation and tradition, we would have no idea of Him.[104] Gaspard Langenhert's *Philosophus Novus* urged that Christian philosophy should reject Descartes and Aristotle altogether, and Plato as well, since it was clear that theology "presupposed" the existence of God and that without faith the theologian cannot "prove" Him.[105] In 1728, the abbés Blondel and Louvail proposed that belief in God was achieved by faith alone and that only by virtue of Christ did we learn of "an infinitely perfect being," a Creator, or a Providence.[106] In a century whose Catholic minds were enjoined to demand *évidence,* competing claims took a heavy toll: in the church itself, the assertion was being made ever more boldly that perhaps such *évidence* could not be had.

We now arrive, after many an allusion, at the "problem" of Jean Meslier. He *must have* read Bayle, wrote the otherwise impeccable Pierre Rétat, since a critique of our knowledge of Providence is at the heart of his system.[107] Such critiques were everywhere! He read "only several books, and those above all that would be found in the most modest clerical library as guarantors of the faith," wrote Jean Fabre, and thus "this peasant and self-taught curé, liberated from dogma but not from scholasticism, cleared for himself the path of a merciless atheism."[108] It was precisely in works that were "guarantors of the faith" that the most searing refutations of proofs of God's existence could be found. We perhaps know a few things about Jean Meslier. He may have been born and have died in the country, but he was not "self-taught": he studied at the great seminary at Reims in the late seventeenth century, where Jansenist-versus-Jesuit and Cartesian-versus-Thomist passions ran high. A manuscript source with no axes to grind, written after the *Testament* had been found, described something of Meslier's intellectual world: initially drawn to Descartes, he came to know the Jesuits and even dined with them in Paris, and became a friend of the Jesuit Buffier; Buffier prevailed on Meslier to read the abbé Houtteville's treatise on Christianity; among Meslier's few books, the 1713 edition of Fénelon's treatise on the existence of God.[109] Although the argument about theological contributions to atheism stands with or without such a manuscript, Buffier, Houtteville, and the 1713 edition of Fénelon in fact all bear the imprint of the debates we have addressed here. Let us examine, briefly, these "guarantors of the faith."

Who was Buffier? He was a Jesuit philosopher who not only rejected all a priori proof of God after vigorous analysis, but who conceded that the a posteriori proofs, though persuasive, lacked "absolute *évidence*." All "complete demonstration," Buffier urged, presupposed nondemonstrable "first truths," beyond reason or the senses, among which he included the "principle" that order "could not be the effect of chance." To ask for demonstration of such principles, Buffier averred, was malicious.[110] Who was the abbé Houtteville? He was a theologian who had concluded that Pascal was correct in his emphasis on the need to have faith to know God, since, in Houtteville's words, "it is not by metaphysical and abstract proofs" that men achieved "complete conviction." Would-be demonstrations of God relied too much on "imagination" (the a priori proofs) or on "the senses" (a posteriori proofs) "to extend to first principles." It was not by reason or the senses, but "by the heart" that God's existence could be known.[111] What was the 1713 edition of Fénelon? It was an edition in which the editor, the Jesuit Tournemine, furious at Fénelon's willingness to use Cartesian proofs in addition to Thomistic ones, prefaced the work with a "Treatise on Atheism," showing how Cartesian and Malebranchist thought could lead only to materialism and atheism.[112] Perhaps the "problem" of Jean Meslier is no problem at all.

How strange to have to say it: one cannot know what Catholic France produced without knowing Catholic France! The church, in its extraordinary diversity of beliefs and institutions, taught everyone, from Meslier, to Voltaire, to Diderot. Its causal agency, except as catalyst and target, virtually has been removed from Enlightenment history, as R. R. Palmer complained long ago.[113] It was the *potentia* out of which so much Enlightenment actuality was realized, and its tensions or contradictions (whichever you prefer) were the stuff of much disbelief. The church in France had rid its kingdom of Protestants, but it could not banish its own divided minds. Whatever its intellectual authority, and whatever its consensus on the *content* of the preambles and articles of its faith, the contentious public breakdown of a dominant philosophical paradigm created or helped to create an opportunity for dramatic change and the emergence of antithetical beliefs. Disagreement about conclusions captures our fancy; disagreement about how and why one reaches conclusions is perhaps the far deeper and more revolutionary phenomenon.

Notes

1. The first major study of the many clandestine manuscripts of the first half of the eighteenth century in France is Ira O. Wade, *The Clandestine Organization and Diffusion of Philosophic Ideas in France from 1700 to 1750* (Princeton, 1938), which established a solid initial knowledge of the nature and dissemination of clandestine manuscripts and offered a stimulating and often prescient agenda for further inquiry and interpretation. These manuscripts are diversely heterodox, primarily deistic, and, in the main, explicitly opposed to atheism. The past fifteen years have witnessed a great deal of interest in the manuscripts, including publication of several critical editions, most notably an invaluable edition of Meslier's atheistic *Testament* by Jean Deprun, Roland Desné, and Albert Soboul, eds., *Oeuvres complètes de Jean Meslier,* 3 vols. (Paris, 1970–72). For a good sense of the nature of current research into the (above all) bibliographic, attributional, and "ideological" questions occupying most students of the manuscripts, see the many essays in Olivier Bloch, ed., *Le Matérialisme du XVIIIe siècle et la littérature clandestine* (Paris, 1982). While excellent work is being done on the diffusion of the manuscripts, too much attention is being paid to insoluble issues of attribution, and there is an undue emphasis on the manuscripts both as a mental world somehow "apart" from their surrounding culture and as "causes" or anticipations of later phenomena. In some cases, mere readers' notes are being treated as original (rather than useful) documents in their own right. For the particular purposes of my larger study, I am above all interested in the etiology and content of two sorts of manuscripts: those that are explicitly atheistic and those that propose or imply philosophical systems ambiguous enough to raise interesting questions about atheism. In contrast to what one would expect from the secondary literature, there is a significant number of manuscripts that are simultaneously materialistic and deistic. These latter, more numerous than the explicitly atheistic manuscripts, are antispiritualist, but emphatic in their beliefs in and "proofs" of a Creator who endowed and conserves matter and who intelligently and benevolently designed the world that followed from matter's operations. The manuscripts I put in my two prime categories, in addition to Meslier's manuscript, are Bibl. de l'Arsenal MSS. 2239 (#2), 2257 (#2), 2558 (#2);

Bibl. Mazarine MSS. 1168 (#2), 1183, 1190, 1192 (#6), 1194 (#1), 1197 (#4); B.N. MSS. fonds français, 9658, 13208. Boulainvillier's notes on his readings, and in one instance his conversations, are not without interest: B.N. MSS. nouv. acq. fran., 11071–11076.

2. Lucien Febvre's classic *Le problème de l'incroyance au XVIe siècle: La religion de Rabelais* (Paris, 1942; rev. ed., Paris, 1947; Eng. tr.) overstates the case of the "unthinkability" of atheism for the sixteenth century, examines only a minute portion of the learned world, and confuses certain cognitive and psychological issues, yet succeeds somehow in being essentially correct. The English translation of Febvre's work, *The Problem of Unbelief in the Sixteenth Century: The Religion of Rabelais,* tr. B. Gottlieb (Cambridge, Mass., 1982), is preferable to the French editions, being more precise in its citations and translations from the Latin than the original and revised French editions. All of the attempted counter-examples in François Berriot, *Athéismes et athéistes au XVIe siècle en France,* 2 vols. (Lille, 1977), are self-evidently references to "ungodliness," swearing, blasphemy, theistic heterodoxy, or other "sin," not to atheism; these raise exceptionally interesting (and perhaps unanswerable) questions about the relationship of "marginal" life-styles and behavior to belief, but the one thing missing from Berriot's study of atheism is atheism. For an extended discussion of Febvre and Berriot, see the introduction to Alan Charles Kors, *Atheism in France, 1650–1729,* vol. I (Princeton, 1990). For other approaches to and conceptions of the problem, see also *Actes du colloque international de Sommières,* André Stegmann, ed.: *Aspects du libertinisme au XVIe siècle* (Paris, 1974); Antoine Adam, *Le Mouvement philosophique dans la première moitié du XVIIIe siècle* (Paris, 1967) and *Théophile de Viau et la libre pensée française en 1620* (2d ed., Geneva, 1965); Michael J. Buckley, S.J., *At the Origins of Modern Atheism* (New Haven, 1987); Henri Busson, *La pensée religieuse française de Charron à Pascal* (Paris, 1933) and *La religion des classiques (1660–1685)* (Paris, 1948) and *Les sources et le développement du rationalisme dans la littérature française de la renaissance* (rev. ed. Paris, 1957); Cornelio Fabro, *God in Exile: Modern Atheism. A Study of the Internal Dynamic of Modern Atheism, from Its Roots in the Cartesian 'Cogito' to the Present Day,* tr. Arthur Gibson (New York, 1968) (tr. from Fabro's *Introduzione all'ateismo moderno* [1964]); Tullio Gregory, *Theophrastus redivivus: Erudizione e ateismo nel seicento* (Naples, 1979); Tullio Gregory, G. Paganini, et al., *Ricerche su letteratura libertina e letteratura clandestina nel seicento* . . . (Florence, 1981); Hermann Ley, *Geschichte der Aufklärung und des Atheismus* (Berlin, 1966); Fritz Mauthner, *Der Atheismus und seine Geschichte im Abendlande* (Stuttgart and Berlin, 1921); René Pintard, *Le libertinage érudit dans la première moitié du XVIIe siècle,* 2 vols. (Paris, 1943); J. S. Spink, *French Free-Thought from Gassendi to Voltaire* (London, 1960); and D. P. Walker, *The Ancient Theology: Studies in Christian Platonism from the Fifteenth to the Eighteenth Century* (Ithaca, N.Y., 1972), 132–63.

3. The "commonplace" atheists were Protagoras, Critias, Diagoras (of Melos), and Theodorus. Many added Epicurus, Bion, and Lucretius.

4. Aristotle, *Topica,* VIII. xiv [163b 1–19]. The E. S. Forster translation of the *Topica* in Aristotle, *Organon,* vol. II (Cambridge, Mass., 1960), seems reasonably consistent with the Latin of the seventeenth-century Du Val edition: "In dealing with any thesis we must examine the argument both for and against, and having discovered it we must immediately seek the solution; for the result will be that we

shall have trained ourselves at the same time both for question and for answer. If we have no one else with whom to argue, we must do so with ourselves. Also one must choose arguments relating to the same thesis and compare them; . . . for the result is that one is put on one's guard against contrary arguments." Virtually every text on philosophical method of the seventeenth-century collèges and universities approved of this model.

5. Following the sequence of the text, see, for example, the excellent works by Aram Vartanian, *Diderot and Descartes: A Study of Scientific Naturalism in the Enlightenment* (Princeton, 1953); J. S. Spink, *French Free Thought from Gassendi to Voltaire* (London, 1960); Paul Vernière, *Spinoza et la pensée française avant la Révolution*, 2 vols. (Paris, 1954), and Pierre Rétat, *Le Dictionnaire de Bayle et la lutte philosophique au XVIIIe siècle* (Paris, 1971); on Meslier, see below.

6. G. Canziani and Gianni Paganini, eds., *Theophrastus Redivivus*, 2 vols. (Florence, 1981–82). Jerome Vercruysse's observation that "the philosophical milieux of the 18th century seem to ignore the *Theophrastus Redivivus* almost totally" seems exact: J. Vercruysse, "Le *Theophrastus Redivivus* au 18e siècle: mythe et réalité," in T. Gregory, et al., *Ricerche su letteratura libertina . . . Atti del convegno di studio di Genova*, 30 ottobre–1 novembre 1980 (Florence, 1981), 297–303.

7. D'Holbach "discovered" the metaphysical side of Hobbes on a trip to England in the mid-eighteenth century, and translated the *Treatise of Human Nature* into French. Diderot wrote that he was first introduced to the philosophical Hobbes by this, and quite swept away. See Diderot, *Correspondance*, G. Roth, ed., vol. XII (Paris, 1965), 45–47.

8. See, for example, Jean Nicolai, O.P., ed., *Summa Theologica S. Thomae Aquinatis . . .* (Paris, 1663) Ia. Quest. 2, Art. 2. As Nicolai, doctor of theology from the University of Paris, and *premier régent* of the *grand couvent des Jacobins*, explained to his readers, ibid., 4–5, note P, God was apparent, and faith pertained to that which was not apparent. This was occasionally but very infrequently contested in seventeenth-century France. Many agreed with Dom François Lamy, O.S.B., *Les Premiers Elémens des sciences . . . proportionnés à la portée des commerçans . . .* (Paris, 1706), 68–94, that reason must first establish the existence of God for any faith to be possible; since faith was submission to God's word, belief in Him by faith would be submission to the word of a being whom you did not know to exist. Paraphrasing Henry Holden, the priest Louis Ellies Dupin (doctor of theology from Paris, professor of philosophy at the *Collège Royal*, and sympathizer of the Jansenists) noted that belief in God was considered "a preamble necessary to the Faith, rather than an Article of Faith, since it is impossible to believe any Article because of the authority of God who revealed it unless one first supposes [as a certain premise] the existence of God." Louis Ellies Dupin, *Bibliothèque des auteurs ecclésiastiques du dix-septième siècle*, 7 vols. (Paris, 1708), II, 166.

9. This was the almost universal understanding of the eighth session of the Fifth Lateran Council (1513). The widely respected Minim monk Emmanuel Maignan (a theologian, mathematician, and philosopher) in his *Philosophia Sacra* (Paris and Toulouse, 1661; 2d ed., 1672), 85–86, termed any opposition to this view to be, at best, an absolute "theological error," and, most probably, "entirely and expressly against the faith." The celebrated dictum of Romans 1:19–20 was taken by many

to endorse a posteriori demonstration, but the issue of what kind of natural proof was required was wholly open to debate. On the condemnation by the University of Paris of any fideistic claims that God could not be proven by natural reason, see Denifle, ed., *Chartularium universitatis Parisiensis*, vol. II (Paris, 1851), pièce 1124, 576ff. At the First Vatican Council, the church reaffirmed this understanding of the 1513 dictum: "The . . . Church . . . holds and teaches that by the natural light of reason, God . . . can be shown with certainty by means of created things." Further, it pronounced anathema against anyone who "says that the unique and true God, our Creator and Lord, cannot be known with certainty by means of created entities." G. Schneeman and T. Granderath, eds., *Acta et decreta sacrorum conciliorum recentiorum*, 7 vols. (Freiburg, 1892), VII, col. 250 and 255.

10. There is great erudition and depth in the growing historical literature on these phenomena. See, among others, F. Furet and J. Ozouf, *Lire et écrire: L'alphabétisation des Français de Calvin à Jules Ferry*, 2 vols. (Paris, 1977); H.-J. Martin, R. Chartier, and J.-P. Vivet, et al., eds., *Histoire de l'édition française*, 3 vols. (Paris, 1982–); François Lebrun et al., *De Gutenberg aux Lumières* (Paris, 1981); vol. 4 of the *Histoire générale de l'enseignement et de l'éducation en France*; M.-M. Compère and D. Julia, *Les collèges français. 16e–18e siècles* (Paris, 1984); J. Lelièvre, *L'éducation en France du XVIe au XVIIe siècle* (Brussels, 1975); G. Snyders, *La pédagogie en France aux XVIIe et XVIIIe siècles* (Paris, 1972); F. de Dainville, S.J., *L'éducation des Jésuites (XVIe–XVIIIe siècles)* (Paris, 1978); W. Frijhoff and D. Julia, *Ecole et société dans la France de l'Ancien Régime* (Paris, 1975); J. de Viguerie, *Une oeuvre d'éducation sous l'Ancien Régime: Les Pères de la Doctrine chrétienne en France et en Italie, 1592–1792* (Paris, 1985); R. Chartier, et al., *L'éducation en France du XVIe au XVIIIe siècle* (Paris, 1976).

11. Jean-Baptiste de La Grange, Oratory, *Les principes de la philosophie, contre les nouveaux philosophes* . . . (Paris, 1675). These were difficult times for the Oratory, rightly suspected of teaching Cartesianism in its courses and of sympathies toward both Jansenism and the "new philosophy." In 1671, the Faculty of Theology at Paris reiterated the 1624 prohibition against any philosophy departing from Aristotle. In 1675, in a bitter struggle in which the Oratorians were seriously compromised, the University of Angers adopted an absolute prohibition against teaching "the opinions and sentiments of Descartes," to which the royal *conseil d'état* appended the phrase "in any way or manner whatsoever." In that same year, the Benedictines were commanded "to abstain from teaching the new [Cartesian] opinions" about "the essence and nature of bodies . . . actual extension . . . [and] accidents." The congregation of the Oratory must have been relieved to find this Aristotelian in its midst to bear witness to its "orthodoxy," permission to publish being granted in printed approbation by Sainte-Marthe, its reverend-father-general. In a humiliating formal agreement with the rival Jesuits in 1678, the Oratory was forced to admit its "abuses" in philosophical teaching, and to promise to abstain from teaching Cartesian natural philosophy (a promise it would not keep). A similar agreement was imposed on the congregation of Sancta Genovefa, prohibiting "our philosophers" from "teaching the opinions of Descartes." When people needed reminding in 1705 of these bans and promises (and many similar prohibitions), Jean DuHamel, an Aristotelian professor of philosophy at the University of Paris, published them

all in his *Quaedam recentiorum philosophorum, ac praesertim Cartesii, Propositiones Damnatae ac Prohibitae* (Paris, 1705).

12. La Grange, Oratory, op. cit., 7–19, 30–36, 51–176.

13. Among his works from this period see Dom François Lamy, O.S.B., *Vérité évidente de la religion chrétienne . . .* (Paris, 1694); *Les Premiers élémens des sciences . . .* (Paris, 1706) (with its interesting subtitle "proportionnés à la portée des commerçans"); and *L'Incrédule amené à la religion par la raison, en quelques Entretiens où l'on traite de l'Aliance [sic] de la Raison avec la Foy* (Paris, 1710).

14. F. Lamy, O.S.B., *L'Incrédule*, 78–118. In his *Lettres philosophiques* (Paris, 1703), 33–95, Lamy had decried criticism of the Cartesians for relying *too much* on God in their philosophy, characterizing his critics as believing that "it is not philosophizing to have recourse to God for the explanation of natural effects, as if the Author of nature and the unique true cause of all that occurs were something foreign to the explication of these effects."

15. Aristotelians found the parsimonious Cartesian ontology absurd and unable to deal with motion or act; Cartesians found the scholastic ontology of forms and intentional species that were somehow neither material nor spiritual equally absurd and dangerous. Each side sought to show the incompatibility of the other's metaphysic with foundational theology, the simplest way of discrediting a view. For representative anti-Cartesian "reductions to atheism" of Cartesian ontology, see Gabriel Daniel, S.J., *Voyage au Monde de Descartes* (2d ed., Paris, 1691), 144–53; Jean DuHamel, *Réflexions critiques sur le système Cartésien de la philosophie de Mr. Régis* (Paris, 1692), passim, and, especially, 220–25, 330–44; the priest J. Galimard, *La philosophie du prince, ou La véritable idée de la nouvelle et de l'ancienne philosophie* (Paris, 1689), 53–216; Rodolphe Du Tertre, S.J., *Réfutation d'un nouveau système de métaphysique,* 3 vols. (Paris, 1715), I and II, passim. Since Aristotle had believed in the eternity of matter, Cartesians and other anti-Aristotelians—especially among the Benedictines, Oratorians, and Franciscan Capuchins—found the reduction to atheism of his system easy to accomplish in their countless commentaries on patristic literature, condemnations of pagan errors, and histories of philosophy. Bayle, to say the least, was not the first to do this in his celebrated note G to the article "Zabarella." For less subtle discussions, see Jean de Launoy, *De varia Aristotelis in Academia Parisiensi fortuna* (3d ed. Paris, 1662); and Valerien Magnus, O.F.M., Capuchin, *Principia et specimen philosophiae axiomata; . . . atheismus Aristotelis; . . .* (Cologne, 1652). Vartanian, *Diderot and Descartes,* v, correctly defines the very heart of Enlightenment materialism as the belief "that matter and its inherent modes of behavior have brought about all things, or at least . . . that all things are to be explained by recourse to matter and its properties," but his assumption that the Cartesians themselves brought about such materialist conclusions misses the actual process of "transmission." Bibl. de l'Arsenal MSS. 2558 (#2) and Bibl. Mazarine MSS. 1168 (#2) are interesting examples of how Cartesian and Aristotelian reductions of each other's systems to atheism find their place in the atheistic literature.

16. The study of approbations and permissions is a neglected part of the history of seventeenth-century theology and philosophy, especially important given the intensity of divisions among Catholic schools of thought each with eminent

defenders. Even in times requiring the greatest prudence, authors knew where to turn for needed approbations, and there were distinct groups of Aristotelian, Cartesian, Malebranchist, and fideistic theological and philosophical censors and superiors who could be counted upon to grant permissions to works that competing schools found both libelous and, indeed, essentially dangerous to the faith.

17. See the English translation of the *Ratio Studiorum* by A. R. Ball, in Edward A. Fitzpatrick, *St. Ignatius and the Ratio Studiorum* (New York and London, 1933), 119–254. In addition to his edition of the *Summa Theologica* (with over ten thousand marginal glosses), the Dominican scholar Nicolai published Aquinas's commentary on the synoptic gospels, on the four books of the *Sentences,* and the quodlibetal discussions. Between 1650 and 1670, there was a remarkable outpouring of critical editions of St. Thomas, commentaries upon his work, and published courses on his philosophy and theology. Among the most notable and successful of the latter were the multivolumed works of Jean-Baptiste Gonet, O.P., *Clypeus theologiae thomisticae contra novos ejus impugnatores* (Bordeaux, 1659–69); Pierre Labat, O.P., *Theologia scholastica secundum illibatam S. Thomae doctrinam . . .* (Toulouse, 1658–61); Jérôme De Medicis, *Formalis explicatio Summae theologicae divi Thomae Aquinatis . . .* (Paris, 1657); Antoine Regnault, *Doctrinae Divi Thomae Aquinatis . . .* (Toulouse, 1670); and, in French, abbé N. de Hauteville's ten-volume *La théologie de saint Thomas . . .* (Paris, 1670) (de Hauteville was a doctor of Theology from the University of Paris).

18. See above, nn. 11 and 13.

19. In Louis Thomassin, Oratory, *La méthode d'étudier chrétiennement et solidement la philosophie par rapport à la religion chrestienne et aux Ecritures* (Paris, 1685), 165–93 and 288–584, for example, whose author was deeply sympathetic to both Descartes and Malebranche, the errors of Aristotle were contrasted sharply and repeatedly with the purity of Plato, whose consistency with St. Augustine and Christian teaching was always emphasized. Bonaventure d'Argonne, Carthusian, *Traité de la lecture des Pères* (Paris, 1688; reissued Paris, 1691), 64–83, stressed the Fathers' clear preference for Plato over Aristotle, in contrast to the current scholastic "condemnation of modern Platonists."

20. These demonstrations are found in the third and fifth meditations in René Descartes, *Meditationes de Prima Philosophia in qua Dei existentia et animae immortalitas demonstratur* (Paris, 1641; 2d ed., 1642).

21. Although Aquinas addresses the question of proof of God's existence diversely in a variety of places, the "Five Ways" came to be synonymous with his theology, and are found in any edition of the *Summa Theologica,* 1a. Question 2, Article 3.

22. Bibl. de l'Arsenal MSS. 2558 (#2), 101–102.

23. Charles de Saint-Evremond, *Oeuvres Mêlées,* new ed., 5 vols. (Amsterdam, 1705), I, 184–85.

24. Gabriel Daniel, S.J., *Voyage au monde de Descartes* (Paris, 1691), 163–75. Daniel's work was published first in Paris, 1690, and Amsterdam, 1690; the 1691 edition was identical to that of 1690. A revised edition of Paris, 1702, added a section on Descartes's theory of animals. Daniel was librarian of the Parisian Jesuits in Paris and *historiographe du roi.* He also wrote extensively against Pascal.

25. François-Marie Assermet, O.F.M., *Theologia scholastico-positiva* . . . , tome I: . . . *De Theologiae Principibus, Prolegomenis, De Deo Uno, Ejusque Attributis* (Paris, 1713), III–12. Assermet was a self-proclaimed disciple of Duns Scotus, not Aquinas.

26. Robert Basselin, *Dissertation sur l'origine des idées, où l'on fait voir contre M. Descartes, le R.P. Malebranche et MM. de Port-Royal, qu'elles nous viennent toutes des sens et comment* (Paris, 1709).

27. The Jesuits eventually distanced themselves from Locke, but they initially had reviewed Pierre Coste's 1700 translation of the *Essay* quite favorably, calling Locke "a penetrating mind, who meditates much, and who proves [his propositions]"; see *Journal de Trévoux*, jan.–fév. 1701, 116–31. They particularly enjoyed and approved of his arguments that the idea of God could only come from the senses.

28. Pierre-Daniel Huet, *Censura Philosophiae Cartesianae* (Paris, 1689), 101–36. The *Censura* enjoyed many reprintings and a fourth edition by 1694. It was republished in several editions in the 1720s. At the time he wrote it, Huet was bishop-designate of Soissons.

29. Antoine Ravaille Regnault, O.P., *Doctrinae Divi Thomae Aquinatis tria Principia cum suis Consequentiis* . . . , 3 vols. (Toulouse, 1670), I, 118–20. Regnault was also known as Antonio Reginaldo.

30. Jean DuHamel, *Lettre de Monsieur Du Hamel . . . pour servir de réplique à monsieur Régis* (Paris, 1699), 7. This was written in response to the great Cartesian Pierre-Sylvain Régis's *Réponse aux Réflexions critiques du M. Du Hamel sur le système Cartésien de la Philosophie de M. Régis* (Paris, 1692), whose title referred to DuHamel's *Réflexions critiques sur le système Cartésien de la philosophie de M. Régis* (Paris, 1692), whose title referred to Régis's *Système de Philosophie*, 3 vols. (Paris, 1690). Régis would also become embroiled with Huet over the latter's *Censura*. Régis, barred from the universities, gave very successful private lectures on Cartesianism. DuHamel was professor of philosophy at the Collège de Plessis-Sorbonne at the University of Paris, and a member of the redoubtable Maison et Société de la Sorbonne.

31. Jacques-Nicolas Colbert, *Philosophia vetus et nova ad usum scholae accommodata* . . . , 4 vols. (Paris, 1678), II, 488–98. This work appeared during the same year that saw Colbert received as a member of the Académie Française. In 1691, he became archbishop of Rouen. He was a doctor of theology from the Sorbonne. Despite his fundamental Aristotelianism, his philosophical text was not without sympathies toward Plato and the philosophical sides of Augustine.

32. Michel Morus, *De existentia Dei et Humanae Mentis Immortalitate Secundum Cartesii et Aristotelis Doctrinam Disputatio* (Paris, 1692), 56–79, 196–313.

33. François Perrin, S.J., *Manuale Theologicum sive Theologia Dogmatica et Historica ad usum seminariorum* (Toulouse, 1710), 5–9.

34. As Daniel, S.J. op. cit. (n. 24 above), 174–75, put it, "the perfection of an idea is not measured by the nobility of the object it represents, but by the manner in which it represents it, which being very imperfect in the case in question, cannot be infinite." See also Morus, op. cit. (n. 32 above), 292–93. Huet, loc. cit. (n. 28 above), argued that the assumption that the "object" of an idea was identical with the actual being it purported to represent was precisely the question at issue. Since ideas were merely "modifications of our minds," they all could be attributed to

finite causes. For DuHamel, *Réflexions critiques,* 12–16, 68–78, the distinction between "formal" and "objective" being was "confused" and "false." Since the "virtue of representing" was "merely an attribute" of "the formal being of ideas," the two were inseparable. A proper definition of the formal being of ideas, for DuHamel, entirely vitiated Descartes's "proof": it was the passive power to represent and modify imperfectly. See also Perrin, loc. cit.

35. DuHamel, loc. cit.

36. Régis, *Réponse aux Réflexions . . . de Du Hamel,* 40–42.

37. DuHamel, *Lettre . . . de réplique à . . . Régis,* 7.

38. Colbert, op. cit. (n. 31 above), II, 488–98.

39. Huet, loc. cit. (n. 28 above). See also Morus, op. cit. (n. 32 above), 71–79, 238–47, 292–313.

40. See, for example, Assermet, loc. cit.; Etienne Petiot, S.J., *Démonstrations théologiques pour établir la foy chrestienne et catholique . . .* (Metz, 1674), 19; and Guillaume Dagoumer, *Philosophia ad usum scholae accommodata,* tome III: *Metaphysica* (Paris, 1703), 235–39. Dagoumer was professor of philosophy at the prestigious Collège d'Harcourt. He served as rector of the University of Paris for the unusually long periods of 1711 to 1713 and 1723 to 1725, and as administrative head of the collège d'Harcourt from 1713 to 1730.

41. Daniel, S.J. op. cit. (n. 24 above), 174–75. In the new edition of the *Voyage* (Paris, 1702), 524–25, Daniel expressed his astonishment at the need to continue discussing proofs so "pitiable and ridiculous." As in the case of atheism, continued adherence to Descartes's proofs, he believed, could only be explained as a failure of will.

42. DuHamel, ed., *Quaedam recentiorum philosophorum, ac praesertim Cartesii, Propositiones damnatae ac prohibitae* (Paris, 1705), 33–34.

43. Adrien Baillet, *La Vie de Monsieur Des-Cartes,* 2 vols. (Paris, 1691), II, 283–85, 507; see also I, 181. Baillet studied his theology with the Franciscans, taught at the seminary-collège de Beauvais, sympathized profoundly with the Jansenists, and wrote extensively on saints, earning an outstanding reputation in hagiography.

44. Régis, *Réponse aux Réflexions . . . de Du Hamel,* 71–79.

45. *Histoire des Ouvrages des Savans,* XVI (1700), 220–22. The author of this polemic was Isaac Jacquelot, a Huguenot Cartesian theologian much admired in France; see his *Dissertations sur l'existence de Dieu . . .* (The Hague, 1697), "Préface." Jacquelot was convinced that Cartesianism was a great barrier to atheism since it established a perfect being, where other systems allowed the word God to be used so "equivocally" that it could mean "no more than that of the matter of the universe." A posteriori proofs for him were tied to senses that in no way could provide the idea of God. He wrote in his preface that "People say in vain that [the existence of God] is a principle that should not be discussed pro and con. It would be wonderful if that were the case, but it is not."

46. F. Lamy, O.S.B., *Le nouvel athéisme renversé . . .* (Paris, 1696), 5–8.

47. Régis, *Système de Philosophie* I, 59, 79–87. Huet, *Censura,* 130–34, asked the Cartesians how anyone could dare believe "that God is what he thinks," reminding them that "Great philosophers in the past examined their idea of Divinity and concluded diversely that God was plural, corporeal, bounded by shape, mortal

or *non-existent*" (emphasis added). Régis replied at length, replicating all of the debates, in his *Réponse au livre qui a pour titre P. Danielis Huetii . . . Censura Philosophiae Cartesianae . . .* (Paris, 1691), subtitled, with full Cartesian self-confidence, "serving as explanation of all parts of philosophy, above all metaphysics." By 1692, however, in his *Réponse aux Réflexions . . . de . . . Du Hamel*, 5–8, he obviously felt in some difficulty concerning the "objective being" of ideas, for he reminded his audience with uncharacteristic defensiveness that "philosophers are free to define words as they wish, provided they are explicit about it."

48. Denis de Sallo, sieur de La Coudraye, *Traitez de métaphysique demontrée selon la méthode des géomètres* (Paris, 1693), "Préface" [xxii–xxviii]. La Coudraye, known also as Sallo, was the founder and first publisher of the *Journal des Sçavans*.

49. Régis, *Réponse . . . Huetii . . . Censura*, 219–51.

50. It is difficult to convey the combinations of awe and rapture on the one side, dismay and anger on the other, with which Catholics in the two or three generations before the Enlightenment read and discussed Malebranche. Pascal, Arnauld, Bossuet, and Fénelon all had admirers; Malebranche had disciples.

51. See, for example, Malebranche, Oratory, *De la Recherche de la vérité*, in André Robinet, gen. ed., *Oeuvres complètes de Malebranche* (hereafter *O.C.*), 21 vols. (Paris, 1958–70), II, 19, 103–4; and *Conversations chrétiennes*, in *O.C.*, IV, 14–30; and *Entretien d'un philosophe chrétien et d'un philosophe chinois sur l'existence et la nature de Dieu*, in *O.C.*, XV, 11–18.

52. Malebranche, *Rech. de la vér.*, in *O.C.*, II, 371–72; see also IV, 14. In the *Entretiens sur la métaphysique et sur la religion*, *O.C.*, XII, 56, he repeats the standard Cartesian accusations against the scholastics, that their insistence that we do not grasp perfection denies them any conclusion for a perfect being from their own proofs: "It is as if you would ask, is there a 'Blictri,' that is to say, a certain thing, without knowing what."

53. Malebranche, *Rech. de la vér.*, *O.C.*, II, 90–95.

54. Ibid., 96–101.

55. He debated with Arnauld in many works and journals. For the quotation, see his *Réponse au Livre des vraies et fausses idées*, *O.C.*, VI, 169. See also his *Réponse . . . à la troisième lettre de M. Arnauld . . .*, *O.C.*, IX, 947–50; and his *Réponse . . . à M. Régis*, ch. 2, *O.C.*, XVIII (part 1). See also *Journal des Sçavans*, 1694, 291–98 (28 juin, Arnauld's first letter), 302–9 (5 juillet, Arnauld's second letter), 311–22 (12 juillet, Malebranche's first reply), 326–36 (19 juillet, Malebranche's second reply).

56. Henri Lelevel, *La vraye et la fausse métaphysique, où l'on réfute les sentimens de M. Régis, et de ses adversaires, sur cette matière* (Rotterdam, 1694), 22–39.

57. Antoine Arnauld, *Des vraies et des fausses idées, contre ce qu'enseigne l'auteur de la Recherche de la vérité* (Cologne, 1683), 285–88. See also his *Troisième lettre . . . au R. P. Malebranche* (1698), published in Malebranche, *O.C.*, IX, 1027–41. For educated France, the spectacle of debate between these two giants was gripping.

58. Malebranche, *Rép. aux vraies et fausses idées*, *O.C.*, VI, 165.

59. Malebranche, *Rech. de la vér.*, *O.C.*, I, 441–42, 449–50; II, 96–101, 371–72.

60. Respectively, Malebranche, *O.C.*, VI, 166–167; XII, 53–54; and (the *Traité de l'amour de Dieu*) XIV, 11–12.

61. Jean-Claude Sommier, *Histoire dogmatique de la religion; ou, la Religion prouvée par l'autorité divine et humaine, et par les lumières de la raison*, 3 vols. (Paris, 1708–11), I, 23–25.

62. Pierre Poiret, *L'Oeconomie divine . . .*, 7 vols. (Amsterdam, 1687), II, 568–73.

63. Perrin, S.J., *Manuale theologicum*, 5–9.

64. Rodolphe Du Tertre, S.J., *Réfutation d'un nouveau système de métaphysique proposé par le P.M. . . .*, 3 vols. (Paris, 1715), I, 277–319.

65. On Hardouin's activity, see the account by Malebranche's truly persecuted Jesuit supporter, Y. M. André, S.J., in Malebranche, *O.C.*, XIX, 840–42, and XX, 213–14, and see Hardouin's menacing letter to André in ibid., XIX, 823, where he wrote of his several years of trying to convince André and Du Tertre that "Malebranchism . . . was atheism." Hardouin's teaching notes can be found in B.N., MSS. fonds français, 14705–14706. His views were published in his *Athei Detecti*, in Hardouin, S.J., *Opera Varia* (Amsterdam, 1733), 1–243, but already had been made public in print by La Pillonnière, *L'Athéisme découvert par le R. P. Hardouin . . .* (s.l., n.d. [1715]), which was reprinted by Thémiseul de Saint-Hyacinthe, *Mémoires littéraires*, 2 vols. (The Hague, 1716), II, 403–35.

66. Malebranche, *Entretien d'un phil. chrét. et d'un phil. chin.*, *O.C.*, XV, 3–7.

67. Régis, *Réponse . . . Huetii . . . Censura*, 245.

68. Lelevel, *Vraye et fausse métaphysique*, 39–40.

69. Dom Robert Desgabets, O.S.B., *Critique de la Critique de la Recherche de la vérité . . .* (Paris, 1675), 86–88.

70. Régis, *Seconde réplique de M. Régis à la Réponse du R. P. Malebranche . . .* (Paris, 1694), art. 23.

71. *Journal de Trévoux*, juillet 1708, 1134–43 and décembre 1708, 1905–2004.

72. Du Tertre, S.J., op. cit., 23–58 (n. 64 above).

73. B.N. MSS. fonds français, 14075, fol. 239, and 14075–14076, passim.

74. Poiret would travel a road through fideism to extreme mysticism, and La Pillonnière a road through fideism to Protestantism.

75. See the Dortous de Mairan-Malebranche letters in Malebranche, *O.C.*, XIX.

76. Basile de Soissons, O.F.M., Capuchin, "Traité de l'existence de Dieu . . . ," paginated separately [45 pp.] at the end of vol. I of his *Fondement inébranlable de doctrine chrétienne . . .*, 3 vols. (Paris, 1680–83).

77. Nicolas L'Herminier, *Summa Theologiae ad usum scholae accommodata*, 3 vols. (Paris, 1701–1703), I, 24–55. (There was a second edition published in Paris, 1718–19.) L'Herminier taught theology at Paris from 1699 until 1710. Meslier's arguments are often close to L'Herminier's; see, for example, Meslier, op. cit., II, 207–8.

78. N. Anaclet du Havre, O.F.M., Capuchin, *Sujet de conférences sur la théologie positive . . .*, 3 vols. (Rouen, 1712), I, 61–62; the "authorities" are given on I, 48–49.

79. See, for example, Longobardi and Couplet on China; Jean de Léry, Jean Mocquet, and René Laudonnière on the Indians of the southern parts of North America and of South America; Marc Lescarbot, Samuel Champlain, and Paul le

Jeune, S.J., on the Indians of New France; François Cauche on Madagascar; Antoine Biet on the Isle de Cayenne; Claude d'Abbéville, O.F.M., Capuchin, on the Isle de Maragnan; Paul Rycaut on the Ottoman Empire (tr. into French in 1670); and Simon de La Loubère on Siam.

80. Jean-Baptiste Du Tertre, O.P., *Histoire générale des Antilles habitées par les français*, 4 vols. (Paris, 1667–71), II, 499–502.

81. Le Jeune, S.J., *Relation de . . . 1635* (Paris, 1636), 210–13; Lescarbot, *Histoire de la Nouvelle France* (Paris, 1609), 683; La Loubère, *Du Royaume de Siam . . .*, 2 vols. (Amsterdam, 1691), I, 222–23; and Rycaut's *Histoire de l'état présent de l'Empire Ottoman . . .*, M. Briot, tr. (Paris, 1679), 237–39.

82. L. Le Comte, S.J., *Eclaircissement sur la démonstration faite . . . des Nouveaux mémoires de la Chine* (s.l., 1700), 14.

83. See, for example, among the works discussed in France, J. H. Foppius and W. Vogt, *De Atheismo Philosophorum Gentilium Celebriorum* (Bremen, 1714); N. H. Gundling, *Observationum Selectarum . . .* (Leipzig, 1707); Anton Reiser, *De Origine, Progressu et Incremento Antitheismi . . .* (Augsburg, 1669); Theophile Spizelius, *De Atheismi Radice . . .* (Augsburg, 1666); and, from England, J. T. Philipps, *Dissertatio Historico-Philosophica de Atheismo . . .* (London, 1716).

84. J. F. Buddeus, *Theses Theologicae de Atheismo et Superstitione . . .* (Jena, 1717). Buddeus's work was in a third Latin edition by 1737 and was translated into French in 1740.

85. See, for example, Benjamin Binet, *Idée générale de la théologie payenne . . .* (Amsterdam, 1699), 30–85, or R. W. Boclo, *Dissertatio philosophica, de Gentilium Philosophis Atheismi Falso Suspectis . . .* (Bremen, 1716).

86. Alexis Gaudin, Carthusian, *La distinction et la nature du bien et du mal . . .* (Paris, 1704), "Préface" and 1–160. Gaudin's work, published with the approbation of the Oratorian La Marque Tilladet, cited St. Augustine rather than Descartes or Malebranche.

87. Jacques Bernard, *De l'excellence de la religion*, 2 vols. (Amsterdam, 1714), I, 94–100. Bernard was a Huguenot widely read in France.

88. Henri-Marie Boudon, *Oeuvres complètes*, 3 vols. J.-P. Migne, ed. (Paris, 1856), I, 367–424. (This is a critical edition of the works of the celebrated grand archidiacre d'Evreux.)

89. Abbé Armand de Gérard, *Le véritable chrestien qui combat les abus du siècle . . .* (Paris, 1679), 76–117; and *La philosophie des gens de cour* (Paris, 1680), 33–35.

90. Henri Lelevel, *Entretiens sur ce qui forme l'honneste homme et le vray sçavant* (Paris, 1690), 61–98, 221.

91. J.-B. Bossuet, *Oeuvres de Bossuet* [Institut de France edition], 4 vols. (Paris, 1849), I, 414–17; II, 715–24.

92. Abbé de Choisy and abbé Dangeau, *Quatre dialogues* (Paris, 1684), 142–55.

93. Abbé Jean Rousseau, *Traité moral de la divine providence envers ses créatures . . .* (Paris, 1694), 80–348.

94. Pierre de Villemandy, *Traité de l'efficace des causes secondes contre quelques philosophes modernes . . .* (Leiden, 1686), 4–5.

95. Dom André Roze, O.S.B., *Nouveau sistême par pensées sur l'ordre de la nature* (Paris, 1696), "Avertissement" and 1–21.

96. Jean Filleau de la Chaise, *Discours sur les Pensées de Pascal* (Paris, 1672), 45–59. Many think that Philippe DuBois-Goibaud is the actual author of this *Discours.*

97. J.-B. Massillon, *Oeuvres complètes,* 4 vols., ed. abbé E.-A. Blampignon (Bar-le-Duc, 1865), I, 111–19. Massillon was bishop of Clermont.

98. Blaise Pascal, *Pensées de M. Pascal sur la religion* . . . (Paris, 1670) [B.N. Imprimés D.85078]. This is the so-called "Port-Royal edition," with a preface by Etienne Perier. See, in particular, 55–65, 136–45, 150–58.

99. The remarkable sequence of approbations, singular both for the number, length, and substance of these usually brief and formulaic permissions, follows immediately after the "Préface."

100. Ibid., "Préface."

101. Jean Filleau de la Chaise, op. cit., 5–16.

102. N. Desmolets, Oratoire, ed., *Continuation des Mémoires de littérature et d'histoire,* vol. 5, part 2 (Paris, 1728), 271–331.

103. See P.-D. Huet, *Demonstratio Evangelica,* (2d ed. Paris, 1690), "Praefatio" nos. 3 and 4, and his posthumous and notorious *Traité philosophique de la faiblesse de l'esprit humain* (Paris, 1723).

104. Dom Robert Desgabets, O.S.B., op. cit., 85–89.

105. Gaspard Langenhert, *Philosophus Novus,* 4 tomes in 1 vol. (Paris, 1701–1702), I, 13–73.

106. Abbé L. Blondel and abbé J. Louvail, *L'Idée de la religion chrétienne* . . . (Paris, 1728), 1–4.

107. Pierre Rétat, *Le Dictionnaire de Bayle et la lutte philosophique* . . . , 239–42. This is an incidental matter for Rétat, whose central theses are compelling.

108. Jean Fabre, "Jean Meslier, tel qu'en lui-même . . . ," *Dix-Huitième Siècle* 3 (1971), 107–15.

109. Bibliothèque de l'Arsenal, MSS. 2558, no. 1, 1–5. My acceptance of the authenticity of this manuscript would not be unproblematic for some, although there seems no reason whatsoever to doubt either its genuineness or its factual content. Voltaire derived his "life of Meslier" either by *abridging* this source or, more likely, by abridging a common source of his "life" and this document.

110. See Claude Buffier, S.J., *Traité des premières véritez et de la source de nos jugemens, où l'on examine le sentiment des philosophes sur les premières notions des choses* (Paris, 1724); and *Elémens de métaphysique* . . . (Paris, 1725).

111. Abbé Claude-François Houtteville, *La religion chrétienne prouvée par les faits* . . . (Paris, 1722), cliii–clviii.

112. René-Joseph Tournemine, S.J., "Réflexions . . . sur l'athéisme . . . ," in Fénelon, *De l'existence de Dieu* (Paris, 1713). Tournemine was the editor of the *Journal de Trévoux,* in which, instructed by the powerful Le Tellier (confessor to Louis XIV), he apologized to Malebranche for this injury (nov. 1713, 2029–30). Even here, however, he could not restrain himself from adding that "God said, 'I am that I am.' God did not say, 'I am all that is. I am being-in-general.'"

113. R. R. Palmer, *Catholics and Unbelievers in Eighteenth-Century France* (Princeton, 1939; repr. New York, 1961).

Lawrence Stone

8. Honor, Morals, Religion, and the Law: The Action for Criminal Conversation in England, 1670–1857

Introduction

Few historical topics are harder to handle with clarity, sensitivity, and accuracy than shifts in the sensibilities, mental structures, or moral codes that govern human behavior. In the first place one is usually dealing—certainly in the West since the sixteenth century—with moods and systems of value that may appear to be prevalent at certain times but are never universally held and are always in unstable competition with others. Second, each social grouping tends to live in its own mental world, which is sometimes quite similar to those of other social classes, but is never quite the same and is sometimes strikingly different. Third, there is always movement of ideas between different groups, sometimes only one way, from the top down or the bottom up, and sometimes in both directions; thus, elite culture and popular culture are forever either pulling apart or coming together or interacting with each other. Fourth, while the historian interested in this type of change can locate sometimes subtle, sometimes very obvious, shifts in perceptions, sensibilities, and codes, there are always pioneers and laggards, innovators and holdovers, so that the picture is never clear-cut and the date of any shift from one code to another cannot be established with any precision. For example, at some point, European societies moved away from a deep religious faith which was accompanied by total acceptance of the moral propriety and political necessity of persecuting even to death anyone who preferred another faith or none at all. In the end the political nation everywhere gradually adopted an easygoing deism, regarding God as a remote divine watchmaker, and accepted a belief in the moral rightness and practical necessity of religious toleration. But this was a process that in most of Europe took up to two centuries to accomplish, and each society moved at a different speed from the others. Similarly, the shift among the elite from a mental world based on concepts of patriarchy, hierarchy, honor, and shame to one based on the commercial values of the marketplace and individualistic ideas about freedom of choice also occurred very slowly over one or two centuries, even in the single society of England. Some changes in these areas were expressed in legal form and were quite dramatic in their apparent significance, but the timing of their general acceptance and use is another matter.

Some of the changes involved a prolonged tug of war over several centuries between old values and new ones, for example between honor and money, or between the duty of obedience to parents and the right of individual choice over the selection of a spouse. Nor were the trends by any means always linear, but often ebbed and flowed erratically. Moreover, since at all periods passionate beliefs are usually held only by small, well-organized minorities, the majority swing helplessly to and fro in the middle, unable to do much to affect the trajectory of history. As historians, we are therefore perforce dealing with minority mindsets, which over time become the mindsets of the majority.

As a result, it is extremely difficult to demonstrate that a significant change in moral codes did actually take place, while admitting at the same time that the change was slow, hesitant, and irregular; that its social, geographical, and even psychological spread was limited; and that the dominant code was always under challenge from others. It is only with the benefit of hindsight that the full meaning and significance of some of these shifts can be perceived and demonstrated through changes in the use or meaning of words and signs.

Finally, the historian of moral codes and mental worlds faces the intractable problem of the interpretation of texts, all of which have their drawbacks. The most reliable are clearly memoirs, correspondence, autobiographies, and the depositions of witnesses and pleadings of legal counsel in court cases. The former reveal moral positions, and from the rhetoric of the latter, of political speeches and pamphlets, of works of political economy, and of the sermons of prominent theologians, it is possible to deduce the predominant cultural values. Observed behavior, such as adultery, is a concrete fact, if it can be documented, but the motivation behind it is always open to interpretation. Works of imaginative literature, such as widely read novels, plays, or poetry, offer useful guides to public opinion, since the mere fact of their success suggests that they may be molding and reinforcing, as well as mirroring, certain values.

Most dubious of all is prescriptive advice literature about ideal morality and behav'or, such as religious sermons or polemical pamphlets. First, it is hard to tell whether they were widely read and admired, or largely ignored; indeed, in some cases the modern historian often has an uneasy feeling that he may well be the first reader seriously to examine the text. Second, there is always a very wide gap between theory and practice, between uplifting moral sentiments and crass day-to-day behavior. Sexual and marital behavior is affected not only by intimate feelings and violent passions, but also by ideas about community cohesion and individualism, and the desirable distribution of property; by attitudes toward love, courtship, marriage, sexuality, and divorce—to say nothing of the fact that it provides most of the raw material for that all-important bonding ritual of gossip.

The prime purpose of this particular study is to examine and explain changes over time in the delicate and uneasy balance between a wide range of conflicting values and moral codes concerning issues that touch some of the most sensitive nerves in any society: how best to protect the patrilinear descent of the titles and property of great families; how to defend the hierarchy of society and the control of husbands and fathers over female sexuality; how to regulate the commerce between the sexes; and how to define and deal with sexual irregularities. Few subjects arouse more passionate debate and affect more profound aspects of individual psychology and public policy.

The second object is to study the transmission of culture and the reciprocal effects upon the transmission of changing means and modes of communication, and the technical details of the law. The argument concerning the latter suggests a reciprocal relationship between the enacted law and social, economic, and cultural forces. The enacted law creates a framework that remains ostensibly unchanged, thanks to legal conservatism, the mediating institutions of the judicial administrative machinery itself, and the personal beliefs of influential judges.[1] Underneath the facade of conservative rhetoric and unchanging procedures, however, the latent function of an existing law may be totally transformed in order to meet changing circumstances. These circumstances are themselves created in part by massive alterations in the quantity and content of published accounts of legal trials, and in part by changing concepts of honor and morality.

The Nature of the Action

It should be explained that England was the only Protestant country which at the Reformation did not adopt a system of divorce for female adultery, male cruelty, and possibly desertion. Plans for divorce for adultery or cruelty were drawn up under Cranmer's leadership in the reign of Edward VI, abandoned under Mary, and never revived under Elizabeth since they were embedded in a radical revision of the canon law which was anathema to the moderate Protestants then in power, and also to Elizabeth herself. There was a formal affirmation in 1597–1604 by church and state of the principle of the indissolubility of marriage. Thereafter the only option open in England was the traditional Catholic one of formal separation from bed and board without permission to remarry, granted by an ecclesiastical court on grounds of adultery or cruelty. The one exception to this rule of the indissolubility of marriage was the complex and expensive procedure of a private act of Parliament for divorce with permission to remarry. This slowly evolved in the late seventeenth century in order to allow childless men of rank and property to prevent their titles and estates from passing to illegitimate children fathered by the lovers of their adulterous wives. The third legal procedure, which developed at the same time as the Parliamentary divorce, was an action by a husband against his wife's lover for financial damages.

The other legal feature which made England very different from the rest of Europe was that between 1670 and 1730 both ecclesiastical and lay local legal authorities abandoned the effort to punish adultery as a sin and a misdemeanor. The reasons for this double abandonment are complex and obscure, mostly connected with the failure of the great moral crusade of Puritanism in 1660 and the granting of religious toleration in 1689. In the late seventeenth century, the two superior courts of common law, the King's Bench and Common Pleas, moved in to fill the gap created by this abdication by extending the range of the action of trespass, which had previously been used as a remedy for mayhem, battery, or wounding. It was now made to cover an action by a husband against the seducer of his wife, the seduction being described as a "criminal conversation," despite the fact that it was neither criminal nor a conversation, in the normal sense of the word. The jury either acquitted the defendant, which rarely happened, or awarded the plaintiff damages and costs, which often amounted to very large sums indeed. This crucial decision-making process by the jury took astonishingly little time. A verdict which might not only ruin a woman's reputation but also destroy a man's career, reduce him to a pauper, or cast him indefinitely into exile or a debtors' prison, was normally made in a matter of minutes. The defendant had four options. He could pay the damages in full; he could come to terms with the plaintiff (if he had not already secretly done so); he could go to prison and live off the income of his real estate; or he could sell all his goods or convey them in trust to others, and flee the country before, during, or immediately after the trial. He could then live in exile off the proceeds of the sale of his goods and the income of his real estate, which could not be touched.

The Principles of the Action

There were several principles that underlay the action. The first was that the common law should and could provide facilities for litigants to obtain monetary damages for any tort, even when it did not involve physical violence or financial loss. The common law judges were prepared to extend the range of actions for trespass and actions on the case in order to include psychological injuries due to a wife's adultery, just as they had done at the same period for injuries due to a daughter's seduction and a suitor's breach of promise. They made these expansions possible by the use of legal fictions, such as the loss to the father of the economic services of a seduced daughter; the loss to a woman of financial prospects by a breach of promise of marriage; and the use of force and arms in the seduction of a wife, who, since she had no legal personality, could not possibly give her consent to an act of adultery. By so doing, they offered a legal alternative to the largely abandoned jurisdiction of the ecclesiastical courts over the definition of sexual morality and the punishment of transgressions. They established a legal action which was to last for almost 200 years.

But it was one thing to set up a legal procedure, and another to get the public to use it. The critical change which made it morally possible for a member of the landed elite to bring a crim. con. action was a shift in attitudes toward male honor, which began in the late seventeenth century. Previously, the injured husband had been accustomed to resorting to murder, open violence, or a challenge to a duel in order to obtain satisfaction. For in such societies honor in a man is defined by sexual potency and shame by cuckoldry; honor in a woman is defined by sexual purity and shame by adultery.[2]

In the late seventeenth and early eighteenth centuries, there began a slow process of redefinition of loss of male honor thanks to which the fact of being branded as a cuckold was transformed into an injury which could be compensated for by monetary damages publicly awarded in a court of law. It is difficult to imagine clearer evidence of the beginning of a shift from an honor and shame society to a more commercial society than this change in the socially acceptable remedy for cuckoldry from physical assault or a duel to a widely publicized crim. con. suit. Litigation for monetary damages is a commercial activity, taking place in a legal market.

The first to raise the moral issue of dueling or litigating over female adultery in England were the late seventeenth-century playwrights, who suggested satirically that the crim. con. action was developed in part in order to protect peaceable or timid cuckolds from being killed in duels by truculent seducers of their wives. In 1698, when pointedly reminded by his wife's lover that the latter wore a sword, Vanbrugh's Sir John Brute protested feebly: "Wear a sword, Sir?—And what of that, Sir?—He comes to my house; eats my meat; lies with my wife; dishonours my family; gets a bastard to inherit my estate. And when I ask a civil account of all this, 'Sir,' says he, 'I wear a sword.'"[3]

The evidence suggests that after about 1670, a culture of litigation slowly began to evolve as a competitor with a still flourishing culture of machismo. This evolution was in part a product of the growth of the nation state in the sixteenth and seventeenth centuries, during which time it slowly weaned the aristocracy and squires from their earlier lawless and violent ways, and persuaded them to transfer their disputes to "wars in Westminster Hall."[4] But if unregulated personal violence was largely suppressed, the code of the duel lived on and even experienced a temporary revival among some members of the army officer class who came to maturity during the endless wars with France of the late eighteenth and early nineteenth centuries, although even here his fellow officers now often regarded a challenger as "a damned fool."

For example, in 1814 Sir Henry Mildmay fell passionately in love with Countess Rosebery, and her husband became sufficiently alarmed both to forbid him access to the house and ostentatiously to cut him in the street. Sir Henry then devised a plan for a reconciliation with the suspicious husband. His idea was to provoke Lord Rosebery to "call him out" to a duel. He would first let the latter fire at him—apparently assuming that he would not shoot to kill, or would miss—and then he himself would deliberately fire into the air. By doing so, he calculated that he would oblige Lord Rosebery "by the etiquette among men of honour, to bow to him and notice him in the street," which would perhaps lead to a reconciliation and a renewal of access to the house. Nothing came of the scheme, so Sir Henry smuggled himself into Lady Rosebery's bedroom and was caught there in flagrante delicto. He was prosecuted for crim. con. and suffered the huge damages of £15,000. Unable to pay such a sum, he was forced to flee the country with Lady Rosebery to avoid either financial ruin or arrest for debt. Clearly what wounded Sir Henry most was being cut in the street, and both his action in planning a duel and that of Lord Rosebery in suing for damages show how the two moral codes ran side by side in the early years of the nineteenth century. In this case, the code of the duel was only a pipe dream and the reality was the crim. con. damages.[5]

A major reason for the persistence and growth of the crim. con. action in the eighteenth century was the elevation of the concept of property to a central position in political ideology and legal practice and, taken in its broader sense, its expansion to cover almost everything from the right to vote to the holding of an office. It was only a small extension to include a wife's body in this capacious definition of property. As a result, although marriage was widely regarded as a holy state based on mutual love, there was nevertheless nothing odd or shocking to eighteenth-century sensibility in the assertion in 1789 that "A man's wife may be deemed no less his property than his money," or in the statement by a judge in 1756 that the seduction of somebody else's wife was "the highest invasion of property."[6]

On the other hand, a wife did not acquire a similar right over the body of her husband, despite the mutual exchange of vows at the wedding ceremony. The conventional defense of this inequity was given by a lawyer for a plaintiff in a case in 1803: "Casual revelry and immorality in the husband . . . cannot be productive of defrauding the children or his wife by introducing a spurious offspring, which the infidelity of the wife may lead to."[7] As the Roman jurist Gaius observed in the second century AD: "Maternity is a fact. Paternity is merely an opinion."

It should be noted that neither the undoubted contemporary anxiety about the seduction of young virgins from poor but respectable families which was so marked a feature of the literature of the last half of the eighteenth century, nor modern notions of a male chauvinist trade of a wife's chastity for money, are appropriate ways of viewing the ethical principles which underlay the crim. con. action. What seems to be clear is that the very tentative adoption by some of the aristocracy of the crim. con. action in the 1690s was evidence of a drive to reinforce male contractual control over female chastity, another being the contemporary reluctant acceptance of Parliamentary divorce for female adultery. A Parliamentary Divorce Act in the late seventeenth and early eighteenth centuries always included formal bastardization of illegitimate children and permission to the man to remarry in order to beget legitimate heirs to title and property. All this took place at a time when there raged intense political debates over the nature and application of theories of contract, which were used by Mary Astell and Lady Chudleigh to support ideas about female equality of rights. The former asked in 1706: "If absolute sovereignty be not necessary in a state, how comes it to be so in a family? Or if in a family, why not in a state?"[8] Whig theories of contract and the sanctity of property, thus, on the one hand provided support for a reinforcement of male patriarchy, while on the other they laid the intellectual foundations upon which criticism of this patriarchy could build.

Because of the high legal costs, the plaintiffs in crim. con. actions were all men of means. Before 1750 they were almost entirely from the leisured classes, but thereafter included clergy, the military, businessmen, and even shopkeepers (Fig. 8.1).[9] The defendants, on the other hand, were drawn from all social levels, from stable boys to royal dukes, but the great majority came from the same classes as the plaintiffs, if only because seducers were so often social acquaintances, friends, or business or professional associates.

The first action involving a nobleman was the crim. con. suit brought by the Duke of Norfolk in 1692. He was the premier duke in England, and his action created a sensation, especially when the jury awarded him only derisory damages because of his own notorious adulteries. His motive was that he was desperate to get a Parliamentary divorce in order to remarry and beget children to inherit his great estates and ancient titles. It is significant of the slowness with which the culture of litigation replaced the culture of the duel that the duke's lawsuit failed to stimulate a rapid growth of the action. In fact, it was little used during the next half century, only about fourteen cases being known between 1690 and 1732. One reason was that most cuckolded husbands from the middling sort found it more profitable to pursue the traditional strategy of exercising threats of litigation and exposure as blackmail to obtain private cash payments from a wife's lover rather than to embark on the tedious, costly, and public process of suing for damages. For example, in 1701 a tailor found a man called Mounteney in bed with his wife. He threatened to sue Mounteney at common law and brought in his attorney to negotiate with him. He started with a demand for £10, but was prepared to come down to £5 "for the injury he received." The money had been paid and the two men had become "very intimate" by the time the ecclesiastical officials heard about it and sued Mounteney for adultery. The latter told a friend: "I have fucked a woman in Duffield and they are going to put me into the court for it," despite the

Figure 8.1. "The Danger of Crim. Con.," 1797. Courtesy of Library of Congress.

fact that both he and his new friend the tailor were now denying that any impropriety had taken place or that any compensation had been exacted.[10]

The reason for the slowness of the development of the action among the elite was that many of them were still ashamed of washing their dirty linen in public and of exposing themselves to the world as cuckolds. The evolution of the action therefore came to depend heavily on it becoming a commonplace event, due to the publicity devoted to it.

Publicity and the Action

In the last half of the eighteenth century, these trials began to attract more and more attention, thanks to widespread publicity in print. This process of commercialized publication was facilitated by three developments. The first was a striking improvement in the technique of stenography which was developed in the 1750s.[11] The second was the enormous expansion of the numbers of newspapers and new books and pamphlets published, which occurred from 1740 onward. The third was the shift of opinion in English elite and official quarters from regarding sex as a sin to regarding it as an interesting and amusing aspect of life. The collapse of the moral controls of the church courts after the Act of Toleration in 1689, the decline of Puritanism, the expiry of the licensing laws in 1695, and the general secularization of thought in the eighteenth century all facilitated not only the publication of a few items of pure pornography, such as *Fanny Hill,* but also large numbers of full transcripts of detailed evidence produced in trials for adultery. The very language of extramarital sexual relations was softened, a love affair becoming an "intrigue" and an act of adultery an act of "gallantry."

The reporting of trials for separation in the ecclesiastical courts on grounds of adultery, crim. con. actions in the common law courts, and divorce cases before Parliament were only part of a much wider explosion of reporting of legal cases in the eighteenth century. Accounts of individual cases and collections of the more sensational items began in about 1690, and grew from a trickle to a flood in the 1770s. These stenographic records of trials focused mainly upon their human interest and their prurient detail, supplied by the witnesses testifying to looking through keyholes, or holes they had bored in the wainscot, listening to creaking beds, and inspecting bed linen. A pamphlet reporting on the first prominent crim. con. case, that of the Duke of Norfolk and John Germain in 1692, set an example for future publications in the detailed description by a chambermaid of an act of coitus interruptus practiced by Germain and the duchess.[12] This material clearly circulated widely, both among the general reading public eager for sexual titillation and especially among the elite, like Horace Walpole, who were also avid for gossip about the sex lives of their friends and acquaintances. There can be no doubt that their scandalous content was the principal cause for their success.

But there was more to these reports of cases than mere sexual titillation. There was intense interest in the human drama of the narrative, the discrepancies in the evidence, the moral and factual differences between the two stories told by husband and alleged seducer, the rhetorical feats of the rival counsels, and at the climax the always unpredictable assessment of the damages by the jury. Crim. con. reportage thus served all the purposes of a modern television sitcom. It was a morality play, ostensibly designed to expose and castigate the vices of the rich, but one deliberately couched in immoral terms. As a result, in about 1820, at the height of the Queen Caroline affair, Leigh Hunt said that he "might look upon the British public as contantly occupied in reading trials for adultery."[13] *The News of the World* of the 1980s thus has a very long history behind it.

This tide of publicity had two completely opposite results. One was to disseminate among the public at large knowledge about separation suits and crim. con. actions and Parliamentary bills of divorce. By making such actions better known, it therefore made them more acceptable, and thus directly stimulated the surge of litigation after 1750. It is no accident that two of the most distinguished lawyers of eighteenth-century England, Lords Mansfield[14] and Erskine,[15] made their fortunes and careers out of the huge publicity which surrounded the more sensational crim. con. cases. Moreover, some families took advantage of the press to plant their own version of the affair in periodicals and newspapers, or even to commission privately printed pamphlets, sometimes running to hundreds of pages.

The second result of the publicity was exactly the reverse, to frighten off some potential litigants. Family honor was still a crucial factor in influencing elite behavior, and a crim. con. suit could threaten the reputation of all parties. The husband was exposed to the world as a cuckold; the wife was branded as a whore, without a chance to defend herself; and the lover was often revealed as a false friend. Because of this sense of personal and family shame, many persons of property and standing shrank from allowing the intimate details of their private lives to become "the talk of the town." The withering blast of publicity engendered by these suits was a major inducement to many unhappy couples to take the path of private separation rather than that of public litigation.[16] On the whole, however, the statistics indicate that the publicity did more to stimulate use of the action than it did to frighten off potential litigants.

The Apogee of the Action, 1770–1830

The widespread literary perception that female adultery in respectable circles was on the increase in the late eighteenth century is matched by the dramatic explosion of recorded crim. con. cases, which began in the 1770s and peaked in the thirty years from 1790 to 1829 (Table 8.1 and Fig. 8.2). There are two possible explanations for this rise in the number of crim. con. cases. The one is that it reflects a real increase in wifely adultery in respectable circles. The other is that it reflects no more than changes in habits of litigation and bears no relation to any alteration in sexual behavior. Lamentations at the exceptional sexual turpitude of the age are a common theme in almost all times and places, but at this period they seem to

TABLE 8.1.   Recorded Criminal Conversation
Actions 1680–1849

Decade	Numbers
1680–89	2
1690–99	2
1700–1709	3
1710–19	3
1720–29	5
1730–39	7
1740–49	7
1750–59	17
1760–69	18
1770–79	36
1780–89	37
1790–99	73
1800–1809	52
1810–19	49
1820–29	47
1830–39	44
1840–49	c. 35

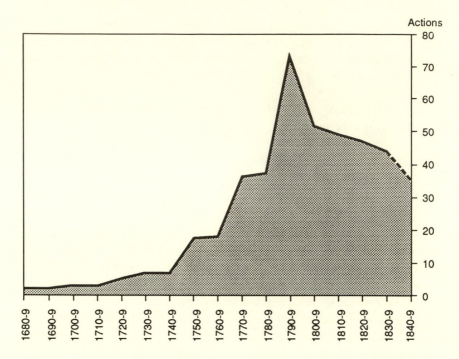

Figure 8.2. Recorded criminal conversation actions, 1680–1849.

have been peculiarly common. There was a widespread conviction in the 1790s, first that sexual immorality was on the increase and second that this depravity was particularly prevalent among the elite of high title and great wealth, the explanation being that standard eighteenth-century source of anxiety, the growth of idleness and luxury. It took a foreign observer to bring a different perspective to the question. L. Simond observed in 1811 that "Upon the whole there is more conjugal fidelity in England than in most other countries, and these crim. con. prosecutions calumniate the higher ranks of society."[17] Who was right in this dispute?

There is no doubt that in the late eighteenth century a large proportion—perhaps a half—of the recorded litigants in these actions were still drawn from the ranks of the landed elite, esquires and above. It is also true that the defendants in these suits were very frequently military or (far more rarely) naval officers. But the idea of an indolent and degenerate landed elite indulging in widespread adultery and wife-swapping is largely fantasy. Only 4 percent of the men holding titles of peer or baronet at the peak of the crim. con. boom between 1770 and 1830 were involved on one side or the other in these actions or in Parliamentary divorces. This is not a negligible figure and is undoubtedly far higher than the proportion in other classes of the society. But it bears little relation to the hysterical claims that a tide of sexual immorality was engulfing the aristocratic classes. Of course, this tells us nothing about the sexual habits of the husbands, which were almost certainly much more promiscuous than those of their wives, but perhaps no different from what they had been a century or two centuries before.

If one looks first at possible causes for a real rise in the amount of wifely adultery, there can be no doubt that the changes in equity law to protect the property of wealthy married women now offered some cushion—at least for the rich—against the financial penalties for marital infidelity. This may have made it easier for wives among the elite to commit adultery, secure in the knowledge that their property was safe. But the property of the 90 percent of wives without a marriage settlement remained wholly at the mercy of the husbands, so that for them the financial consequences of adultery remained as catastrophic as ever. What can hardly be doubted, however, is the influence of the rise of affective individualism, and the ideal of the companionate marriage. This had existed since the sixteenth century, with the concept of "holy matrimony," but became increasingly dominant in the system of values in elite and upper-middle-class circles in the middle and late eighteenth century.[18] This new sensibility is clearly revealed in court, where after 1770 counsel for husbands petitioning Parliament for divorce now laid most emphasis upon the loss of "the comforts of matrimony" rather than the threat to property by bastardy or the loss of control over a wife's body.[19] On the other hand, if more women were expecting more out of marriage than ever before, and if they did not find the love, sexual satisfaction, friendship, and companionship they had anticipated, it is possible that they were more apt to look elsewhere for it. In most cases it was the indifference or infidelity or cruelty of the husband which began the dissolution of the marriage, and the adultery of the wife was only a last reactive stage of the process.[20]

Both of these explanations for the rise in crim. con. actions involving the possibility of a real increase in wifely adultery seem plausible, but neither is entirely convincing. It is therefore necessary to turn to possible reasons for greater resort to the crim. con. action after 1770, even if the level of adultery remained constant. It seems clear that the most important reason was that it was a product of a concurrent rise in Parliamentary di-

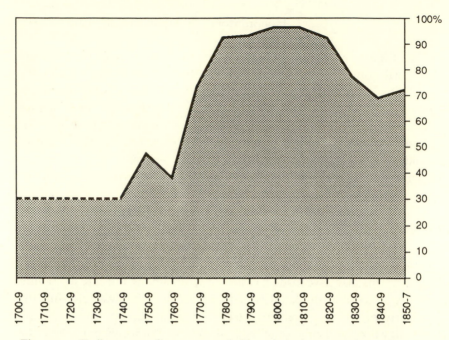

Figure 8.3. Parliamentary divorces preceded by criminal conversation actions, 1700–1857.

TABLE 8.2. Parliamentary Divorces Preceded by Crim. Con. Actions 1750–1857[1]

	Parliamentary Divorces	Crim. Con. Actions	Percent
1700–49	14	4	30
1750–59	15	7	47
1760–69	13	5	38
1770–79	34	25	73
1780–89	12	11	92
1790–99	43	39	93
1800–09	23	22	96
1810–19	27	26	96
1820–29	25	23	92
1830–39	35	27	77
1840–49	55	38	76
1850–59	29	21	72
Total	325	248	76

1. S. Wolfson, "Divorce in England 1700–1857," *Oxford Journal of Legal Studies* V, 1985, Table 4 and Appendix 1A. There are rather different figures, but the identical trends, given for petitioners for Parliamentary divorces in S. Anderson, "Legislative Divorce," in *Law, Economy and Society 1750–1914,* ed. G. R. Rubin and D. Sugarman (Abingdon, 1984), Table III, p. 439.

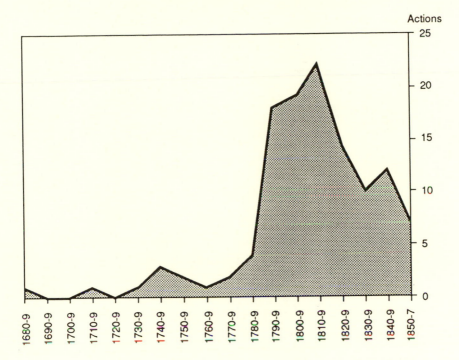

Actions

25

20

15

10

5

0

1680-9 1690-9 1700-9 1710-9 1720-9 1730-9 1740-9 1750-9 1760-9 1770-9 1780-9 1790-9 1800-9 1810-9 1820-9 1830-9 1840-9 1850-7

Figure 8.4. Damages over £2,000 in criminal conversation actions, 1680–1857.

vorces. Success of a bill for a Parliamentary divorce increasingly depended on the previous award of substantial damages by a jury in a crim. con. case at common law (Table 8.2 and Fig. 8.3). As a result, an increasingly common motive of the plaintiff in bringing a crim. con. suit was not to recover damages but to use the suit purely in order to facilitate a Parliamentary divorce.

Another probable cause for the rise in the number of crim. con. cases was the dramatic increase in the size of damages awarded by juries in the decades between 1780 and 1830, when the number of awards over £2,000 rose precipitously (Fig. 8.4 and Table 8.3). Rather than settle on a private separation, many aggrieved husbands must have been tempted to go to court in the hope of winning one of the rich prizes in the lottery of jury awards. Since the wife was formally barred from any role in the action, unable to testify, to be represented by counsel, or to bring witnesses, the chances of success for the plaintiff were good.

TABLE 8.3.   Damages Over £2,000 in Crim. Con. Actions

Decade	£2,000–2,999	£3,000–4,999	£5,000–9,999	£10,000+	Total
1680–89			1		1
1690–99					–
1700–1709					–
1710–19			1		1
1720–29					–
1730–39				1	1
1740–49	1		1	1	3
1750–59	2				2
1760–69	1				1
1770–79				2	2
1780–89	2	1	1		4
1790–99	4	6	5	4	19
1800–1809	3	4	4	7	18
1810–19	7	5	4	6	22
1820–29	4	3	7		14
1830–39	5	4		1	10
1840–49	5	3	3	1	12
1850–59	4	3			7
Total	38	29	27	23	117

The Assessment of Damages

In awarding damages for crim. con., juries were instructed to take a number of factors into consideration, the relative weight attached to each of which changed significantly over time. As we have seen, the action began in the late seventeenth century in order to provide monetary recompense for that intangible, loss of honor, and was reinforced by the idea that the wife and her body were the property of her husband. The principal fear was pollution of blood in a patrilineal primogenitural society. Before about 1760, the most important consideration was whether or not the wife already had or was about to give birth to an illegitimate child who, under the conditions of the settlement of the family estates, might inherit property, name, and title. If the husband had no legal offspring of his own, he was naturally very anxious for a divorce act in order to disinherit any bastard children of his wife; and in order to achieve that he needed a favorable verdict and sizable damages in his crim. con. suit.

After about 1750, however, the core of the action shifted to "the loss of comfort and society of his wife," that is deprivation of her sexual, maternal, managerial, and social services.[21] The value of all this clearly turned on the terms upon which the couple had lived before the act of adultery. In consequence, after 1750 the assessment of the size of the damages became crucially dependent upon evidence of the degree of happiness of the marriage before that event—something the court was singularly ill-equipped to investigate, since the wife was allowed neither to appear in court nor bring witnesses in her defense.

This aspect of the action became more and more important after about 1770 as sensibilities changed, largely under the influence of the novel, so as to increase the emphasis upon marital happiness. The argument now ran that the greater the happiness before the adultery, the larger should be the monetary compensation for its loss. Counsel therefore now also talked more freely about sexual pleasure, or the absence of it, Erskine in 1794 exclaiming enthusiastically in court that "nothing, certainly, is more delightful to the human fancy than the possession of a beautiful woman in the prime of health and youthful passion."[22] There is, of course, nothing new in this idea, but its expression in court seems new. Because of this increased emphasis on marital happiness, attention was drawn to the question of whether the marriage had been arranged by parents or friends, or whether it had been a love match based on mutual choice. Rarely mentioned in the first half of the century, by the 1790s great attention was being given, by both the prosecution and the defense counsel, to this question of arranged marriage or marriage by free choice. Other circumstances which increased the damages were the personal qualities of the adulterous wife. For example, in 1796 her husband's counsel pointed out that Lady Westmeath was "of most respectable family and connexions, polished education, high accomplishments and great beauty of person."[23]

Lurking behind every suit for crim. con. lay the question of the moral responsibility of the plaintiff in driving his wife into the arms of another man. In 1800 Sir William Scott, later Lord Stowell, stated publicly that he thought that in ninety-nine cases out of a hundred the blame for a wife's adultery lay first with the husband for his neglect, cruelty, or adultery; then with the wife for her lack of moral courage to resist temptation; and last of all with her lover, the defendant in a crim. con. case.[24] This was an opinion supported by other experienced lawyers and judges at this time, for example, Lord Erskine, who had been counsel, almost invariably for the plaintiff husband, in every major crim. con. case for over twenty years.[25]

In consequence, after about 1770 evidence of earlier quarrels, alienation, or indifference reduced the claim for damages.[26] Rejected by a jury in

1769, the first successful use of a prior separation of beds to block the award of large damages to a plaintiff occurred in 1788. The defendant's counsel, the ubiquitous Thomas Erskine, called on his usual rhetoric to sway the jury:

> he would not sleep in the same bed with her, as if she had been seized with some loathsome disorder. She was obliged to lie in a solitary bed without the consolation, without the friendship, and without the society of her husband, who was snoring, by himself, in the opposite side of the house.

So moving was this appeal for pity for a neglected wife in the new age of affective individualism that the jury awarded the derisory damages of 1s.[27]

Still more damaging to the claims of a plaintiff was a prior full separation, as a result of which the couple had already parted company before the adultery. By 1790, as reparation for "loss of comfort and society" took priority over loss of honor and damage to property, the question was asked whether a prior private separation deed actually barred a later suit for crim. con. Over this issue, as over others, the position adopted by the common law courts shifted erratically according to the personal views of the chief justices, and before 1820 did not follow any clear trend which can be linked to external forces or shifts in concepts of honor or shame, or the value placed on marital comfort.[28]

In both the ecclesiastical courts and in Parliament, evidence of adultery by the husband automatically disqualified him from any right to sue for either separation or divorce. This legal principle of "recrimination"—of rebutting a charge against a wife by a similar charge against a husband—had long been standard by canon law.[29] At common law, however, during the late seventeenth and eighteenth centuries adultery by the husband was treated as a mitigating circumstance in the assessment of damages, but not as an absolute bar to the action. Although the common law courts later hardened their attitude toward adultery by the plaintiff husband, they still had not fallen into line with the church courts or Parliament in considering it as an absolute bar when the action was finally abolished by Parliament in 1857.[30]

The prior relationship of the two men in the case, the husband and the wife's lover, could seriously influence the size of the damages awarded. If the lover was a bare acquaintance of the husband, then no breach of friendship and hospitality had taken place. If, on the other hand, he had been an old family friend on regular dining terms and free to stay the night whenever he chose, then the breach of faith was regarded as very serious.[31]

A famous crim. con. action which turned upon the issue of betrayal of personal male friendship was one initiated by Lord Abergavenny in 1730 against Mr. Lyddell. On catching Lyddell in bed with Lady Abergavenny, the house steward reproached him for his treachery: "For you, Sir, to come so frequently in such a show of friendship, and to wrong his lordship after such a manner as you have done, is a crime for which you can make no satisfaction." Overcome with remorse, Lyddell replied: "I am a vile wretch. For God's sake do not speak to me." Lady Abergavenny went into shock, cried, "I shall be ruined"—and died twenty-six days later. It is hardly surprising that the report of this case was constantly reprinted for over a century, since it was such a gripping moral epic of sin, guilt, repentance, and punishment. The early death of the lady seemed like divine retribution, and Mr. Lyddell's immediate sense of shame and humiliation came long before his later financial ruin, brought about by the award of damages to the staggering amount of £10,000.[32]

Where and how the seduction took place was also not without its importance. It is significant that by far the largest number of recorded acts of adultery, of which there are several hundred, took place in the drawing room or the dining room. Other acts occurred while riding in a coach, or in a secluded spot in the countryside, or at a bagnio, or a hotel.[33] It was quite rare that the wife and her lover were willing to break the taboo of violating the marriage bed itself, which was regarded as a serious sexual insult to the husband. Whenever this happened, much was made of it at the trial.[34]

The strongest correlation of all is between the status and wealth of the plaintiff and the amount of the damages awarded to him. The first reason for this is the extreme importance of the concept of honor in stimulating and maintaining the crim. con. action, which has already been discussed. The well-born were not only thought to have more honor—and more property—to lose than the vulgar, but also to have more sensitive feelings and therefore on both counts to need greater compensation. In 1804 Baron Smith instructed the jury to pay attention to the rank of the plaintiff, due to the greater "delicacy of sentiment and punctilio of honour engendered by the refined habits which belong to opulence and distinction."[35]

Another important consideration was whether the seduction was the result of a deliberate and premeditated campaign or merely a sudden, overwhelming gust of passion. Thus it told against Captain Sykes, when sued by a fellow officer for crim. con. with his wife, that he had remarked to a friend some months before, "I should like to debauch that woman."[36]

The extent to which the rank and wealth of the defendant was to be taken into consideration was more controversial. At the top of the scale there was general agreement that rich noblemen should be made to pay heavily for their acts of gallantry, especially with married women of genteel birth. The one glaring exception to this rough correlation between size of the damages and the rank of the defendant were occasions when the latter was of utterly contemptible status, a poor servant who had become the lover of a rich and well-born woman. In cases such as these, judges and juries combined to levy savage damages ranging from £200 to £5,000, in order to compensate not only for the breach of trust between servant and master, but more especially for the threat to social hierarchy involved in so grossly unequal a pairing. Since the servants in question were all earning less than £30 a year, the damages were clearly intended to put them in gaol for life. The intense indignation demonstrated by litigants, judges, jury, and the public in general at the breach of trust between master and servant, and at the breach of the rules of social rank endogamy, outweighed the self-evident fact that in the initial stages of these affairs, the servants must have been merely the youthful victims of sexually frustrated or predatory middle-aged women. These servants were so far below their superiors in rank, power, and wealth that they could not possibly have dared to make the first move, except perhaps very tentatively by the use of body language.[37]

One of the most vexed questions concerning the award of damages in crim. con. actions was whether or not the jury should take into consideration the defendant's poverty. On the one hand, one could argue that being poor should not create immunity from punishment for the seduction of a married woman nor diminish the just compensation due to the husband. On the other hand, there was the fact that, according to the English law of debt, inability to pay would lead to arrest, which might in some cases result in imprisonment for life in a debtors' gaol. Should a jury in a civil suit de facto condemn a man to life imprisonment? During the eighteenth century, judges and juries remained uncertain how to settle this question, but after about 1820 judges began to direct juries to adjust the damages to the defendants' capacity to pay. For example, in 1823 a judge told the jury that "I would . . . guard against awarding such (damages) as would incarcerate the defendant in gaol for life."[38]

The Moral Panic of the 1790s

In 1788 Lloyd Kenyon was appointed Lord Chief Justice, and promptly inaugurated a reign of terror against adulterers in the Court of King's Bench.

Lord Kenyon came to crim. con. actions with four powerful convictions. The first was that sexual irregularity was a vice of such enormity as to threaten the very fabric of society. The second was that moral turpitude was spreading, but that it could be curbed by the award of punitive damages on an unprecedented scale. The third was that the income of the defendant was totally irrelevant to the size of the damages. His standard advice to the jury was that "he who cannot pay with his purse must pay with his person"—that is, by imprisonment for debt due to the plaintiff for damages. The fourth and last was that in crim. con. actions, judges and juries had a responsibility not merely to recompense the plaintiff in a private suit, but to set an example to the nation by the infliction of exemplary punishment upon the defendant. From 1788 to his death in 1802, Lord Kenyon, aided and abetted by the forensic lawyer Thomas Erskine, contrived to turn the crim. con. action into moral theater, using the rhetoric of doom and damnation to convince juries to set an example by awarding crippling damages (Table 8.3 and Fig. 8.4).

Popular fears about the social consequences of the alleged growing sexual depravity among the elite were reinforced to no small extent by contemporary events and alleged historical precedents. References were continually being made to the contribution of the growth of elite adultery to the Fall of Rome and the French Revolution. Commentators also drew attention to the association in revolutionary France in the 1790s of political terror and the sexual freedom provided by the new laws permitting divorce virtually on demand.[39] In a case in 1800 which involved a defender who had lived in France, his counsel went out of his way to stress that his client "does not stand here as an advocate of French vices, which have been employed in corrupting the morals of this nation." This "pollution behavior" is the normal response of any society under stress, the manifestations of which are strenuous attempts to create order in a disorderly world by the imposition of rigid codes of behavior.[40] As a result of this paranoia, it was possible for Lord Kenyon for thirteen years to turn a private civil suit for personal damages into a public criminal suit to punish vice and set an example to society.

The Results of the Moral Panic

The first result of the dramatic rise in the size of crim. con. damages was exactly what was intended by judge and jury. It added the seduction of a married woman to the list of ways by which a man could lose a fortune. But the rise in the size of damages in the middle and late eighteenth century had other consequences which were wholly unexpected and morally disturbing. One was that the potential damages were so enormous that some husbands and wives were tempted to conspire together to entrap a wealthy man, catch him in the act of seduction, sue him for crim. con., and then quietly share the damages between them. The novelists had long anticipated such a development. In 1751 Fielding in *Amelia* has Mr. Trent rent his wife to a lord in return for a promise of promotion to office, which is not fulfilled. He then, with two witnesses, catches them in bed, and exerts blackmail by threatening a crim. con. action. When challenged to a duel by the lord, he refuses to fight, explaining frankly: "My Lord, it would be the highest imprudence in me to kill a man who is now become so considerably my debtor."[41] There is no hint that Fielding intends his readers to regard this statement as dishonorable. It thus can stand as a symbol of the shift in concepts of honor from the early seventeenth to the mid-eighteenth centuries.

A far more serious threat to the integrity of the crim. con. system than connivance in adultery for the purpose of blackmail was the well-known and openly admitted fact that by the 1790s in an increasing number of cases, perhaps a majority, the action was now collusive: by prearrangement the damages were paid by the defendant to the plaintiff and then secretly returned back to him. This procedure developed partly due to a growing moral repugnance at taking such tainted money, but mostly because of a decline in belief in the religious basis for the indissolubility of marriage. The plaintiff, his wife, and the defendant now saw nothing immoral in conspiring together to obtain an uncontested divorce so as to allow all parties to remarry. As a cuckolded husband suing for crim. con. damages observed in 1811: "I am not in want of money, but of a divorce."[42]

Based on these prior agreements, the two uncontested suits in King's Bench and an ecclesiastical court and an uncontested bill of divorce in Parliament would all go forward, the three parties being very careful to conceal all traces of their double collusion. After the Divorce Act was passed, the money was returned to the lover by the husband, the ex-wife married the lover, and the husband found himself another wife. The result in practice was a divorce by mutual consent, for the purpose of starting two new legal households. In the debate in Parliament in 1800 over a bill to prevent the marriage of a divorced wife to her lover, Lord Eldon claimed that nine out of ten cases of crim. con. were based on "the most infamous collusion." He went on to complain, "As the law stands, it is a farce and a mockery, most of the cases being previously settled in some room in the City, and juries are called to give exemplary damages, which damages are never paid to, nor expected by, the injured husband."[43]

This collusion, which spread like a cancer through the whole crim. con. process, provides a classic example of how unintended consequences arise from changes introduced for totally different purposes—in this case, in order to punish sexual immorality. Heavy damages remained overtly functional merely for the handful of husbands who were not only determined to secure for themselves the money awarded to them, but who also actually succeeded in doing so. They were covertly functional for the very much larger number of husbands, wives, and lovers who now had no moral scruples about conspiring to use the action to obtain divorce by mutual consent but did have moral scruples about making money out of their wives' shame. In this respect there was a revival—or reemergence into the open—of that sense of honor which until 1692 had prevented members of the elite from using the crim. con. action. They now used the action, but secretly refused to touch the money.

Another wholly unanticipated result of the imposition in crim. con. actions of huge punitive damages far in excess of the capacity of the defendant to pay was that more and more defendants sought refuge in flight into exile abroad. These were men involved in that minority of cases in which, for motives of greed or revenge, the plaintiff refused collusion and was determined to enforce collection of the damages, if necessary by having the defendant arrested and gaoled. As a result, by the 1830s, in about a quarter of all the crim. con. cases which were followed by Parliamentary divorce, the writ could not be served, or if it was the damages were not collectible, usually because the defendant had sold all his assets and fled the country, often taking the plaintiff's wife with him.[44] By 1800 Calais and Boulogne were said to be full of fugitives from crim. con. actions.

The Moral Reaction 1800–57

Because of these unintended and very unwelcome consequences of the frequent award of very large damages in crim. con. actions, a moral reaction to the whole procedure set in after about 1800. Even before he died in 1802, Lord Kenyon's judicial colleagues felt obliged to challenge the turning of a private common lawsuit into a public criminal one by the award of punitive damages. But it took a layman, Sir George Turner, to put Lord Kenyon in his place during a debate in the House of Commons in 1800: "A learned gentleman has talked of exemplary damages being given. To talk of exemplary damages in civil actions is to talk exemplary nonsense. Who told juries that they were to be the *custodes morum*? The man who stated this doctrine was responsible for the effect it produced."[45] The first clear evidence of a moral reaction against the crim. con. procedure was the growing reluctance of plaintiffs to accept such tainted money as damages. During the debate in the House of Lords over the adultery bill in 1800, the Duke of Clarence referred to "the pretty generally known fact that the husband who, by suing for pecuniary damages, obtains a verdict, is considered not a very honourable man if, when he receives them, he puts them in his own pocket, instead of returning them to the purse of the defendant."[46] As the counsel for the Honorable Edward Foley put it in his suit against the Earl of Peterborough in 1799, his client had no desire "to carve out his lordship's fortune to put it in his own pocket."[47]

Many now wanted to modify or get rid of the crim. con. action itself, but if it were merely abolished, adulterers would in future go unpunished. The idea of making adultery a criminal offense had long been recognized as a possible alternative to the now discredited crim. con. action for damages. As a palliative, four attempts were made in Parliament between 1771 and 1809 to pass legislation which would prevent the guilty party in a divorce case for adultery from marrying her lover. With the enthusiastic support of the bishops, but a good deal of opposition from libertine lay peers, all passed in the House of Lords. But all were rejected by the House of Commons,[48] almost entirely because of the strength of sentiment already felt by 1800 in influential circles about the need for greater legal equality in the treatment of women. Preventing the adulterous wife from remarrying her lover would merely add insult to injury by driving her into concubinage or prostitution instead.

As time went on, more and more thoughtful men and women began to realize that in a crim. con. suit a wife could be falsely charged by a husband anxious only to be rid of her, or falsely blamed for enticement, or falsely accused of previous promiscuity by a lover anxious to mitigate the damages awarded against him. In all these circumstances, she was legally helpless to make known her side of the case. Nor in a suit at common law was it open to her to bring before the court evidence of her husband's prior adulteries, cruelty or indifference to her, as was the case in the church courts or Parliament. In 1850 Thackeray wrote a poem entitled "Damages Two Hundred Pounds" which attacked this male monopoly of the crim. con. action:

British Jurymen and husbands, let's hail this verdict proper.
If a British wife offends you, Britons, you've a right to whop her.
. . . You may strike her, curse, abuse her: so declares our law renowned.
But if after that you lose her—why, you're paid two hundred pounds.[49]

In 1809 Lord Erskine, who for 30 years had pleaded, nearly always on the side of the plaintiff, in "almost every case of this sort," admitted that "much of his knowledge could not come before the court" since the wife's story could not be presented to it.[50]

At the same time as educated public opinion was demanding greater justice for women, it was also shifting away from the traditional view of women primarily as property and toward the concept of marriage as a contract for the development of domestic happiness and affective individualism. As a result, in their direction to a jury about the criteria upon which to assess damages, judges began changing the balance of factors to be taken into account. Less emphasis was given to questions of status and wealth and more to those of the moral worth of the wife, her chastity, probity, devotion as a mother to her children and as friend and companion to her husband, as well as on her educational accomplishments, her physical beauty, and her competence as a household manager. Moreover the lover was now pilloried more as a homewrecker, a destroyer of domestic bliss, and less as one who owed reparation to the husband for his loss of honor or as a trespasser upon his private property.[51]

Another element in causing the fall after 1820 in the number of excessive damages awarded was changing attitudes toward penology and punishment. This humanitarian movement caused judges to oppose the idea of deliberately planning to leave a man to rot in prison because of his inability to pay huge damages. According to the new ethic, this was a perversion of the whole legal system of awarding damages. As a result, in 1838 Parliament passed a law limiting imprisonment for inability to pay damages to two years.[52] Thus both lawyers and politicians were being affected by the new climate of penal reform.

Typology of Change

Between 1600 and 1860 educated public opinion underwent several quite startling reversals over the way to treat adultery by a married woman. Before about 1670, the seduction of a wife was perhaps the most serious offense one man could commit upon the honor of another. In elite circles, where honor was held in particularly high esteem, it was morally accepted that the offense should be avenged by personal violence, whether spontaneous and untrammeled or ritualized as a duel.

The second phase began in about 1670 as the ecclesiastical courts started to collapse and the local lay courts to lose interest in punishing adulterers. To fill this gap and to reduce the area of private violence the common law Courts of King's Bench and Common Pleas expanded the use of the writ of trespass to cover the seduction of a wife. Since the action was based on the award of monetary damages for loss of honor by the seduction of a wife, even the limited use of the crim. con. action symbolized the beginning of a shift among some elements of the landed elite from a moral code based on honor and shame to one based also on the rights of property by a husband in the body of his wife, and his moral right to monetary compensation for any trespass upon it. This shift can be paralleled in other spheres of life, for example in electoral politics. Before the 1670s the prime objective of a candidate was to avoid the loss of honor incurred by open defeat in an election and corruption of electors was minimal. As a result, publicly contested elections were few, and the electorate rewarded by no more than ample food and drink. After the 1670s the rage of party dramatically increased the number of contested elections and thus of losers, while electoral bribery with cash became commonplace. There again, honor began to give way to money, although both were to remain in competition for a very long while.[53]

The third phase began in about 1770, when three simultaneous and related developments began to take place. The number of suits shot up, partly because of an actual increase of adultery by wives in elite circles, but mostly because a successful crim. con. action had become a necessary prerequisite to a Parliamentary divorce, the numbers of which were also increasing. Like the motives behind crim. con. actions, those behind Parliamentary divorces were also changing in the last half of the eighteenth century. Petitioners now began to drop arguments about the importance of a remarriage in order to beget heirs, and Parliamentary Acts no longer included clauses for the bastardization of illegitimate children. After 1800, the preservation of patrilineal property rights ceased to be the main issue. The emphasis was now upon the loss of "the comforts of matrimony," caused by separation without remarriage. These changes in legal arguments show how concern for companionship was now tending to drive out cruder concepts of property rights.

The fourth phase was visible by 1800, overlapping with and building on the third, and took the form of a many-faceted moral reaction against the crim. con. action. This moral reaction included a rejection of the treatment of female adultery as a public crime and the restoration of the crim. con. action to its original role as a remedy for a private injury; a denial of the morality both of trading marital happiness for money and of condemning a defendant to prison for debt for an indefinite period; a growing demand among both educated women and lawyers for greater legal equality between the sexes; and a shift in the argument for retention of the double sexual standard from one based on property rights over persons and fear of illegitimate progeny to one based upon differential male and female sexual psychology. It was now argued that a man commits adultery as an act of pure sensuality, but a woman only as a by-product of an emotional commitment. Only the latter is therefore a serious threat to the stability of the marriage. Under the influence of the greater emphasis placed upon the ideal of the companionate marriage and the new sentimentalization of female chastity, the seduction of a married woman came to be regarded less as an invasion of male property rights than as an attack on domestic happiness.

Thanks to rising secularization, and a decline in the ethical authority of the Anglican Church, by the late eighteenth century there had arisen a quite new pragmatism in professional and upper-middle-class circles in attitudes toward divorce, as a result of which secret collusion in order to obtain freedom to remarry for all three partners in the sexual triangle became morally acceptable. Among the titled aristocracy, however, fear of provoking social revolution, the results of Evangelical piety, and the spread of the ideal of domesticity, caused their almost total withdrawal after 1830 from their former highly conspicuous participation in both crim. con. cases and Parliamentary divorces (Table 8.4).

By the 1840s the acceptance of monetary compensation for a husband's loss of matrimonial comfort and happiness was generally looked upon with disgust. Lord Lansdowne in 1857 summed up the current attitude when he declared in Parliament: "These proceedings are founded on the monstrous assumption that the affection of a wife is to be treated as the loss of an ordinary chattel, and is to be compensated in pounds, shillings and pence."[54] Thus what had seemed perfectly reasonable to all in the late eighteenth century had now become "a monstrous assumption." By 1857 the sole justification still offered for it was, as Lord Chancellor Cranworth put it, "not as a *solatium* for injured feelings, but in the case of persons to

TABLE 8.4.   A. Men of Title Granted Parliamentary Divorces[1]

	Total	Titled	%
1700–49	13	6	46
1750–69	28	3	11
1770–1829	103	30	18
1830–57	118	2	2

B. Men of Title Involved in Crim. Con. Actions

| Date | Total Actions | Men of Title | | | % Total Plaintiffs & Defendants | % of Men of Title |
		Plain-tiffs	Defen-dants	Total		
1700–49	23	6	7	13	46	28
1750–69	29	2	4	6	58	10
1770–89	68	10	9	19	136	14
1790–1809	124	14	14	28	248	11
1810–29	96	17	14	31	192	16
1830–57	c. 80+	2	5	7	c. 160	4
1700–1857	c. 420	51	53	104	c. 840	

1. S. Wolfson, op. cit., p. 166, Table 3 and Appendix III.

whom damages in a pecuniary point of view might be important," for example, in paying for a poor man's legal expenses.[55] Conflicts between English moral codes about marriage and divorce over two centuries and the slow shifts from one dominant code to another and then to a third are exemplified with remarkable clarity by these changing justifications for the crim. con. action.

By the 1850s the great law lords were particularly opposed to the crim. con. action because of the withering criticism it received from their Continental colleagues. The future Lord Chancellor, Lord Campbell, spoke for them all when in 1857 he said bitterly: "I am ashamed of it. I have been taunted with it by foreigners, and have blushed when I was obliged to confess that such was the law of the land."[56] The two things foreign jurists seem to have known about the English were that husbands sold their wives like cattle at auction with halters round their necks and that they made a financial profit from their wives' adultery. Both confirmed the stereotype of the English as a nation of shameless shopkeepers.

This near universal contempt into which the crim. con. action had fallen by the mid-nineteenth century was thus a result of the coming together of five rather different strands of thought. First, in the new moral atmosphere of Evangelical religion and Benthamite individualism, hardbitten judges, lawyers, and litigants all took the view that there was something morally repellent in making a financial profit out of a wife's adultery. This transaction was particularly odious, since it blurred that characteristic Victorian distinction between the private and the public spheres, the domestic hearth and the marketplace. Second the growing protests by liberal thinkers like John Stuart Mill, pious Christians like William Gladstone, and indignant and eloquent upper-middle-class women like Caroline Norton had persuaded significant segments of elite male society that something had to be done to provide women with greater equality before the law. The total exclusion of wives from crim. con. actions was now recognized as a striking example of judicial gender injustice. Third, the puritanical anti-vice sentiment, which in 1857 was sufficiently powerful to push through a tough Obscene Publications Act, also generated indignant protests against the rich copy offered to the semipornographic press by the intimate details of sexual activity revealed by witnesses in crim. con. trials. Fourth, all the lawyers concerned with the action were convinced that it had become a mere legal charade, in most cases the result of prior collusive agreements between the husband, the wife, and her lover to conceal the truth and obtain damages merely to clear the way for a divorce by mutual consent, followed by a secret return of the money. Fifth, demands for reform of this action and the setting up of a new common law Court for Matrimonial Causes and Divorce were merely a minor aspect of a massive Benthamite overhaul of the whole court system, the legal procedures, and the enacted law itself. This resulted above all in a unification and rationalization of the law, involving the near destruction of the ecclesiastical courts and the amalgamation of equity and common law. This great transformation was driven forward by reform-minded lawyers and judges organized in the Law Amendment Society.

In 1857 the only obstacle to the abolition of the crim. con. action was the total lack of consensus on what to put in its place. As Lord Cranworth said: "If you abolish an action for criminal conversation, what do you propose as a substitute? That is the real practical difficulty."[57] Turning adultery into a criminal misdemeanor exposed husbands to prosecution equally with wives, which made many men very uneasy. Moreover, criminalizing adultery would do nothing to provide poor persons with money to help pay for their legal costs in obtaining a divorce. This intractable problem tied up Parliament for many days during the spring and summer of 1857, and the result was an ambiguous standoff. In the Divorce Act of that year one clause inserted by the House of Lords abolished the action, while another inserted by the House of Commons in practice partly revived it, but under another name and in a very much sanitized and less objectionable form. For all intents and purposes the old, disgraceful, and uniquely English legal action for crim. con. was dead, although it lingered on in Ireland well into the twentieth century.

Causes of Change

The first influence affecting the rise and fall of the crim. con. action was that of the press. As has been seen, the growth of printed pamphlets, law reports, and newspaper accounts of crim. con. trials coincided with the great rise in the use of the action and the spread of the litigants down to the professional and middle classes. The prominent role of the action in public discussion between 1790 and 1857 was due in large part to this publicity, most of it intended to appeal to prurient interest, but some of it to a professional interest in case law. On the other hand the post-1790 reaction against the action as itself immoral since it involved an exchange of money for honor, was also a negative response to this publicity. The growing hostility in some quarters to the pornographic aspects of these publications was also very prominent in the debate over the abolition of crim. con. in Parliament in 1857 (Figs. 8.5, 8.6).

Secondly, changes in law and litigation raise the question of the relationship of the enacted law and society and the degree to which the former is a semi-independent historical variable.[58] There can be no doubt that the crim. con. action began in the late seventeenth century because of a desire by the common lawyers to extend their business and be able to offer a remedy for any tort. In consequence the crim. con. action was invented to offer competition with the ecclesiastical courts in punishing adultery and thus to capture at least a small share of the business concerning marital affairs.

Nor is there any doubt that the common lawyers were only too pleased to take on these new responsibilities. Partly they enjoyed the increase in business and profits, partly they regarded oral crossquestioning in open court as a much more reliable method of hunting out the truth than the

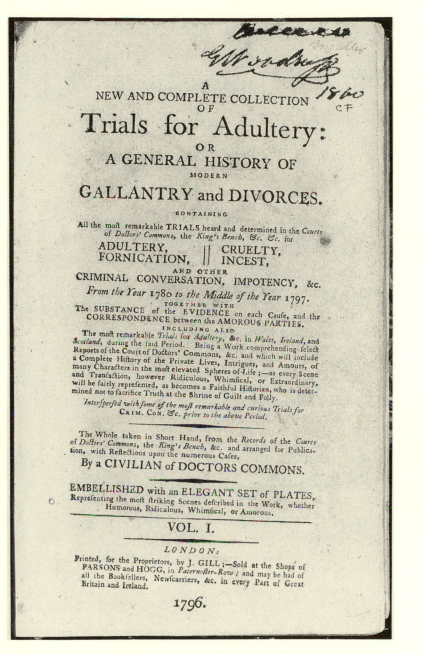

A
NEW AND COMPLETE COLLECTION
OF
Trials for Adultery:
OR
A GENERAL HISTORY OF
MODERN
GALLANTRY and DIVORCES.

CONTAINING

All the moſt remarkable TRIALS heard and determined in the *Courts of Doctors' Commons*, the *King's Bench, &c. &c.* for

ADULTERY,   CRUELTY,
FORNICATION,   INCEST,
AND OTHER
CRIMINAL CONVERSATION, IMPOTENCY, &c.

From the Year 1780 *to the Middle of the Year* 1797.

TOGETHER WITH

The SUBSTANCE of the EVIDENCE on each Cauſe, and the CORRESPONDENCE between the AMOROUS PARTIES.

INCLUDING ALSO

The moſt remarkable *Trials* for *Adultery, &c.* in *Wales, Ireland,* and *Scotland,* during the ſaid Period. Being a Work comprehending ſelect Reports of the Court of Doctors' Commons, &c. and which will include a Complete Hiſtory of the Private Lives, Intrigues, and Amours, of many Characters in the moſt elevated Spheres of Life;—as every Scene and Tranſaction, however Ridiculous, Whimſical, or Extraordinary, will be fairly repreſented, as becomes a Faithful Hiſtorian, who is determined not to ſacrifice Truth at the Shrine of Guilt and Folly.

Interſperſed with ſome of the moſt remarkable and curious Trials for CRIM. CON. &c. *prior to the above Period.*

The Whole taken in Short Hand, from the *Records* of the *Courts* of *Doctors' Commons,* the *King's Bench,* &c. and arranged for Publication, with Reflections upon the numerous Cafes,

By a CIVILIAN of DOCTORS COMMONS.

EMBELLISHED with an ELEGANT SET of PLATES,
Repreſenting the moſt ſtriking Scenes deſcribed in the Work, whether Humorous, Ridiculous, Whimſical, or Amorous.

VOL. I.

LONDON:

Printed, for the Proprietors, by J. GILL;—Sold at the Shops of PARSONS and HOGG, in *Paternoſter-Row;* and may be had of all the Bookſellers, Newſcarriers, &c. in every Part of Great Britain and Ireland.

1796.

Figure 8.5. *A New and Complete Collection of Trials for Adultery* (London, 1797), title page. Courtesy of Harvard Law School Library.

PREFACE.

THE great Defire which Readers of every Defcription entertain for well-reported Cafes of ADULTERY, FORNICATION, SEDUCTION, and all Kinds of CRIMINAL CONVERSATION, and the uncommon Avidity with which former Accounts of the kind have always been received, together with the Benefits likely to accrue to the Public, by laying before them authentic Relations of the *heavy Damages*, and other fatal Confequences unavoidably attendant on *illicit Amours*, have induced the Editor hereof to felect and procure from the Records of the Courts, the moft remarkable Trials of this Nature, from the Year 1780 to the prefent Time, including genuine Narratives of ILLEGAL ELOPEMENTS, UNEQUAL MARRIAGES, CALEDONIAN EXCURSIONS, PRIVATE INTRIGUES, AMOURS, &c. with faithful Copies of the feveral Exhibits, LOVE LETTERS, SONNETS, &c. which are, on thefe Occafions, the general *Telegraphs* of Love from one Party to another.

A Publication of this Kind will, it is prefumed, afford no lefs Improvement than Entertainment. Accounts of Vices,

1   A 2   the

Figure 8.6. *A New and Complete Collection of Trials for Adultery,* preface. Courtesy of Harvard Law School Library.

written depositions and replies to written interrogatories that were the practice in the ecclesiastical courts. The legal rivalry was undoubtedly present and was openly expressed. It therefore might seem plausible to attribute some part of the late-seventeenth-century invention of the crim. con. action to a power grab by the common lawyers, especially since the action turned out to be even more incapable of eliciting the truth and preventing collusion than the much-criticized canon law procedure.

On the other hand, the common law judges in the late seventeenth century moved very cautiously into the crim. con. business, deliberately raising the qualifications for plaintiffs and almost never issuing an injunction against an ecclesiastical court. At an early stage, they expressed grave doubts about the wisdom of exposing matrimonial differences in open court and of leaving the decision about such delicate matters to the tender mercies of an ignorant jury, which last problem they got around by using only a select jury of prominent householders handpicked by the sheriff of London. They also restricted the use of the crim. con. action largely to the middle and upper classes, by insisting that such an action, like an action for bigamy, be based on incontrovertible evidence of a legal marriage.[59] But before the 1753 Marriage Act, very large numbers of marriages, especially among the poor, were either contract marriages or clandestine marriages, carried out without banns or license and without official registration, and therefore not capable of legal proof.

Whatever their motives and their degree of enthusiasm or lack of it, there can be no doubt that the invention of the action changed public perceptions and sensibilities. If there had been no crim. con. action available, the Duke of Norfolk in 1692 and other nobles who later followed his example would not have been tempted to turn their own dishonor into something to be compensated in a courtroom by the award of monetary damages. The mere fact of this shift from the duel to the courtroom is symbolic of the beginning of a shift of mental attitudes about honor. This remains true, even if the principal motive of the duke and of many others after him was to improve his chances for a Parliamentary divorce rather than to be revenged upon a seducer, and even if the duel survived well into the nineteenth century.

To a significant extent, therefore, the law itself helped to mold opinion and mentality by offering monetary damages for an insult to honor. During the course of the eighteenth and nineteenth centuries, there undoubtedly occurred very significant changes in the open and latent function of the action. There were major changes in the rhetoric used by counsel in open court to justify the action and to encourage or discourage the jury in assessing the use of the damages. These changes show that it was shifting sensibilities among the public at large, which first drove the system to its peak and then brought about its subsequent decline.

When it came to the abolition of the action as part of the 1854–57 divorce bills, the role of a power struggle between different sections of the legal profession is clear beyond doubt. The original purpose of the bills was to remove so much jurisdiction from the ecclesiastical courts that for all intents and purposes they would be obliged to shut down. The divorce bill removed all matrimonial business to a new common law/equity court, and a concurrent bill designed to go with it removed to a new probate court all business concerning wills. Moreover, it was the law lords who persuaded the House of Lords to abolish the crim. con. action as something which brought discredit upon the profession and made them ashamed to meet their Continental colleagues. And it was the House of Commons, less dominated by lawyers, which invented a new procedure to substitute for the abolished crim. con. action by which a husband suing for divorce could, as an option, sue the co-respondent for damages, to be allocated by the judge between endowment for his children, maintenance for his wife, payment of his legal costs, and compensation for his loss of companionship. The self-interest of lawyers thus played a far more prominent role in the abolition of crim. con. than in its creation.

Ostensibly the courts operated as independent entities, indifferent to the waves and eddies of public opinion that washed over and around them, although a few of the judges, like Lord Mansfield, were activists who openly stated their belief that it was the duty of a judge to modify case law to meet changing societal needs and values. In fact, the judges and lawyers who operated the system were members of a wider society, bound together by a common university experience, a reading of the same newspapers and periodicals, and a shared sociability in London clubs and fashionable drawing rooms. During the seventeenth century, they adopted contemporary ideas about contract, patrilinear descent of property, and the sexual double standard. During the eighteenth century they were influenced by ideas about possessive individualism, a market economy, the secular Enlightenment, affective individualism, Romanticism, and fear of the French Revolution. During the first half of the nineteenth century they were influenced by Benthamism, demands for legal justice for women, and Liberalism, all of which ideologies played a prominent role in the debates over divorce and crim. con. in the 1850s. In this context it is appropriate to recall that

Jeremy Bentham attributed his life-long passion for legal reform to an early reading about a notorious mid-eighteenth century case involving fraudulent marriage, bigamy, and collusive crim. con. litigation, which convinced him of the gross irrationalities and inequities of all branches of the English legal system as then constituted.[60]

On the other hand, the evolution of the crim. con. action is also open to a functionalist explanation. What looks at first sight like an irrational, illogical, and immoral legal action turns out, on close inspection, to have been ideally suited to the need of the key participants in the process; the elite males who were the plaintiffs and the barristers and judges who staffed the courts. The action could also, as we saw in the case of Lord Kenyon in the 1790s, satisfy occasional popular outbursts of moral rectitude. At first, in the early eighteenth century, the crim. con. action gave elite husbands a powerful tool with which to enforce the sexual fidelity of their wives and to punish any men who poached on this particular piece of domestic property. It also opened the way for the plaintiffs to Parliamentary divorces if they wanted to start new families. After collusion became normal in the late eighteenth century, the action allowed the most adulterous of husbands to get around the law so as to obtain a divorce, so that all three members of the sexual triangle could happily remarry. Meanwhile, morality was ostensibly upheld, the seduction of married women ostensibly punished, and the common lawyers, barristers, attorneys, and solicitors became rich and famous for their roles in these highly publicized court dramas. The fact that what was revealed in court bore little relation to the real situation was a positive advantage to all concerned, except those with strong views about the evils of collusion to defraud the law.

These changes in the latent functions of the action to satisfy the leading participants satisfactorily explain why it survived until 1857.

Its abolition in 1857 can also be explained on the same functional grounds. The law lords and common lawyers had become ashamed of the trading of honor for money, the blatant collusion and perjury behind most litigation, and the injustice of barring wives from any opportunity for self-defense in court. By giving the action up, they gained more power and business by seizing from the ecclesiastical courts control over all litigation concerning matrimonial affairs as well as the probate of wills.

The wealthy laity were also well satisfied with the change. It was now easier and cheaper for them to obtain divorces without passing through the squalid procedure of the crim. con. action. The third interest group, the clergy and laity who stood for middle-class Victorian Evangelical morality and who were well represented in Parliament were also satisfied by the continued punishment of the seducer by a new system of damages, now fully controlled by the court. Thus the guilty continued to be punished up to 1970, while the law of divorce was steadily accommodated to changing social needs and moral perceptions. This paper therefore lends support to a functionalist interpretation of the law in terms of the interests of both its professional administrators and of the principal litigants.

When all is said and done, however, the driving forces behind the rise and fall of the crim. con. action from the 1690s to 1857 were deep shifts in the culture of the elite and of the "middling sort," affecting laymen, judges, lawyers, and reporters alike. There was certainly no direct and simple shift from one moral code to another, but rather a series of overlapping stages, involving competition and conflict between rival sensibilities and attitudes. In the end, however, clearly identifiable changes in the predominant moral code did occur. The story provides a revealing example of how, over a period of two hundred years, slow-moving changes in the most widely accepted definitions of honor and morality, connected to the rise of a market economy and of a substantial, well-educated middle class, could entirely transform both attitudes toward, and the practical effects of, an ostensibly unaltered legal action. Both the legal action and the attitudes to it, moreover, appear to have been unique to England and strikingly different from those prevailing anywhere else in Scotland, America, or the continent of Europe.

This chapter is a summary of one chapter in a book titled *Road to Divorce: England 1530–1987,* to be published by the Oxford University Press, Oxford.

Notes

1. For this last point, see C. W. Francis, "The Structure of Judicial Administration, and the Development of Contract Law in Seventeenth Century England," *Columbia Law Review* (1983) 83.

2. J. Pitt-Rivers, *The Fate of Schechem* (Cambridge, 1977), 23; see also *Honour and Shame,* ed. J. G. Peristiany (London, 1966).

3. J. Vanbrugh, *The Provoked Wife* (1697), V, i; for an example in real life, see *Town and Country Magazine* 4 (1772), 122.

4. For the slow conquest of violence by the English State, see L. Stone, *The Crisis of the Aristocracy 1558–1641* (Oxford, 1965), ch. 5.

5. *The Times,* 12 May 1815, p. 3.

6. *The Bon Ton Magazine* 21 (1789), 24; quotation from J. M. Beattie, *Crime and the Courts in England 1660–1800* (Princeton, 1986), 95.

7. Pentland v. Crick, 1803, Royal Irish Academy, Haliday Pamphlets 849, p. 9.

8. M. Astell, *Reflections on Marriage* (London, 1730), 106–7.

9. S. Anderson, "Legislative Divorce—Law for the Aristocracy," in *Law, Economy and Society 1750–1914,* ed. G. R. Rubin and D. Sugarman (Abingdon, 1984), 420–34; S. Wolfram, "Divorce in England 1700–1857," *Oxford Journal of Legal History* 5 (1985), 164, Table 3.

10. Office v. Mounteney, Lichfield Joint Record Office, Lichfield C.C., B/C/5 (1701); Office v. Hulme, loc. cit., B/C/5 (1708); Office v. Barker, loc. cit., B/C/5 (1707).

11. T. Skelton, *A Tutor to Tachygraphy* (London, 1642) and *Tachygraphy* (London, 1647); T. Gurney, *Brachygraphy* (London, 1750); S. Taylor, *An Essay . . . of Stenography* (London, 1786); I. Pitman, *Stenographic Shorthand* (London, 1837); see P. A. Pickering, "Class Without Words: Symbolic Communication in the Chartist Movement," *Past and Present* 112 (1986), 144–62 (at 148–49).

12. *Further Depositions . . . in the Affair of the Duke and Duchess of Norfolk* (London, 1692), 16.

13. *Correspondence of J. H. Leigh Hunt,* ed. Thornton Hunt (London, 1862), I, 157. I owe this quotation to Thomas Laqueur.

14. Cibber v. Sloper, 1738; J. Campbell, *Lives of the Chief Justices* (London, 1849), II, 341–43; M. Nash, *The Provoked Wife* (New York, 1973), 137–63; Anon., *Adultery Anatomized,* I, 109–52; F. Truelove, *The Comforts of Matrimony* (London, 1739); Anon., *Trials for Adultery till 1760* (London, 1760), VII, 3–39.

15. Sir Thomas Erskine, *Speeches,* ed. J. Ridgway, IV, passim; J. Campbell, *Lives of the Lords Chancellors* (London, 1846), VI, 530.

16. See *A New and Complete Collection of Trials for Adultery* (London, 1797), I, 5.

17. L. Simond, *Journal of a Tour and Residence in Great Britain,* 2 vols. (New York, 1815), I, 34.

18. L. Stone, *Family, Sex and Marriage in England 1500–1800* (London, 1977), chs. 6–8; R. Trumbach, *The Rise of the Egalitarian Family: Aristocratic Kinship and Domestic Relations in Eighteenth-Century England* (New York, 1978); J. Lewis, *In the Family Way: Childbearing in the British Aristocracy 1760–1860* (New Brunswick, 1986), ch. 1.

19. S. Anderson, op. cit., 422.

20. See J. Lewis, op. cit., ch. 1.

21. Defined by Thomas Erskine in 1794 in Howard v. Bingham, in *Speeches of Lord Erskine,* ed. J. Ridgway (London, 1847), IV, 308.

22. Ibid., 309.

23. *A New and Complete Collection of Trials for Adultery* (London, 1797), I, 3–4.

24. *Hansard,* 2d Series, 24, col. 1285.

25. *Speeches of Lord Erskine,* IV, 279.

26. For a few examples of the use of the unhappy marriage argument, see *London Chronicle,* 1788, i, 238; 1789, i, 7; *Crim. Con. Gazette,* London, 1830, I, 53, 93.

27. *London Chronicle,* 1788, i, 238.

28. Parkes v. Cresswick, 1825, *Crim. Con. Gazette,* II, 139; Sullivan case, 1825, J. F. MacQueen, *Appellate Jurisdiction of the House of Lords* (London, 1842), 638; Graham v. Wright, 1827, *Crim. Con. Gazette,* 644; Cherer v. Marriot, 1827, F. Plowden, *Crim. Con. Biography* (London, 1839), II, 316.

29. L. Shelford, *A Practical Treatise of the Law of Marriage and Divorce* (London, 1841).

30. Stuart v. Blandford, 1801, *London Chronicle*, 1801, i, 509; Astley v. Garth, F. Plowden, *Crim. Con. Biography*, II, 237–40; *Crim. Con. Gazette*, I, 45.

31. For cases in which the counsel for the plaintiff laid special stress on the breach of friendship by the defendant, see, for example, Baring v. Webster, 1822, Beresford v. Bective, 1816, Duberley v. Gunning, 1789, *Crim. Con. Gazette*, I, 207, 61, 77; for other examples of the use of the breach of friendship argument by counsel in crim. con. cases, see *London Chronicle*, 1798, 178; 1800, i, 524; 1802, i, 426; *A New and Complete Collection of Trials*, I, 5 (Westmeath v. Bradshaw, 1796), 3 (Biscoe v. Gordon, 1794); *Crim. Con. Gazette*, I, 21–22, 45, 70, 77; II, 126, 207, 283; *Town and Country Magazine*, 1786, 345.

32. R. Halsband, *Letters of Lady Mary Wortley Montagu* (Oxford, 1965–67), II, 295 note; *Trials for Adultery from 1760*, VII; *A New and Complete Collection of the Most Remarkable Trials for Adultery* (London, 1780), I; *A Collection of Trials . . . ,* II, 89–94; F. Plowden, *Crim. Con. Biography*, I, 26–36; *Crim. Con. Gazette*, II, 13–14; *Crim. Con. Actions and Trials* (London, n.d.), 89–94.

33. Coaches were such common places for sexual activity that in 1698 a bill introduced into Parliament against "vice and prophaneness" contained a clause specifically prohibiting "unlawful commerce" in hackney carriages. (J. Oldmixon, *History of England* [London, 1735], 175. I owe this reference to Dr. David Hayton.)

34. Loveden v. Loveden, Lambeth Palace, Court of Arches MSS, D 1312.

35. Massey v. Marquis of Headfort, 1804, Royal Irish Academy, Haliday Pamphlets 872 (1) p. 89.

36. Anon., *Trials for Adultery Since 1780* (London, 1799), I, 3, 14.

37. The cases were: Dormer v. Jones, 1715; Clavering v. Gremley, 1738; Ennever v. (a cowman), 1753; Morgan v. Hall, 1754; Larking v. Juson, 1792; Wilmot v. Washbourne, 1793; Middleton v. Rose, 1794; Fowler v. Hodges, 1807; ? v. McCarthy, c. 1800s; Gregson v. Theaker, 1809; Talbot v. ? (a groom), 1852.

38. Lord Beresford v. Earl Bective, 1816, *Crim. Con. Gazette*, I, 63; Baring v. Webster, 1822, ibid., II, 207; Swetenham v. Macaghton, 1823, ibid., 62. See also Flight v. Willat, 1823, Anon., *A Familiar Compendium of the Law of Husband and Wife* (London, 1831), 41–43; MacQueen, *Appellate Jurisdiction*, 495, 657.

39. Walford v. Cooke, 1789; *The Trial of Mr. Cooke* (London, 1789), B.L. 518.C 18(4), pp. 41–49; *Town and Country Magazine* 21 (1789), 340; Parslow v. Sykes, 1789; *The Trial of Captain Sykes* (London, 1789), B.L. 1132.q.102, pp. 11, 17, 19–22; *A New and Complete Collection*, I, 12, 27–28, 36, 40, 44–46; T. Brasbridge, *The Fruits of Experience* (London, 1824), 239; see also Moorson v. Clark, 1791, *London Chronicle* (1791), i, 571; see also Barttelot v. Hawker, 1790, *The Trial of Samuel Hawker* (London, 1790), B.L. 518.1.12(5).

40. Taylor v. Birchwood, 1800, *London Chronicle* (1800), i, 523; For an accurate comment in 1808 on the disastrous effects of the reaction to the French Revolution upon all reform movements in England see *Memoirs of the Life of Samuel Romilly* (London, 1840), II, 90; M. Douglas, *Purity and Danger: an Analysis of Concepts of Purity and Taboo* (London, 1970).

41. H. Fielding, *Amelia* (1751), 2 vols. (London, 1930), 236–38.

42. Defries v. Holden, London Consistory Court, DL/C/189.

43. *The Parliamentary History of England from the Earliest Period to the Year 1803*, 36 vols. (London, 1806–20) (hereafter "*Parlt. Hist.*"), 34, cols. 233, 237, 252, 280.

44. S. Anderson, op. cit., 442; *Journal of the House of Lords*, 1800–passim.

45. *Parlt. Hist.*, 35, col. 322; for similar complaints by C. W. Wynn in the House of Commons in the 1830s, see *Hansard*, 2d ser., 24, col. 1284.

46. *Parlt. Hist.*, 20, p. 277; *Hansard*, 1st ser., 14, 96, col. 326.

47. *Crim. Con. Gazette*, I, 4.

48. *Parlt. Hist.*, 17, col. 185; 20, col. 592; 34, col. 1552; 35, cols. 225, 1268; *Hansard*, 1st ser., 14, cols. 326, 612.

49. W. M. Thackeray, *Works* (London, 1903), XXIV, 226, XXXV, 205–7.

50. *Hansard*, 1st series, 14, cols. 332–33.

51. *Hansard*, 3rd series, 145, col. 491.

52. 1–2 Vict. cap. 110, para. 78.

53. M. Kishlansky, *Parliamentary Selection: Social and Political Choice in Early Modern England* (New York, 1986).

54. *Hansard*, 142, col. 1974.

55. *Hansard*, 145, col. 919.

56. *Hansard*, 145, col. 513.

57. *Hansard*, 145, col. 919.

58. For a general discussion of this problem, see R. W. Gordon, "Critical Legal Histories," *Stanford Law Review* 36–37 (1984), 57–125.

59. Morris v. Miller, 1767, *English Reports* 98, pp. 73–74; Anon, *The Laws Respecting Women* (London, 1777), 318; W. D. Evans, *A General View of the Decisions of Lord Mansfield* (London, 1813), I, 102.

60. *The Works of Jeremy Bentham*, ed. J. Bowring (London, 1843), X, 35.

Contributors

ANN BLAIR is a graduate student in history and history of science at Princeton University. She has written articles on sixteenth-century French education and the astronomy of Tycho Brahe; her dissertation will deal with Jean Bodin and the tradition of encyclopedism in the late Renaissance.

INGA CLENDINNEN is senior lecturer in history at LaTrobe University in Melbourne, Australia. She is the author of *Ambivalent Conquests: Maya and Spaniard in Yucatan, 1517–1570* (Cambridge, 1987).

ANTHONY GRAFTON is Andrew W. Mellon professor of history at Princeton University. He is the author of *Joseph Scaliger: A Study in the History of Classical Scholarship* I (Oxford, 1983) and the co-author (with Lisa Jardine) of *From Humanism to the Humanities* (Cambridge, Mass., 1986).

WILLIAM HUNT is associate professor of history at St. Lawrence University. He is the author of *The Puritan Moment* (Cambridge, Mass., 1983).

LISA JARDINE is professor of Queen Mary College, London. She is the author of *Francis Bacon: Discovery and the Art of Discourse* (Cambridge, 1974) and *Still Harping on Daughters* (Hassocks, 1983) and the co-author (with Anthony Grafton) of *From Humanism to the Humanities* (Cambridge, Mass., 1986).

DONALD R. KELLEY is professor of history at the University of Rochester and editor of the *Journal of the History of Ideas*. His books include *Foundations of Modern Historical Scholarship* (New York, 1970), *François Hotman* (Princeton, 1973), and *The Beginning of Ideology* (Cambridge, 1981).

ALAN CHARLES KORS is professor of history at the University of Pennsylvania. He is the author of *D'Holbach's Coterie: An Enlightenment in Paris* (Princeton, 1976).

LAWRENCE STONE is Dodge professor of history at Princeton University and the founding director of the Shelby Cullom Davis Center for Historical Studies. His books include *The Crisis of the Aristocracy, 1558–1641* (Oxford, 1965), *The Family, Sex and Marriage: England 1500–1800* (New York, 1977), and (with Jeanne C. Stone) *An Open Elite? England, 1540–1880* (Oxford, 1984).

LUCETTE VALENSI is Maître de Recherche at the Ecole des Hautes Etudes en Sciences Sociales. She is the author of *On the Eve of Colonialism,* tr. K. Perkins (New York, 1977), *Tunisian Peasants in the Eighteenth and Nineteenth Centuries,* tr. B. Archer (Cambridge, 1985), and (with Abraham Udovitch) *The Last Arab Jews* (London and New York, 1983).

Index